T0226198

Lecture Notes in Computer Science   10898

Commenced Publication in 1973
Founding and Former Series Editors:
Gerhard Goos, Juris Hartmanis, and Jan van Leeuwen

Editorial Board

More information about this series at http://www.springer.com/series/7409

Mounir Mokhtari · Bessam Abdulrazak
Hamdi Aloulou (Eds.)

Smart Homes
and Health Telematics

Designing a Better Future:
Urban Assisted Living

16th International Conference, ICOST 2018
Singapore, Singapore, July 10–12, 2018
Proceedings

 Springer

Editors
Mounir Mokhtari
Institut Mines Télécom Paris/CNRS
Paris
France

Hamdi Aloulou
Digital Research Centre of Sfax
Sfax
Tunisia

Bessam Abdulrazak
Universite de Sherbrooke
Sherbrooke, QC
Canada

ISSN 0302-9743   ISSN 1611-3349   (electronic)
Lecture Notes in Computer Science
ISBN 978-3-319-94522-4   ISBN 978-3-319-94523-1   (eBook)
https://doi.org/10.1007/978-3-319-94523-1

Library of Congress Control Number: 2018947349

LNCS Sublibrary: SL3 – Information Systems and Applications, incl. Internet/Web, and HCI

Printed on acid-free paper

This Springer imprint is published by the registered company Springer International Publishing AG
part of Springer Nature
The registered company address is: Gewerbestrasse 11, 6330 Cham, Switzerland

In memory of our beloved friend and colleague Zeugnam Zenn Bien, Professor KAIST, South Korea

"I send all my sympathies for his family and feel sad about this great loss for the scientific community"
Prof. Hélène Pigot, Sherbrooke University, Canada, Chair ICOST 2005 and ICOST 2011

"Really shocked to hear this sad news and this is truly a big loss to our community! I still remember his always smiling face and encouraging words at several meetings with him in South Korea, France, Canada, and the USA"
Prof. Daqing Zhang, Telecom SudParis, France. Chair ICOST 2014

"This is huge loss to our community. My memories of Zenn are still very vivid when he visited Ames with some of us in 2008"
Prof. Carl Chang, IOWA State University, USA, Chair ICOST 2008 and ICOST 2016

"Zenn Bien always supported us and acted as a true mentor. He was always benevolent to us"
Prof. Sylvain Giroux, University of Sherbrooke, Canada, Chair ICOST 2005 and ICOST 2011

"This is truly very sad news and a great loss to the research community. Beyond obituaries, I think a good way to remember Zenn is by celebrating and highlighting his achievements"
Chaired Prof. Sumi Helal, Lancaster University, UK, Chair ICOST 2008 and ICOST 2014

"Sad news for the scientific community. My thoughts are with his family"
Prof. Bessam Abdulrazak, University of Sherbrooke, Canada, Chair ICOST 2011

"It is very sad news and indeed a significant loss for the community"
Prof. Chris Nugent, Ulster University, UK, Chair ICOST'2006

"I am deeply sorry to learn of Professor Bien's passing. I knew Professor Bien more than 20 years. Professor Bien and I taught the same course at Hosei University in Tokyo. Professor Bien was a wonderful person not only as an academic but also as a human being. His passing will be a great loss for us. Please accept our sincere condolences. In deepest sympathy"
Prof. Hisato Kobayashi, Hosei University in Tokyo, Japan

"This is really sad news for me and for our community. I met Zenn in 1999 and I had a strong affection for him since then. This is a big loss for the world. May he rest in peace"
Prof. Mounir Mokhtari, Institut Mines-Telecom, France/CNRS IPAL Singapore, Founder of ICOST conference in 2003

Preface

This year we organized the 16th ICOST conference, an event which has succeeded in bringing together a community from different continents over more than a decade and half and raised awareness about frail and dependent people's quality of life in our societies.

After 15 very successful conferences held annually in three continents (Europe, Asia, and North America), ICOST was hosted in France (2003), Singapore (2004), Canada (2005), Northern Ireland (2006), Japan (2007), USA (2008), France (2009), Korea (2010), Canada (2011), Italy (2012), Singapore (2013), USA (2014), Switzerland (2015), China (2016), and France (2017), the 16th International Conference on Smart homes, Assistive Technologies and Health Telematics (ICOST 2018) was held in Singapore, during July 10–12, 2018. This year the conference was collocated with the World Cities Summit event in Singapore and was considered an official event of the France Singapore Year of Innovation.

ICOST provides a premier venue for the presentation and discussion of research in the design, development, deployment and evaluation of smart urban environments, assistive technologies, chronic disease management, coaching and health telematics systems. ICOST brings together stakeholders from clinical, academic, and industrial backgrounds with end users and family caregivers to explore how to utilize technologies to foster independent living and offer an enhanced quality of life. ICOST 2018 invited participants to present and discuss their experience in the design, development, deployment, and evaluation of assistive and telehealth systems, as well as ethical and policy issues. The conference featured a dynamic program incorporating a range of technical, clinical, and industrial keynote talks, oral and poster presentations, along with demonstrations and technical exhibits.

The theme of the conference this year was "Designing a Better Future: Urban Assisted Living" focusing on the quality of life of dependent people not only in their homes, but also in outdoor living environments to improve mobility and social interaction in the city. Extending the living space with suitable ICT support in terms of smart transportation, mobility, interaction, and socialization is the scientific challenge and promising innovation that the ICOST community decided to tackle. ICTs are not limited only to end users with special needs, but also to caregivers and relatives in charge of taking care of dependent and elderly people. To be more effective and impactful, technologies in different areas, such as IoT (the Internet of Things), big data analytics, smart mobility etc. should target all the stakeholders.

ICOST 2018 was proud to extend its hospitality to an international community consisting of researchers from major universities and research centers, people from industry, and users from 24 different countries. We would like to thank the authors for submitting their current research work and the Program Committee members for their commitment to reviewing submitted papers. The ICOST proceedings have now reached over 150,000 downloads, and are in the top 25% of downloads of Springer LNCS.

We were very pleased to host world-renowned keynote speakers from multiple backgrounds coming from Australia and the USA and we were extremely honored by the confidence of the sponsors in this conference.

This year a special session was held in memory of one of the pillars of ICOST, Prof. Zeugnam Zenn Bien. This session was an opportunity to share our community thoughts and feelings as a means of remembrance and healing. Words cannot express the feelings of our community.

May 2018

Mounir Mokhtari
Bessam Abdulrazak
Hamdi Aloulou

Organization

General Chair

Mounir Mokhtari   Institut Mines Télécom/CNRS IPAL, Singapore

Steering Committee

Mounir Mokhtari   Institut Mines Télécom, France/Director CNRS IPAL
Lab., Singapore
Sumi Helal   Lancaster University (2017–present),
University of Florida (1998–2017)
Bessam Abdulrazak   University of Sherbrooke, Canada
Hamdi Aloulou   University of Monastir, Tunisia; Institut
Mines-Telecom, Paris, France

Scientific Advisory Board

Carl K. Chang   Iowa State University, USA
Daqing Zhang   Institut Mines Télécom, Télécom SudParis, France
Hisato Kobayashi   Hosei University Information Technology Research
Center, Japan
Norman Wu   Ministry of Health Holding, Singapore
Christian Roux   Institut Mines Télécom, France

Program Committee

Chairs

Bessam Abdulrazak   University of Sherbrooke, Canada
Hamdi Aloulou   University of Monastir, Tunisia; Institut
Mines-Telecom, Paris, France

Members

Abdallah M'Hamed   Telecom SudParis - Evry, France
Abdenour Bouzouane   University of Quebec at Chicoutimi, Canada
Angelique Chan   DUKE@NUS, CARE Centre, Singapore
Belkacem Chikhaoui   Télé-Université du Québéc, Canada
Benoît Encelle   Lyon 1 University, IUT Lyon 1, France
Carl K. Chang   Iowa State University, USA
Charles Gouin-Vallerand   Télé-Université du Québéc, Canada
Chris Nugent   University of Ulster, UK
Christian Roux   Institut Mines Télécom, France

Philippe Fraisse	University of Montpellier, CNRS LIRMM (UMR 5506), France
Rami Yared	University of Sherbrooke, Canada
Roger Zimmermann	NUS, Singapore
Stefanos Kollias	University of Lincoln, UK
Salim Hima	ESME-SUDRIA, France
Stephane Renouard	CTO EnergieIP, Paris, France
Sun Jun	ISTD, Singapore University of Technology and Design (SUTD), Singapore
Timo Jamsa	University of Oulu, Finland
Vincent Augusto	Institut Mines Télécom, Mines Saint-Etienne, France
Xiaolan Xie	Institut Mines Télécom, Mines Saint-Etienne, CNRS Limos Saint-Etienne, France
Ye-Qiong Song	University of Lorraine, France
Yves Demazeau	CNRS, France
Zuraimi Sultan	SinBerBEST, Berkeley Education Alliance for Research in Singapore (BEARS), Singapore

Organizing Committee

Chair

| Antoine de Marassé Enouf | CNRS IPAL, Singapore |

Members

Hamdi Aloulou	University of Monastir, Tunisia; Institut Mines-Telecom, Paris, France
Martin Kodys	Institut Mines-Télécom, CNRS IPAL, Singapore
Ibrahim Sadek	Institut Mines-Télécom, CNRS IPAL, Singapore
Angela Saenz	CNRS IPAL, Singapore

Sponsors

Image and Pervasive Access Lab, CNRSUMI 2955, Singapore
Institut for Infocomm Research, Singapore
National University of Singapore, Singapore
Institut Mines Télécom, Paris, France
National Center for Scientific Research, France
University of Sherbrook, Canada

Contents

XIV   Contents

Smart Environment Technology

Short Contributions

E-health Technology Design

Can Technology Improve Medication Adherence in Older People with Dementia?

Najwan El-Saifi[1,2(✉)], Wendy Moyle[1,2], Cindy Jones[1,2],
and Haitham Tuffaha[1,3]

[1] Menzies Health Institute Queensland, Griffith University,
Nathan, Brisbane, QLD 4111, Australia
najwan.el-saifi@griffithuni.edu.au,
{w.moyle,c.jones,haitham.tuffaha}@griffith.edu.au
[2] School of Nursing and Midwifery, Griffith University,
Nathan, Brisbane, QLD 4111, Australia
[3] Centre for Applied Health Economics, School of Medicine, Griffith University,
Nathan, Brisbane, QLD 4111, Australia

Abstract. Older people with dementia often depend on caregivers to manage their medications. The complexity of medication regimens in this population can impede medication adherence (i.e., taking medications as prescribed), which may compromise the effectiveness of treatment and increase the cost and burden of illness. Different technological devices have been used to improve medication adherence, however, these devices are often not evidence-based or designed with end-user involvement, thereby affecting their acceptability by people living with dementia and their caregivers. This in turn, can influence the effectiveness and uptake of such devices. This study aims to explore the challenges of medication adherence for both older people with dementia and their caregivers to guide the development of future technological solutions that can be effective, practical and sustainable.

Keywords: Medication adherence · Dementia · Technology · Medication aids
Webster packs

1 Introduction

Dementia is a disorder that is characterised by a decline in one or more cognitive domains including memory, language, visuospatial skills, personality or behaviour, and manipulation of acquired knowledge. Dementia is a challenging syndrome with profound health and quality of life repercussions for people with the condition and their family caregivers [1]. Caregivers for people with dementia are at an increased risk for financial burden, stress, depression, social isolation and physical morbidities [2]. As a major global health problem, it was estimated that around 50 million people were living with dementia worldwide in 2015, this figure is expected to reach 75 and 135 million in 2030 and 2050 respectively due to continuous population growth and ageing [3]. Worldwide, the annual estimated direct costs of dementia were US$815 billion in 2015 [4].

Older people with dementia experience age-related physiological changes and often have multiple comorbidities that require treatment with medications. This can lead to disability and increased dependence on caregivers to help them with daily activities including medication administration [3]. Nevertheless, the complexity of medication regimens and the other care responsibilities caregivers have to undertake simultaneously can lead to suboptimal medication adherence. Medication adherence, as defined by the World Health Organisation (WHO), is the extent to which a person's behaviour of taking medication corresponds with agreed recommendations from a health care provider [5]. Suboptimal medication adherence can impact health outcomes and healthcare costs as it compromises the effectiveness of treatment thus increasing the burden of disease [6]. A recent study estimated the annual economic cost of non-adherence to range from $949 to $44,190 per person in 2015 US$ [7].

There has been an increasing interest in developing technologies to assist patients and caregivers in improving medication adherence in several ways including providing appropriate medication information, education, organising medications, dispensing and dose reminding [8]. Technologies to improve medication adherence can fall under three primary categories [9]: (1) Pill monitoring technology which includes pill bottles with electronic smart caps, smart blister packaging and digital pills; (2) Mobile health technology, which is the use of smartphones and other wireless technology in medical care [9, 10]; and (3) online resources and social media. However, these technologies are mostly commercial, lack an evidence-base, and have been designed and developed by engineers or programmers without sufficient end-user involvement [9]. Hence, the solutions provided through these technologies might not be practical or acceptable to people living with dementia and their caregivers, which in turn can influence the effectiveness and cost-effectiveness (i.e., value for money) of existing technologies in real-world practice [9]. Thus, it is important in the development of any technological solution to consider end-users' needs and healthcare systems' requirements for safe, effective and cost-effective products [11, 12]. Therefore, there is a strong need to empirically identify the challenges caregivers face during medication administration to develop technological solutions that are patient-centred, effective and sustainable to help people with dementia and their caregivers make the best use of medications.

The aim of this study is to explore the challenges of medication adherence faced by both caregivers and people with dementia during medication administration from the caregivers' perspective. This information will be used to help guide the development of future technological solutions to improve medication adherence in older people with dementia.

2   Methods

Semi-structured telephone interviews were conducted with family caregivers of older people with dementia living in the community, with any type and stage of dementia. A convenient sample of family caregivers was recruited. Family caregivers were invited through national caregiver support agencies. Interested family caregivers contacted the lead researcher, and a time for the interview was then arranged. The study was approved by Griffith University Human Research Ethics Committee (Reference no: 20017/150)

The interviews sought to explore the challenges or problems that influenced medication adherence and how these challenges could be addressed. Interview questions were developed based on literature reports of the factors influencing medication adherence in this population [13]. The interviews were conducted by the lead researcher from an office at Griffith University during September and October 2017. The interviews were digitally recorded and lasted between 30 to 65 min. Participants provided their verbal consent at the beginning of the telephone interview. A range of demographic information about each participant was also collected at the beginning of the interview. Participants were no longer recruited when no further attributional themes arose.

The interviews were transcribed verbatim. Transcripts were checked against the original digital recordings for accuracy and all identifying information was removed. An inductive thematic analysis based on Braun and Clarke's method was conducted by two researchers, discussed and confirmed with the other authors [14]. The method started with data familiarisation by reading and re-reading the data allowing the generation of initial codes across the entire dataset [14]. The codes were collated into potential themes which were checked and reviewed, followed by the generation of clear definitions and names for each of the themes [14].

3 Findings

Ten caregivers were interviewed. The majority of caregivers were spouses (70%), older than 65 years (60%), females (80%), and retired (60%). Two major themes emerged from the telephone interviews that describe the challenges faced during medication administration: (1) human challenges and (2) technology challenges. Exemplar quotations from caregivers are provided to support the themes outlined.

3.1 Human Challenges

This theme involved two sub themes; people with dementia's experience with self-medication through caregivers' perspective, and caregivers' experience.

People with Dementia's Experience from Caregivers' Perspective
Caregivers talked about their care recipients' experience with medications. People with dementia face various problems at different times during their caregiving depending on the stage of dementia, cognitive functioning and changing capacities of the person with dementia. In the early stages, people with dementia struggled with not only remembering to take their medications but also whether they had taken the medications or not, which had the potential to lead to overdosing. These changes affected their autonomy in medication management and required the involvement of caregivers. C_1: *"She had a checklist she would get part way through it and forget and not know whether she'd had one or not…It was just simply that she couldn't follow through and so it became critical that someone else i.e. me in this case, look after the medication."*

Caregivers' Experience

Caregivers found administering medications very difficult and challenging alongside the progression of dementia, as the disease affected the person with dementia's understanding, behaviour and sense of trust; hence, care recipients become less trustful of people, and as a result they resist taking medications. For example, one caregiver stated C_6: *"She would never take them, she always refused to take a tablet. She thought we were poisoning her. Sometimes she would just not even know who I was so she wouldn't take it because she didn't know who it was."*

Caregivers considered the understanding of dementia and treatment options a core element in medication management that could help to ensure medication adherence. They expressed anxiety and concerns about administering medications in the safest way possible. C_6: *"Because if you don't know about the medications and stuff it's scary. You don't want to think you're going to kill someone if you do it wrong."* Information provided from medication information downloaded from the internet was not found to be useful. The medication information was described as being too long, complex, and written in technical terminology that most caregivers would not understand, as a result they perceived that they might miss important information. C_1: *"So the information is inconsistent and very much the medication data sheets that you download from the web, as good as they are for some kinds of people, for a carer who doesn't necessarily have the background they're useless. They go on, far too much information without having the critical information that you need for the particular person that you're dealing with."*

3.2   Technology Challenges

This theme involved two sub themes; traditional technology and modern technology.

Traditional Technology

Caregivers reported the use of different strategies to facilitate the process of medication management, such as the use of containers, dosette boxes and Webster or blister packs. They reported one of the challenges of pill boxes or containers faced by their care recipients was the perplexity of filling these with medications. Caregivers expressed their dissatisfaction with the boxes they got at the pharmacy, as these simple three compartment morning, noon, and night boxes only worked for the basics. In particular, managing these boxes becomes cumbersome where there were multiple medications, and when some of the medications were too big fit the box or required refrigeration. Nonetheless, half of the caregivers used Webster or blister packs, and they found them C_7: *"Very helpful"* and C_{10}: *"The easiest thing".* Explicitly, these were deemed most useful in the early stages of dementia where the care-recipients may take their medications from the packs under caregivers' supervision. The best features of Webster packs as stated by caregivers, were being divided into compartments for different times (morning, lunchtime or evening), and containing the list of all the medications, the strengths and the amount to be taken. Thereby, making it easier to give or let their care-recipients have them on time, with no need for the caregivers being involved in the preparation. C_3: *"In our case I don't think there's any better way because it's coming straight from the pharmacy and I don't have to do it and I don't have to have those tablets lying around in the house. So, to me that's probably about the best way."*

However, caregivers who didn't use the blister packs, justified the reasons as being both expensive and nuisance, since things kept changing. Even they found the blister pack to be daunting, as it was full of tablets that could confuse the person with dementia, which raised concerns for caregivers about the risk of getting the medications mixed up. C_1: *"I don't think Webster packs would be adequate because people get mixed up on what day it is... there's some medications in one of Webster pack boxes so they take that regardless of what time it is because I need to follow it all the way through, one after, one after."* Also, one caregiver added the availability of cheap versions of the same concept of blister pack, that might not be sufficiently well-designed, then suggested C_9: *"Perhaps there should be one specifically designed for dementia people."* Nevertheless, other caregivers mentioned that their main issue was to remember giving the medications on time, which might be difficult when they are busy doing other tasks; therefore, there is a need for a reminder along with the use of Webster packs. Some caregivers set alarms on their mobile phones to remind them of the medication time, as stated by C_4: *"It is not where the medication is. It is remembering to actually get to it."* Others used yellow post-it-notes stuck on different places in their house as a reminder to give the care-recipient their medications.

Modern Technology

Caregivers talked about the use of modern technology in several situations. For instance, some caregivers set medication alarms on their smartphones, others sought medical information from the internet using computers, smartphones or tablets. However, few caregivers didn't feel positive towards computers or technology, which they found complicated, challenging and confusing. Furthermore, they added that the care-recipients themselves could not be involved in the use of technology, as they had lost the ability to use anything that was related to technological understanding, and this happened from the early stages of dementia. C_5: *"He couldn't learn to master the basic skills of a very basic mobile phone."* C_9: *"My husband was a brilliant scientist. He doesn't even use the computer now. He uses the wrong devices for turning on television or the inverter or the radio."* The caregivers preferred a one-to-one approach where someone could talk to them in plain English and help them understand the condition and the required medications.

Caregivers were asked to share their thoughts on technology and whether it could help them to achieve medication adherence. They reported that technology uptake would be different for different people. Additionally, a single solution would not be appropriate for all caregivers but rather a solution that is tailored to each caregiver's needs was required. C_1: *"It's a problem that's not going to be solved by a single tool. Whatever solution, it needs to be multifaceted."*

The majority of caregivers thought of smartphones when they discussed technology, as they perceived that smartphones had become part of everyone's life, and a lot of people carried mobile phones and connected regularly to them. They also indicated that a mobile application might be useful, as it could be programmed to manage the challenges of medication management. C_4: *"An app would cover everything, an app that could manage medication for dementia people where the caregiver could download the person's details, what tablets they take, what hours they take the tablet, and the app would do the magic reminder for each tablet."* Although many older people use mobile phones, one caregiver thought that older caregivers might not be sufficiently comfortable with the concept of an app and suggested C_9: *"The Fitbit concept, because it's multifaceted and that would be something that a caregiver could comfortably utilise as a watch, something on a wrist strap that would have all those things, including an alarm."*

Regardless of the type of the technology, caregivers spoke of the need to build relevant health education into the tool or device, where information provided should be in plain and simple English, also to have links to additional information for people who wanted to know more. In addition, a reminder system and a dementia forum where caregivers could talk, support each other and share their experiences would be useful. When considering technology-based solutions, all caregivers concurred, that in order to be encouraged to use a technological device, it should be attractive, simple, easy to understand, easy to operate and user friendly. C_2: *"You've got enough to worry about with what's going on without having to worry about how to work everything else, so it has to be basic."* C_1: *"It needs to work with me not me work with it."* They also added if it would be for the person with dementia, it needed to be simple, bright and of a decent size so that it would not be fiddly to hold.

4 Discussion

In this study, we have explored the challenges faced during medication administration from the caregivers' perspective. The qualitative nature of the study provided a deep insight into the process of medication administration and the challenges caregivers of people with dementia face which can affect medication adherence. These were described within the two major themes: human challenges and technology challenges. We have shown that medication administration process represents a big challenge for people with dementia and their caregivers. This is consistent with what we know about dementia as a progressive condition, where people with advanced disease experience significant memory loss and behaviour changes and, consequently, become less capable of being autonomous in their treatment [13], increasing the burden on their caregivers.

The participants in the interviews expressed their need for the right information to know how to manage their care-recipients' medications as well as for effective and practical means to help them remember giving medications on time. Understanding dementia and the progressive changes in the people's cognitive capacities and behaviour is critical to mitigate the reasons behind their resistance to taking medications. However, seeking reliable concise information was one of the hardest things as all the information were in medical terms and so complicated. Therefore, caregivers should be empowered by providing them with the relevant information in a simple and clear way. Participants in the telephone interviews expressed mixed opinions about existing aids and reminders (e.g. Webster packs); however, the interviews revealed a great potential for modern technology (e.g. computers, tablets and smartphones) to provide the necessary information to empower caregivers and to help them administer medications as prescribed. With the rapid development of technology to assist seniors and their caregivers, and in a time where the use of smartphones, tablets and computers is ubiquitous, the use of technology in enhancing medication adherence in this population is promising. Technological solutions may help caregivers safely administer medications to their care recipients and lessen the burden placed on them. However, the technology should be a multi-compartment dose organiser with a built in reminder. It should also have an educational component that provides clear information about the medication. To facilitate the technology uptake, it should be effective, affordable and user friendly i.e. easy to operate, decent size to be carried everywhere and catchy. Importantly it should be designed right from the conceptual stage with the input of end-users. It should also be able to be integrated into existing technologies such as smart home systems where a collection of inter-related software and hardware components can be used to monitor behaviours such as medication adherence and physiological status and to send reminders to take medications.

The present study extends our understanding of adherence to medication providing an evidence-based explanation for medication non-adherence in older people with dementia, which is instrumental for intervention development. Notwithstanding, this is the first step in the intervention development process. Further steps should be followed including the development of a valid design for a technological solution, translating the design into a practical device and the evaluation of the technology in terms of effectiveness and cost-effectiveness. Of note, technology based solutions in this setting might be a cost-effective option because of the relatively low cost of delivery and the potential to reduce resources consumed by the health system (e.g., healthcare provider's time) or out-of-pocket expenses by caregivers [9]. Demonstrating effectiveness and value for money will enhance the chances for the uptake of the technology and make it a sustainable choice for health care systems. Therefore, there has been an increasing interest by manufacturers in conducting pre-market (i.e., early) economic evaluations to know whether it is worthwhile investing in a given technological product. In addition, this can help manufacturers identify future research needs to support their products and inform the right price that is profitable but at the same time affordable for individual users and health organisations.

5 Conclusion

The number of people with dementia is on the rise and there is an increased need to optimise their therapeutic outcomes. Caregivers play a major role in the medication management of people with dementia, but they face several challenges. Evidence-based and user-centred technological solutions can address these challenges and help people with dementia make the best use of their medications.

References

1. Australian Institute of Health and Welfare. Dementia in Australia Canberra: AIHW (2012). http://www.aihw.gov.au/WorkArea/DownloadAsset.aspx?id=10737422943
2. Brodaty, H., Donkin, M.: Family caregivers of people with dementia. Dialogues Clin. Neurosci. 11(2), 217–228 (2009)

3. World Health Organisation. The Epidemiology and Impact of Dementia Current State and FutureTrends (2015). http://www.who.int/mental_health/neurology/dementia/dementia_thematicbrief_epidemiology.pdf
4. Alzheimer's Disease International. The Global Impact of Dementia: An analysis of prevalence, incidence, cost and trends. https://www.alz.co.uk/research/WorldAlzheimerReport2015.pdf
5. World Health Organisation. Adherence to Long-Term Therapies - Evidence for Action 2003, 30 May 2016. http://apps.who.int/medicinedocs/en/d/Js4883e/7.2.html
6. Kocurek, B.: Promoting Medication Adherence in Older Adults and the Rest of Us. Diabetes Spectr. **22**(2), 80–84 (2009)
7. Cutler, R.L., Fernandez-Llimos, F., Frommer, M., Benrimoj, C., Garcia-Cardenas, V.: Economic impact of medication non-adherence by disease groups: a systematic review. BMJ Open **8**(1), e016982 (2018)
8. Center for Technology and Aging. Technologies for Optimizing Medication Use in Older Adults. http://www.techandaging.org/MedOpPositionPaper.pdf
9. Marsch, L.A., Lord, S.E., Dallery, J.: Behavioural Healthcare and Technology: Using Science-Based Innovations to Transform Practice. Oxford University Press, Oxford (2015)
10. Hamine, S., Gerth-Guyette, E., Faulx, D., Green, B.B., Ginsburg, A.S.: Impact of mHealth chronic disease management on treatment adherence and patient outcomes: a systematic review. J. Med. Internet Res. **17**(2), e52 (2015)
11. Markiewicz, K., Van Til, J., Ijzerman, M.: Early assessment of medical devices in development for company decision making: an exploration of best practices. J. Commer. Biotechnol. **23**(2), 15–30 (2017)
12. Rothery, C., Claxton, K., Palmer, S., Epstein, D., Tarricone, R., Sculpher, M.: Characterising uncertainty in the assessment of medical devices and determining future research needs: characterising uncertainty in the assessment of devices. Health Econ. **26**, 109–123 (2017)
13. El-Saifi, N., Moyle, W., Jones, C., Tuffaha, H.: Medication adherence in older patients with dementia: a systematic literature review. J. Pharm. Practice (2017). https://doi.org/10.1177/0897190017710524
14. Braun, V., Clarke, V.: Using thematic analysis in psychology. Qual. Res. Psychol. **3**(2), 77–101 (2006)

Human Centered Design Conception Applied to the Internet of Things: Contribution and Interest

Quentin Chibaudel[1](✉), Bellmunt Joaquim[2](✉), Lespinet-Najib Véronique[1](✉), and Mokhtari Mounir[2](✉)

[1] Cognitique et Ingénierie Humaine (CIH), Laboratoire Intégration du Matériau au Système (IMS) - UMR CNRS 5218, École Nationale Supérieure de Cognitique (ENSC), Institut Polytechnique de Bordeaux, Talence, France
{quentin.chibaudel,veronique.lespinet}@ensc.fr
[2] Imaging and Pervasive Access Lab (IPAL) UMI CNRS 2955, Institut for Infocomm Research (I2R/A*STAR), Singapore, France
{Joaquim.bellmunt,mounir.mokhtari}@ipal.cnrs.fr

1 Introduction

Internet Of Things (IoT) is increasingly used throughout the world in different fields. But it does not have a standardized definition [28]. Several definition can be proposed. IoT corresponds to *"objects with virtual identity and personality, working in a smart environment and using smart interfaces to connect and communicate in some various context"* [3]. IoT is a sum of entities that are used to exchange information in different contexts. This is a network of connected objects communicating between them to extend their functionalities [17]. The IoT is larger than just a system: it is a system of system. Each one can be divided in sub-system and assimilated to a specific technology [5]. The IoT is *"a dynamic infrastructure of a global network. This global network has auto-configuration capacities based on standards and communication protocols interoperable. In this network, physical and virtual objects have identities, physical attributes, virtual personalities and smart interfaces and they are integrated to the network in a transparent way"* [31].

Currently, approach to develop IoT is almost exclusively technical. Yet, this way of conception is insufficient. *"The IoT is a socio-technical system"* [6] that may have different form according choices that will be done by our societies [8]. Until now, IoT development was dominated by technical vision [34]. Few efforts were made about the study of the social, political or organizational impact [28]. One of the IoT main scope is the accessibility [26]. There is a need for a cross-disciplinary framework. It represents all the aspect of technological systems including, among other things, users [29]. As a socio-technical system IoT can show a specific kind of complexity. It is a hybrid system made of different elements that interact with each other [34]. A holistic approach to analyze the system is central to develop IoT [27]. *"Such choices, on the social, cultural and behavioral impacts of how we develop, manage and evolve the IoT, will be critical to its success"* [28].

A paradox is appearing. One the main objective of the IoT is to increase accessibility in our society. Yet, insufficient account is taken of human factor in developing IoT tools. There is a lake of accessibility. It needs to be improved.

On the side of technical approach, Human-Centered Design (HCD) methodology is to reach this goal. *"Human-centered Design is an approach to interactive systems development that aims to make systems usable and useful by focusing on the users, their needs and requirements, and by applying human factors/ergonomics, usability knowledge, and techniques. This approach enhances effectiveness and efficiency, improves human well-being, user satisfaction, accessibility and sustainability; and counteracts possible adverse effects of use on human health, safety and performance"* [18]. Using this methodology helps conceivers to take in account user's needs and adapt the tool. One example is interesting to study: elderly people (i.e. people who are more than 65 years old) [24]. There are more and more elderly people around the word. For example, in 1994, the part of elderly people was 9%. In 2014, it was 12%: the part increased of 33% ! Experts estimate this part to be 21% in 2050: a multiplication by two [32]. But *"our lives are longer but not without disabilities"* [9]. And, *"living longer does not mean living with good health"* [22]. Changes that form and influence the aging process are complexes [19]. Several definitions may be proposed.

From a biological point of view, the aging process is associated with an important diversity of molecular and cellular injuries [30]. These injuries decrease physiological resources and general capacities of a person. Modifications are not linear nor constant. For example, elderly people have more difficulties in monitoring their cognitive functions than younger people. And, there is a higher standard deviation for elderly people than young people [33]. Aging process also has noxious consequences on motor and sensorial skills [11]. Modifications are specific to each person [30]. They are related to the environment where the person is living and his behavior [24]. It is important to consider not only medical nor biological considerations but also social condition of living. The aging process also corresponds to *"all the mechanisms that progressively decrease capacities of an organism to deal with all the requirements of the environment and maintain the integration of the organs that ensure vital functions"* [20]. The living environment can accelerate or reduce this phenomenon. For example, new technologies can help to prevent deficiencies caused by the aging process [2]. To sum up, the aging process can be defined as *"a normal phenomenon, progressive, irreversible, unequal, heterogeneous and with noxious consequences of the person"* [15].

As age increase, there is a higher prevalence of chronic diseases or functional limitations [7]. If aging leads to disabilities, it is not a synonym of disease. Most of the time, environment is a curb to accessibility. It is not adapted nor accessible. Accessibility corresponds to the possibility to access a place, a service or an information [13]. An accessible space is defined by an absence of exclusion and an arrangement of the public space for everyone [10]. Accessibility is also considered as all barriers that prevent people from full participation to daily life activities [12].

A problem is appearing. On one side, there are more and more elderly people in our society. And their number is going to increase significantly. But environment is not accessible for them. A tool might be relevant to improve accessibility for them: the IoT. IoT methodologies are often technical and not always adapted to elderly people's needs. HCD methodology is a relevant approach. The aim of this paper is to applied a HCD methodology to an IoT tool destinated to elderly people to improve accessibility and adapt it. We are going to present a HCD methodology, called AMICAS, applied to an existing and already tested IoT tool: UbiSmart. First, AMICAS methodology will be described. Then, we will explain how UbiSmart system works and how we applied the AMICAS methodology to it. Finally, before discussing the advantages and the limits of this new approach, we will explain how this work will help us to improve the accessibility for elderly people.

2   Methodology

To study accessibility, a global approach is required: environment, human and material must be considered [4]. Methodology applied here is called AMICAS: "Approche Methodologique Innovante de Conception Adaptee Systemique" (Innovative and Methodological Approach of Adapted and Systemic Conception). AMICAS methodology is a HCD methodology and a holistic approach [25]. All the factors (cognitive capacities, motor and sensorial skills) can be considered. We applied this methodology following different steps:

1. theoretical study of the approach
2. adaptation of the methodology to the situation considered
3. implementation of the method
4. exploitation of the results

2.1   Description of the Original Methodology

There are three main steps in the AMICAS methodology. Each step is divided is several sub-steps. The step 1 is called "definition and application of analysis grids". This step is illustrated on the Fig. 1
There are six grids for the first step:

- grid A - definition of the context: identify the different element that compose the user's environment
- grid B - definition of the common situations and preconditions to realize them: identify different actions that the user daily realizes. Definition of the prerequisites (cognitive, sensorial and motor) to achieve the action
- grid C - definition of user's profile: define users in terms of deficiency (cognitive, sensorial and motor), needs and strengths
- grid D - definition of cognitive, sensorial and motor precondition to participate to the evaluation: define cognitive, sensorial and motor prerequisites to allow a person to participate to the evaluation

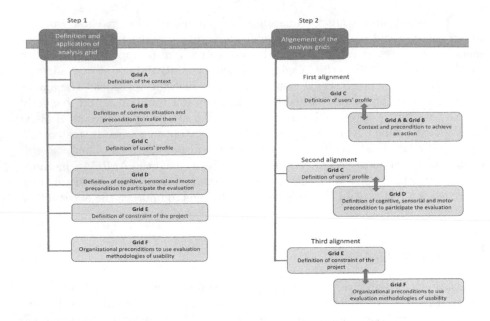

Fig. 1. Description of the different grids for the first step

- grid E - define project's constraints: identify constraints is terms of access to the users and resources available (time, money, ect)
- grid F - organizational preconditions to use evaluation methodologies of usability: define organizational elements to put in practice a relevant methodology of evaluation

Elaboration of the different grids is an iterative process. They can be adapted according the context ([25]). The step 2 is called "alignment of the analysis grids". There are three alignments for the second step:

- alignment 1: comparison of user profile (grid C) with the context (grid A) and situations studied (grid B). The aim of this comparison is to put in the light difficulties and constraint for a user to realize a task. After this step, we are able to propose adapted solutions
- alignment 2: in this alignment, we compare the user profile and the prerequisites needed to participate to the evaluation. With this comparison, we get the list of the methodology adapted for the situation and/or how they can be adapted to the context
- alignment 3: with this alignment, we get the methodologies that can be effectively used according the conditions of the project (cultural aspects, money, resources, etc.)

The step 3 is an iterative process between conception and validation of the tool.

2.2   Description of UbiSmart

UbiSmart is an IoT tool developed to improve accessibility for elderly people. Elderly people need four main requirements in their daily life activities: remembering daily living task; maintain social links; participate to social activities; boosting feeling of safety [23]. Some of them, like participate to social activities, are linked with the accessibility. This tool is currently tested in France and in Singapore. Current UbiSmart system is composed of 6 sensors: 3 motion sensors, 2 door sensors and one sleep sensor. They collect data and an algorithm interpret them to detect an activity. The work done was based on technical recommendations about the hardware and the software [21]. Few work was done about the service and the knowledge. By using AMICAS, we are able to propose adaptation on the system and the service and improve the accessibility.

2.3   Adaptation of the Methodology for UbiSmart

AMICAS methodology can be adapted according the project and the situation [25]. For the study of UbiSmart, some adaptations have been made only on the step 1 and 2 as illustrated on the Fig. 2

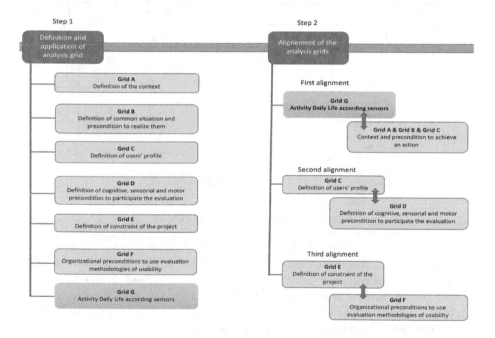

Fig. 2. Illustration of the AMICAS methodology adapted

To participate to the evaluation, the participant had to be cognitively abled; English or mandarin speaking; volunteer. The protocol agreement respected the ethical politic fixed by the Singaporean government. In this situation there is only one user profile. It means grid C was fixed by the condition. Therefore on the step one, a new grid G was added. On the step two, the alignment 1 was modified. The aim is to try to explain the differences between the real behavior of an elderly person and the behavior proposed by UbiSmart.

3   Results

4 participants have been interviewed. They all respected the conditions to participate and were all volunteers. Grids of the first step were established. To establish these grids, observations were made on participant's apartments. After the grids were established, alignment were made.

3.1   Alignment 1

For the grid A, a map with the localization of the different sensors was made as shown on the Fig. 3.

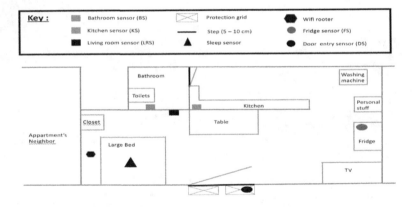

Fig. 3. Cartography of an apartment

For the grid B, based on the interview and the current list implemented in UbiSmart, a list of common daily life activities was proposed. Foreach activity, a list of prerequisites was proposed. The Fig. 4 illustrates that for the cooking activity. A schema of the sensor to detect an activity was added on the grid C: it corresponds to the sensor's state during an activity.

The grid C proposed on the Fig. 5 describes the user profile. Based on the element noted during the observation, lists of cognitive, sensorial and motor capacities, needs and strengths were proposed.

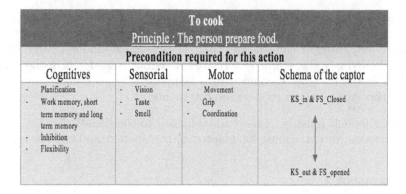

To cook			
Principle : The person prepare food.			
Precondition required for this action			
Cognitives	Sensorial	Motor	Schema of the captor
- Planification - Work memory, short term memory and long term memory - Inhibition - Flexibility	- Vision - Taste - Smell	- Movement - Grip - Coordination	KS_in & FS_Closed ↕ KS_out & FS_opened

Fig. 4. precondition for the cooking activity.

People living in Senior Activity Center		
Deficiencies		
Cognitives	Sensorial	Motor
- Language - Attention - Flexibility - Planification - Inhibition - Short term memory, work memory	- Decrease of sensorial capacities	- Decrease of motor fitness (to walk, to stand, …)

Fig. 5. illustration of the user profile associated to Grid C

3.2   Study of Two Representative Activities: To Cook and to Have Meal

For the activity "to cook", sensor's state are modified. According the sensor activated, we can know whom user is concerned and its localization in its apartment and how long he is staying in a particular room. With this information, ubiSmart determines the activity. For the cooking activity, the time spent in the kitchen is limited to 20 min. There is a succession of activation between the kitchen sensor and the fridge sensor.

The cross of these grids allows us to put in light several elements about the interpretation of the user's behavior and about the data treatment.

First, UbiSmart can interpret some behavior as unusual whereas there are not. For example, according to the grid C, the person has difficulties to stand for a long time. We can imagine that, while the rice is cooking, the person wants is sat. At this moment, the living room sensor is activated. It does not mean there is a problem. Plus, the user may have cognitive deficiencies especially about work and short memory and scheduling. It means they can put more than 20 min to prepare food: if they forgot where are the ingredients or if they need to change their organization, it will be longer.

Currently, the activity "have meal" is detected according several conditions: this activity is rear the cooking activity. It is considered that the person is eating in its kitchen. The sensor kitchen is activated and the living room one is not. According the map proposed on the grid A and considering that the user cannot stand for a long time, we can consider that the person eats in its living room. As a result, the living room sensor is activated. It is not considered in the current algorithm. It will consider it as an absurd behavior.

With this cross, we can propose improvements:

– behavior models must be revised and adapted to the situation
– interpretation of datas must be adapted to the context and the person

3.3   Alignment 2

To realize the alignment 2, grid C illustrated on the figure Fig. 6 was used. To realize the grid D, a website was used: https://useusers.ensc.fr/ (in French only) [25]. It is a system dedicated for professionnals to help to sort and find HCD methodologies adapted to the situation (context, users) [25]. The Fig. 6 represents the interface of the tool. In our situation: we have access to our final users; we are working on the evaluation phase to propose improvements; users have some sensorial (hearing and visually) deficiencies; users have cognitive (communication and think) deficiencies; users have some motor deficiencies (mobility). Results are illustrated on the Fig. 6.

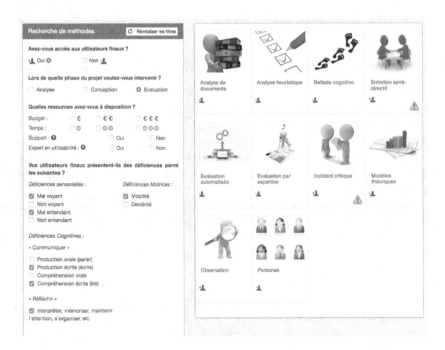

Fig. 6. Result of the methodology that can be used for the evaluation (in French only))

According the user profile and the context, a list of methodology illustrated on the Fig. 6 can be used. Among this list, some methodologies will not be able to be used because of the constraint of the project.

3.4   Alignment 3

This alignment could not have been done for the moment. Indeed, budget are still to be defined. Plus, this tool is currently used in France and in Singapore: a study of the laws in this two countries has to be done. This study is focused on the collection and the treatment of the data. According our the possibilities, some methodologies will not be able to be used in both countries (what are the common authorization ? what are the differences ?). For example, in Singapore, there is no specification about sensitive data. In France, there are restriction about sensitive data. There is no authorization to diffuse data about health situation. Document analysis about the health condition is possible in Singapore so we can apply this methodology in Singapore. But not in France. We need to find methodologies adapted for each legislation.

3.5   Enhancement of the Accessibility

To conclude, we have shown the interest of using a HCD methodology for an IoT tool to improve accessibility for elderly people. We propose recommendations to offer a better service: better interpretation of the elderly person's behavior and critical situation. Plus, we hope to help user to deliberate from technological barriers. With a better interpretation of data, we will help care services to take in charge the elderly person by offering an adapted service. Then, this will also help elderly people to be fully part of their care: the modification proposed should allow user to know if there is a problem or not and may help elderly to know when they need care and take initiative about that.

3.6   Next Steps to Come

Now, we need to modify the algorithm and test it. To test it, a first list of methodologies can be used. We have to study some more aspects to define more precisely the methodologies that are going to be used to evaluate the recommendations made.

4   Discussion

The IoT is a socio-technical system. Methodologies to develop it must not only be technical but also human centered design. Here, we have illustrated a specific methodology (AMICAS) on a specific tool (UbiSmart). We have shown how to apply this methodology to increase accessibility. We got positives results and perspectives even if some limits appeared during the study.

4.1   Advantages

First, a human centered design methodology allows designers and developer to take in account more elements (especially the environment) and adapt the tools. Thus, we have made two kind of improvements: we can identify some behavior that may look absurd while they are not. And we can propose an adaptation of the data treatment and have more relevant results. This recommendations should be adapted to user and help them using the system. Now, these recommendations have to be tested. According the results, we will be able to know if they recommendation were relevant and how we can still improve UbiSmart. The iterative process is a strength for this evaluation. If we are wrong, with the tests, we will be able to propose alternatives. If we are right, we will be able to propose new improvements and new tests.

4.2   Limits

Even if we have positive perspectives with, some elements are still to be improved. The AMICAS methodology consider general profiles. Yet, every situation is specific. The difficulty of access for this population is explained by "the singularity of the situation" [1]. For example, in the consideration of the limit of time that the system considers the resident has a problem, is specific to each person. For one person, the problem can be declared after 10 min of unactivity. For another one, the problem can be declared after 1 h of unactivity. We need to find a way to adapt the daily life activity system recognition respecting privacy. Technical approach must not be neglected. Recommendations might be very hard to be put in practice. We also need to think a way of coordinating the two ways of thinking: there is not on one side the HCD methodology and, on the other one, the technical methodologies. For more efficiency, we need to put in practice this two methodologies on parallel and coordinate them.

4.3   Perspectives of Evolution

Whatever methods are finally adopted, there is a need of multidisciplinary approach. Technical methodologies need to add human factors elements to propose accessible tools. And vice-versa: human centered design methods need to understand technical challenges to conceive functional tools. To do that, future users must be involved in the conception as soon as the project begins. Their needs must be collected and understood to propose functional and accessible functional. Plus, the aging phenomenon raise some more questions. Someone who is not yet suffering from incapacities or is losing autonomy is considered as frailty. It is a major factor of incapacity and mortality [14]. With the aging, their capital decreases. That is the reason why elderly people have more cognitive troubles [16]. Considering that, a work about their free will needs to be done. The solution cannot be dictated. Yet, their health must be preserved. Their choices and wishes must not be neglected. A human centered design methodology could help to take in consideration this kind of problems.

References

1. Azéma, B., Martinez, N.: Les personnes handicapées vieillissantes: espérances de vie et de santé; qualité de vie. Rev. française des affaires sociales. **2**(2), 295–333 (2005)
2. Baltes, P.B., Freund, A.M., Li, S.-C.: The Psychological Science of Human Ageing. Cambridge University Press, Cambridge (2005)
3. Bassi, A., Horn, G.: Internet of things in 2020: a roadmap for the future. Eur. Common. Inf. Soc. Media **22**, 97–114 (2008)
4. Belio, C.: Handicap, cognition et représentations. Ph.D. thesis, Bordeaux 2 (2012)
5. Benghozi, P.-J., Bureau, S., Massit-Folea, F.: L'internet des objets. quels enjeux pour les européens? (2008)
6. Bijker, W.E.: Of Bicycles, Bakelites, and Bulbs: Toward a Theory of Sociotechnical Change. MIT Press, Cambridge (1997)
7. Briançon, S., Guèrin, G., Sandrin-Berthon, B.: Les maladies chroniques. Actualités Dossiers En Santé Publique, pp. 11–53 (2010)
8. Brunet, R., Ferra, R., Théry, H.: Les mots de la géographie, dictionnaire critique. GIR RECLUS/La Documentation française (1992)
9. Bussière, C.: Recours aux soins de santé primaires des personnes en situation de handicap: analyses économiques à partir des données de l'enquête Handicap-Santé. Ph.D. thesis, Université Paris-Saclay (2016)
10. Chaudet, B.: Handicap, vieillissement et accessibilité. Exemples en France et au Québec. Ph.D. thesis, Université Paris-Saclay (2016)
11. Covelet, R.: Prendre enfin conscience des enjeux des déficits sensoriels des personnes âgées. Gérontol. soc. **30**(4), 249–262 (2007)
12. Despouy, L.: Human Rights and Disabled Persons. United Nations (1993)
13. Folcher, V., Lompré, N.: Accessibilité pour et dans l'usage: concevoir des situations d'activité adaptées à tous et à chacun. Le trav. hum. **75**(1), 89–120 (2012)
14. Fried, L.P., Tangen, C.M., Walston, J., Newman, A.B., Hirsch, C., Gottdiener, J., Seeman, T., Tracy, R., Kop, W.J., Burke, G., et al.: Frailty in older adults: evidence for a phenotype. J. Gerontol. Ser. A Biol. Sci. Med. Sci. **56**(3), M146–M157 (2001)
15. Gohet, P.: L'avancée en âge des personnes handicapées contribution à la réflexion. Rapport, Paris (2013)
16. Grossman, M., et al.: The Demand for Health: A Theoretical and Empirical Investigation. NBER Books, New York (1972)
17. Gubbi, J., Buyya, R., Marusic, S., Palaniswami, M.: Internet of things (IoT): a vision, architectural elements, and future directions. Future Gener. Comput. Syst. **29**(7), 1645–1660 (2013)
18. ISO: Ergonomics of human-system interaction: Part 210: Human-centred design for interactive systems (2010)
19. Kirkwood, T.B.L.: A systematic look at an old problem. Nature **451**(7179), 644 (2008)
20. Ladislas, R.: Le vieillissement. faits et théories (1995)
21. Marinc, A., Stocklöw, C., Braun, A., Limberger, C., Hofmann, C., Kuijper, A.: Interactive personalization of ambient assisted living environments. In: Smith, M.J., Salvendy, G. (eds.) Human Interface 2011. LNCS, vol. 6771, pp. 567–576. Springer, Heidelberg (2011). https://doi.org/10.1007/978-3-642-21793-7_64
22. Martel, L., Bélanger, A.: Une analyse de l'évolution de l'espérance de vie sans dépendance au canada entre 1986 et 1996. Rapport sur l'état de la population du Canada 1998–1999, pp. 164–186 (1998)

23. Mokhtari, M., Aloulou, H., Tiberghien, T., Biswas, J., Racoceanu, D., Yap, P.: New trends to support independence in persons with mild dementia-a mini-review. Gerontology **58**(6), 554–563 (2012)
24. OMS: Rapport mondial sur le vieillissement et la santé (2016)
25. Roche, A.: Proposition d'une méthode de conception systémique d'interface homme-système adaptée aux situations de multihandicap. Ph.D. thesis, Université de Bordeaux (2015)
26. Seydoux, N., Drira, K., Hernandez, N., Monteil, T.: Rôle d'une base de connaissance dans semiotics, un système autonome contrôlant un appartement connecté (2016)
27. Shin, D.-H.: A socio-technical framework for cyber-infrastructure design: implication for Korean cyber-infrastructure vision. Technol. Forecast. Soc. Change **77**(5), 783–795 (2010)
28. Shin, D.: A socio-technical framework for internet-of-things design: a human-centered design for the internet of things. Telemat. Inform. **31**(4), 519–531 (2014)
29. Sommerville, I., Dewsbury, G.: Dependable domestic systems design: a socio-technical approach. Interact. Comput. **19**(4), 438–456 (2007)
30. Steves, C.J., Spector, T.D., Jackson, S.H.D.: Ageing, genes, environment and epigenetics: what twin studies tell us now, and in the future. Age Ageing **41**(5), 581–586 (2012)
31. Sundmaeker, H., Guillemin, P., Friess, P., Woelfflé, S.: Vision and challenges for realising the internet of things. Clust. Eur. Res. Proj. Internet Things, Eur. Comm. **3**(3), 34–36 (2010)
32. UNO: World population ageing 2013. Department of Economic and Social Affairs PD (2013)
33. Robert, L., West, R.L.: An application of prefrontal cortex function theory to cognitive aging. Psychol. Bull. **120**(2), 272 (1996)
34. Winter, J.: The internet of things: scenarios for a human-centered design and policy process. In: Conference Paper Presented at the World Futures Studies Federation 40th Anniversary Conference, Bucharest. Romania, June 2013

Designing a Product Service Platform
for Older People: From Needs to Requirements

Roberto Menghi[✉], Alessandra Papetti, Sara Carbonari,
and Michele Germani

Department of Industrial Engineering and Mathematical Sciences,
Università Politecnica delle Marche,
Via Brecce Bianche, 12, 60131 Ancona, Italy
{r.menghi, a.papetti, sara.carbonari,
m.germani}@univpm.it

Abstract. Helping older people to remain in their homes and to be more autonomous and less isolated, escaping from the potential related depression, is a global challenge. To support people 'age in place', the paper proposes a specific data collection to establish the possible requirements of a novel Product Service Platform for wellbeing and health of older people. The study of a community of older people over 75 who live in their homes has allowed acquiring the knowledge of their main needs and characteristics. Two focus groups with experts dealing with the ageing population were then set up to define: (a) how to design an IT artifact that meets end-users needs and (b) the services that a Product Service Platform should provide.

Keywords: Product service platform · Healthcare · Elderly · Survey
Smart environments

1   Introduction

In the context of demographic changes in developed countries, the population of older people will increase significantly in the coming decades. The population trend until 2050 shows a relevant increase of older people. In Europe it is expected an increase about 50% from 2000 to 2050 and among these a sudden rise of ultra-octogenarians people [1]. In addition, the basic healthcare model is often considered inappropriate and insufficient for providing adequate services and fulfilling the needs of people, in particular, of older people [2]. This highlights an evident need to improve the current healthcare model that cannot support such an older people increase with high-quality services. Moreover, the common family model has been changing through years: from a patriarchal model to a more distributed model, where normally sons live far away from their parents due to job opportunities [3]. So, present caregivers necessary appeal to people external to the family. Nevertheless, this is a short-term solution that does not improve the quality of life of older people and represents a considerable cost for the entire family. According to this environment, it has clearly emerged that older people who live alone need to have a new assistance model, more adequate not only from a healthcare point of view, but also from a social perspective.

© Springer International Publishing AG, part of Springer Nature 2018
M. Mokhtari et al. (Eds.): ICOST 2018, LNCS 10898, pp. 23–34, 2018.
https://doi.org/10.1007/978-3-319-94523-1_3

During the last years, scientific research has been trying to find solutions to the growing problem about older people home care. Smart objects [4], robots [5], smart environments [6] and platforms [7] have been developed. However, the research is often technology oriented and neglects the end-user needs. It does not consider the expressed and latent needs of older people and all stakeholders involved in the old people's healthcare.

The aim of this paper is to define the main requirements of a potential Product Service Platform, designed to improve older people living conditions. A deep analysis on a sample of Italian older people living at home has been conducted, followed by a focus group with experts dealing with the ageing population to discover what the main needs of the older people sample are. Finally, a further focus group was conducted on the obtained results to identify functional and non-functional requirements of the platform to enhance the collaboration between all stakeholders.

2 State of the Art

Many statistical studies have been carried out to analyze the older people conditions and needs, focusing also on specific aspects of their daily life. Findings support the assumption that depression and resilience are consistent intermediary factors of the relationship between family function and Quality of Life (QoL) among older people [8]. Those at home reported higher care satisfaction than those in nursing homes did [9]. Moreover, living alone was associated with less preventive care use and worse health. It is important to provide more social and economic support for older people living alone to increase their preventive health care service utilization and improve their health status [10]. Moreover, in countries, like Italy, where the primacy of family support of the older people has been decreasing in recent years, relationship-centered approaches play a key role [11]. According to this evidence, this work focuses on elderly people living at home and aims to improve the current care model, looking for the right tradeoff between people and technologies.

During the last years, the technological evolution has supported the rising issue of older people healthcare [12]. The IoT technologies diffusion has allowed the creation of tailored devices – smart objects – for monitoring different human parameters, such as blood pressure, heart rate, glycaemia, etc. and design elderly smart homes [4, 6, 13]. Ni et al. review the main devices, techniques and models to support developers and service providers to construct and deploy tailored services to enhance independent living for the elderly in smart homes [14]. Also, the communication systems have been improved to guarantee the connection of people far from home [15] or to design personalized services [16]. Along with these devices, also more invasive systems have been designed, such as assistance robots for the older people [5], to support them constantly along their daily activities. Many studies emphasize the potential benefits the use of ICT has particularly for older people [17]. It has been proved that web-based interventions can provide accessible support to family caregivers to offset declines in their health and wellbeing [18]. However, older people group is seen as one in which the possibilities regarding these technologies are marginalized by issues of access and use. The goals set up for IoT enabled technology in personalized healthcare systems are not easily reachable, and there are still many issues to deal with [19]. Although smart homes non-evasively enhance home care for the elderly and people with disabilities, to provide an adequate information flow between stakeholders is still an open challenge [20]. Providing older people with a health-coordinating center that integrates and manages the various data from various devices and then provides comprehensive and easily understandable feedback is crucial [21]. Another useful instrument is the service platform, which can be regarded as an IT artifact that enables, shapes and supports the business processes needed to deliver products and services and improve the value proposition of those who use the platform [22]. The services provided by a platform are various. Many commercial platforms propose services for activity coaching, nutrition, sport, serious games or assistance. Usually, a platform allows an older person to be more proactive in their health and wellbeing and it could be customized depending on the person's desires and needs. The general aim is to enable a community-based approach to ageing at home. Moreover, a platform usually monitors the health conditions of the user: if someone has a fall in the house, a caregiver or a doctor would be alerted, thanks to the IT devices installed in the house, connected to the platform. This aspect suggests the need to rethink the Product Service Platform designed, at the same time, for older people, for caregivers, and for all possible entities that could be related to them, improving the healthcare or providing more adequate services. Although PSS applications can have a huge potential in healthcare industry, research around this topic are very scant [23]. To address this lack, the paper aims at studying and analyzing a specific urban living environment and the inclusion of frail people in the society in order to define the main requirements that the future healthcare should satisfy.

3   Method

To discover what are the main requirements of a Product Service Platform for health and wellbeing, a survey of older people and two focus groups have been conducted. Two data collection methods have been used to analyze the health status of the community and to identify user needs and the criticalities of actual social healthcare model. The study was done from January 2017 to October 2017 as show in Fig. 1.

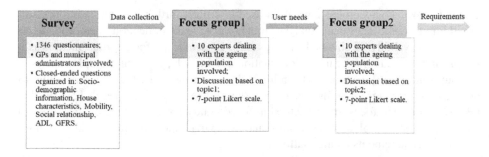

Fig. 1. Methodological approach used to define platform requirements

Survey. The study involved the inhabitants of the inner areas of the Marche region, which has similar characteristics of great part (approximately 60%) of Italian territory. In particular, the following eight municipalities have been considered: Belmonte Piceno, Falerone, Francavilla d'Ete, Massa Fermana, Mogliano, Montappone, Monte Vidon Corrado, Servigliano. These territories are affected by depopulation and lack of territorial enhancement. This is mainly due to the distance from the socio-economical centers and the consequent decline in personal services. In comparison with regional indicators, the reference area is characterized by a community with a higher average age (47 years), a higher incidence of older people over 75 (2459 inhabitants, which represent the 16,7% of the population), and a lower number of people belonging to the segment of the active population (35–54 years). Older people over 75 who still live in their own homes have been chosen as sample. 1346 of the 2459 inhabitants were randomly selected and analyzed in the questionnaire.

The data collection involved General Practitioners (GPs) and municipal administrators who know participants well and interact with them almost every day. The survey consisted of closed-ended questions organized in the following sections:

- Socio-demographic information such as year of birth, gender, residence, etc.
- House characteristics (type, location, presence of mobility aids, etc.) to gather information about its accessibility;
- Mobility in terms of availability and use of car and benefit of volunteer transportation services;
- Social relationships, considering the participation to religious and/or recreational activities;
- Katz Index of Independence in Activities of Daily Living (ADL) that permits to assess the functional status of older adults as a measurement of their ability to perform activities of daily living independently (i.e. bathing, dressing, toileting, transferring, continence, feeding);
- Geriatric Functional Rating Scale (GFRS), which is used to evaluate the functional capacity of an elderly patient, identifying who are able to function alone or with some assistance from those who require institutionalization [24].

Missing data rates among questionnaires were low ($\leq 1\%$): only 13 questionnaires were excluded.

Focus Group. Focus groups have been used to collect further qualitative information in addition to the statistical analysis (quantitative data collection method) and to improve the validity of obtained findings [25]. In detail, the focus group method is a simple and useful tool for gaining information and knowledge using multiple experts in a group setting [26]. Compared to individual session methods, focus groups allow to obtain a larger range of skills and knowledge and to legitimize a result [27]. In this research work, the focus group method as a secondary research objective was used to validate the statistical analysis results and to extract the first functional and non-functional requirements of the platform.

Two rounds of focus group meetings were organized. Experts dealing with the ageing population from a practical and a research point of view were involved in each meeting. The experts involved in the focus group are shown in the Table 1.

Table 1. Focus group participants

Participants	Number	Mean age
General practitioners	5	56.2
Researchers of elderly research hospital	2	44.5
Informal caregivers representatives	2	61.5
Supporters of voluntary associations involved with older people	2	65.5
Mayors of the local community	6	52.2
University researchers	3	37.3

The focus group sessions have lasted about three hours, conducted by the same facilitator and it have been recorded and transcribed for analysis. According to a content-oriented research, the facilitator encourages the discussion among focus group members to acquire specificity, scope and depth. The focus group meetings consisted of an initial presentation followed by a question & answer session and the evaluation. In detail, the discussions were focused on two questions and the participants' answers were measured using a 7-point Likert scale (i.e., 1 = absolutely not, and 7 = absolutely).

4   Survey of Older People

The sample, which reflects the characteristics of the target population, includes 1333 inhabitants (55.4% females) from 75 to 103 years with a median age of 83 years.

Most of respondents (65.6%) live in single-family homes in the center or district. Few families have mobility aids (3.5%) although multiple floor houses prevail (70%). More than half of older people who lives in an isolated house (18.6%) do not have a car. This could affect their isolation and loneliness, especially if men.

The importance of active ageing and independent living is highlighted by the number of people over 75 who live alone (20%) or as a couple (24%), as shown in Fig. 2. Moreover, the family seems to still be the main caregiver of older people.

A quarter of respondents reported finding difficulty in at least one ADL, which makes them dependent on others. The more severe the impairment is (difficulty with 5–6 ADL), the more likely it is the presence of informal caregivers (Fig. 3). It also emerged a strong correlation between the Katz Index of Independence in ADL and age, chronic diseases and cognitive problems. Conversely, no relationship emerged with gender. According to the trend to leave the parental home by young people, it is likely that the need of high quality home help services and more skilled caregivers increases.

Social interactions play a key role in health, and vice versa. As shown in Fig. 4, the onset of the disabilities affects the isolation and loneliness of older people who spend a lower time in religious and recreational activities. In turn, the reduction of social connections can be associated with lower levels of self-rated physical health and interfere with mental functioning, sleep, and well-being, increasing the risk of illness and death. Health and community services should be improved to satisfy different needs and promote the active aging.

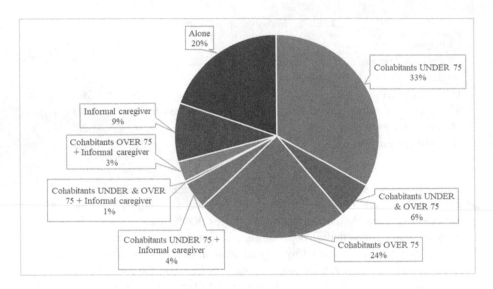

Fig. 2. Older people cohabitants

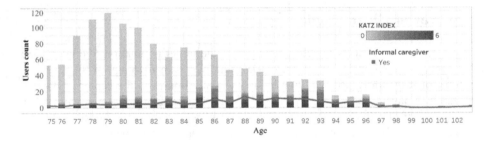

Fig. 3. Katz ADL in relation to age

According to the life expectancy trend, older people tend to stay healthy longer. Considering the GFRS (Fig. 5), 75.3% of respondents is able to function alone (class 1), 5.1% is able to function with some assistance (class 2), and the 19.6% needs of institutionalization (class 3). These results highlight that the majority of people are able to live independently within the community if provided of an adequate support. Moreover, it is worth to notice how the depression state (*) seems to be an "indicator" of the frailty status, remarking the need to stimulate older people.

Despite the diffusion of Internet of Things, it also emerged that the technology is little exploited to help older people maintaining their independence: only the 23% of them has got internet at home and this percentage drops drastically (7%) considering older people who live alone or as a couple.

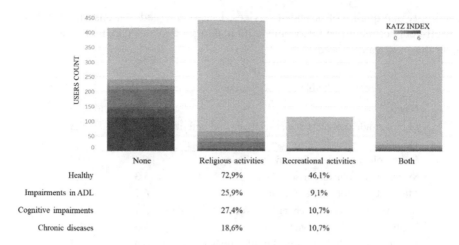

	None	Religious activities	Recreational activities	Both
Healthy		72,9%	46,1%	
Impairments in ADL		25,9%	9,1%	
Cognitive impairments		27,4%	10,7%	
Chronic diseases		18,6%	10,7%	

Fig. 4. How the health conditions affect the older people isolation

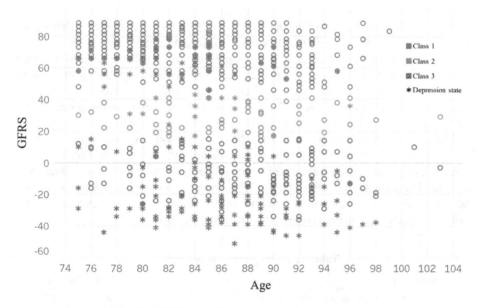

Fig. 5. GFRS according to age and depression state

5 Focus Group

The first focus group focused on the definition of the older people's needs through the question "*What are the main needs of older people living at home?*" and the evaluation of the survey results.

The highest ratings (see Table 2) are related to the improvement of older people's social relationships as main way to reduce the health decline, and to the increase accessibility and quality of provided services. It also emerged that ensuring the safety and well-being of older people together with making the role of GPs more effective are among the most valued needs.

Table 2. Focus group – user needs

Needs	Mean value	SD
Improve older people's social relations and activities	6.6	0.5
Optimize community resources	5.5	1.2
Ensure older people safety and wellbeing	6.4	0.7
Systematize voluntary associations	5.3	1.8
Make the GP role more effective	6.1	1.0
Improve information exchange between stakeholders	5.1	1.5
Improve home help services	5.5	1.1
Increase accessibility and quality of provided services	6.5	0.5
Improve the community's economic exchanges	5.1	1.0

Next to that, almost all participants highlighted the need for all stakeholders (i.e., government, health and social providers, formal/informal caregivers) to work together to help older people stay at home as long as possible. In detail, the need to optimize community resources, to integrate volunteer associations into the care system, and to improve the exchange of information and economic exchanges in the community has been identified. All the participants have a strong believe about the usefulness of the platform for a broad range of potential end-users.

The second focus group issue was: *"What requirements should the platform have?"*. Eight main requirements have emerged from the focus group discussion (see Table 3). Although the average score of all requirements is quite high, some differences emerged. Participants mentioned tailor-made services, multichannel communication and physical and virtual access are the most advantageous requirements. User healthcare conditions monitoring is also indicated as useful.

Table 3. Focus group – requirements

Requirements	Mean value	SD
Detailed information about community activities	4.9	1.1
Tailor-made services	6.3	0.7
Marketplace for products and services	5.6	1.3
Multichannel communication	6.1	0.7
User healthcare conditions monitoring	5.8	1.0
Integration with existing information systems	5.5	1.3
Managing administrative activities (e.g. reservation, bills payment)	5.3	1.1
Physical and virtual access (e.g. office, call center, web)	6.2	0.9

On the other hand, more detailed information, the help in managing administrative activities (e.g. reservation, bills payment) and the development of a marketplace are seen as the least beneficial options for the elderly. They are not technology-savvy and need support with the platform. Some participants (i.e., 3) pointed out that the platform is not suitable for current older people (i.e., 75+), because they are not familiar with technology, but rather for older people of the next few years. Moreover, it emerged that almost all participants could use the platform to find the proper information to help their relatives and to find health and wellbeing goods (e.g., wheelchair, walker). Four participants stated that a platform for remote communications does not improve the quality of life of older people. Only direct interaction with people of the community and not mediated by technology can improve and mitigate the isolation of the older people. As a further suggestion, two participants proposed a specific intervention for the creation of community nurses who, coordinated by the platform, intervene both at the elderly's home and in nursing homes.

During the discussion the participants also expressed a list of non-functional requirements and the potential pitfalls to be taken into account. In detail, among the non-functional requirements of the platform were reported: easy to use and accessible for everyone (n = 10), high data protection and privacy management (n = 9) and continuously updated (n = 8). Among the most mentioned barriers are: high complexity (e.g., big data mining, multiple accesses management and different systems integration) (n = 9), the poor familiarity with the technology of today's old people (n = 9) and the development of a new tool mainly driven by technology rather than human-centered (n = 5).

6 Discussion

Data analysis pointed out the needs and wishes of the older people and provided some relevant outcomes useful to improve the current welfare model. The design requirements of a new PSP aimed to optimize the existing services and to add new services in order to satisfy untreated needs have been defined. As shown in Fig. 6, the platform is based on a user-centered approach aimed to promote the active aging and the independent living of older people. It consists of five main pillars:

- Accessibility & Optimization. The platform should provide a single access point to multiple services through different modalities (office, call center, web) in order to make them enjoyable by as many people as possible, simplifying bureaucratic processes, increasing people awareness and overcoming technological barriers. It should also be useful for local authorities to optimize the provided services, identify unexpressed needs and reduce healthcare expenditure;
- Tailored services, which allows satisfying older people needs. Finding the right trade-off between technology (e.g. smart devices, telemedicine platforms, holter, etc.), caregiver support (e.g. homecare assistance), and society involvement (e.g. volunteer network, social events, etc.) plays a key role to ensure people wellbeing and overcome disabilities, isolation, depression, etc. A set of rules to match the user's profile with the platforms services should be defined in order to create tailored projects and make sure that they fit well with the needs of individuals;

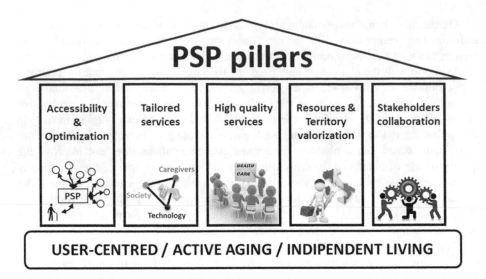

Fig. 6. Product Service Platform pillars

- High quality services, which are the targets of the PSP. For example, it should be a useful tool to monitor the elderly health (e.g. telemedicine devices) and to detect in advance the decline of certain chronic diseases. GPs will not focus on established diseases and/or disability, but will implement a preventive approach that can slow down functional decline for older people. For this aim, a set of indicators and thresholds should be defined;
- Resources & Territory valorization. The PSP should reduce the gap between supply and demand and provide a good opportunity for local companies to offer their services in a reliable and effective way (e.g. shopping delivery). A proper resources management and training allows increasing caregivers, operators, and volunteer skills and increase the territory attractiveness;
- Stakeholders collaboration, including citizens (i.e. older people and formal/informal caregivers), service providers (i.e. public and private companies in the health and wellbeing domain) and local governments. It allows creating an efficient network that ensures a proper information flow and an integrated products/services supply.

According to the survey carried out, the services to be implemented in a PSP should be the following:

- Help in daily activities: support in hiring caregivers, support in administrative procedures and payments, help in housework and gardening;
- Healthcare support: home healthcare (e.g., request of nurse, physiotherapist, etc.), specialized medical transport, management and reservation of medical check-ups;
- Social activities support: transport to the main social centers (e.g., community centers, bars, social place, shops, etc.), organization of social events (e.g., cards tourney, dinner party, meetings, etc.) and activation of creative workshops for maintaining an active status (e.g., with kids, handicrafts, pet care);

- Patient monitoring: connected IoT devices to monitor the older person's parameters (e.g., heart, blood sugar, falls, diet, etc.) and to detect issues about safety, security, health status, and domestic accidents.

The platform should be easily expandable, scalable, and exportable, allowing adding new services and new categories (based on the application context) making future expansions easy. It brings together all the stakeholders involved in old people's care, making it easy to meet the (latent) needs and (as yet unknown) services of a community. It allows the development of new community actions, with focus on interconnections, in the "Smart Village" domain.

7 Conclusion

The paper aims to investigate the requirements of a novel PSP for wellbeing and health of older people. The survey was carried out by focusing on older people over 75 who still live in their own homes. A sample of 1333 individuals has been analyzed in terms of socio demographic characteristics, home and services accessibility, participation to social activities, and health conditions. In addition, twenty experts dealing with the ageing population from a practical and a research point of view were involved through two focus groups. Users' needs and platform requirements were thus determined. The outcomes suggest that the platform should be designed on five main pillars to promote the active aging and the independent living of older people: Accessibility & Optimization, Tailored services, High quality services, Resources & Territory valorization and Stakeholders collaboration.

Future works will focus on development and experimentation of the proposed PSP.

References

1. Rees, P., van der Gaag, N., de Beer, J., Heins, F.: European regional populations: current trends, future pathways, and policy options. Eur. J. Popul. **28**(4), 385–416 (2012)
2. Saltman, R.B., Figueras, J., World Health Organization: European health care reform: analysis of current strategies (1997)
3. Wang, C., Sen, A., Plegue, M., Ruffin IV, M.T., O'Neill, S.M., Rubinstein, W.S., Acheson, L.S., Yoon, P.W., Valdez, R., Irizarry-De La Cruz, M., Khoury, M.J.: Impact of family history assessment on communication with family members and health care providers: a report from the Family Healthware™ Impact Trial (FHITr). Prev. Med. **77**, 28–34 (2015)
4. Mshali, H., Lemlouma, T., Moloney, M., Magoni, D.: A survey on health monitoring systems for health smart homes. Int. J. Ind. Ergon. **66**, 26–56 (2018)
5. Breton, L., Coignard, P., Kemoun, G., Hernot, A., Pichot, N., Fattal, C.: Study relevance of an assistance robot for the elderly in institution. Ann. Phys. Rehabil. Med. **58**, e55–e56 (2015)
6. Gullà, F., Ceccacci, S., Menghi, R., Germani, M.: An adaptive smart system to foster disabled and elderly people in kitchen-related task. In: Proceedings of the 9th ACM International Conference on PErvasive Technologies Related to Assistive Environments, p. 27 (2016)

7. Etchemendy, E., Baños, R.M., Botella, C., Castilla, D., Alcañiz, M., Rasal, P., Farfallini, L.: An e-health platform for the elderly population: the butler system. Comput. Educ. **56**(1), 275–279 (2011)
8. Lu, C., Yuan, L., Lin, W., Zhou, Y., Pan, S.: Depression and resilience mediates the effect of family function on quality of life of the elderly. Arch. Gerontol. Geriatr. **71**, 34–42 (2017)
9. Kwak, C., Lee, E., Kim, H.: Factors related to satisfaction with long-term care services among low-income Korean elderly adults: a national cross-sectional survey. Arch. Gerontol. Geriatr. **69**, 97–104 (2017)
10. Lijuan, L.I.U., Kun, S.H.A., Weimin, R.E.N., Yue, W.A.N.G.: Living alone, health and preventive care use among the elderly in Shanghai, China. J. Med. Coll. PLA **28**(4), 219–227 (2013)
11. De Belvis, A.G., Avolio, M., Spagnolo, A., Damiani, G., Sicuro, L., Cicchetti, A., Ricciardi, W., Rosano, A.: Factors associated with health-related quality of life: the role of social relationships among the elderly in an Italian region. Public Health **122**(8), 784–793 (2008)
12. Kuo, M.H., Wang, S.L., Chen, W.T.: Using information and mobile technology improved elderly home care services. Health Policy Technol. **5**(2), 131–142 (2016)
13. Peruzzini, M., Germani, M., Papetti, A., Iualè, M.: Design of sustainable smart homes for elderly. Int. J. Des. Sci. Technol. **22**(1), 7–26 (2016)
14. Ni, Q., García Hernando, A.B., de la Cruz, I.P.: The elderly's independent living in smart homes: a characterization of activities and sensing infrastructure survey to facilitate services development. Sensors **15**(5), 11312–11362 (2015)
15. Boll, F., Brune, P.: Online support for the elderly–why service and social network platforms should be integrated. Procedia Comput. Sci. **98**, 395–400 (2016)
16. Spagnoletti, P., Resca, A., Sæbø, Ø.: Design for social media engagement: insights from elderly care assistance. J. Strateg. Inf. Syst. **24**(2), 128–145 (2015)
17. Hernández-Encuentra, E., Pousada, M., Gómez-Zúñiga, B.: ICT and older people: beyond usability. Educ. Gerontol. **35**(3), 226–245 (2009)
18. Wasilewski, M.B., Stinson, J.N., Cameron, J.I.: Web-based health interventions for family caregivers of elderly individuals: a scoping review. Int. J. Med. Inform. **103**, 109–138 (2017)
19. Qi, J., Yang, P., Min, G., Amft, O., Dong, F., Xu, L.: Advanced internet of things for personalised healthcare systems: a survey. Pervasive Mob. Comput. **41**, 132–149 (2017)
20. Alaa, M., Zaidan, A.A., Zaidan, B.B., Talal, M., Kiah, M.L.M.: A review of smart home applications based on Internet of Things. J. Netw. Comput. Appl. **97**, 48–65 (2017)
21. Kim, H.S., Lee, K.H., Kim, H., Kim, J.H.: Using mobile phones in healthcare management for the elderly. Maturitas **79**(4), 381–388 (2014)
22. Evans, D.S., Hagiu, A., Schmalensee, R.: Invisible Engines: How Software Platforms Drive Innovation and Transform Industries. MIT Press, Cambridge (2008)
23. Xing, K., Rapaccini, M., Visintin, F.: PSS in healthcare: an under-explored field. Procedia CIRP **64**, 241–246 (2017)
24. Liotta, G., Scarcella, P., Mancinelli, S., Palombi, L., Cancelli, A., Marazzi, M.C.: The evaluation of care needs in elderly people: the use of Geriatric Functional Evaluation Questionnaire. Annali di igiene: medicina preventiva e di comunita **18**(3), 225–235 (2006)
25. Creswell, J.W., Clark, V.L.P.: Designing and Conducting Mixed Methods Research (2007)
26. Caplan, S.: Using focus group methodology for ergonomic design. Ergonomics **33**(5), 527–533 (1990)
27. Massey, A.P., Wallace, W.A.: Focus groups as a knowledge elicitation technique: an exploratory study. IEEE Trans. Knowl. Data Eng. **3**(2), 193–200 (1991)

Ativo: A Data Inspired Design Used to Manage Energy Expenditure for Heart Failure Patients

Idowu Ayoola[1,2(✉)] and Bart Bierling[1]

[1] Department of Industrial Design, Eindhoven University of Technology,
LaPlace 32, 5612AZ Eindhoven, Netherlands
i.b.i.ayoola@tue.nl
[2] Onmi B.V., Eindhoven, The Netherlands

Abstract. We present three subsequent case studies to design for heart-failure patients at home. The process resulted in the design of Ativo—a tool to help heart-failure patients with their energy management. The research was done using a Jawbone Move activity tracker to obtain data from two heart-failure patients for three weeks each. During the three weeks period, a cultural probe was conducted twice in combination with patient interviews to collect information and data on their daily activities. Another probe was used to test the viability of the concepts. The data obtained captured the critical events that may have gone unnoticed, which helped us to make a design rationale. A conceptual prototype was created and validated with a heart-failure patient using the cognitive walkthrough method. We received positive responses showing that the patient liked to have alternative ways of tracking her energy level throughout the day. After a month, the patient reported continuous benefits from the awareness derived from using the prototype.

Keywords: Chronic patients · Energy expenditure · Daily steps
Heart-failure patients

1 Introduction

Heart-failure (HF) is a life-changing disease. When a patient suffers from heart-failure, their heart function diminishes significantly. Lifestyle changes include the management of modifiable risk factors such as smoking, dietary, activity, etc. [4]. Energy depletion is one of the most confronting problems for HF patients due to their health condition [3]. A walk to get the mail can already be tiresome for them. This often results in stress or depression [3].

This paper describes a case-study of HF patients through a design-research process using probes to gather information and data. We use three different types of probes to collect data from two different patients. Two inquiries focused on gathering data and information and one probe was made to test the concept viability. The next sections describe the inquiries and the design process.

© Springer International Publishing AG, part of Springer Nature 2018
M. Mokhtari et al. (Eds.): ICOST 2018, LNCS 10898, pp. 35–43, 2018.
https://doi.org/10.1007/978-3-319-94523-1_4

2   State-of-the-Art

De Activiteitenweger by Meander Medische Centrum (www.meandermc.nl) is
a tool used by the occupational therapists in the Netherlands to help patients
manage their physical energy usage. They adapted this tool for HF patients to
help them reduce fatigue. Users can create points for various activities and could
spend an optimum number of points per day. This method has shown to help
patients to balance their energy expenditure. Although there are numerous other
approaches to support patients with their energy expenditure, in this work, we
like to follow a data-driven approach to understand the challenges these patients
usually encounter in their daily living. We employ the use of a wrist-worn activity
tracker to monitor daily step-counts and sleep patterns. The system proposed
in [5] can also help us to capture data from other sources. However, our work
presented here is limited to the use of a Jawbone (www.jawbone.com) activity
tracker.

3   Probes and Interviews

3.1   Understanding in Context

Objective. The goal of the first inquiry (Probe 1) is to understand the general
behaviour of an HF patient through his daily activity pattern.

Method. We involved an HF patient as referred by his therapist at Catharina
Hospital in Eindhoven. The patient is male, 75 years of age and diagnosed with
HF for over two years. At intake, the patient signed informed consent and was
provided with an activity tracker (Jawbone Move, www.jawbone.com), which he
wore for three weeks. The tracker collected data on step counts and sleep cycles
when worn. He started to use the device on March 20. He did not wear the
tracker properly for two days March 21 and 22. He forgot to wear the tracker
at night (or forgot to turn on sleep mode). In the morning, he did not wear
the tracker for the first hour. An intermediate interview was planned after 1.5
weeks. A post evaluation was planned after three (3) weeks to discuss his activity
patterns.

Results. We obtained a visualisation of the data using the smartphone application of the Jawbone. We observed irregular sleeping patterns, suggesting that
the patient's sleep was persistently interrupted 3–4 times at night. Figure 1 is the
visualisation that shows the sleeping cycles where the patient woke at four (4)
instances as indicated by the yellow segments. Figure 2 shows the step counts
for each day, over the period the tracker was worn. According to the tracker,
there was a relatively low activity level from March 20–29. There was a sporadic
increase in step counts from March 31, which was reasonably maintained till
April 9. We see that there was a significant drop in activity on April 5 and 6.

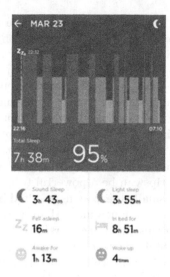

Fig. 1. Screenshot of Jawbone mobile application showing the user's sleep pattern.

Discussion. The follow-through interviews helped us to understand more about the patient's experiences and behaviour at home. The observations from the data were used as conversation starters to help explain insightful events. The patient revealed that he experienced shortness of breath at night and occasionally woke to the toilet due to his health condition. He visited the hospital on March 19 for a regular checkup. At the checkup, he mentioned his incessant symptoms that were evident in his sleeping pattern. Due to the patient's report, the number of diuretics administered was lowered. The diuretics helped him to quickly lose body fluid, which has a side effect of lightheadedness. This symptom is common as explained in [2]. According to the patient's report to us, the medication was lowered around March 28, which explains his increase in activities in the

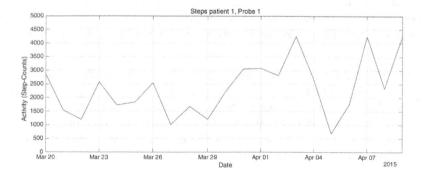

Fig. 2. Chart from the first probe showing the patient's activity pattern according to the data from Jawbone.

subsequent days. On April 5 and 6, he stayed home to follow the international UCI world tour (www.uci.ch), the cycling programs on TV that took place in Belgium and Spain respectively. For this reason, he moved less on these days.

The patient's ability to manage his physical energy level was central to his daily behaviour and perception of health. The patient expressed that small changes in his behaviour usually had an impact on his energy level, thus affecting his activities after that. E.g., he explained how he intentionally left out vacuuming under the chair to minimise how much energy he physically used. When he avoids the places for which he would have to lean over he could clean his entire house. More examples were given during the hospital visiting hours. Incorporating these experiences or tips can be a powerful tool to support patients self-management. Most of these small observations resulted in a significant difference that can enable the patient to do much more than he would typically do.

Discussing the data and insights with nurses was also useful; they valued the information that was obtained. According to the nurses, the data collected can be valuable for them to indicate the activity trends up to date. They also emphasised that it may motivate the patient in managing his activities on a daily basis.

3.2   Energy Expenditure

Objective. The second study (Probe 2) focused on finding how physical energy can be estimated based on the type of activities that occur. We also liked to know the corresponding step-counts for each kind of activity.

Method. We recruited a 45-year-old female from the Catharina Hospital in Eindhoven. She was diagnosed with heart-failure in 2014. She was considered a stable patient according to her HF nurse. She was fairly active compared to most patients, and she loved to hike. We adopted the diary table method [1] for the patient to register her daily activities. The diary contained the activity names, time of the activities and a feelings rating for each day. Feelings were rated on a 5-item-Likert scale (items "1", "3", and "5" corresponded to worst, normal, and best respectively). She used the Jawbone Move to keep track of her daily step counts and sleep cycles. A follow-up interview was planned after two weeks.

Results. The patient collected data for two weeks. The number of steps taken varied widely depending on the activity performed. According to the activity data from Jawbone (Fig. 3), she preferred to alternate her active days as she hiked between 12,000 and 16,000 steps in a day and did little other activities. Alternatively, she walked between 1,000 and 3,000 steps and combined with other activities like visiting family or friends.

Discussion. The feelings rating gave a better indication of how much more she could sustain her energy level. Discussing how she interpreted the scores was

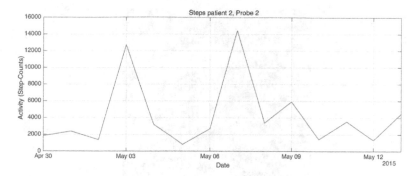

Fig. 3. Chart from the second probe showing the patient's activity pattern according to the data from Jawbone.

the following: "1" would mean that she would not do much more than the bare essentials for that day. Scoring a "3" would mean normal since her diagnosis, and "5" was excellent, almost like she did before her diagnosis. The activity data helped us to observe her daily pattern and can help her to better plan her activities.

4   A Design Preposition for Self-management

Given the knowledge gained in the previous studies (Sect. 3), we proposed a mobile application called Ativo, to help patients keep track of their physical energy expenditure, and help them to self-manage their activities. The design aimed to map everyday activities patterns using the data derived from the activity tracker. This mapping is then used to advice the patient in planning their daily activities.

The concept of Ativo was developed in two iterations. A walk-through session was conducted with an HF patient to evaluate the initial design.

4.1   The Initial Design

The initial design of *Ativo* consisted of three components (Fig. 4). The first component showed the live status, the second allowed the user to rate her current wellbeing with a slider, and the third is an agenda that helped the user to plan her activities. The Agenda view featured three concentric circular meters to indicate the left-over physical energy, the amount of time the user can still be active, and an approximation of how many steps can be done for the rest of the day. The amount of energy left is dependent on several variables—active time, steps done and the rating of current wellbeing. All three components were contained within a single scroll-pane.

Fig. 4. Image showing the initial design for the Ativo mobile application.

4.2 The Improved Design

Here we utilised multiple screen views instead of the scrolling view to show the contents. The first screen (Fig. 5, left) showed a quick overview when the user opens the app. The other screens provided more options to plan and reveal the energy expenditure pattern.

The medical personnel (expert) considered the new version helpful for them to review the measurements during check-ups, and hopefully will help to identify regular patterns. The expert mentioned that the overview screen might also reflect the changes in medications when the energy depletion patterns are observed. In this version, time was not taken into account in estimating the physical energy usage, and the expert also stated that energy is spent even when inactive, which means that the application should take this into account in the future.

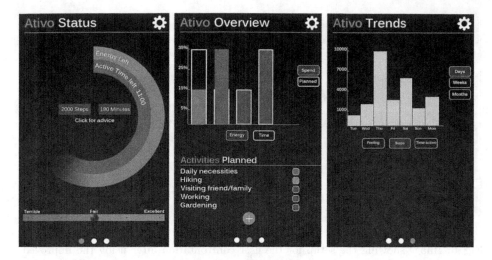

Fig. 5. Image showing the improved design for the Ativo mobile application.

4.3 Walk-Through Using Ativo

A user confrontation was organised to test the improved version. The primary objective was to examine the viability of the concept and if it would be useful for the user. Figure 6 shows the setup applied. The first question requested the user to indicate his or her main activity performed so far. This was important because the type of activity performed has a great influence on the number of steps achieved. The second question was rating the participant's general feelings concerning their energy levels, and the third requested the number of steps taken so far (as measured by the activity tracker). The fourth screen is an indication or advice for the patient and shows how much energy the user would approximately have left. The user was also notified of the possibility that the estimation may be inaccurate and should not base her activities on the indication.

The same heart-failure patient employed in the second inquiry used this app for seven days as if it was completely functional. She was encouraged to freely view the app at moments needed at least once a day but without any obligations. We liked to know when she desired to see her calculated energy level. We requested her to note down few parameters when viewing the app using a diary table. First is the *time* and *date*. Second is the number of steps, how she felt and the indication the app gave. Lastly, was to note if the indication was close to what she felt.

The data from the diary showed that the patient looked at the mobile app after her morning activities (10:00–13:00 h) to see her progress and at the end of the day 17:00–21:00 h to have an overview of the day. In total, she used the mobile app 1–3 times per day. The patient was positive about the usage of the app since it provided a possibility to quantify her energy expenditure as a means to reflect. According to the patient, the estimations were not always accurate. Nevertheless, she stated: "this application already made me more conscious of

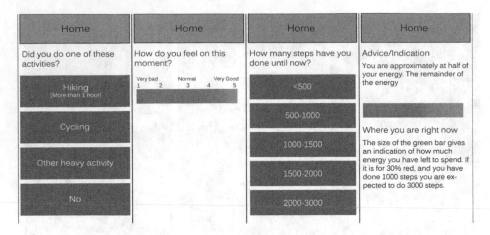

Fig. 6. Image showing the setup for the user confrontation after using the improved Ativo mobile application.

my energy and helped me plan my day better than before". After a few weeks, she again reported, "it was very informative to participate, and I still profit in my daily life from participating... I got a better understanding of my energy usage and gained awareness of my energy consumption during my activities".

5   Summary

This paper presents a descriptive study and may guide future research. The presented case studies gave inputs to the design phase; the obtained data gave insight into the daily life of two heart-failure patients. During the process, there were interviews with potential stakeholders. In total, four interviews with two heart-failure nurses were conducted. The involvement of the different stakeholders also helped to enrich the design process.

This data-inspired-design approach and method in involving prospective users, has helped us in identifying the nuanced behavioural patterns, which will otherwise go unnoticed. By analysing the activity patterns, we found that when the medication was lowered, the first patient achieved more step-counts than previously. Besides the report of the patient, by using the activity tracker, the physical energy levels were measurable and visible to everyone (patient and the caregiver/expert).

The third user inquiry, which tested the *Ativo* design concept gave inputs in identifying the patient's needs. Although the energy expenditure estimation method used was inaccurate due to unaccounted factors (e.g., activity duration, energy expenditure due to elevations, etc.), the design still achieved a favourable outcome; making the user aware of his or her physical energy levels and thinks of using it consciously. Besides making the patient more aware of their energy expenditure, *Ativo* is also meant to help patients balance their energy expenditure between fun and energizing activities and for example household chores. In addition, the value of sharing advice with patients how activities like vacuuming can be done with less energy should not be underestimated. Although the application of wrist-worn activity trackers posses limitations to the type of activities that could be monitored, other means can help to capture these activities, such as using a diary logger. The future design of *Ativo* will consider this option. Despite the early stage of development, the *Ativo* concept has been given interests by the patients and experts, which makes it worth further research. The future design should aim to improve the energy estimation method used in this study. Additional data and information like heart-rate, stress, and activities that do not involve walking could enhance the accuracy of energy estimation. Future steps should continue to involve the prospective users and stakeholders.

Acknowledgments. We thank the patients who participated in the study for several weeks and appreciate their invaluable input. We extend our thanks to the two nurses from Catharina Hospital for their feedback and their help in including the patients.

References

1. Bratteby, L., Sandhagen, B., Fan, H., Samuelson, G.: A 7-day activity diary for assessment of daily energy expenditure validated by the doubly labelled water method in adolescents. Eur. J. Clin. Nutr. **51**(9), 585 (1997)
2. Felker, G.M., Lee, K.L., Bull, D.A., Redfield, M.M., Stevenson, L.W., Goldsmith, S.R., LeWinter, M.M., Deswal, A., Rouleau, J.L., Ofili, E.O., et al.: Diuretic strategies in patients with acute decompensated heart failure. N. Engl. J. Med. **364**(9), 797–805 (2011)
3. Ingwall, J.S., Weiss, R.G.: Is the failing heart energy starved?: on using chemical energy to support cardiac function. Circ. Res. **95**(2), 135–145 (2004)
4. Mokdad, A.H., Forouzanfar, M.H., Daoud, F., Mokdad, A.A., El Bcheraoui, C., Moradi-Lakeh, M., Kyu, H.H., Barber, R.M., Wagner, J., Cercy, K., et al.: Global burden of diseases, injuries, and risk factors for young people's health during 1990–2013: a systematic analysis for the global burden of disease study 2013. Lancet **387**(10036), 2383–2401 (2016)
5. Wetzels, M., Ayoola, I., Bogers, S., Peters, P., Chen, W., Feijs, L.: Consume: a privacy-preserving authorisation and authentication service for connecting with health and wellbeing APIs. Pervasive Mob. Comput. **43**, 20–26 (2018)

Context and Behavior Recognition

Technological Approach for Early and Unobtrusive Detection of Possible Health Changes Toward More Effective Treatment

Firas Kaddachi[1]([⊠]), Hamdi Aloulou[2], Bessam Abdulrazak[3], Philippe Fraisse[1], and Mounir Mokhtari[4]

[1] Montpellier Laboratory of Informatics, Robotics and Microelectronics (LIRMM), Montpellier, France
firas.kaddachi@lirmm.fr
[2] Digital Research Center of Sfax, Sakiet Ezzit, Tunisia
hamdi.aloulou@gmail.com
[3] University of Sherbrooke, Sherbrooke, Canada
bessam.abdulrazak@usherbrooke.ca
[4] Institut Mines-Telecom (IMT), Paris, France
mounir.mokhtari@mines-telecom.fr

Abstract. Aging process is related to serious decline in physical and cognitive functions. Thus, early detection of these health changes is important to improve classical assessments that are mainly based on interviews, and are insufficient to early diagnose all possible health changes. Therefore, we propose a technological approach that analyzes elderly people behavior on a daily basis, employs unobtrusive monitoring technologies, and applies statistical techniques to identify continuous changes in monitored behavior. We detect significant long-term changes that are highly related to physical and cognitive problems. We also present a real validation through data collected from 3-year deployments in nursing-home rooms.

Keywords: Aging-related decline · Early health change detection
Unobtrusive technologies · Statistical change-detection techniques

1 Introduction

The world population is aging. Elderly people aged 65 and over represent 12,4% in 2000, and will represent 20,6% by 2050 [1]. Physical and cognitive decline is much more common with age, and considerably affect quality of life of elderly people. Therefore, detecting these health changes in early stages of their evolution is essential to increase treatment efficiency. Nowadays, geriatric methods have limitations in terms of diagnosing all possible changes on a daily basis. In order to complete classical observations, we propose an approach that provides objective technological observations of daily living. We employ unobtrusive

© Springer International Publishing AG, part of Springer Nature 2018
M. Mokhtari et al. (Eds.): ICOST 2018, LNCS 10898, pp. 47–59, 2018.
https://doi.org/10.1007/978-3-319-94523-1_5

technologies that monitor elderly people over long periods, in order to identify significant long-term changes in their health conditions.

Among a variety of aging-related physical and cognitive diseases (*e.g.,* Parkinson, Alzheimer, Bipolar Disorder), dementia affects 13% of aged 80–84 and more than 30% of those over 85 [2]. In order to diagnose aging-related diseases, geriatricians mainly use scales and questionnaires, such as Mini Mental State Examination (MMSE) to identify memory impairments [3], Get-up-and-Go scale to understand mobility problems [4], Mini Nutritional Assessment (MNA) to evaluate nutritional status [5], Autonomie Gerontologique et Groupes Iso-Ressources (AGGIR) to detect autonomy loss [6] and Behavioral Pathology in Alzheimer's Disease (BEHAVE-AD) to follow-up behavioral anomalies [7].

Geriatric scales and questionnaires are insufficient to follow-up progression of all possible health changes on a daily basis. Health conditions change from day to day, and geriatricians chiefly rely on incomplete and imprecise patient feedbacks during infrequent office visits [8]. For example, 75% of dementia cases are undiagnosed by geriatricians during office visits [9].

Early detection of health changes is a keystone for more advanced assessment and earlier intervention [10]. Consequently, elderly people have more chance to treat diseases in early stages of their evolution, regain affected functions and reduce disease impact on their independent living. Without early detection of Alzheimer Disease, it is expected that Alzheimer patient number will be 4 times higher in 2050 more than 2002 [11].

Interest in smart technologies has been increasing toward better adaptation of health care services in the geriatric field [12]. Smart technologies deployed at home and in city provide new objective observations of daily living that complete classical medical observations. Elderly people are also accepting the integration of technologies in their life to remain independent as long as possible and delay their entry to nursing home [13]. Nowadays, elderly people show acceptability for unobtrusive technologies that are deployed in the environment, more than intrusive technologies, such as wearable sensors [14].

We propose a technological approach for long-term behavior monitoring and detection of possible health changes that are highly related to physical and cognitive problems [15,16]. We employ unobtrusive technologies (*e.g.,* movement and door sensors) that do not interfere with natural behavior and do not affect individual privacy.

Following, Sect. 2 highlights contributions of our approach compared to state of the art. Sections 3 and 4 present our methodology and implementation, including details on our technique to translate geriatric needs, our analysis algorithms to compute geriatric indicators and metrics, and statistical techniques for change detection. Sections 5 and 6 discuss our 3-year validation through real data collected in nursing-home deployments, and conclude this paper.

2   Related Work

In addition to geriatric methods for health change detection [3–7], technological methods allow to improve health change detection and revolutionize health care services. Multiple environmental technologies (*e.g.*, movement, light, humidity and pressure sensors) and wearable technologies (*e.g.*, smart watch, smart bracelet with RFID and accelerometers) are deployed at home and in city to collect new observations of daily living that complete classical medical observations. We can distinguish 4 categories of existing technological approaches.

2.1 Short-Term Health Change Detection

This category focuses on detecting short-term changes occurring in specific time periods. For example, Aloulou et al. employ pressure, proximity and motion sensors to identify wandering at night, showering for too long, leaving the wash-room tap on and toilet falls [17,18]. Bourke et al. apply machine learning techniques to distinguish between normal mobility and falls, by asking elderly people to wear tri-axial accelerometer [19].

Our technological approach targets analysis of overall behavior over long periods. We consider multiple behavior dimensions and their long-term evolution in time. So, we focus on behavior changes that take weeks or months to establish new behavior patterns, and are more challenging to detect [20].

2.2 Offline Health Change Detection

Another category analyzes collected data offline, and investigates health changes after their occurrence. For example, a scientific study asks for human with mobility problems to wear fit-bit pedometer, and compares physical activity data before and after participating in training sessions [21]. The goal of this study is to investigate training impact at the end of the experimentation.

Our technological approach targets early health change detection with an online analysis of collected data. We analyze sensor data on a daily basis, in order to detect health changes in early stages of their evolution and send real-time notifications to geriatricians.

2.3 Inter-individual Health Change Detection

A further category focuses on inter-individual health changes by comparing different populations with or without a target disease, in order to identify significant geriatric indicators that require close monitoring. For example, researchers compare the social behavior of intact and Mild Cognitive Impairment (MCI) patients to investigate problems in speech using webcams [22], and phone use by deploying landline-phone monitors [23]. It was reported that MCI patients speak more words and receive significantly less phone calls.

Our technological approach targets monitoring of geriatric indicators and detection of possible changes at temporal scale. We investigate intra-individual changes compared to past personal habits.

2.4   Intrusive Health Change Detection

This category employs intrusive technologies to monitor elderly people; e.g., researchers propose wearable pulse sensors to identify Diabetes-related pulse changes [24], wearable smart watches to monitor heart beats [25], and mobile applications to take food photos and monitor nutritional habits [26].

Nowadays, it is often challenging for elderly people to operate wearable sensors in real home settings [14]. Acceptability issues are also reported regarding mobile applications and daily online-based questionnaires [27]. Therefore, our technological approach employs unobtrusive technologies that discretely operate at home and in city, do not interfere with natural behavior of monitored participants and do not require additional manual efforts.

3   Methodology

Our technological approach for early and unobtrusive detection of possible health changes is strongly related to geriatric needs of our stakeholders, such as geriatricians, family members, elderly people and nursing home. Therefore, we start with identifying their important geriatric needs; e.g., completing geriatrician observations, taking care of relatives living away, feeling safe at home and creating a link between nursing home and isolated elderly people.

Based on validated geriatric references, we investigate significant geriatric indicators (e.g., physical, cognitive, social and nutritional activities) that translate identified geriatric needs and can be monitored via ambient technologies. We analyze monitored geriatric indicators following different dimensions (e.g., time, number and duration metrics) in order to detect significant changes in monitored behavior. We also investigate the cause of detected changes based on medical, personal and context information, in order to validate the correct translation of geriatric needs. Furthermore, we collect stakeholder feedbacks to validate their engagement and evaluate the impact of our approach.

3.1   Geriatric Needs

Based on our stakeholder interviews and several scientific references, our technological approach starts with identifying essential geriatric needs:

- **Geriatricians:** these stakeholders are interested in monitoring activities of daily living that occur outside their office and are important for their medical assessment [8]. Our technological approach completes their medical observations with objective technological observations.
- **Family members:** are also important stakeholders, and need to take care of their relatives living away from them. They are interested in receiving significant information about activities of daily living and changes in health status [25]. They prefer unobtrusive technologies that do not affect individual privacy [28].

- **Elderly people:** represent our main stakeholders, and require to feel safe at home without intrusive supervision. They refuse technologies that affect individual privacy [28], and do not prefer wearable technologies that require manual efforts [14].
- **Nursing home:** is an important stakeholder, and is interested in creating a link with isolated elderly people at home. The main concern is to delay entry to nursing home and maintain independent living at home [13].

3.2 Geriatric Indicators and Monitoring Technologies

In order to translate identified geriatric needs, and based on validated geriatric references (*e.g.,* MMSE [3], Get-up-and-Go [4], MNA [5], AGGIR [6] and BEHAVE-AD [7]), we determine geriatric indicators that can be monitored via ambient technologies (Table 1).

Table 1. Examples of geriatric indicators and unobtrusive monitoring technologies

Category	Indicators	Technologies
Activities of daily living	Household, prepare meals, dressing, hygiene, urinary and fecal elimination	Environmental movement, door, bed, vibration, pressure, proximity, temperature, humidity, light sensors
Mobility	Move indoors and outdoors, get up, turn around, walk	
Cognition	Learn, speak, manage financial situation	Smart TV, scale, medicine box
Social life	Communicate with others, use means of transport, shopping, collective free time activities	In-phone-embedded GPS, accelerometer, gyroscope, step detector, proximity sensor

3.3 Geriatric Metrics

We detect significant changes points in the time evolution of monitored geriatric indicators using statistical techniques. Therefore, we need to quantify these indicators using different metrics, such as number, duration and time.

Among geriatric metrics, *number* quantifies the quantity of executing activities of daily living; e.g., we compute the number of toilet entries in order to identify abnormal increases that are associated with urinary infection. In addition, *duration* quantifies how long these activities are executed; e.g., we measure the duration of sleep periods in order to evaluate the impact of prescription sleep drugs. Furthermore, *time* indicates when activities are executed; e.g., we follow-up visit times to detect possible social isolation of elderly people.

3.4   Validation

We rely on correlating medical (*e.g.,* diagnosed health problems and hospital-izations), personal (*e.g.,* feeling pain and having sleep impairments) and context (*e.g.,* weather conditions and changing living environment) observations with technologically-observed health changes to investigate their origin. We also collect stakeholder feedbacks (*e.g.,* acceptability, engagement and effectiveness) in order to validate their involvement and evaluate the impact of our approach.

4   Implementation Approach

We develop our technological approach as a new service ChangeTracker [15,16] in our ambient assisted living platform UbiSMART [17,18]. UbiSMART collects environmental sensor data to monitor elderly people at home and in city, in order to notify family members and geriatricians about health anomalies. Following, we discuss the Model-Controller-View architecture of ChangeTracker service (Fig. 1):

– **Model** acquires sensor data for permanent storage. In fact, our gateways (*e.g.,* Raspberry Pi) receive locally-collected sensor data and send them via Internet access points to our remote database.

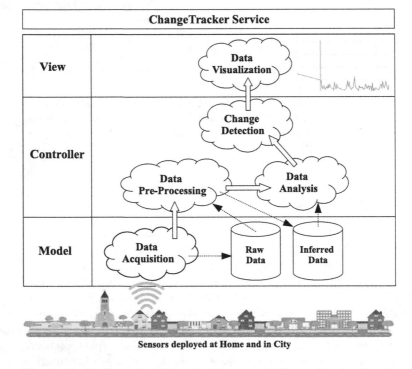

Fig. 1. Model-Controller-View Architecture of ChangeTracker Service

- **Controller** directly accesses model layer to read sensor data on a daily basis, and write inferred data using data-preprocessing algorithms; e.g., these algorithms read toilet-sensor data and infer daily frequency of toilet entries. We also apply statistical algorithms to detect significant changes in inferred data; e.g., we investigate changes in toilet entries that are associated with urinary infection.
- **View** shows inferred data and detected change points for users. They can recall all past data, get more detailed information about change points and correlate different indicators to better understand health status. In addition, they can configure real-time notifications and monthly reports.

Applied statistical change detection techniques (i) allow to analyze data online to detect changes in early stages of their evolution, (ii) differentiate between transient and continuous changes in time evolution, and (iii) require less training data compared to machine-learning techniques. Following, we present statistical techniques investigated in our research:

- **Z-Score** computes the distance from a moving window mean to the mean of all past data in units of the standard error [29]. A change occurs if absolute value of computed distance is higher than a threshold.
- **Bootstrap** calculates the differences between data values and data mean to determine the magnitude of the change [30]. 1000 bootstraps are generated by randomly re-ordering original data. If at least 95% of these bootstraps have a lower magnitude of change, a change occurs.
- **CUSUM** technique determines important parameters (*e.g.,* mean and standard deviation) based on reference data [31]. It recursively computes cumulative sums for positive and negative deviations to determine change points.
- **SD-Band** calculates a band with bounds equal to 1 standard deviation above and below the mean [32]. A change occurs, if consecutive deviations exist outside the defined band.
- **PELT** minimizes the Likelihood Ratio Test, in order to infer number and position change points. This technique uses Penalized Likelihood, by defining a penalty function to determine the optimal candidate change points [33].

5   Validation

In order to validate our technological approach for early health change detection, we deploy unobtrusive technologies (*e.g.,* movement and door sensors) in 10 nursing-home rooms. Despite the basic information collected by these sensors (*i.e.,* presence and absence of movements, and door openings and closings), we extract significant information of health conditions on a daily basis, such as toilet entries, sleep interruptions, visits, activity level and time out of room. We detect long-term changes in these parameters that are highly associated with physical and cognitive functions.

5.1 Data Collection

We collect raw data using Marmitek MS13E movement sensors deployed in each bathroom, toilet and bedroom (Fig. 2). We also deploy Marmitek DS90 door sensors at main entries. Employed sensors use X10 communication protocol. For data transmission, we use Raspberry-Pi gateway equipped with X10 receiver and an Internet access point. In total, we recruit 10 participants having an average age of 90 years old and living in a French nursing home (Table 2).

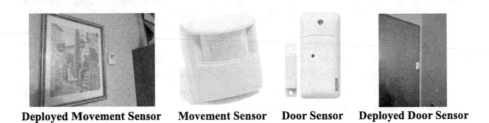

Deployed Movement Sensor   **Movement Sensor**   **Door Sensor**   **Deployed Door Sensor**

Fig. 2. Deployment of movement and door sensors in nursing home rooms

Table 2. Participant gender, age and monitoring period

Participant	Gender	Age	Start	End	Period(months)
A	M	90	2014-09-23	2015-02-13	4
B	M	90	2015-03-15	2015-08-03	4
C	M	84	2015-09-10	2018-02-26	29
D	F	85	2014-09-23	2015-08-06	10
E	F	98	2015-08-13	2018-02-26	30
F	F	87	2014-09-23	2017-01-18	27
G	F	90	2014-09-23	2018-02-26	41
H	F	95	2014-09-14	2015-06-03	8
I	F	95	2015-06-04	2018-02-26	32
J	F	90	2017-04-04	2018-02-26	10

5.2 Data Analysis

We pre-process raw data online to infer daily information on health conditions. Movement and door sensor data allow to compute toilet entries, sleep interruptions, time out of room, activity level and visits. We also exclude days with no sensor data due to technical problems or hospitalizations, in order to avoid detecting insignificant changes in analyzed indicators.

We weight analyzed indicators according to presence time at room, in order to prevent detecting irrelevant changes; e.g., toilet entries might decrease because of spending less time at room, and not because of going really less frequently to toilet. Therefore, we divide each day into 24 h blocks and compute detected movement number in each block. We exclude consecutive blocks with no movements that are followed and preceded by main door openings. These blocks represent time when the participant is outside his room.

We also weight analyzed indicators according to time being alone, in order to avoid recognizing insignificant changes; e.g., activity level increases due to presence of multiple persons at room, and not due to real increase of individual activity level. Therefore, we compute activity periods for each room section by identifying sequences of movements with time difference less than 30 s. We look for parallel activity periods that occur in at least two different room sections (e.g., toilet, bathroom and bedroom) at the same time. These parallel activity periods indicate the presence of multiple persons.

Consequently, toilet entries are equal to N/T, where N is the number of movements detected in toilet when person is alone at room and T is the time alone at room. Furthermore, sleep interruptions are quantified by S/D where S is the number of movements detected between 0 h and 6 h when person is alone at room and D is the time alone at room between 0 h and 6 h. In addition, activity level is measured by M/T where M is the total number of detected movements when person is alone at room. Moreover, time out and visits represent the duration when the person is outside his room or receiving visits respectively.

5.3   Results and Discussion

In total, we detected 249 changes for our 10 participants with an average of 1.14 change per month for each participant. The medical nursing-home team continuously records significant health events, in order to investigate the cause of detected changes. Detected changes are either the result of health problems (e.g., Participant J becomes less active due to mobility problems (Fig. 3)), or health improvements (e.g., Participant J becomes more active thanks to treatment of knee problems (Fig. 3)) with respective rates of 66.06% and 33.94%.

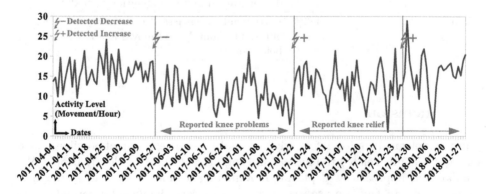

Fig. 3. Detected changes in activity level of participant J

We send real-time notifications about detected changes from 2 to 10 days after change occurrence, in order to be sure that detected changes are really continuous and to provide an opportunity for early change explication. Table 3 gives more information about investigated causes of detected changes.

The medical team prefers to receive monthly reports to correlate multiple changes and better investigate their origin. Moreover, we organize personal interviews with caregivers and elderly people each 4 months. We evaluate the precision of our statistical techniques by computing the percentage of detected changes with retrieved medical explication. Unexplained changes can be either really not significant due to false detection, or related to undiagnosed health problems. Among investigated techniques, Bootstrap provides the best precision of 83.87% compared to Z-Score, CUSUM, SD-Band and PELT with 57.14%, 26.29%, 39.29% and 32.38% respectively. In deed, Bootstrap is more robust to outliers and detects relevant changes that are missed by other statistical techniques.

Table 3. Investigated causes and examples of detected changes

Cause	Rate	Example
Physical problems	4.07%	Participant D goes out less frequently due to foot problems
Nutritional problems	5.88%	Participant E enters more frequently to toilet due to diarrhea
Emotional problems	4.07%	Participant F has more sleep impairments due to husband's death
Multiple health problems	26.24%	Participant G is less active due to toothache, cough and respiration problems
Context changes	1.81%	Participant C has more sleep impairments due to room change
Health improvements	33.94%	Participant J becomes more active thanks to treatment of knee problems
Cognitive problems	20.36%	Participant E is abnormally more active due to disorientation and hallucination periods
Death	3.62%	Participant A has less sleep interruptions, goes out less frequently and moves less few months before death

6   Conclusion

Our technological approach for early and unobtrusive detection of possible health changes is highly related to physical and cognitive decline for elderly people. We validate our approach by deploying movement and door sensors in 10 nursing-home rooms. In fact, we use sensor data to extract significant information on health conditions, such as toilet entries, sleep interruptions, time out of room, activity level and visits. We also apply statistical techniques to detect long-term changes in monitored indicators.

We received positive feedbacks from nursing home appreciating the usefulness of our service. It does not only allow to monitor elderly people behavior but also provides daily analysis. Detected changes significantly correlate with health status. Nursing home also recommends to extend our deployments in individual houses.

In the context of the European project City4age [34], we are improving our work. City4age targets detection of frailty and mild cognitive impairments using IoT technologies deployed in urban areas. It provides elderly people with services of continuous monitoring and tailored intervention.

Acknowledgement. We give our special thanks to Saint Vincent de Paul nursing home in Occagnes, France. Our deployment in this nursing home is also supported by VHP inter@ctive project and the Quality Of Life chair.

Our work is part of the European project City4Age that received funding from the Horizon 2020 research and innovation program under grant agreement number 689731.

References

1. Bureau, U.S.C.: United States Census Bureau: International Data Base (2018)
2. Ferri, C.P., et al.: Global prevalence of dementia: a Delphi consensus study. Lancet **366**(9503), 2112–2117 (2005)
3. Cockrell, J.R., Folstein, M.F.: Mini-mental state examination. In: Principles and Practice of Geriatric Psychiatry, pp. 140–141 (2002)
4. Mathias, S., et al.: Balance in elderly patients: the "get-up and go" test. Arch. Phys. Med. Rehabil. **67**(6), 387–389 (1986)
5. Vellas, B., et al.: The mini nutritional assessment (MNA) and its use in grading the nutritional state of elderly patients. Nutrition **15**(2), 116–122 (1999)
6. Lafont, S., et al.: Relation entre performances cognitives globales et dépendance évaluée par la grille aggir. Revue d'épidémiologie et de santé publique **47**(1), 7–17 (1999)
7. Reisberg, B., et al.: Behavioral pathology in Alzheimer's disease (BEHAVE-AD) rating scale. Int. Psychogeriatr. **8**(S3), 301–308 (1997)
8. Wilson, D., et al.: In-home assessment of the activities of daily living of the elderly. In: Extended Abstracts of CHI 2005: Workshops-HCI Challenges in Health Assessment (2005)
9. Holsinger, T., et al.: Does this patient have dementia? JAMA **297**(21), 2391–2404 (2007)
10. Boockvar, K.S., Lachs, M.S.: Predictive value of nonspecific symptoms for acute illness in nursing home residents. J. Am. Geriatr. Soc. **51**(8), 1111–1115 (2003)
11. Sloane, P.D., et al.: The public health impact of Alzheimer's disease, 2000–2050: potential implication of treatment advances. Annu. Rev. Public Health **23**, 213–231 (2002)
12. Rantz, M., Skubic, M., Miller, S., Krampe, J.: Using technology to enhance aging in place. In: Helal, S., Mitra, S., Wong, J., Chang, C.K., Mokhtari, M. (eds.) ICOST 2008. LNCS, vol. 5120, pp. 169–176. Springer, Heidelberg (2008). https://doi.org/10.1007/978-3-540-69916-3_20

13. Rantz, M.J., et al.: The future of long-term care for the chronically ill. Nurs. Adm. Q. **25**(1), 51–58 (2000)
14. Demiris, G., et al.: Older adults' attitudes towards and perceptions of 'smart home' technologies: a pilot study. Med. Inform. Internet Med. **29**(2), 87–94 (2004)
15. Kaddachi, F., Aloulou, H., Abdulrazak, B., Fraisse, P., Mokhtari, M.: Unobtrusive technological approach for continuous behavior change detection toward better adaptation of clinical assessments and interventions for elderly people. In: Mokhtari, M., Abdulrazak, B., Aloulou, H. (eds.) ICOST 2017. LNCS, vol. 10461, pp. 21–33. Springer, Cham (2017). https://doi.org/10.1007/978-3-319-66188-9_3
16. Kaddachi, F., et al.: Technological approach for behavior change detection toward better adaptation of services for elderly people. BIOSTEC **2017**, 96 (2017)
17. Aloulou, H., et al.: An adaptable and flexible framework for assistive living of cognitively impaired people. IEEE J. Biomed. Health Inform. **18**(1), 353–360 (2014)
18. Aloulou, H., et al.: Deployment of assistive living technology in a nursing home environment: methods and lessons learned. BMC Med. Inform. Decis. Mak. **13**(1), 42 (2013)
19. Bourke, A.K., et al.: Fall detection algorithms for real-world falls harvested from lumbar sensors in the elderly population: a machine learning approach. In: 2016 IEEE 38th Annual International Conference of the Engineering in Medicine and Biology Society (EMBC), pp. 3712–3715. IEEE (2016)
20. Lally, P., et al.: How are habits formed: modelling habit formation in the real world. Eur. J. Soc. Psychol. **40**(6), 998–1009 (2010)
21. Sprint, G., et al.: Unsupervised detection and analysis of changes in everyday physical activity data. J. Biomed. Inform. **63**, 54–65 (2016)
22. Dodge, H.H., et al.: Web-enabled conversational interactions as a method to improve cognitive functions: results of a 6-week randomized controlled trial. Alzheimer's Dement.: Transl. Res. Clin. Interv. **1**(1), 1–12 (2015)
23. Petersen, J., et al.: Unobtrusive phone monitoring as a novel measure of cognitive function. Alzheimer's Dement. J. Alzheimer's Assoc. **10**(4), P366–P367 (2014)
24. Reddy, V.R., et al.: PerDMCS: Weighted fusion of PPG signal features for robust and efficient diabetes mellitus classification. In: HEALTHINF, pp. 553–560 (2017)
25. Sashima, A., et al.: A telecare system on smart watches that communicate with wireless bio sensors. In: HEALTHINF, pp. 429–434 (2017)
26. Dalakleidi, K., et al.: A modified all-and-one classification algorithm combined with the bag-of-features model to address the food recognition task. In: HEALTHINF, pp. 284–290 (2017)
27. Magill, E., Blum, J.M.: Personalised ambient monitoring: supporting mental health at home. In: Advances in Home Care Technologies: Results of the Match Project, pp. 67–85 (2012)
28. Perera, C., et al.: Big data privacy in the Internet of Things era. IT Prof. **17**(3), 32–39 (2015)
29. Basseville, M.: Statistical methods for change detection. In: Control Systems, Robotics and AutomatioN-Volume XVI: Fault Analysis and Control, p. 130 (2009)
30. Taylor, W.A.: Change-point analysis: a powerful new tool for detecting changes (2000). http://www.variation.com/cpa/tech/changepoint.html
31. Mesnil, B., Petitgas, P.: Detection of changes in time-series of indicators using CUSUM control charts. Aquat. Living Resour. **22**(2), 187–192 (2009)

32. Bland, J.M., Altman, D.G.: Comparing methods of measurement: why plotting difference against standard method is misleading. Lancet **346**(8982), 1085–1087 (1995)
33. Killick, R., et al.: Optimal detection of changepoints with a linear computational cost. J. Am. Stat. Assoc. **107**(500), 1590–1598 (2012)
34. City4Age: Elderly-friendly city services for active and healthy aging (2018). http://www.city4ageproject.eu/

Automatic Identification of Behavior Patterns in Mild Cognitive Impairments and Alzheimer's Disease Based on Activities of Daily Living

Belkacem Chikhaoui[1](✉), Maxime Lussier[2], Mathieu Gagnon[3], Hélène Pigot[3], Sylvain Giroux[3], and Nathalie Bier[2]

[1] Department of Science and Technology, TELUQ University, Montreal, Canada
belkacem.chikhaoui@teluq.ca
[2] École de réadaptation, Faculté de médecine, Université de Montréal, Montreal, Canada
{maxime.lussier,nathalie.bier}@umontreal.ca
[3] Domus Laboratory, University of Sherbrooke, Sherbrooke, Canada
{mathieu.gagnon,helene.pigot,sylvain.giroux}@usherbrooke.ca

Abstract. The growing number of older adults worldwide places high pressure on identifying dementia at its earliest stages so that early management and intervention strategies could be planned. In this study, we proposed a machine learning based method for automatic identification of behavioral patterns of people with mild cognitive impairment (MCI) and Alzheimer's disease (AD) through the analysis of data related to their activities of daily living (ADL) collected in two smart home environments. Our method employs first a feature selection technique to extract relevant features for classification and reduce the dimensionality of the data. Then, the output of the feature selection is fed into a random forest classifier for classification. We recruited three groups of participants in our study: healthy older adults, older adults with mild cognitive impairment and older adults with Alzheimer's disease. We conducted extensive experiments to validate our proposed method. We experimentally showed that our method outperforms state-of-the-art machine learning algorithms.

1 Introduction and Related Work

New research has shown that early signs of dementia can be detected 10 years before the formal diagnosis is made [12]. At this time, individuals start showing dysfunctions in complex activities of daily living (ADL) such as managing one's finances [2,4,12,21]. However, differentiating these early signs of dementia from normal cognitive aging requires an in-depth knowledge of the subtle differences observed in ADL function in these two populations. Considering the expected increase in prevalence of dementia in the coming years worldwide, it is urgent that we refine measures used to document ADL changes in the aging population

© Springer International Publishing AG, part of Springer Nature 2018
M. Mokhtari et al. (Eds.): ICOST 2018, LNCS 10898, pp. 60–72, 2018.
https://doi.org/10.1007/978-3-319-94523-1_6

so that appropriate prevention strategies can be put into place to minimize the repercussions of these diseases on the individuals and their family.

ADL dysfunctions in aging have been generally measured with questionnaires and performance-based assessments that generally fail to capture the person's actual performance and difficulties in everyday life [3,6,14,15]. An alternative and innovative approach to questionnaires consists in measuring the performances of participants while they carry out ADL and instrumental ADL (IADL) with the aid of sensor technologies allowing a non-invasive and continuous monitoring. Data gathered by the sensor technologies could allow for standardized quantitative and fully automated evaluation and contribute to the functional evaluation of a therapist.

A few studies using this newer evaluation approach have shown encouraging results in detecting MCI in older adults [1,8,9,16,19]. For example, Cook et al. [8,19] used machine learning techniques to analyze behavior data of healthy older adults and adults with Parkinson's disease using wearable sensors. The authors found that differences between healthy older adults and adults with Parkinson's disease exist in their activity patterns, and that these differences can be automatically recognized. Dawadi et al. [9] used different machine learning algorithms namely principal component analysis, support vector machines, and logistic regression to quantify activity quality of healthy and cognitively impaired people in a smart home environment. The authors achieved reasonable results in differentiating between the two classes: healthy and cognitively impaired people. Jekel et al. [16] investigated smart home environment to assess ADLs for dementia diagnosis. Two groups of people: healthy and mild cognitive impairment were recruited to perform instrumental ADLs. Differences were observed for making a phone call, operating the television, and retrieving objects. The MCI group showed more searching and task-irrelevant behavior than healthy group. However, no machine learning algorithms were employed to differentiate between these two groups, and only statistical tests were used.

The main goal of the present study is to analyze smart home sensor data for automatic identification of behavioral patterns of people with mild cognitive impairment and Alzheimer's disease based on activities of daily living. Three groups of people were recruited in our study: healthy, MCI, and AD, which allows to collect rich data, and makes the identification of behavioral patterns more challenging. The contributions of the papers are summarized in the following points:

1. Identify automatically behavioral pattern of people with mild cognitive impairment and Alzheimer's disease using machine.
2. Perform experiments in two smart homes with different sensors types and setup to analyze ADLs and identify behavioral patterns.
3. Collect real data from three groups of participants: healthy, MCI, and AD.
4. Conduct extensive experimental tests to validate our proposed approach.

The rest of the paper is organized as follows. Section 2 introduces our proposed approach such as data collection procedures, dataset description, machine learning technique for data analysis and results obtained. Section 3 presents a comparison of our machine learning method with state-of-the-art methods. A discussion is presented in Sect. 4. Finally, Sect. 4 presents our conclusions and highlights future work directions.

2   Proposed Approach

In this section, we describe our proposed approach for early detection of AD by analyzing sensor data collected during ADL's completion. Before introducing our approach, we will first describe the experimental setup in terms of participants and data collection procedures.

2.1   Participants

Two sites were used for recruiting participants: Sherbrooke and Montreal, Canada. A total of 56 participants (24 in Sherbrooke and 32 in Montreal) were recruited in this study. Details of participants and how they are recruited in the two sites are presented as follows:

Participants without cognitive impairment (n = 26), control or healthy, were recruited in Sherbrooke and Montreal, mainly through databases of controlled participants. Inclusion criteria were: (1) to be 65 years of age or older; (2) to obtain normal results in cognitive disorders by age and education, as measured by the Montreal Cognitive Assessment (MoCA) [17]. Exclusion criteria were related to health conditions that could cause cognitive impairment: (1) History of cerebral involvement (head trauma, stroke, encephalopathy); (2) Uncontrolled diabetes or hypertension; (3) Presence of psychiatric disorders: schizophrenia, bipolar disorder, anxiety or depression; (4) delirium in the last six months; (5) Intracranial surgery; (6) Vitamin B12 deficiency or ethylism; (7) Use of medication that can influence cognition and alertness (hypnotics, neuroleptics, or anticonvulsants); (8) Physical impairments limiting the ability to move alone and safely in the intelligent apartment.

Participants with mild cognitive impairment (MCI) (n = 22) were recruited via the Montreal Geriatric University Institute (IUGM) and the Institute of Geriatric University of Sherbrooke (IUGS) via lists of participants. Inclusion criteria were: (1) to be 65 years of age or older; (2) have a diagnosis of MCI. This diagnosis was confirmed, in accordance with the current MCI criteria, [13,18] by one of the two outpatient clinics, one at the IUGM institute and one at the IUGS institute. The exclusion criteria were the same as those of healthy participants.

2.2   Procedure

Participants were instructed to carry out five activities of daily living detailed on a sheet of paper. Four of the selected activities[1] were validated in previous studies [11] and one (obtaining information on the phone) was based on the IADL

---

[1] Here we use the words "activity" and "task" interchangeably.

Profile Bottari et al. [5]. Participants were asked to complete the five tasks in any order but within 45 min to increase the pressure, based on the procedure of the Six Elements Test of Shallice and Burgess [20]. Extension could be provided to allow for the completion of the tasks. The objective was to highlight the planning and adaptation capacities to the novelty of the participants. Tasks were selected so that older adults without cognitive impairment should be able to perform all tasks without much difficulty, but that older adults with MCI or AD could experience difficulties in some tasks. Task 1: Place personal belongings (bag and coat) in the wardrobe; Task 2: Prepare a light meal (prepare an egg, two toasts with jam and a hot beverage with milk and sugar; set up the table; clean the tools); Task 3: Clean the bathroom (flush the toilet, wash the mirror and washbasin with a cleaner); Task 4: Telephoning for information on bus departures between Montreal and Toronto; Task 5: Answer the phone that will ring during the experiment and perform the task indicated by the caller, i.e. fold and store three pieces of clothing placed in the room. Each task took place at different room of the smart home.

Participants were free to choose the order and planning of tasks. The instruction sheet was available at all time so to allow compensation for participants with memory deficits. While performing the tasks, the experimenters were instructed to intervene as little as possible, but may intervene if he/she considers that a situation is unsafe, if the participant had been stuck on the same task for a long time, or if the participant hastily declares to be finished and did not attempt all tasks. If they were to intervene, they had to provide graduated indices in order to guide the participant as little as possible.

2.3   Datasets

The data collected during experiments represent sensor data as shown in Table 1.

Table 1. Example of sensor data collected in a smart home at Sherbrooke.

Date	Time	Sensor name	State/Value	Participant
2014-12-03	09:00:00	InfraRedSensor16	ON	MCI
2014-12-03	09:00:10	InfraRedSensor17	ON	MCI
2014-12-03	09:00:30	DoorSensor12	OPEN	MCI
2014-12-03	09:01:01	DoorSensor13	OPEN	MCI
2014-12-03	09:01:09	InfraRedSensor20	ON	MCI
2014-12-03	09:01:20	HotWaterSensor-B	ON	MCI
2014-12-03	09:01:50	ColdWaterSensor-A	ON	MCI

In the Sherbrooke smart home, we count different types of sensors such as infrared sensors, contact sensors, pressure sensors, and debimeter sensors installed in different locations as shown in Fig. 1(a). Whereas in the Montreal

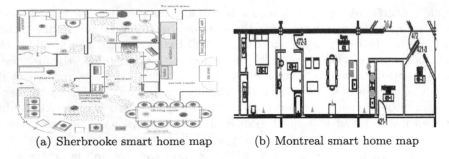

(a) Sherbrooke smart home map   (b) Montreal smart home map

Fig. 1. Sherbrooke and Montreal smart home maps and sensor locations.

smart home, we have three types of sensors: contact sensors, electric sensors and motion sensors as shown in Fig. 1(b).

Sensors are triggered as participants perform ADLs. Therefore, it will be interesting to analyze sensor data in the order that sensors are triggered. The rational of analyzing data in this way is to have a clear idea about the progression of ADL's completion by participants and the possibility to intervene and assist participants in real time applications when help is needed or errors are detected. As shown in Table 1, each sensor represents a feature with On/Off, 0/1, Open/Close or real value data. These sensors represent features in our dataset. We count 74 features in the dataset collected at Sherbrooke smart home and 12 features in the dataset collected at Montreal smart home. The next section details our method for early detection of AD and MCI by analyzing data related to ADLs.

2.4 Proposed Method

In this section, we present our proposed machine learning method for early detection of Alzheimer. We first present our feature selection method, followed by the learning and test method, and finally the results obtained. These steps are detailed in the following sections.

2.5 Feature Selection

Feature selection is an important step in machine learning to build a good classification model. It allows to select best features for classification tasks. In addition, feature selection allows to reduce significantly the dimension of the data. For example, in the data collected in the smart home at Sherbrooke, we have 74 sensors. However, not all these sensors are useful and discriminant. Therefore, feature selection in this case is helpful to select only the most discriminant sensors that will help differentiate users.

We used different techniques to select the best features such as principal component analysis, Chi-square feature selection, and Latent semantic analysis method. All these methods extract ten (10) common best features. Therefore, we reduced the dimensionality of data from 74 to 10, which will help reduce the computational complexity of the classification task. With 10 selected features, we were able to capture more than 90% of variations present in the data. We did not perform feature selection for the data collected in Montreal smart home since the number of features is small (12 features). Note that features are different in each dataset since sensors are different. Once features are selected, we perform classification using random forests.

2.6 Classification

Several classification methods could be used such as SVM, decision trees, and naive Bayes to perform classification. We selected random forest classifier as it performed well in a wide range of classification tasks [10]. This motivates us to choose random forest to build our classification method. Random forest classifier operates by constructing several decision tree classifiers. The classification results of a random forest are obtained by majority voting over all decision trees. We experimentally setup the number of decision trees to 200 as this number achieves the best classification results compared to 10, 50, and 100 decision trees. We experimentally selected a window size of 90 s with 50 % overlap to count the number of times each sensor is triggered. We do this process for the entire data sequences. The rational of using the number of times each sensor is triggered is to be able to extract meaningful information about behavioral patterns of each category of participants during the completion of ADLs, and how these behavioral patterns will help us to differentiate between each category of participants.

2.7 Leave One Out Cross Validation

We used leave one out cross validation method [22] to evaluate our method. We performed cross validation on data collected at Montreal and Sherbrooke smart homes separately. For example, for data collected at Sherbrooke smart home, we used all data from 24 participants (10 control, 10 MCI, and 4 AD) for training and the data of the remaining participant for testing. We performed the experiment 24 times, excluding one participant at each time. We performed the same experiments with data collected from Montreal smart home with 32 participants (16 control, 12 MCI, and 4 AD). The benefit of such setup is twofold. First, it allows detecting problematic participants and analyzing the sources of some of the classification errors caused by these participants. A problematic participant means his/her activities were performed differently compared to other participants. Second, it allows testing the inter-participant generalization of the method, which constitutes a good indicator about the practicability of our method. Tables 2 and 3 show the classification results obtained for each participant using the F-score measure. Note that the F-score is calculated as follows:
$F - score = \frac{2 \times (precision \times recall)}{precision + recall}$.

Table 2. Classification results obtained using data collected in Sherbrooke smart home.

User	Type	F-score	User	Type	F-score	User	Type	F-score
1	Control	0.886	11	MCI	0.819	21	AD	0.984
2	Control	0.918	12	MCI	0.316	22	AD	0
3	Control	0.934	13	MCI	1	23	AD	0.91
4	Control	0.938	14	MCI	0.484	24	AD	0.976
5	Control	0.965	15	MCI	1			
6	Control	0.903	16	MCI	0.537			
7	Control	0.907	17	MCI	0			
8	Control	0.911	18	MCI	1			
9	Control	0.934	19	MCI	0.468			
10	Control	0.96	20	MCI	0.515			

Table 3. Classification results obtained using data collected in Montreal smart home.

User	Type	F-score	User	Type	F-score	User	Type	F-score
1	Control	0.933	12	Control	0.625	23	MCI	0.667
2	Control	0.8	13	Control	0.947	24	MCI	0.462
3	Control	0.917	14	Control	0.909	25	MCI	0
4	Control	0.917	15	Control	0.8	26	MCI	0
5	Control	0.947	16	Control	0.609	27	MCI	0.4
6	Control	0.857	17	MCI	0	28	MCI	0.222
7	Control	0.615	18	MCI	0.533	29	AD	0.455
8	Control	0.615	19	MCI	0.667	30	AD	0.667
9	Control	0.667	20	MCI	0.154	31	AD	0.72
10	Control	0.609	21	MCI	0.375	32	AD	0
11	Control	0.615	22	MCI	0.235			

As shown in Table 2, in the Sherbrooke smart home, our method is able to differentiate between the three categories of people control, MCI and AD with an average F-score $= 0.761$, which is promising given the small number of participants with AD (4 participants). Note that our method identifies perfectly participants with AD as demonstrated by the high values of the F-score except for one user (User 22 in Table 2) incorrectly classified as a participant with MCI. This means that the behavioral patterns of User 22 are similar to those of participants with MCI so that he/she performs activities in the same way participants with MCI do. Similarly, participant User 17 (MCI) was incorrectly classified as a participant with AD. The behavioral patterns observed in participants with MCI may help identify patients with MCI who are more likely to develop AD given the level of difficulty they experience during the realization of ADLs.

The same observation applies for the patient with AD that performs better in realizing activities of daily living compared to the three other patients with AD. Finally, our method is able to identify perfectly behavioral patterns of control participants as shown in Table 2. The same observation applies for participants with AD except for User 22.

However, the classification results obtained using data collected from the Montreal smart home are not very promising since the average F-score is 0.56, which is slightly better than a random classifier. This can be explained by the small number of wireless sensors used to collect data, which is not enough to differentiate between participants. One important observation here is that all MCI and AD participants with F-score null in Table 3 are incorrectly classified as control participants. Consequently, Users 17, 25, 26 and 32 perform activities similarly to control participants and share similar behavioral patterns.

Note that each category of participants has specific behavioral patterns and performs activities differently. This can be shown by the number of times sensors are triggered for each category of participants for all activities using data from Sherbrooke smart home. Figure 2 shows the number of times sensors are triggered when participants in each category perform ADLs in Sherbrooke smart home.

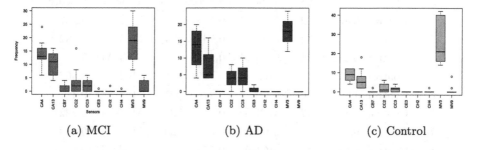

| (a) MCI | (b) AD | (c) Control |

Fig. 2. Number of times sensors triggered for each category of participants. Horizontal axis represent sensor names. Contact sensors names start with C, Movement sensors names start with M.

As shown in Fig. 2, sensors are triggered more frequently in MCI and AD categories compared to control category. Therefore, the behavioral patterns of MCI and AD participants are reflected in the number of times each sensor is triggered for these two categories. For example, sensor CA4 (contact sensor) has been triggered around 20 times for the categories MCI and AD as shown in Figs. 2(a) and (b), while it has been triggered around 10 times for control participants as shown in Fig. 2(c). This can be explained by the fact that control participants find easily utensils and objects used to perform activities compared to the other two categories where participants tried to look for objects everywhere and open different cabinets and drawers to find objects. The same observation applies to the other sensors except for sensor MV3 (movement sensor) that has been triggered more frequently, between 20 and 40 for control participants as shown in Fig. 2(c)

Table 4. Classification results obtained using data collected at Sherbrooke smart home using two categories of participants.

User	Type	F-score	User	Type	F-score	User	Type	F-score
1	Control	0.986	11	MCI-AD	1	21	MCI-AD	1
2	Control	0.947	12	MCI-AD	0.43	22	MCI-AD	1
3	Control	0.935	13	MCI-AD	1	23	MCI-AD	1
4	Control	0.96	14	MCI-AD	0.203	24	MCI-AD	1
5	Control	0.934	15	MCI-AD	1			
6	Control	0.96	16	MCI-AD	0.795			
7	Control	0.964	17	MCI-AD	0.991			
8	Control	0.921	18	MCI-AD	1			
9	Control	0.995	19	MCI-AD	0.846			
10	Control	1	20	MCI-AD	0.523			

Table 5. Classification results obtained using data collected at Montreal smart home using two categories of participants.

User	Type	F-score	User	Type	F-score	User	Type	F-score
1	Control	0.857	12	Control	0.533	23	MCI-AD	0.667
2	Control	0.8	13	Control	0.947	24	MCI-AD	0.182
3	Control	0.917	14	Control	0.909	25	MCI-AD	0.667
4	Control	0.87	15	Control	0.759	26	MCI-AD	0.667
5	Control	1	16	Control	0.476	27	MCI-AD	0.4
6	Control	0.897	17	MCI-AD	0	28	MCI-AD	0.222
7	Control	0.87	18	MCI-AD	0.625	29	MCI-AD	0.583
8	Control	0.615	19	MCI-AD	0.571	30	MCI-AD	0.857
9	Control	0.333	20	MCI-AD	0	31	MCI-AD	0.769
10	Control	0.545	21	MCI-AD	0.632	32	MCI-AD	0.4
11	Control	0.615	22	MCI-AD	0.333			

compared to the other two categories where it has been triggered between 15 and 25 times. This can be explained by the fact that MCI and AD participants wait for help when they were unable to perform activities, compared to control participants who continue performing activities. These are important behavioral patterns for these two categories as they indicate that participants may not initiate the activity, and intervention may be needed at this stage to help them.

We performed other experiments by merging the two categories MCI and AD. Our goal is to identify abnormal behavioral patterns during the realization of ADLs. The advantage of this method is to quickly distinguish between normal participants (control) and participants with cognitive deficits based on their behavioral patterns. Tables 4 and 5 show the recognition results for both categories in Sherbrooke and Montreal smart homes respectively.

As shown in Table 4, our method differentiates perfectly between healthy participants (control) and participants with cognitive deficits (MCI and AD) in the Sherbrooke smart home with an average F-score of 0.891. We can see that User 14 is identified as a participant with MCI-AD with an F-score of only 0.203. This means that this participant performed activities similarly to normal participants compared to other participants with MCI-AD and no abnormal behavioral patterns are observed. The same observation applies for User 12 with an F-score of 0.43. These observations are of great importance since they allow to identify persons with cognitive deficits who are still able to perform ADLs correctly. This will help them to stay engaged in realizing activities, which may allow to delay their cognitive decline. However, as shown in Table 5, our method did not perform well with data collected in the Montreal smart home. This was expected for two main reasons: (1) the small number of sensors used, which creates more confusion between participants, and (2) all MCI and AD participants incorrectly classified by our method were classified as control participants, this means that merging the MCI and AD categories does not help in differentiating between healthy participants and those with cognitive deficits. The results obtained using data from the Montreal smart home suggest that using small number of sensors is not suitable for identifying behavioral patterns and detecting patients with cognitive deficits or recognizing their activities of daily living. The use of very small number of sensors makes the task of detecting participants with cognitive deficits more complicated.

3   Comparison

We compared our method with several state-of-the-art machine learning algorithms such as support vector machines (SVM), Hidden Markov Models (HMM), Bayesian networks (BN), Naive Bayes (NB), decision trees (DT), K Nearest Neighbors (KNN), and multilayer perceptron neural network(mlp). Table 6 shows the comparison results obtained for all methods in terms F-score in both scenarios, i.e. with three categories of participants and two categories respectively using data from Sherbrooke smart home.

As shown in Table 6, our method outperforms all the state-of-the-art machine learning classifiers for both scenarios (three categories of participants and two categories). The HMM models performs poorly in both scenarios. This can be explained by the small sample size of the data as HMM models require more training data to perform well. The SVM model performs well also in both scenarios compared to the other classifiers.

Table 6. Comparison results between our method and state-of-the-art- methods using data collected in Sherbrooke smart home.

Method	Three categories Control, MCI, AD	Two categories Control, MCI-AD
	F-score	F-score
Our method	**0.761**	**0.891**
SVM	0.727	0.822
HMM	0.5	0.655
BN	0.703	0.804
NB	0.71	0.807
DT	0.722	0.817
KNN	0.722	0.809
MLP	0.709	0.787

4   Discussion and Conclusion

In this paper we proposed a method for automatic detection of patients with Alzheimer's and their behavioral patterns based on activities of daily living. We collected real data related to five activities of daily living from fifty-six (56) participants to perform experiments in two different smart homes. We performed feature selection in order to identify the most discriminant features and reduce the dimensionality of the data. The selected features were then fed into a random forest classifier for learning and testing. With a leave one out cross validation method, we were able to identify the three categories of participants (control, MCI and AD) with an average F-score of 0.76 and 0.56 using data collected in Sherbrooke and Montreal smart homes respectively, which is very promising given the small sample of participants with AD. We also empirically demonstrated that our proposed method is suitable in differentiating between healthy participants (control) and participants with cognitive deficits (MCI and AD) behavioral patterns with an average F-score of 0.89 and 0.60 using data collected in Sherbrooke and Montreal smart homes respectively. We were able to extract behavioral patterns of problematic participants who perform activities of daily living differently than the other participants of the same category.

The novel aspect of our research is to evaluate dysfunctions in ADL in normal aging, MCI and dementia conditions on a continuum of ability using a new performance-based approach, using simple sensors but most importantly, efficient machine learning approaches. The experiments performed in this work suggest that the use of a small number of sensors may create confusion between participants and make the identification of participants based on their behavioral patterns more challenging and complicate. This is demonstrated by the results obtained using data of the two smart homes. Indeed, at Sherbrooke smart home, where the relatively large number of sensors allows to create a behavioral profile for each category of participants that helps identify participants. In contrast, the small number of sensors used in Montreal smart home demonstrates the limitation in identifying participants of each category. Consequently, using more sensors allows to capture more variations in activities of daily living, which helps discriminating between participants. In addition, other machine learning methods such as deep neural networks could be used in the future to improve the recognition results as they showed promising results for other datasets [7].

In conclusion, we hypothesized that this method of evaluation may support currently used tools. Future study in the field may contribute to better early detection of dementia and identification of the person's difficulties and needs, which in turn will lead to more tailored interventions.

References

1. Akl, A., Chikhaoui, B., Mattek, N., Kaye, J., Austin, D., Mihailidis, A.: Clustering home activity distributions for automatic detection of mild cognitive impairment in older adults. J. Ambient. Intell. Smart Environ. **8**(4), 437–451 (2016)
2. Fabrigoule, C., Helmer, C., Rouch, I., Dartigues, J.F., Barberger-Gateau, P.: Functional impairment in instrumental activities of daily living: an early clinical sign of dementia? J. Am. Geriatr. Soc. **47**(4), 456–462 (1999)
3. Rainville, C., Letenneur, L., Dartigues, J.-F., Barberger-Gateau, P.: A hierarchical model of domains of disablement in the elderly: a longitudinal approach. Disabil. Rehabil. **22**(7), 308–317 (2000)
4. Letenneur, L., Barberger-Gateau, P., Dartigues, J.F.: Four instrumental activities of daily living score as a predictor of one-year incident dementia. Age Ageing **22**(6), 457–463 (1993)
5. Bottari, C., Dassa, C., Rainville, C., Dutil, E.: A generalizability study of the instrumental activities of daily living profile. Arch. Phys. Med. Rehabil. **91**(5), 734–42 (2010)
6. Dutil, E., Dassa, C., Bottari, C., Rainville, C.: Choosing the most appropriate environment to evaluate independence in everyday activities: home or clinic? Aust. Occup. Ther. J. **53**, 98–106 (2006)
7. Chikhaoui, B., Gouineau, F.: Towards automatic feature extraction for activity recognition from wearable sensors: a deep learning approach. In: IEEE ICDM Workshops, pp. 693–702 (2017)
8. Dawadi, P., Cook, D.J., Schmitter-Edgecombe, M.: Analyzing activity behavior and movement in a naturalistic environment using smart home techniques. IEEE J. Biomed. Health Inform. **19**(6), 1882–92 (2015)
9. Dawadi, P.N., Cook, D.J., Schmitter-Edgecombe, M., Parsey, C.: Automated assessment of cognitive health using smart home technologies. Technol. Health Care **21**(4), 323–343 (2013)
10. Díaz-Uriarte, R., de Andrés, S.A.: Gene selection and classification of microarray data using random forest. BMC Bioinform. **7**(1), 3 (2006)
11. Dutil, E., Forget, A., Vanier, M., Gaudreault, C.: Development of the adl profile. Occup. Ther. Health Care **7**(1), 7–22 (1990)
12. Pérès, K., et al.: Natural history of decline in instrumental activities of daily living performance over the 10 years preceding the clinical diagnosis of dementia: A prospective population-based study. J. Am. Geriatr. Soc. **56**(1), 37–44 (2008)

13. Winblad, B., et al.: Mild cognitive impairment-beyond controversies, towards a consensus: report of the international working group on mild cognitive impairment. J. Intern. Med. **256**(3), 240–246 (2004)
14. Koppel, J., Keehlisen, L., Christen, E., Dreses-Werringloer, U., Conejero-Goldberg, C., Goldberg, T.E.: Performance-based measures of everyday function in mild cognitive impairment. Am. J. Geriatr. Psychiatry **167**(7), 845–853 (2010)
15. Byerly, L.K., Vanderhill, S., Lambe, S., Wong, S., Ozonoff, A., Jefferson, A.L., et al.: Characterization of activities of daily living in individuals with mild cognitive impairment. Am. J. Geriatr. Psychiatry **16**(5), 375–383 (2008)
16. Jekel, K., Damian, M., Storf, H., Hausner, L., Frolich, L.: Development of a proxy-free objective assessment tool of instrumental activities of daily living in mild cognitive impairment using smart home technologies. J. Alzheimers Dis. **52**(2), 509–517 (2016)
17. Bédirian, V., Charbonneau, S., Whitehead, V., Collin, I., Cummings, J.L., Chertkow, H., Nasreddine, Z.S., Phillips, N.A.: The montreal cognitive assessment, moca: a brief screening tool for mild cognitive impairment. J. Am. Geriatr. Soc. **53**(4), 695–699 (2005)
18. Petersen, R.C.: Mild cognitive impairment as a diagnostic entity. J. Intern. Med. **256**(3), 183–194 (2004)
19. Seelye, A.M., Schmitter-Edgecombe, M., Cook, D.J., Crandall, A.: Naturalistic assessment of everyday activities and prompting technologies in mild cognitive impairment. J. Int. Neuropsychol. Soc. **19**(4), 442–452 (2013)
20. Shallice, T., Burgess, P.W.: Deficits in strategy application following frontal lobe damage in man. Brain **114**(2), 727–741 (1991)
21. Sikkes, S.A., et al.: Do instrumental activities of daily living predict dementia at 1- and 2-year follow-up? Findings from the development of screening guidelines and diagnostic criteria for predementia alzheimer's disease study. J. Am. Geriatr. Soc. **59**(12), 2273–2281 (2011)
22. Vehtari, A., Gelman, A., Gabry, J.: Practical bayesian model evaluation using leave-one-out cross-validation and waic. Stat. Comput. **27**(5), 1413–1432 (2017)

Activity Recognition by Classification Method for Weight Variation Measurement with an Insole Device for Monitoring Frail People

Eric Campo$^{(\boxtimes)}$, Damien Brulin$^{(\boxtimes)}$, Yoann Charlon,
and Elodie Bouzbib

LAAS-CNRS, Université de Toulouse, CNRS, UT2J, Toulouse, France
{campo, brulin, charlon, bouzbib}@laas.fr

Abstract. Healthcare has become a major field of scientific research and is beginning to merge with new technologies to become connected. Measurement of motor activity provides physicians with indicators in order to improve patient follow up. One important health parameter is weight variation. Measuring these variations is not obvious when a person is walking. This paper highlights the difficulty of providing reliable weight variation values with good accuracy. To reach this objective, the paper presents ways to classify the activity of walking, in order to propose a method to measure weight variation at the right time and in a good position. Many methods were studied and compared, using Matlab. We propose a classification tree that uses the standard deviation of acceleration magnitude to define normal walking. The algorithm was embedded in an insole equipped with two force-sensing resistors and tested in laboratory.

Keywords: Smart insole · Frail people monitoring · Classification methods
Embedded system · Actimetry · Weight variation measurement
Walking

1 Introduction

Home monitoring of the elderly is a well-identified goal of current health policy that aims to favor home support and prevent loss of autonomy. This policy is essential as life expectancy increases. It also is a strategy that should provide more comfort to those concerned by allowing them to stay at home, while helping to improve global health spending management. Thanks to technological tools, tele-monitoring permits ad hoc follow up in order to detect deteriorating health and facilitate timely assistance. Given the non-intrusive and user-friendly characteristics of recent technologies, it is possible to ensure optimized acceptability in a use case context. Dependency prevention and home support of frail people is a huge challenge. Frailty is an emerging concept that encompasses a high risk of death, and, more generally, of dependency. Correlations between frailty and some health parameters are today clearly established: walking speed, loss of weight, spontaneous activity...Thus, walk monitoring and evaluation are key points potentially predictive of unhealthy evolution among the elderly. Fried and al.

© Springer International Publishing AG, part of Springer Nature 2018
M. Mokhtari et al. (Eds.): ICOST 2018, LNCS 10898, pp. 73–84, 2018.
https://doi.org/10.1007/978-3-319-94523-1_7

criteria [1] currently are largely used in clinical studies to characterize frailty patients. These studies rely essentially on analysis of the physical component of frailty. In fact, Fried and al. criteria that make it possible to identify frailty syndrome are: diminution of walking speed, physical activity decrease or exhaustion and diminution of weekly calorific expenditure (which can be linked to reduced weekly walking distance), reduction of grasping force and involuntary weight loss. This paper is focused on the last criterion by proposing a way to measure weight variation thanks to a connected insole. The insole seems to be a good means to measure walk parameters [2] and weight [3]. A comparative study already has been realized concerning insole-embedded technologies used to measure weight [4]. The question, now, is to determine the moment when the measurement should be done. To do so, we evaluated several existing methods. We focused on supervised approaches, and we evaluated performances of generative and discriminative methods thanks to Matlab software. We discussed obtained results based on data collected during test scenarios in laboratory. The paper is organized as follows: Sect. 2 describes the objective of weight measurement. Section 3 gives classification techniques and an analysis method for spotting signals. Section 4 presents the equipment used for tests. Section 5 shows modelling results. Section 6 introduces the first results of weight measurement. Section 7 ends the paper with a conclusion.

2 Weight Measurement

Weight measurement during walking and its evolution is original. Most instrumented insoles in research projects use force (or pressure) sensors distributed on the insole area to analyze weight distribution under the sole of the foot. Optimally, a single sensor would measure resultant vertical forces over the entire insole area and would be sensitive to high loads. Non-linearity, hysteresis and sensibility criteria could be taken into account with software, thanks to sensor calibration. The most important point concerning weight monitoring is to achieve replicable measurements over time. Vertical forces on the under-foot area depend on walking cadence, stride length and weight of the user. The load measurement does not rely exclusively on these parameters, however. The activity of the user also has an influence. For the same cadence, the weight load is different, depending on whether the patient is walking, running or climbing stairs, for example. Thus, we want here to evaluate the user's mean weight variation (and not absolute weight which can be obtained thanks to the integral of the load curve divided by time) over a certain period of time (a week, for example); the aim is to be able to detect meaningful weight loss (3 kg), which would indicate the risk of diminished physical abilities and, therefore, loss of autonomy for the elderly person. In order to reduce energy consumption, we decided to measure weight variation with a sufficiently reliable algorithm and low computational resources (which it is not possible if we consider absolute weight), several times per day during a few strides, in order to obtain daily averages and to observe significant evolution during a week. To obtain the most replicable measurement, we decided to measure weight variation only during well-known and frequent circumstances – during a "normal" speed walk on a flat surface ("normal" meaning usual for each individual), for example. It is thus necessary to recognize this activity in order to measure weight only when a variation is detected. The principle of the "weight variation" function runs through three steps:

- First: determination of how that particular person walks by measuring his average walking speed with a calibration system developed specifically for measuring speed on a distance of 4 m [5];
- Second: online determination of walking activity. When sufficiently sustained activity is detected, we determine if it is a walking activity close to that identified during the learning phase.
- Third: weight variation calculation. If the activity matches, we retrieve the maximal pressure value during each walking cycle on flat surface. By calculating the average several times each day, we obtain a daily average which allows us to observe and monitor the evolution of weight variation.

3 Classification Techniques for Learning Signals

3.1 Classification Models

Concerning embedded weight variation measurement, we propose a walking activity classification, since this measure, in order to be reliable, must be realized under classic walking conditions. This means walking on a flat surface at "normal" speed (normal meaning the personal usual speed of the monitored patient, not the usual speed of all monitored patients). Indeed, the process will be different if weight is measured during stair climbing, running or walking. It is thus necessary to develop a classification algorithm of activity to discriminate walking from others activities.

Several supervised classification methods exist in the literature [6]: generative methods, discriminative methods [7]. Authors in [8] demonstrate that the discriminative approach usually surpasses the generative approach to classification tasks. Parameters to take into account ideally are simple implementation and reliability (In this type of study, 95% reliability is targeted [9]). The replicable ability also is a crucial point, since measurement will be carried out several times during the day in order to obtain accurate values. Finally, we want to limit energy consumption of the system, so we need to make sure not to choose a method that requires too much computation resource. Use of the supervised method is justified by the fact that activity models are carried out, initially, on a first database before being used in the embedded system. We want to develop an appropriate method on a computer and then to adapt it to real data on the embedded microprocessor.

Supervised methods have a predictive role. Indeed, from a first learning dataset, we will be able to evaluate the distribution of a class of activity without direct measure, by taking into account values linked to the activity. The aim will thus be to minimize the prediction error. Discriminative approach models directly use a classification rule, with $P(Y \mid X)$, Y being the output and X the input. Generative approach models use the joint distribution $P(X, Y)$ and deduce the classification rule afterwards. Generative models differ from discriminative models in that they are complete probabilistic, while the discriminative approach only determines models from conditional probabilities.

Considering that classification and regression do not necessitate joint distribution, discriminative models seem to perform better. Furthermore, generative models typically are more flexible than discriminative ones to express dependencies during complex learning. Most discriminative methods are supervised and may not be extended easily to unsupervised learning (Fig. 1).

Generative models	Discriminative models
- Model of Gaussian mixtures - Hidden Markov model - Bayesian naïve classification - Boltzmann machine	- Logistic regression - Linear discriminant analysis - Support vector machine - Boosting - Linear regression - Artificial Neural Network

Fig. 1. Classification models.

3.2   Analysis Method and Signal Characteristics

In literature, the standard approach consists of selecting a fixed set of indicators [10] and a sliding window with fixed length for gathering data of studied activities [7]. A combination of temporal and frequency parameters seems to be more precise. In literature, numerous indicators extracted from signals for activity classification are used. It is important to have a significant number of signals in order to improve precision. In any case, we need to extract uncorrelated indicators in order to avoid uselessly increasing the system's complexity. In the field of activity recognition, different sensors can be used, with an accelerometer usually the principal choice [11]. Acceleration data often are associated with a pressure sensor to measure weight with an insole [12, 13]. Some articles also mention the use of a barometer to measure elevation or of a gyroscope to measure rotation angle [14].

Center of Pressure (COP): In the literature, it is proposed to watch pressure distribution, in addition to pressure amplitude. In [15], authors look at the evolution of COP (central point of pressure) and speed in order to recognize activities. We do not use enough pressure sensors to take advantage of this system.

Study of front and back foot forces: The system presented in [16] uses pressure sensor mesh on an insole divided into two parts (front and back). The parameters used to recognize activities (sitting, standing, walking) are: subject's weight, estimated force both on left and right insole…

Classification with rejection: In [17, 18], authors propose to recognize activities and postures thanks to a system similar to our smart insole (insole composed of 5 pressure sensors and a 3-axis accelerometer). Data from sensors are sampled at 100 Hz and then brought back to 25 Hz by averaging (as in our case).

Indicators computed on each 2-s sequence of signal are:

- Step pace/step duration
- Mean of signal for one step
- Variance of signal for one step
- Maximum and minimum of signal amplitude for one step
- MAD (Mean Absolute Deviation) for one step
- Energy for one step (for acceleration, mean of the norm for each step)
- Entropy for one step.

Two other parameters are used to form an indicator: relation between maximum acceleration and maximum pressure. Activity recognition is then realized thanks to a learning phase.

4 Instrumentation System

4.1 Equipment

Our system is composed of a development card designed at LAAS-CNRS, an insole equipped with 2 FSR Teksan A401 sensors and a computer with Matlab software (Fig. 2). The development card has been designed in order to lay out the electronics of the smart insole. Microprocessor used is a nRF51822: this System on Chip is composed of a low-consumption radio emitter-receiver at 2.4 GHz. The 3-axis accelerometer chosen is the ADXL362 ultra low consumption. The two pressure sensors are respectively placed in the region of the metatarsal bones and the heel.

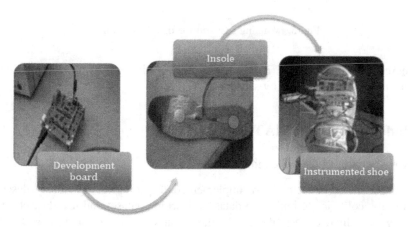

Fig. 2. Instrumentation.

4.2 Measurement Protocol

Data are obtained from raw data collected by sensors in the insole (Fig. 2) during a complete route. The insole sends 100 radio frames per second. A program in C++ allows the saving and the timestamping of received data by a beacon in an Excel datasheet. Retrieved parameters are:

- Acceleration a_x according to X-axis (horizontal and perpendicular to walk direction) in g;
- Acceleration a_y according to Y-axis (horizontal and in walk direction) in g;
- Acceleration a_z according to Z-axis (vertical) in g;
- Acceleration magnitude V_s in g;
- Output tension V_0 of the integrated circuit linked to FSR sensors in V.

The protocol consisted in three different activities in diverse situations (Fig. 3):

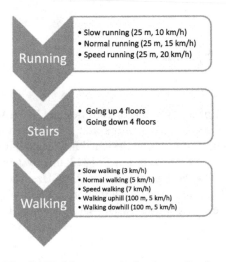

Fig. 3. Walking scenario for data collection.

We searched to determine if it was possible to distinguish these three different activities using data delivered by sensors.

5 Modelization with MATLAB

5.1 Comparison of Classification Methods

For each classification method, we implemented the complete previously described measure protocol twice to build two datasets: learning dataset and test dataset. In our modelling, we divided each dataset in three parts (walking, running and stairs), themselves cut into three sub-parts: duration of walking cycle, amplitude of cycle, cycle areas for pressure and acceleration signal. The learning dataset is thus composed of 60 to 90 walking cycles based on data coming from pressure and acceleration sensors. Among them, 30 to 60 cycles represent walking at different speeds, 15 correspond to running activities at three different speeds and the last 15 cycles are for stairs (up and down). The test dataset is composed of 15 cycles, 5 for each of the three

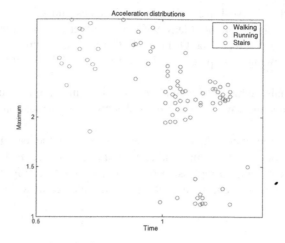

Fig. 4. Distribution of accelerations in learning phase

activities. Each cycle is randomly chosen in the original dataset: no duplication and each cycle belong to only one dataset (learning or test). Thus, we have a learning vector X, a vector Y representing classes and a test vector Z (Fig. 4).

$$X_i = \lceil\ Acc_i\ Time\quad Acc_i\ Max\quad Acc_i\ Area\quad Press_i\ Time\quad Press_i\ Max\quad Press_i\ Area \rceil$$

Each color corresponds to a particular activity, respectively: walking, running and walking up and down stairs.

Main classification methods have been tested with Matlab using several consecutive tries in order to obtain maximum precision for results. Table 1 compares the error rate of each tested method: pressure data only, acceleration data only and pressure and acceleration combined.

Table 1. Comparison of error rates for each method in Matlab.

Methods	Acceleration+Pressure	Acceleration	Pressure Data
LDA lin	5.53%	23.00%	3.19%
LDA quad	8.59%	23.55%	3.77%
LDA custom	9.31%	23.00%	3.19%
Naive Bayes	**5.21%**	**21.04%**	**3.67%**
SVM lin	16.05%	47.64%	8.48%
SVM quad	75.43%	50.53%	69.56%
SVM rbf	7.84%	23.49%	3.36%
Weighted Distances	**5.25%**	**15.99%**	**3.64%**
Reg Tree	7.72%	29.40%	4.83%
Class Tree	**5.32%**	**17.43%**	**2.92%**
k-NN	8.84%	21.89%	3.72%

We can see that Naïve Bayes, Weighted Distances and Class Tree are the most efficient, with a precision rate of at least 95% using either combination of pressure and acceleration or only pressure data. Of them all, Class Tree requires less computational resource while allowing good precision. Thus, we selected this method to develop our algorithm.

After some trials, duration of walking cycles, their maximum value and area have offered good results and have been chosen to design our classification algorithm based on Class Tree.

In the Class Tree approach, leaf represents values of the targeted variable and branching corresponds to the input variable combinations that lead to these values. Matlab software can return a regression or a classification tree (Fig. 5) based on predictors and Y response. Then, the algorithm predicts classes in which Z data belong.

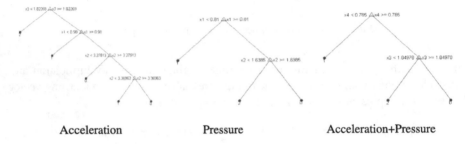

Acceleration   Pressure   Acceleration+Pressure

Fig. 5. Class Tree classification with acceleration and pressure data

5.2 Walking Parameters Measurement

As we saw the redundancy of standard deviations and means with Class Tree, we computed these two indicators for the different walking stages. We proposed a classification tree that uses standard deviation of acceleration amplitude to define way of walking and speed.

Indicators used for strides and cadence are acceleration amplitude (also called Sum Vector V_s^2), its mean and variance.

- Computation of square of sum vector, square of acceleration amplitude:

$$V_s^2 = a_i^2 = a_{xi}^2 + a_{yi}^2 + a_{zi}^2. \tag{1}$$

- Mean computation over a sliding window with w = 25 of the square acceleration amplitude a_q:

$$Moy2 = \overline{a_j^2} = \frac{1}{2w+1} \sum_{q=i-w}^{i+w} a_q^2. \tag{2}$$

- Computation of variance of square acceleration amplitude over a sliding window:

$$Var2 = \sigma^2_{a_i^2} = \frac{1}{2w+1} \sum_{j=i-w}^{i+w} \left(a_j^2 - \overline{a_j^2}\right)^2. \tag{3}$$

$$and \; Var2 = \frac{1}{2w+1} \sum_{j=i-w}^{i+w} \left(V_s^2 - Moy2\right)^2. \tag{4}$$

Variances obtained after modification are presented in Table 2.

Table 2. Variance of square acceleration amplitude depending on the walking stages: up and down stairs, flat surface at three different speeds, in g^2.

Class	Slow (flat)	Normal (flat)	Speed (flat)	Going up	Going down
Running	159	647	1043		
Walking	0.5	3.8	34.4	34.3	110
Stairs				22.4	18.1

Execution of this method is simple since we just have to compute Var2 over a sliding window and request pressure data acquisition related to weight variation, when Var2 is within an optimal space (Fig. 6).

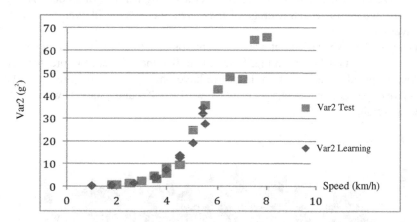

Fig. 6. Variance of square acceleration amplitude as a function of gait speeds, in learning and test phases

Using these characteristics, we have built a database in order to identify each walking stage. We can observe, in Table 2, differences between variances of acceleration amplitude, depending on step stages and then on walking speeds. Each variance is related to a particular speed.

We tested this approach on a treadmill, by varying walking speed. Figure 7 illustrates walking sequentially at 4, 6, 2 and 8 km/h and a return at normal condition (4 km/h). We can notice a huge variation of Var2 depending on speed.

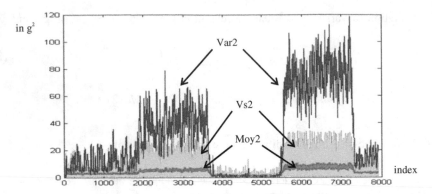

Fig. 7. Evolution of Var2 (Blue), Moy2 (Pink) and Vs2 (Green) depending on walking speed (index 0 to 2000 : 4 km/h, 2000 to 4000 : 6 km/h, 4000 to 5500 : 2 km/h, 5500 to 7500 : 8 km/h, 7500 to 8000 : 4 km/h) in g^2

6   Weight Variation Measurement

Continuous data collection of pressure during stable walking periods on a flat surface showed that we obtained peaks at each step, slightly shifted between the two FSR sensors (front and back of foot). We thus decided to compute an average of the maxima of the two sensors (resultant vertical force) over a sliding window of 25 data. At the end of the day, we computed an average of these averages which allowed us to obtain a daily average.

As a first step, we carried out walking scenarios on a treadmill at 4 km/h speed with different loads in a backpack. In Fig. 8, we can notice the difference in pressure when a new load is added at each stop. In detail, we have phase 1 with no extra load, phase 2 with +2.6%, phase 3 with +4.5%, phase 4 with +5.4% and phase 5 with +7.2% of subject's weight.

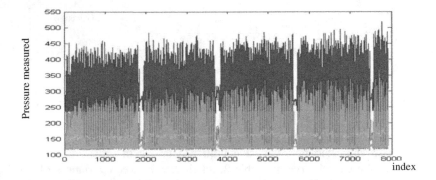

Fig. 8. Pressure variations depending on load

Table 3 summarizes pressure variations, in percentage terms, depending on the load.

Table 3. Evolution of average pressures and their maxima according to applied weights

Index	Additional weight (%)	Maxima average (%)	Average of average (%)
1:1890	0	–	–
1890:3750	+2.6	+2.7	+3.9
3750:5640	+4.5	+4.4	+5.5
5640:7470	+5.4	+4.8	+5.8
7470:7870	+7.2	+7.3	+7.0

We can see that increases, in percentage terms, of maxima averages are close to those for additional loads under real conditions. Indeed, results are better in this case because maximum pressure value is obtained when the foot is flat and contact between foot and the two pressure sensors is highest. This is why we decided to use maxima average pressure to calculate daily average weight variation.

7 Conclusion and Perspectives

We studied, with Matlab, performances (in terms of error rate) on sensor datasets (with acceleration and pressure) of the main classification methods. We proposed a classification tree, using standard deviation of acceleration amplitude, to define the type of walk and a speed. Our proposed approach combines precision, easy implementation, low cost computation and low energy consumption. Results obtained in laboratory are promising. When an elderly person receives an insole, he or she will be asked to walk at normal and fast speed in order to calibrate the insole. Thanks to the Var2 indicator, during this calibration step, we will be able to determine a space with two variances and a 10% (more or less) margin, for example. This space will make it possible to recognize his personal normal walking activity on a flat surface, and, thereafter, to measure weight variation. The interest of automatic measurement at home is that it can be repeated, thereby enabling longitudinal medium and long term monitoring, ensuring systematic measurement in ecological and similar conditions and making it possible to detect meaningful variations in a timely manner. Personalized monitoring of frail people at home should allow care to be adapted earlier, depending on the evolution of frailty indicators, preventing dependency and allowing the elderly to stay at home as long as possible. Developed algorithms may propose walking activity and weight variation monitoring by identifying the appropriate time to implement significant measures. Relative weight variation is targeted. Algorithms' reliability must, henceforth, be tested in real conditions.

References

1. Fried, L.P., Tangen, C.M., Walston, J., Newman, A.B., Hirsch, C., Gottdiener, J., McBurnie, M.A.: Frailty in older adults: evidence for a phenotype. J. Gerontology Ser. A Biological Sci. Med. Sci. **56**(3), M146–M157 (2001)
2. Muro-De-La-Herran, A., Garcia-Zapirain, B., Mendez-Zorrilla, A.: Gait analysis methods: an overview of wearable and non-wearable systems, highlighting clinical applications. Sensors **14**(2), 3362–3394 (2014)

3. Abdul Razak, A.H., Zayegh, A., Begg, R.K., Wahab, Y.: Foot plantar pressure measurement system: a review. Sensors **12**(7), 9884–9912 (2012)
4. Campo, E., Charlon, Y., Brulin, D.: Instrumented insole for weight measurement of frail people. In: Proceedings of the 8th ACM International Conference on PErvasive Technologies Related to Assistive Environments, p. 60, July 2015
5. Charlon, Y., Campo, E., Brulin, D.: Design and evaluation of a smart insole: application for continuous monitoring of frail people at home. Expert Syst. Appl. **95**, 57–71 (2018)
6. Kotsiantis, S.B., Zaharakis, I., Pintelas, P.: Supervised machine learning: a review of classification techniques. Emerg. Artif. Intell. Appl. Comput. Eng. **160**, 3–24 (2007)
7. Huynh, T., Schiele, B.: Analyzing features for activity recognition. In: Proceedings of the 2005 Joint Conference on Smart Objects and Ambient Intelligence: Innovative Context-Aware Services: Usages and Technologies, pp. 159–163, October 2005
8. Ng, A.Y., Jordan, M.I.: On discriminative vs. generative classifiers: a comparison of logistic regression and naive bayes. In: Advances in Neural Information Processing Systems, pp. 841–848 (2002)
9. Tang, W., Sazonov, E.S.: Highly accurate recognition of human postures and activities through classification with rejection. IEEE J. Biomed. Health Inf. **18**(1), 309–315 (2014)
10. Bao, L., Intille, S.S.: Activity recognition from user-annotated acceleration data. In: Ferscha, A., Mattern, F. (eds.) Pervasive 2004. LNCS, vol. 3001, pp. 1–17. Springer, Heidelberg (2004). https://doi.org/10.1007/978-3-540-24646-6_1
11. Panagiota, A., Layal, S., Stefan, H.: Assessment of human gait speed and energy expenditure using a single triaxial accelerometer. In IEEE Ninth International Conference on Wearable and Implantable Body Sensor Networks (BSN), pp. 184–188, May 2012
12. Howell, A.M., Kobayashi, T., Hayes, H.A., Foreman, K.B., Bamberg, S.J.M.: Kinetic gait analysis using a low-cost insole. IEEE Trans. Biomed. Eng. **60**(12), 3284–3290 (2013)
13. Sazonov, E.S., Fulk, G., Hill, J., Schutz, Y., Browning, R.: Monitoring of posture allocations and activities by a shoe-based wearable sensor. IEEE Trans. Biomed. Eng. **58**(4), 983–990 (2011)
14. Pappas, I.P., Popovic, M.R., Keller, T., Dietz, V., Morari, M.: A reliable gait phase detection system. IEEE Trans. Neural Syst. Rehabil. Eng. **9**(2), 113–125 (2001)
15. Shu, L., Hua, T., Wang, Y., Li, Q., Feng, D.D., Tao, X.: In-shoe plantar pressure measurement and analysis system based on fabric pressure sensing array. IEEE Trans. Inf Technol. Biomed. **14**(3), 767–775 (2010)
16. El Achkar, C.M., Massé, F., Arami, A., Aminian, K.: Physical activity recognition via minimal in-shoes force sensor configuration. In: Proceedings of the 7th International Conference on Pervasive Computing Technologies for Healthcare, pp. 256–259. ICST (Institute for Computer Sciences, Social-Informatics and Telecommunications Engineering), May 2013
17. Hynes, M., Wang, H., Kilmartin, L.: Off-the-shelf mobile handset environments for deploying accelerometer based gait and activity analysis algorithms. In: IEEE Annual International Conference of Engineering in Medicine and Biology Society, EMBC 2009, pp. 5187–5190, September 2009
18. Tang, W., Sazonov, E.S.: Highly accurate recognition of human postures and activities through classification with rejection. IEEE J. Biomed. Health Inf. **18**(1), 309–315 (2014)

Categorization of the Context Within the Medical Domain

Hicham Ajami[1(✉)], Hamid Mcheick[1(✉)], Lokman Saleh[2],
and Rania Taleb[1]

[1] Computer Science Department, Université du Québec à Chicoutimi,
555, Boul De l'Université, Chicoutimi, QC G7H 2B1, Canada
{Hicham.Ajami1,Hamid_Mcheick,Rania.Taleb1}@uqac.ca
[2] Computer Science Department, Montréal, Université du Québec à Montréal,
Case Postale 8888, Succursale Centre-ville, Montréal, QC H3C 3P8, Canada
Saleh.Lokman@courrier.uqam.ca

Abstract. The context itself has multiple meanings may vary according to the domain of application. This contextual flexibility was behind the emergence of so such huge number of context definitions. Nevertheless, all the proposed definitions do not provide solid ground for systems developers' expectations, especially in healthcare domain [1]. This issue prompted researchers to divide the context into a set of concepts that would facilitate organizing of contextual knowledge. The conventional taxonomies of context are always too complex, and we need to fight to make them useful in the intended application area. In this paper, we propose a new context classification which covers almost all the context aspects that we may need to develop a tele-monitoring system for chronic disease management.

Keywords: Healthcare · Pervasive computing · Context categorization
Medical context

1 Introduction

The development of healthcare system should be supported by adequate context knowledge. Context and knowledge management is a very important feature to deliver the right service to the right person at the right moment. The conventional taxonomies of context are always too complex, and we need to fight to make them useful in the intended application area. Often, researchers have identified very general taxonomies of context to be used in different domains. However, these taxonomies cannot be applied a in specific domain [2]. Our objective in this paper is to present categorization of context in the medical domain. Such taxonomy aims to represent knowledge that can influence patient status, ensuring access to services and providing necessary monitoring. Although there are a plenty of context structures developed with different approaches, no agreed structure exists can be broadly used for developing telemedicine applications. This work is a new essay to make such structure more consistent. The remainder of this document is organized into three parts. In the first part we present the existing categorizations of the context while the second part describes our perception for

© Springer International Publishing AG, part of Springer Nature 2018
M. Mokhtari et al. (Eds.): ICOST 2018, LNCS 10898, pp. 85–97, 2018.
https://doi.org/10.1007/978-3-319-94523-1_8

medical concepts. The third part provides a case study to design healthcare system for Chronic Obstructive Pulmonary Disease (COPD) patients. Finally, we conclude this research work and give perspectives.

2 State of the Arts

Although everyone has a general idea of what the context is, but it is certainly not easy to find a precise definition of context. There is a lack of standard definitions for this term. However, some common features can be extracted. Rey *et al.* [2] investigate these common characteristics which are discussed and agreed upon by the researchers in the contextual computing. (1) Context does not exist out of context, (2) Context is an information space that serves interpretation and (3) Context evolves, is structured, and shared. The existing work in the field of contextual management in ubiquitous healthcare environment suffers from absence of a detailed description of all dimensions of context. To make more meaningful contribution in this research area we need a good understanding of what are the most important aspects of context in the health care domain. The Table below illustrates the most remarkable categorizations from 1994 to 2016.

Table 1. Dimensions of context.

Authors	Dimensions
Schilit et al. (1994) [6]	Where, who, what
Ryan et al. (1997) [7]	Identity, time, location and environment
Hull et al. (1997) [8]	User identity, locations, vital signs, air quality, network availability
Pasco et al. (1998) [9]	Physical and logical
Franklin et al. (1998) [10]	Person's actions
Abowd et al. (1999) [11]	Primary and secondary context
Chen and Kotz (2000) [12]	Computing, physical, time and user
Petrelli et al. (2000) [13]	The material context and the social context
Gwizdka, (2000) [14]	The internal context and the external context
Klemke et al. (2000) [15]	Organizational, domain content based, personal and physical
Gross and Specht (2001) [16]	Location, Identity, Time, Environment or activity
Hofer et al. (2002) [17]	Physical and logical
Antti Aaltonen (2002) [18]	location, target, calendar, address book, users nearby, history, profile, direction and speed
Henricksen (2003) [19]	Sensed, Static, Dynamic, Derived
Prekop et al. (2003) [20]	Physical and logical
Mayrhofer (2004) [21]	Geographical, Physical, Organizational, Social, Emotional, User, Task, Action, Technological, Time
Wang et al. (2004) [22]	Low level, High level
Chen et al. (2004) [23]	Agents, time, space, events, user profiles, actions and policies.

(continued)

Table 1. (*continued*)

Authors	Dimensions
Brezillon et al. (2004) [24]	Continuous, enumerative, state and descriptive context
Bunningen et al. (2005) [25]	Operational and conceptual
Chaari et al. (2005) [26]	network profile, user description/preferences, terminal characteristics, location and environment
Chang Xu (2005) [27]	Physical and logical
Razzaque et al. (2005) [28]	user, physical, network, activity, material and service context
Miao et al. (2006) [29]	Sensed, profiled and derived
Guan et al. (2007) [30]	Low level, High level
Chong et al. (2007) [31]	Computing, Physical, History, Identity and Time
Zimmerman (2007) [32]	Individuality, time, location, activity and relation
Miraoui et Tadj (2008) [33]	Trigger information, Quality changing information
Arianti Kurti (2009) [34]	User's profile, activity, location/environment
Soylu (2009) [35]	User and environment
Zhong (2009) [36]	User, System, Environment, Social, Time
Tamine et al. (2010) [37]	User, platform and environment.
Rizou et al. (2010) [38]	Low level, High level
Nageba E. (2011) [39]	Physical and abstract
Kim et al. (2012) [40]	5W1H (Who, When, Where, What, Why and How)
Bin Guo (2013) [41]	Individual, social, and urban context
Boughareb et al. (2014) [42]	Device, task, user, document, spatio-temporal, environmental, and event
Ameyed (2016) [43]	Time, space and purpose

2.1 Discussion

Schilit *et al.* [6] categorized context into three conceptual entities based on three common questions: where you are that includes all information related location, common or specific names, addresses and user preferences; who you are with, the information about the people present around the user, and what resources are nearby such as machineries, smart objects, and utilities. Abowd *et al.* [11] introduced one of the most controversial hypotheses of defining context types. They considered location, identity of user, time, and activity as the primary context types, while they defined secondary context as the context that can be extracted using primary context. Pascoe *et al.* [9], Chang *et al.* [27], Hofer *et al.* [17] and Prekop *et al.* [20] divided the context into two main categories, the physical context that can be measured by the physical sensors and the logical context that contains abstract information about the environment or the interaction such as the user's emotional state, goals, etc. In a similar way Wang *et al.* [22], Guan *et al.* [30] and Rizou *et al.* [38] distinguished between two categories of context. First, we have low level or observabale context which represents the information that can be directly obtained from sensors or other sources, and secondly there is high level context or non-observable information that must be inferred from the first kind of context. Petrelli *et al.* [13] have seen context from a different point of view, he considered location, machine, existing platform as material context, while he identified the social aspects or relationship between individuals as part from the social context. In contrast, Gwizdka [14] used two main domains to describe the context. The internal context includes the user's state and the external context encompassing the state of the environment. Chaari [26] added more elements to the basic facets of context in specific application domains: network profile, user description/preferences, terminal characteristics, location and environment. Nageba [39] classified the components of context as physical component such as actor, organization, resource, etc. and abstract component such as process, task, service, messages, parameter, etc. Soylu et al. [35] proposed a hierarchical representation of context with two main roots is defined user and environment. Bunningen *et al.* [25] classified the context into two broader categories: operational and conceptual. The operational category concerns the method of acquisition and execution of context. On the other hand, the Conceptual category is only interested with relationships between the contexts. In the same setting, Zimmerman *et al.* [32] presented a formal extension for context from five fundamental categories: individuality, time, location, activity and relations. Bin Guo [41] introduced new context dimensions that involve individual, social, and urban context. Chen et al. [23] propose a four-dimensional space for context organized into active and passive context, these four dimensions are computing, physical, time and user. Klemke *et al.* [15] presents a simple topology for context with concentrating on the following contextual aspects: organizational, domain content based, personal and physical. Miraoui *et al.* [33] have organized contextual information in two classes: trigger information whose change in value causes automatic release of services provided by the pervasive system and quality changing information whose change in value causes the change of service's format. Brezillon *et al.* [24] proposed values-based categorization: continuous context, enumerative context, state context and descriptive context. Kim el al. [40] mobilizes 5W1H as the minimum information that is necessary to process physical and logical contextual information. Who (Identity), Where (Location), When (Time), What (Activity), Why and How. Boughareb *et al.* [42] proposes a new context taxonomy gathering what they consider all possible dimensions of context such as device, task, user, document, spatio-temporal, environmental, and event. Franklin *et al.* [10] illustrate their context as the person's actions. Where that action will have very different synonym depending on the situation it is used in. Antti Aaltonen *et al.* [18] considered the context as a group of following variables: location, target, and calendar, address book, users nearby, history, profile, direction and speed. Tamine et al. [37] modeled the context by the triplet: user, platform and environment. Henricksen [19] proposed four categories of context: sensed context includes data-acquired directly from sensors, static or permanent information that do not change over time, dynamic information that changes over time and finally derived information that can be obtained using the first three categories. As part of efforts to find a useful categorization, some authors [7, 8, 11, 16, 21, 25, 28, 29] lists aspects of context as combinations of three, four or six elements from the composition we mentioned before.

3   Dimension of Medical Context

Like the creation of any new strategy, the process of developing the medical context should start with a clear understanding of healthcare domain. This requires going beyond all-too-common taxonomies that they don't provide practical sense of context. Structuring context information in the form of categories is a very important to organize contextual knowledge. The set of context information presented above clearly demonstrates that what is considered as context depends on what needs to be described [45]. Therefore, the proposed models discussed in the preceding section offer a general structure that should be extended to suit the medical domain. A domain specific vocabulary may raise the level of abstraction and remove ambiguity by specifying all relevant concepts. The list below outlines the basic entities that respond to requirements of medical context.

3.1   Person

The persons within this healthcare environment are classified according to their functions (e.g. patients, physicians, and social). To build such medical context we need first to identify roles and responsibilities of each person, provided patients remains the concentration key point, for which all actions and decisions are directed [26]. Since patient can be characterized by their physical and psychological attributes, the person category can be subdivided into physical parameters and psychological parameters.

3.2   Profile

Person concept is also directly responsible for modeling the profile of the user in the medical domain. Person's profile consists of a set of basic characteristics that should be considered by a system developer to provide a suitable ubiquitous healthcare customized to the needs of the patient (e.g. Demographic, preferences). The personal profile of patient is needed, in order to automatically perform adaptations that meet the user's necessities [27].

3.3   Time

The medical applications, especially remote patient monitoring focuses on end-to end transmission in real time. Thus, computing systems should be aware of the time to support urgent decision or to record certain events. Usually, in telemedicine, the data measurements are used for immediate response based on real time analytics. Time, when applied to data transfer, can configure bandwidth reservation in networks, thereby enabling faster analytics, low latency for real time operation and timely delivery of critical messages [41]. Furthermore, Klein *et al.* [44] stressed on the importance of time synchronization for context aware applications to infer a user's situation with more accuracy because the contextual information is often aggregated from multitude of physical and virtual sensors.

3.4   Location

In addition to the previous contextual factors, location awareness is considered the backbones of all context aware systems [43]. With the location awareness, patients' tracking becomes easier and they can be transported to a hospital or a medical center when they need urgent intervention. This helps explain why pervasive healthcare applications require the determination of location of patient. Location often provides much deeper, more meaningful and identifiable description about the physical characteristics of the place which may have an impact on the patient's health status (e.g. the altitude harms some types of patients). There are three different ways to represent location: (1) geographic coordinate, (2) named spaces (e.g. room), and (3) relative location (e.g. describe the position of an object in relation to surrounding objects) [46].

3.5   Activity

Today, there is a growing demand of automated recognition of human activities in the health-care domain. Tracking the current situation of the users in smart space allows extending the applications with new features that may give more accurate and consistent results [48]. Furthermore, using the activity context could be useful to warn the user if they were increasing their levels of exercise in an exaggerated manner to prevent exacerbations or any serious complications.

3.6   Technology

This category covers any human-built thing, whether hardware or software application. This part includes computing hardware devices such as Mobile, Personal Digital Assistants (PDAs) or sensors. Technology context not only refers to computing resources but also to issues such as connectivity to a network, platform characteristics [11, 17]. In this setting, Jaydip et al. [3] refer to the importance of mobile connectivity or persistent wireless access and quality of service (e.g., the available bandwidth) to deliver healthcare service. Furthermore, these technologies cover as well the biomedical equipment used by the patients, basically there are three types of devices in the medical environment [45]: (i) fixed infrastructure equipment such as heating, ventilation and air conditioning, (ii) support equipment (e.g. microbiological sterilization and disinfection, laboratory equipment and analytical instruments) and (iii) medical equipment (e.g. vital signals monitor that includes blood pressure, cardiac monitors, respiration rate, pulse oximeters, oxygen saturation, pressure, and temperature) in addition to electrocardiogram, defibrillators, ventilators and computerized tomography.

3.7   Environment

The next context factor to consider when deciding to create a framework to assist healthcare provider organizations is the environment. Ubiquitous healthcare systems must recognize too, that small changes either indoor or outdoor in the environmental factors can have great impact on the patient's behavior [47]. Such a context may include humidity, temperature, pollution and pressure etc. Disease progression can be found in relation to many environmental factors [48]. For example, cold and hot weather could irritate chronic Illness symptoms and pose significant risk to chronic obstructive pulmonary disease (COPD) patient [3], also exposure to air pollutants may increase the chances of developing acute respiratory infection [46].

3.8 Real Time Data

Real time data includes signals taken by biomedical equipment or environmental sensor. Real-time data is used to control both the environmental and physical conditions. Broadly, we might take the mental status in implementation of a continuous control system by adding a set of questionnaires that they answer using a specified set of responses. Furthermore, this category includes a host of sites that have real time weather, air, water, and satellite information.

3.9 History

Historical information contains all a patient's medical history and its long-term follow-up. In practice, this part of the context should contain sufficient information about physical exam findings and prior diagnostic test results, family diseases, regular and acute medications. This parameter could help healthcare professionals to take proper decision [46]. Moreover, using historical context might improve future performance of healthcare systems. In assessing the historical context, we found that this concept (1) grants the ability for treatment to be supervised and monitored, (2) provide the possibility to exchange full health information about a patient. Therefore, that leads to a higher quality of care.

3.10 Disease

Disease context is presented as causal attribution that describes the relations among the symptoms, causes, and treatment [43]. Equally, to present services completely customizable according to patient status, a class of human disease is needed. This category will enrich the existing taxonomy of medical context by linking diseases with appropriate medications, consequently that would provide efficient administration for the treatment [5]. A treatment subclass is associated with multiple components such as type of treatments, condition and effect. Furthermore, disease profile may comprise a combination of severity, duration, stage, and physical feature etc. [45].

3.11 Task

Essentially, care providers use the context to perform task or actions and interact with patients to control precarious or suspicious situations. Hence, action is considered an essential element of the proposed categorization. According to Lasierra et al. [5] medical tasks will comprise four different types: monitoring task, analysis task, planning task and execution task. The relation between these tasks is governed by a set of conditions expressed using rules.

3.12   Event

Likewise, event can be part of task, but we prefer to define it as an independent concept to detect expected events when occur. To put it more simply, we could say that such concept is very necessary because of the nature of the remote health care system, which takes as input the physical attributes that indicate the existing conditions to make the analysis of more complex incidents, e.g. exacerbation.

3.13   Organization

Healthcare organization is a generic term refers to any healthcare entity (hospital, clinic, etc.). Organization is responsible for the management and delivery of healthcare services, by making decision, performing processes and using resources. For example, (1) define and monitor the delivery process of the service care, (2) assign a care provider and a medical equipment when required for a patient, (3) manage and allocate human and physical resources between services and (4) manage collaboration with other centers [5].

3.14   Policies

Context categorization provides a conceptual framework for understanding of context at the application-level. Therefore, this context can be further used at application-level for management of policies. Such as policies include security, integrity, confidentiality and availability, as well as end patient's privacy. Due to the sensitive nature of this information, we believe that is important to satisfy strict privacy and security requirements. The security refers to guarantee reliable message transmission where all security systems should be equipped with mechanisms that can be used to resolve error and carrying information via well-protected channels. Likewise, privacy of information is necessary to establish policies for user and resource to assign permissions such who owns health information, and how restricted is access to it [47].

4   Case Study: Medical Context of COPD

To motivate the use of our model, we introduce in the following an example of context as a pattern of chronic disease. Context of COPD is designed to provide personalized care plans for patients to identify symptoms, risk factors, and effective self-management of COPD. The graphical representation below (Fig. 1) contains the domain-specific context of COPD. These domain-specific components can be interchangeably compatible with any kind of chronic diseases. The context elements listed in this cluster is an example of a domain-specific context consisting of 51 context elements related to COPD. We must mention here that this domain specific context information is not intended to provide an exhaustive representation of the context in the COPD domain, it is simply to show the context elements for the domain as identified in our content analysis of context. Practically, COPD could be a relevant example when designing tele-monitoring system in the healthcare domain. This implementation is

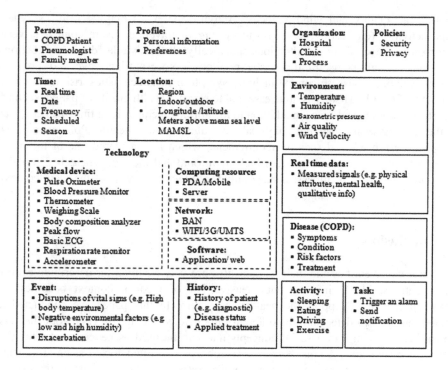

Fig. 1. Domain specific context for COPD

used to identify to which extent current taxonomy approach can generate telemedicine services adapted to the current contextual needs of patients. The structure of the COPD context comprise group of 14 entities used for analyzing such specific health problem. In this work, we created a custom context based on fourteen types of real world concepts that intelligent system should consider when reasoning over COPD context. Thus, Fig. 1 provides a clearer and deeper view of COPD domain. The figure reflects the way we read and our perception and understanding of typical hierarchical structure of the context categories.

Each of these categories has several subcategories that retains to itself of a list of internal context elements. Person context contains the subcategories patient which can be seen as an axial centric point of the medical context, besides physician and family member. Profile context includes personal information about COPD patient and his care providers. Time context may comprise current time to intervene in a timely manner as well as terms related to date and seasons. Location context could be outdoor and indoor place such as home, office, park etc. Technology context is the pervasive network of technologies that surrounds people, added to it the medical devices for monitoring human vital signs, such as body temperature, heart rate, respiration rate, blood pressure, pulse oxygenation, and blood glucose. Environmental context contains all factors that affects COPD patients such as temperature, humidity, barometric pressure, air quality and wind Velocity. Activity context is ranging from everyday home activities (e.g. eating, sleeping) to driving or traveling. Event context is very important to detect abnormal situations specifically all that is related to exacerbation. Task context could be useful to describe monitoring process, trigger events or provide recommendations. Disease context includes symptoms, characteristics, risk factors and treatment of COPD. History is quite essential to register health profile of patient such as diagnosis, lab tests, and scans in addition to the applied therapy. Real time data consists of the instantaneous data e.g. physical attributes, mental health. Policies context establish the privacy and security requirements which is considered one of the most important pillars of medical services both traditional and modern. These benchmarks are valid to any type of illnesses, since only the internal contents of the main context parameters need to be changed.

5   Conclusion

Since real world entities and their relationships are very essential for describing events and situations, identifying a comprehensive list of medical context becomes an important matter to support the healthcare system. In this paper, we conducted a detailed analysis to determine the different dimensions of context. This work dissects the medical domain into a set of concepts that can be used as general terms for the design of healthcare systems. Recent research has identified location, environment, time, person and activity as the most crucial parameters for describing real-world things. Our taxonomy of medical context relies on fourteen components that besides the previous parameters, contains also other items such as the task, history, data, event, disease, organization and policies. This new categorization would be a guideline and an effective strategy that may help developers to find their context structure. The organization of context content is an important issue to consider during creating context awareness system in healthcare environments. This study provides further contribution to the field of ubiquitous computing. For future work we will continue to explore and investigate how the idea of context categorization can provide more features for context awareness system.

References

1. Kurti, A.: Exploring the multiple dimensions of context, Ph.D. thesis, Växjö University Press (2009)
2. Rey, G., Coutaz, J.: The Contextor Infrastructure for Context-Aware Computing. Engineering HCI research group, CLIPS IMAG, Grenoble, France, June 2004
3. Sen, J., Ukil, A.: A QoS-aware end-to-end connectivity management algorithm for mobile applications. In: Proceedings of the Third Annual ACM Bangalore Conference, Bangalore, India, pp. 1–9, 22–23 January 2010
4. Dey, A., Abowd, G., Salber, D.: A conceptual framework and a toolkit for supporting the rapid prototyping of context-aware applications. Human-Computer Interaction (2000)

5. Lasierra, N.: A three stage ontology-driven solution to provide personalized care to chronic patients at home. J. Biomed. Inform. **46**, 516–552 (2013)
6. Schilit, B.: Disseminating active map information to mobile hosts. IEEE Netw. **8**(5), 22–32 (1994)
7. Ryan, N.: Enhanced Reality Fieldwork: The Context-Aware Applications in Archaeology, vol. 23 (1997)
8. Hull, R., Neaves, P., Bedford-Roberts, J.: Towards situated computing. In: 1st International Symposium on Wearable Computers, pp. 146–153 (1997)
9. Pascoe, J.: Adding generic contextual capabilities to wearable computers. In: 2nd International Symposium on Wearable Computers, pp. 92–99 (1998)
10. Franklin, D.: Spring Symposium on Intelligent Environments, Technical report SS-98-02, pp. 155–160 (1998)
11. Dey, A.K., Abowd, G.D., Wood, A.: CyberDesk: a framework for providing self-integrating context-aware services. Knowl.-Based Syst. **11**, 3–13 (1999)
12. Chen, G.: A survey of context-aware mobile computing research, vol. 1, no. 2.1, pp. 2–1. Technical report TR2000-381, Dartmouth College (2000)
13. Petrelli, D.: Modeling context is like taking pictures. In: CHI2000 Workshop (2000)
14. Gwizdka, J.: What's in the context. In: CHI2000 Workshop (2000)
15. Klemke, R.: Context framework. In: Proceedings of the International Conference on Practical Aspects of Knowledge Management, 30–31 October, Basel, Switzerland (2000)
16. Gross, T., Specht, M.: Awareness in context-aware information systems. Tagungsband der 1. Fachübergreifenden Konferenz "Mensch & Computer", Bonn, Germany (2001)
17. Hofer, T.: Context-awareness on mobile devices – the hydrogen approach. In: Proceedings of the 36th Annual Hawaii International Conference on System Sciences, pp. 292–302 (2002)
18. Aaltonen, A.: A Context Visualization Model for Wearable Computers. SEMWEB (2002)
19. Henricksen, K.A.: Framework for Context-Aware Pervasive Computing Applications. Ph.D. thesis, University of Queensland, Queensland (2003)
20. Prekop, P., Burnett, M.: Activities, context and ubiquitous computing. Comput. Commun. **26**(11), 1168–1176 (2003)
21. Mayrhofer, R.: An Architecture for Context Prediction. Ph.D. thesis, Johannes Kepler University of Linz, Austria, October 2004
22. Wang, X.H., Dong, J.S., Chin, C.Y., Hettiarachchi, S.R.: Semantic space: an infrastructure for smart spaces. IEEE Pervasive Comput. **3**(2), 32–39 (2004)
23. Chen, H.A.: An Ontology for Context-Aware Pervasive Computing Environments, vol. 18, no. 3, pp. 197–207. Cambridge University Press (2004)
24. Brézillon, P.: Learning and explanation in a context-based representation: Application to incident solving on subway lines (2004)
25. Van Bunningen, A.H., Feng, L., Apers, P.M.: Context for ubiquitous data management. In: Ubiquitous Data Management, 2005, UDM 2005, International Workshop on IEEE, pp. 17–24, April 2005
26. Chaari, T., Laforest, F., Celantano, A.: Design of context-aware applications based on web services. Technical report, LIRIS UMR 5205 CNRS/INSA de Lyon/Université Claude Bernard (2004)
27. Chen, F.J., Warden, A.C., Chang, H.T.: Motivators that do not motivate: the case of Chinese EFL learners and the influence of culture on motivation. TESOL Q. **39**(4), 609–633 (2005)

28. Razzaque, M.A., Dobson,S., Nixon, P.: Categorization and modeling of quality in context information. In Proceedings of the IJCAI 2005, Workshop on AI and Autonomic Communications. Edinburgh, Scotland (2005)
29. Miao, Y., Tao, X., Shen, Z., Liu, Z., Miao, C.: The equivalence of cognitive map, fuzzy cognitive map and multi value fuzzy cognitivemap. In: IEEE International Conference on Fuzzy Systems (2006)
30. Guan, J., Xiang, P., McBride, R., Bruene, A.: Achievement goals, social goals and students' reported persistence and effort in high school PE. J. Teach. PE **25**, 58–74 (2006)
31. Chong, S.K.: Contextaware sensors and data muling. In: Context Awareness for Selfmanaging Systems (Devices, Applications and Networks) Proceeding, pp. 103–117. VDE-Verlag, Berlin (2007)
32. Zimmermann, A., Lorenz, A., Oppermann, R.: An operational definition of context. In: Kokinov, B., Richardson, Daniel C., Roth-Berghofer, Thomas R., Vieu, L. (eds.) CONTEXT 2007. LNCS (LNAI), vol. 4635, pp. 558–571. Springer, Heidelberg (2007). https://doi.org/10.1007/978-3-540-74255-5_42
33. Miraoui, M., Tadj, C., Amar, C.B.: Architectural survey of context-aware systems in pervasive computing environment. Ubiquit. Comput. Commun. J. **3**, 1–9 (2008)
34. Kurti, A.: Exploring the multiple dimensions of context: Implications for the design and development of innovative technology-enhanced learning environments. Stockholm University, 28 May 2009
35. Soylu, A., De Causmaecker1, P., Desmet, P.: Context and adaptivity in pervasive engineering. J. Softw. **4**(9), 992–1013 (2009)
36. Jun-zhong, G.: Context aware computing. J. East China Normal Univ. (Nat. Sci.) **5**, 1–20 (2009)
37. Tamine-Lechani, L., Boughanem, M., Daoud, M.: Evaluation of contextual information retrieval effectiveness: overview of issues and research. Knowl. Inf. Syst. **24**(1), 1–34 (2010)
38. Rizou, S.: A system for distributed context reasoning. In: 2010 Sixth International Conference on Autonomic and Autonomous Systems (ICAS), pp. 84–89, March 2010
39. Nageba, E.: A model driven ontology-based architecture for supporting the quality of services in pervasive telemedicine applications. In: Proceedings the 3rd International Conference on Pervasive Computing Technologies for Healthcare, London UK, pp. 1–8. IEEE Computer Society, April 2009
40. Kim, S.: Smart learning services based on smart cloud computing. Sensors **11**(8), 7835–7850 (2011)
41. Guo, B.: The Internet of Things to embedded intelligence. World Wide Web **16**(4), 399–420 (2013)
42. Boughareb, D.: Context in information retrieval. In: International Conference on Control, Decision and Information Technologies (CoDIT), France, 3–5 November 2014
43. Ameyed, D: Modélisation et spécification formelle de contexte et sa prédiction dans les systèmes diffus. Ph.D. thesis, L'École de technologie supérieure (ETS) (2016)
44. Klein, B.N.: On the importance of time synchronization for context aware applications. Ph.D. thesis, Kassel University Press (2011)
45. Bardram, J.: Applications of context-aware computing in hospital work. In: Proceedings of 2004 ACM Symposium on Applied Computing, pp. 1574–1579. ACM Press (2004)
46. Levandoski, J., Sarwat, M., Eldawy, A., Mokbel, M.: LARS: a location-aware recommender system. In: ICDE, pp. 450–461 (2012)

47. Xu, X., Tang, J., Zhang, X., Liu, X., Zhang, H., Qiu, Y.: Exploring techniques for vision based human activity recognition: methods, systems, and evaluation. Sensors **13**(2), 1635–1650 (2013)
48. Ajami, H., Mcheick, H., Elkhaled, Z.: Survey of health care context models: prototyping of healthcare context framework. Dans: Summer Simulation Multi-Conference (SummerSim 2016), Montreal, Quebec, 24–27 July 2016

Well-being Technology

A Hybrid Framework for a Comprehensive Physical Activity and Diet Recommendation System

Syed Imran Ali, Muhammad Bilal Amin, Seoungae Kim,
and Sungyoung Lee[✉]

Department of Computer Science and Engineering, Kyung Hee University,
Seoul, South Korea
{imran.ali,seoungae,sylee}@oslab.khu.ac.kr,
m.b.amin@ieee.org

Abstract. The quantified self-movement has gained a lot of traction, recently. In this regard, research in personalized wellness support systems has increased. Most of the recommender systems focus on either calorie-burn or calorie-in take objectives. The achievement of calorie-burn objective is through physical activity recommendations while diet recommendations geared towards calorie-in take objectives. A very limited research is performed which track and optimize objectives for both calorie-burn and calorie-in-take, simultaneously based on well-known wellness support guidelines. In this regard, we propose a hybrid recommendation framework, which provides recommendations for physical activity as well as diet recommendation in order to support wellness requirements of a user in a comprehensive manner.

Keywords: Recommender system · Self-quantification
Wellness support system

1 Introduction

Over the years, there has been a huge surge in wellness support systems. These systems have varied capabilities from a relatively simple step count feature to a more complex wellness regiment-management [1]. Another reason for this renewed interest is due to availability of wearable and mobile technologies. These technologies assist not only in innovative application development but also do so in research such as in development of hybrid frameworks and subsequent field studies for their efficacy evaluation [2].

In order to induce a sustainable healthy behavior a number of aspects related to wellness require consideration. These aspects relate to the comprehensibility of the recommendation regimen and personalization of the recommendations. Existing popular wellness management systems such as Misfit shine [3] Jawbone Up [4] Fitbit Flex [5] provide recommendations based on very limited set of parameters e.g. steps count and slept hours, hence there is a room for a more comprehensive and personalized recommendation framework, which is capable of providing actionable recommendations, based on a number of personalized parameters. The scope of our research is limited to

© Springer International Publishing AG, part of Springer Nature 2018
M. Mokhtari et al. (Eds.): ICOST 2018, LNCS 10898, pp. 101–109, 2018.
https://doi.org/10.1007/978-3-319-94523-1_9

providing wellness support services focused on middle-age users through a knowledge based recommendation framework.

1.1 Expert-in-the Loop

Expert-in-the loop framework is yet another important consideration, which is under-researched in recommendation systems dealing with wellness support. This aspect of the recommender system deals with incorporating the domain expert curated information e.g. curated educational contents, for enhancing the general awareness of the user related to his/her peculiar less desirable habits. Moreover, domain experts e.g. nutritionists, can provide valuable input in menu construction for dietary recommendations. In this regard, our proposed framework deals with three key aspects of a wellness support regimen i.e. educational recommendation, physical activity recommendation, and dietary recommendation within the purview of enhancing the wellness of a target user pool.

Educational Recommendation: Educational recommendations assist in enhancing the awareness level of the user regarding the wellness domain. Moreover, factual nuggets embedded in the recommendation note also provide a rationale for adopting a balanced and active lifestyle that is elaborated by providing activity and dietary recommendations.

Physical Activity Recommendation: The physical activity recommendation is targeted to meet objectives stipulated in the calorie-burn goal. Whereas, the estimated calorie-burn goal is computed based on wellness guidelines in an automated manner. In this regard, the personalization element of the recommendation is also incorporated by assessing the contextual situation of the user at a given time of recommendation [6].

Dietary Recommendation: Dietary recommendation caters for the specific needs of a user in terms of calorie-in take requirements, as estimated from wellness guidelines, and health conditions e.g. diabetic patients are recommended low-glycemic food items. Another important factor of dietary recommendation regimen is the incorporation of local/territorial food information regarding the unsuitability of certain food items for consumption due to seasonal or viral containments. Expert(s) constructs menu-sets for each goal category and the system after multi-factor filtration provides the final recommendation [7].

2 Related Work

There has been an extensive research performed in the area of wellness related recommender systems. These systems are geared towards either physical activity based recommendation or dietary recommendation. Comprehensive systems, as an area of inquiry, the recommendation systems targeting both physical activity and dietary recommendation, are under-researched. In this section, we will provide an overview of an array of recommender systems. Our main focus is on the comprehensive recommender systems.

Recommendation systems, which provide recommendations regarding physical activity normally, employ user's contextual information. Contextual information based on different parameters such as location, current activity, weather information, etc. is poised to provide a holistic situational context. Such a situational context may be explored to determine various important factors such as user interruptibility and suitability of a recommended physical activity for the given user context.

Dietary recommender systems specifically focus on the calorie-in-take goal. Moreover, these systems provide user with recommendation, which includes food items that collectively contribute in achieving the stated goal. Goal maybe user defined or expert recommended based on health condition and suitability constraints. In this regard, both expert advised menu-sets and system generated menu-sets maybe used. Our proposed framework has adopted the former approach.

Acquiring an elaborate contextual user information is not straightforward. Moreover, it necessitates the inclusion of supporting modules which can provide accurate and timely contextual information about a user e.g. location, current activity, emotional state, etc. Although, the inclusion of such supporting modules may add to the complexity of the system, it is a requisite step towards the comprehensibility of the recommender system. Hence, when available the recommendation framework should be able to utilize such contexts as aforementioned. Following are some of the existing systems for physical activity recommendation.

PRO-Fit is a personalized physical activity recommender. It provides personalized workout session recommendations. Contextual data is collected through accelerometer. This data is later synchronized with user's weekly plans [8].

The Runner [9] is another popular recommender systems for users who prefer running activity, geared towards the wellness needs of a specific group of users. It provides both physical activity and nutritional recommendations to users. Although it processes an array of contextual parameters, its physical activity recommendation is primarily oriented towards running.

A web based compressive recommender system is proposed by [10]. The proposed system is capable of processing a wide array of contextual parameters such as demographic information, health conditions, religious information, etc. Since sensory data is not taken into account, therefore system falls short of dynamically adapting to contextual requirements of the user.

Faiz et al. [11] proposed a comprehensive wellness support system for patients suffering from diabetic ailments. Semantic technologies such as ontology engineering is investigated in this work in order to provide wellness related recommendations.

A comprehensive web-based recommendation system and a six-week evaluation study is performed by [12]. This system is evaluated based on technology acceptance model. Although system is capable enough to cater for the basic needs of its targeted user group, it lacks comprehensibility in terms of handling a wide array of contextual factors e.g. user's location.

Aforementioned are a sample of studies, which addressed wellness support through designing comprehensive recommender systems/frameworks. Although most of the studied systems in this research are capable enough to address basic user needs, their comprehensibility in terms of processing multi-factor contextual information and assisting user in adopting healthy habituation (e.g. user awareness towards wellness through educational nuggets) is lacking.

In the subsequent section, we propose a comprehensive wellness support system which caters for educational, active-lifestyle and nutritional needs of a targeted user group.

3   Proposed Framework

Our proposed system is composed of a number of modules. These modules are divided into two categories i.e. main module and supporting modules. Main module represents the main working engine of the framework while the supporting modules provide services to the main module. Hence, the main business logic of the recommender resides in the multi-stage recommender system module as depicted in Fig. 1.

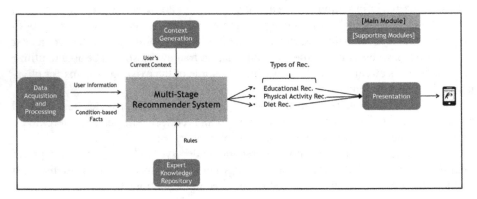

Fig. 1. Abstract level overview of the main and supporting components of the proposed framework

Data Acquisition and Processing module acquires data from the sensory devices e.g. mobile phone, processes the required information and persists it. Moreover, this module is also tasked with storing personal information about the user i.e. demographic information, preferences related information, etc. A monitoring application resides in this module which tracks user's activities, food consumption (entered manually) and calculates a multi-factor vector regarding user's food consumption so far and activity-level. Each factor vector corresponds to a particular "situation".

Context Generation module processes sensory raw data into meaningful user contexts such as user's current activity, location of the user, weather conditions, user's emotional state, etc. This information is very valuable for providing context-aware physical activity based recommendation.

Expert Knowledge Repository module stores expert knowledge in terms of production rules. These rules are based on fact vectors. Against different situations there are different kinds of recommendations. These generic recommendations are stored in IF-THEN form i.e. IF clause of the rule captures the situation part while THEN clause denotes recommendation given by an expert in the given situation.

Presentation module deals with interfacing with the user's device i.e. mobile phone. A recommendation package is sent to the Presentation module. Presentation module presents the generated recommendation in a user-friendly manner.

Multi-stage Recommender System is the main module which deals with processing the provided contextual information along with user profile, and situational information in order to provide a comprehensive recommendation. Stage-I of the module deals with calculating user's calorie-burn, in-take goals and a generic set of physical activity recommendation. It also has a case-based reasoning mechanism through which it infers the most appropriate rule from the knowledge base. Stage-II deals with refining the recommendation in a more personalized manner. For physical activity recommendation, Stage-II recommender creates a context matrix through which it infers which of the activities can be recommended to a user at a given time. Moreover, it is tasked with selecting the most appropriate menu-set based on goal, situational-fact vector, and user preferences. Providing educational recommendation is also the task of this component.

In Fig. 2, a working scenario of the recommender system is depicted. Where S1 and S2 correspond to users in two different stages. S1 users are only provided Educational Recommendation for the first week. Educational recommendation is in the form of a text message, along with curated educational material in terms of web links, pictures, and video links, etc. Users in S2 category are provided with physical activity and dietary recommendation.

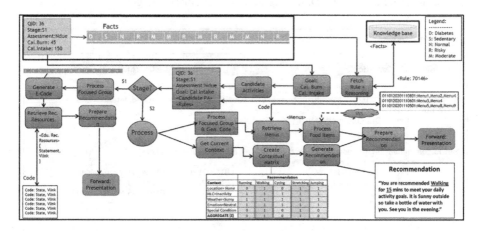

Fig. 2. Execution scenario for educational, physical activity and dietary recommendation

3.1 Rule-Structure for Interpretation and Recommendation Generation

Knowledge base contains rules which are used for generating recommendations. Rule has components i.e. condition part, recommendation part, and an optional description part. Condition part corresponds to the situational vector which encapsulates a user's current situation in terms of physical activity, health status, weight status, fat consumption level, salt and sugar consumption level, protein consumption and food and vegetables consumption, etc. Recommendation component of the vector deals with the subset of the conditions in the situation which are risky and require a recommendation for improvement.

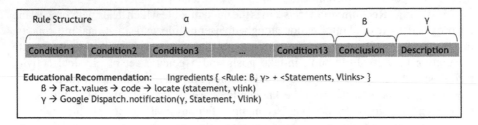

Fig. 3. Rule utilization for educational recommendation

For example, if fat consumption and BMI of the user are abnormal then these two conditions would be part of Recommendation component. Description part of the rule accommodates a free text observation by the domain expert. Figures 3 and 4 depicts how a rule is utilized a different kinds of recommendation i.e. educational, physical activity, and dietary. It is important to note that an index mechanism is used to locate menu-sets for dietary recommendation. A code is generated based on conditions values augmented with the category of the calorie-in-take goal. Category of the goal is divided into four groups i.e. A, B, C, D, having mutually exclusive ranges.

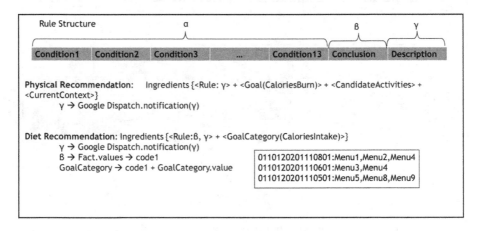

Fig. 4. Rule utilization for both physical and dietary recommendation

3.2 Two-Stage Context-Aware Physical Activity Recommender

Multi-stage recommendation module has two sub-components i.e. Stage-I and Stage-II recommenders. In order to generate a physical activity recommendation first goal is computed for the given user. This goal is based on the formulae provided in wellness guidelines. Subsequently, MET based formula is used to calculate different physical activities and their durations which can meet the stipulated goal. This generic information along with contextual information is fed to Stage-II recommender. This component, generates a contextual matrix. This contextual matrix is computed based on surveyed results in which users were asked to provide their input regarding the suitability of a particular physical activity in different contexts. For example, Running was deemed not suitable when user is in Home while Stretching was deemed a reasonable recommendation in this context. Once a recommended activity is determined then it is conveyed in a user friendly way. This process is depicted in Fig. 5.

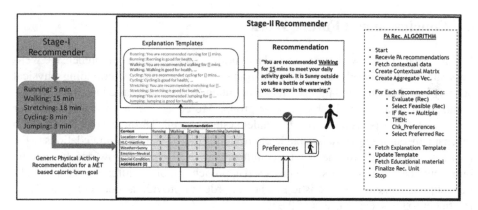

Fig. 5. Scenario for a physical activity recommendation

A similar recommendation mechanism is used for diet recommendation. Stage-I recommender computed the calorie-in-take goal of a user. Category of the goal is determined and all the expert curated menu-sets associated with the category are retrieved. If there are multiple menu-sets then in order to select one menu-set a filtration process is invoked. This filtration process takes into account the user disliked food items in each candidate menu-set and those food items which are tainted and have a government advisory for abstinence. The menu-set which has the least such food items as aforementioned is selected for a final recommendation. The process of dietary recommendation is depicted in Fig. 6.

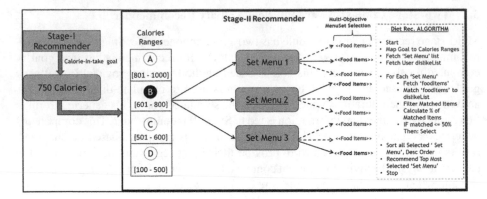

Fig. 6. Scenario for dietary recommendation

4   Conclusion and Future Work

In this research work we have proposed a hybrid framework for a comprehensive wellness support framework. Our proposed framework is capable of providing physical activity based recommendation, dietary recommendation as well as educational recommendations to a selected targeted user group. Moreover, we have also catered for personalization aspects of the recommender system as well. Through expert-in-the loop mechanism, our framework is capable of providing educational recommendations to the user base. A multi-factor menu-set recommendation is also geared towards the specific nutritional needs of the users. The proposed approach combines different facets of wellness support systems in a holistic manner in order to provide a more comprehensive treatment to the specific needs of the users.

In future, we would like to extend our work in a number of directions. Educational contents can be pre-curated automatically for the expert and later domain expert can sift through the pre-curated recommendations. A feedback mechanism maybe introduced which monitors whether user has acted upon the given recommendation or not and record user's opinion regarding the generated recommendation. In terms of menu-set selection, a more automated approach may be investigated which can generate reasonable menu-sets under certain constraints.

Acknowledgement. This research was supported by the MSIT (Ministry of Science and ICT), Korea, under the ITRC (Information Technology Research Center) support program (IITP-2017-0-01629) supervised by the IITP (Institute for Information & communications Technology Promotion)" and by the Korea Research Fellowship Program through the National Research Foundation of Korea (NRF) funded by the Ministry of Science and ICT (NRF-2016H1D3A1938039).

References

1. Chan, V., Ray, P., Parameswaran, N.: Mobile E-health monitoring: an agent-based approach. Commun. IET **2**(2), 223–230 (2008). https://doi.org/10.1049/iet-com
2. Asabere, N.Y.: Towards a viewpoint of context-aware recommender systems (CARS) and services. Int. J. Comput. Sci. Telecommun. **4**(1), 10–29 (2013). http://www.ijcst.org/Volume4/Issue1/p4_4_1.pdf
3. Misfit: Fitness Trackers & Wearable Technology – Misfit.com. https://misfit.com/. Accessed 6 Mar 2018
4. AliphCom dba Jawbone (2014). https://jawbone.com/up. Accessed 6 Mar 2018
5. Fitbit (2018). https://www.fitbit.com/kr/home. Accessed 6 Mar 2018
6. Verbert, K., Manouselis, N., Ochoa, X.: Context-aware recommender systems for learning: a survey and future challenges. In: IEEE Transactions. http://ieeexplore.ieee.org/abstract/document/6189308/
7. Gómez-Sebastià, I., Moreno, J.: Situated agents and humans in social interaction for elderly healthcare: from Coaalas to AVICENA. J. Med. Syst. (2016). http://link.springer.com/article/10.1007/s10916-015-0371-7
8. Dharia, S., Jain, V., Patel, J., Vora, J., Chawla, S., Eirinaki, M.: PRO-Fit: a personalized fitness assistant framework. In: 28th International Conference on Software Engineering and Knowledge Engineering. SEKE, Redwood City (2016). https://doi.org/10.18293/seke2016-174
9. Donciu, M., Ionita, M., Dascalu, M., Trausan-Matu, S.: The runner–recommender system of workout and nutrition for runners. In: 13th International Symposium on Symbolic and Numeric Algorithms for Scientific Computing, pp. 230–238. IEEE (2011)
10. Charles, E., Stanley, D., Agbaeze, E.: Knowledge-based diet and physical exercise advisory system. Int. J. Sci. Res. (IJSR) **14**(7), 2319–7064 (2013). http://www.ijsr.net/archive/v4i7/SUB156493.pdf. ISSN (Online Index Copernicus Value Impact Factor)
11. Faiz, I., Mukhtar, H., Khan, S.: An integrated approach of diet and exercise recommendations for diabetes patients. In: e-Health Networking, Applications (2014). http://ieeexplore.ieee.org/abstract/document/7001899/
12. Omar, A., Wahlqvist, M.: Wellness management through Web-based programmes. J. Telemed. Telecare (2005). http://journals.sagepub.com/doi/abs/10.1258/1357633054461985

A Personalized Health Recommendation System Based on Smartphone Calendar Events

Sharvil Katariya[✉], Joy Bose, Mopuru Vinod Reddy,
Amritansh Sharma, and Shambhu Tappashetty

Samsung R&D Institute, Bangalore, India
{sha.katariya, joy.bose, vinod.mopuru, amr.sharma,
shambhu.t}@samsung.com

Abstract. Many e-health services are available to users today, but they often suffer from lack of personalization. In this paper, we present a system to generate personalized health recommendations from various providers, based on classification of health related calendar events on the user's smartphone. Due to privacy constraints, such personal data often cannot be uploaded to external servers, hence the classification and personalization has to run on the client device. We use a server to train our model to classify calendar events using SVM and fastText, while the prediction is run on the client device using the trained model. The class labels from the classified calendar events, weighted in order of recency, are used to build a vector, which we treat as a representation of user interest while personalizing the recommendations. This vector is used to re-rank health related recommendations obtained from third party providers based on relevance. We describe the implementation details of our system and some tests on its accuracy and relevance to provide relevant health related recommendations. While we used the calendar app to classify events, our system can also be extended for other apps such as messaging.

Keywords: Health recommendation system · e-Health · Calendar
Classifier · FastText · SVM

1 Introduction

There are currently many health apps and services available to users to keep track of their health, medical appointments etc. There are also many types of recommendation systems to recommend services interesting to the user. However, they lack in knowledge of the exact task the user intends to do in any given moment. The calendar application, being personal to the user, gives an insight into the actual activity the user is performing. For example, a recommendation system can know that a given user is in a hospital or clinic, but only the calendar can inform whether they are in the clinic for a general health checkup or a specialized test or getting treatment for a pre-existing condition, in each case of which a different personalized recommendation might be appropriate. On the other hand, the calendar data and health data often cannot be uploaded to a remote server without ensuring that strict privacy regulations are met.

© Springer International Publishing AG, part of Springer Nature 2018
M. Mokhtari et al. (Eds.): ICOST 2018, LNCS 10898, pp. 110–120, 2018.
https://doi.org/10.1007/978-3-319-94523-1_10

In this paper, we present a system to classify health related calendar events on the user's smartphone, using it to generate more personalized recommendations to complement an existing recommendation service based only on the user's interests. Our system is trained on a server to classify calendar events into one of a few given health related categories such as hospital visit, pregnancy or exercise. The trained model is downloaded to the client device on the user device, with no personal data being uploaded to any server. The system is used to re-rank health related recommendations obtained from third party health service providers, using the calendar-classified events to decide how much a given recommendation is relevant for the user. Thus, it can generate personalized health related recommendations.

Figure 1 gives the high-level architecture of our calendar based health recommendation personalization system.

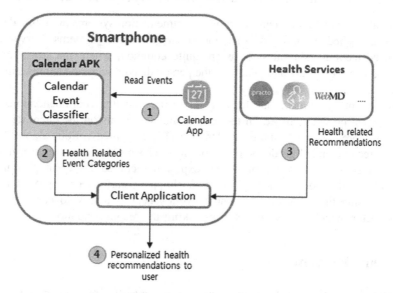

Fig. 1. Architecture of the health recommendation system based on classifying calendar events.

The rest of this paper is structured as follows: in the following section we survey related work in health service recommendation systems and in personalization of recommendations. Section 3 contains the outlines of our method, along with some implementation specific details. Section 4 presents results of some tests on the classification accuracy. Section 5 concludes the paper.

2   Related Work

2.1   Related Work in Personalized Healthcare Services on Smartphones

There have been a number of efforts in the area of personalized health services delivered through smartphones or through the web. Eysenbach [1] defined the term e-health as an interdisciplinary area, giving a list of 10 points how such services can be useful for various stakeholders like doctors, patients, government etc. Germanakos [2] reviewed web based e-health services and described a mobile agent approach for the same. Liu [3] surveyed e-health systems delivered on iOS devices. Free [4] also surveyed work in the area of e-health.

Such services have been used in a variety of medical use cases such as smoking cessation [5], treatment of chronic diseases [6], health monitoring for elderly [7], diabetes treatment [8] and so on.

However, these existing approaches do not include the data available in smartphone apps like calendar to personalize the recommendations for each health service user. Such data can also provide valuable information to the user.

2.2   Related Work in Personalized Recommendations on Mobile Devices

There has also been a lot of recent work on recommendation systems in mobile devices. Ricci [9] published a survey of such mobile recommender systems. Server based personalized recommendation systems are quite common, where the server collects information about the users and generates the personalized recommendations using this information.

However, in this paper, our focus is to re-rank health recommendations from various content providers based on the user's calendar events on the client device, to make them more relevant to the users. Jannach [18] compared various algorithms for re-ranking recommended products, based on the user's context or short-term interests within a given session. Algorithms they explored included Bayesian personalized ranking [19] and co-occurrence of items in shopping carts. Our approach can be thought as using the categorized calendar event labels as a way to derive the user interests vector, which is then used for re-ranking the recommendations.

3   System Overview

In this section, we describe the components of our system for recommending calendar events, as well as the steps followed in each module. Our system has two main components, the first one to categorize the user's calendar event into one of a few health related categories, the other to use this to re-rank recommendations from one or more healthcare providers. They are described in the following two subsections.

3.1   Calendar Event Categorizer Module

This module is responsible for taking as input calendar events of the user, and categorizing them into one of a fixed number of categories related to health. The output of this module is passed to the recommender systems module, which then uses it to recommend relevant health related services.

3.1.1   Creating a Training Dataset of Calendar Events Related to Health

The initial task is to create a training dataset of health related calendar events. One of the problems we faced is that calendar data, being private to the user, is not publicly available. And the few public calendars that we found (public Google calendars [10] of some hospitals and health clinics [11]) were not adequate for our requirements, since they were more about public events in those health clinics rather than patient related. So we had to create the dataset manually (Fig. 2).

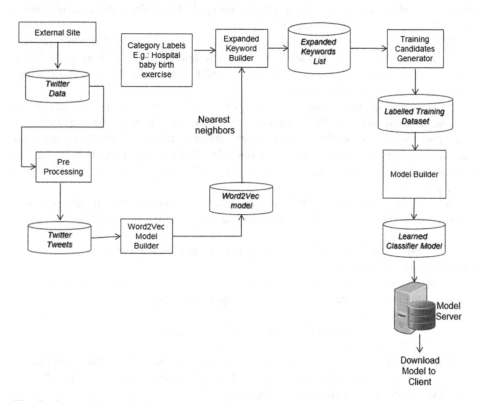

Fig. 2. Steps of the calendar event categorizer module to train the model on the server side.

For simplicity, we select the following categories related to health:

- exercise: sports like golf, ski, tennis, gym, kickboxing, yoga, cycling, fitness class, swimming, cardio, crossfit, pilates, workout
- relaxation: massage, spa, meditation, reflexology, aromatherapy
- beauty: cosmetics, make up, liposuction, anti acne, anti aging, skin creams, hair products, teeth whitening, cosmetic surgery
- diseases: diabetes, flu, cold, headache, weight loss, allergies
- medicines: prescription medicines, alternative medicines, herbal, homeopathy, ayurveda, vitamins, antibiotics, nutrition supplements

- health checkup: full body checkup, x ray, mammogram, ultrasound, eye test, blood test, kidney test, blood pressure, sugar test, urine test
- baby birth: prenatal check, pregnancy, birth control, IVF, midwife
- hospital: chiropodist, physio, acupuncture, dentist, GP, dental, pediatrician, dermatologist, medical operation, psychiatrist, counselling, surgery
- none: for events that do not fit in the other categories

For each category, we first use the category names as seed words. Then we find the nearest neighbors of those seed words by using a Word2Vec model trained on a monthly dump of the Twitter stream [12].

We chose the Twitter dataset to find nearest neighbors for the following reason: Calendar event titles and Twitter tweets have a few things in common: both are typically short text (twitter has a 140-word limit) and are likely to contain slang, shortcuts and common misspellings.

After getting the nearest neighbor words, as well as synonyms and hyponyms of the seed words using WordNet [13], we manually create the dataset by making sentences using those words and aiming to get as much variations as possible, to be close to real life calendar titles. Examples of (calendar title, class label) tuples in our training dataset include: ('diabetes', diseases), ('Maternity check', baby birth), ('Gym session', exercise).

We also manually label the training dataset to one of our health related categories, along with the label of 'none' for sentences that do not belong to any of the categories.

3.1.2 Training a Machine Learning Model on the Server Using the Training Dataset

After creating the labelled dataset of health related events, we fit a machine-learning model to the labelled dataset. This training step runs on the server.

$$Model.fit(calendar\_titles, class\_labels) \tag{1}$$

We used Java libraries for two common machine learning algorithms that can be used on client devices: SVM (libSVM [14, 15]) and a Java port [16] for Facebook's FastText library [17] for comparison (Fig. 3).

3.1.3 Downloading the Trained Model to the Client Device

Once the model is trained on the server using our labelled training dataset, we download the trained model as a JAR file to the client device, which is an Android smartphone.

3.1.4 Extracting Recent Calendar Event Titles and Classifying Them Using the Trained Model

On the Android smartphone, we write an app that takes N most recent calendar event titles from the calendar app as input and uses the trained model to classify them on the server as one of the health related categories, along with the confidence of the prediction.

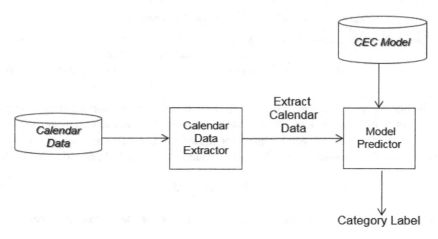

Fig. 3. Steps of the calendar event categorizer module to predict the calendar event category using the previously trained model, on the client device.

$$Predicted\_class\_label, confidence$$
$$= model \cdot predict\_probability(new\_calendar\_title) \quad (2)$$

The same algorithm (SVM or FastText [17]) is used for the prediction as was previously used for the training of the model. The output of the app, which is a category label for the calendar event, is passed to the recommender systems module. Here we ignore the case where two or more categories have sufficient confidence values and select only the category with the highest confidence.

3.1.5   Creating a Calendar Events Weighted Vector

We assume here that for generating recommendations, recent calendar events are more important, than calendar events that are further in the future. Therefore, we define a decay factor α (where $\alpha < 1$) for future calendar events, and use it for weighing the importance of the calendar event. For every successive day after the current day, the weighting factor goes down by the amount α. Table 1 shows how the weight vector w is calculated for some sample calendar events, in order of recency. Here, w_{ij} is the weight vector component associated with calendar entry j for class i.

Table 1. A table of example calendar event titles with categories and weight, $\alpha = 0.9$

Date	Calendar event title	Class label	Weight
1 March	Dental checkup	Health checkup	1.00
1 March	Birthday party	None	1.00
2 March	Pregnancy test	Baby birth	0.90
3 March	Gym visit	Exercise	0.81
4 March	Baby ultrasound scan	Baby birth	0.73

Table 2. Weights of each class for the events in Table 1.

Exercise	Relaxation	Beauty	Diseases	Medicine	Health check-up	Baby birth	Hospital	None
0.81	0.00	0.00	0.00	0.00	1.00	1.63	0.00	1.00

We then compute the sum of weights for each event category and generate a weight vector A (size of which is K*1 where K is the number of event categories, here K = 4) which gives the weight of each category for re-ranking the recommendations. Table 2 shows the resultant weight vector A, whose value is [0.81, 0, 0, 0, 0, 1.0, 1.629, 1.0].

$$A_i = \Sigma_j w_{ij} (where\ class\_label = i) \tag{3}$$

Where i = 1, 2, ... K for the ith class, j = 1, 2,.. N for the jth calendar event

3.2   Recommender System Module

The recommender system module takes as input the recommendations from one or more service providers (including health services as well as other third party services) and re-ranks them as per the categorized calendar events.

This module follows the following steps:

3.2.1   Extracting Recommendations from Service Providers

The first part of our recommender system is creating the recommendation dataset from various content providers. One option is to use public APIs from providers of recommendations such as Groupon. Another option is to scrape the recommendations data if it is available publicly on e-commerce websites, or use a public dataset such as available on Kaggle.

For the current work, we scraped the titles of special offers, coupons and recommendations from the following providers: GroupOn Health and Fitness category, GroupOn Walgreens related offers, GrabOn (an India based provider) offers in the health category. After preprocessing, we built a dataset of 206 recommendation titles from these sources.

We then run some preprocessing on the recommendations to get rid of stop words etc. and extract only the first 1 or 2 sentences from the text of the recommendation.

3.2.2   Categorizing Recommendations Based on Relevance to Calendar Events

We use the same trained model that was previously used for calendar events categorization (Sect. 3.1.2), to predict the category of the recommendation along with its prediction confidence. This ensures that the recommendation category is the same as one of the calendar event class labels.

$$Predicted\_class\_label, confidence$$
$$= model.predict\_probability(recommendation\_text) \tag{4}$$

From this, we compute a matrix B of size N*K, where N is the number of recommendations and K the number of classes. We use a 1-hot encoding to represent each recommendation in matrix B, where the confidence value of the highest confidence class is preserved and the rest of the values are set to 0. For each recommendation, we compute the one hot array representing the predicted class with confidence. Table 3 gives an example of the matrix entry for some sample recommendations.

Table 3. Matrix entries for some sample recommendation titles

Recommendation title	Class label	Confidence	Matrix row
Up to 62% off Reflexology	Relaxation	0.998	[0, 0.998, 0, 0, 0, 0, 0, 0, 0]
Up to 67% off Charcoal Teeth-Whitening Powders	Beauty	0.998	[0, 0, 0.998, 0, 0, 0, 0, 0, 0]
Up to 59% off LASIK Eye Surgery	Hospital	0.919	[0, 0, 0, 0, 0, 0, 0, 0.919, 0]
Up to 49% off Rock Climbing Class Package	Exercise	0.859	[0.859, 0, 0, 0, 0, 0, 0, 0, 0]
Purplle Sign Up Offers: Flat 15% OFF On First Order	None	0.879	[0, 0, 0, 0, 0, 0, 0, 0, 0.879]

3.2.3   Re-ranking Recommendations

Finally, we take the cross product of array B (matrix of prediction confidence vectors for each recommendation) of size N*K and array A (array of calendar event class labels weighed by date) of size K*1. This gives us a vector of size N*1, representing the confidence vector for each recommendation.

$$recommendation\_confidence = B * A \qquad (5)$$

We then select the top M recommendations from this resultant vector, representing the recommendations with the highest confidence as per the calendar event, and present it to the user in a sorted order of recommendations.

In the following section, we present the results of some tests to measure the accuracy of the calendar categorization and validate the recommendations (Fig. 4).

4   Experimental Setup and Results

For our experiment, we used a dataset of 4895 manually created and labelled events. The events were labelled across the health related categories along with none category (hospital, exercise, none, etc.). We tested on the Samsung Galaxy S8 smartphone running Android 7.0 (SDK version 24), with a client app written in Java 1.7. We used a 70:30 split in the training vs testing data. As mentioned, we tested on two different models (SVM and fastText).

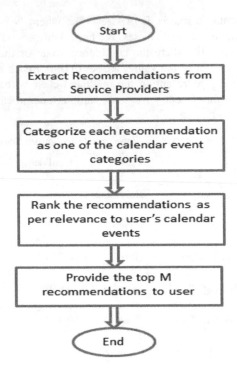

Fig. 4. Flowchart of the system for recommending the most relevant recommendations based on calendar events

4.1 Calendar Event Categorization Using the fastText Library

Table 4 shows the classification results with the fastText library [16, 17]. We performed stop-word removal on the calendar titles data before passing to the fastText library. We obtained an average F1 score of 0.93.

Table 4. Classification results for the calendar event categoriser module using fastText

Category	Precision	Recall	F1 score	Support
Baby birth	0.86	0.92	0.89	13
Exercise	0.92	1.00	0.96	35
Beauty	0.83	0.83	0.83	6
Diseases	1.00	0.83	0.91	6
Medicines	1.00	1.00	1.00	6
Health checkup	1.00	0.50	0.67	6
Hospital	0.95	0.91	0.93	23
Relaxation	0.88	1.00	0.93	7
None	0.98	0.98	0.98	43
Avg/Total	0.94	0.94	0.93	145

4.2   Calendar Event Categorization Using libSVM Library

Table 5 shows the classification results using the SVM model. We use a TF-IDF vectorizer to compute the TF-IDF values before passing it as input to the libSVM library. We use a linear SVC for the training with coefficient C = 5.0. Here the average F1 score obtained is 0.73, somewhat lower than that obtained using fastText.

Table 5. Classification results for the calendar event categoriser module using libSVM

Category	Precision	Recall	F1 score	Support
Baby birth	1.00	0.69	0.82	13
Exercise	0.59	0.97	0.73	35
Beauty	1.00	0.33	0.50	6
Diseases	0.67	0.33	0.44	6
Medicines	0.50	0.50	0.50	6
Health checkup	0.75	0.50	0.60	6
Hospital	0.74	0.74	0.74	23
Relaxation	0.71	0.71	0.71	7
None	0.94	0.72	0.82	43
Avg/Total	0.78	0.73	0.73	145

4.3   Evaluation of the Recommendation System

We generated a dataset of 200 recommendations by scraping from the GroupOn website. We then implemented the recommender module, as described in Sect. 3.2, which ranked and selected the top 20 recommendations as per the users' calendar events.

Finally, to test the relevance of the recommended services, we conducted a user study with 5 users aged between 20–32. To each user we gave 20 URLs, and asked them to rank the URLs as per the relevance to their calendar schedules, with each user given between 10–20 calendar titles belonging to a specific category (beauty, relaxation, exercise). We then computed the correlation of the user rankings with our algorithm generated rankings, using the Spearman correlation coefficient [20]. We obtained an average correlation of 0.4 over the users.

5   Conclusion and Future Work

In this paper, we have presented a system to generate personalized recommendations for health related services, based on calendar events. We described the calendar categorizer module and the recommender module, and obtained good accuracy for the classifier module and recommendation system.

In future, we will seek to interface with healthcare providers to obtain more relevant health related recommendations. We will also experiment with getting data from other apps such as messaging, using it to enrich the health recommendation system.

References

1. Eysenbach, G.: What is e-health? J. Med. Internet Res. **3**(2), e20 (2001). https://doi.org/10.2196/jmir.3.2.e20
2. Germanakos, P., Mourlas, C., Samaras, G.: A mobile agent approach for ubiquitous and personalized eHealth information systems. In: Proceedings of the Workshop on 'Personalization for e-Health'of the 10th International Conference on User Modeling (UM 2005), pp. 67–70, 29 July 2005
3. Liu, C., Zhu, Q., Holroyd, K.A., Seng, E.K.: Status and trends of mobile-health applications for iOS devices: a developer's perspective. J. Syst. Softw. **84**(11), 2022–2033 (2011)
4. Free, C., Phillips, G., Galli, L., Watson, L., Felix, L., Edwards, P., Patel, V., Haines, A.: The effectiveness of mobile-health technology-based health behaviour change or disease management interventions for health care consumers: a systematic review. PLoS Med. **10**(1), e1001362 (2013)
5. Abroms, L.C., Ahuja, M., Kodl, Y., Thaweethai, L., Sims, J., Winickoff, J.P., Windsor, R. A.: Text2Quit: results from a pilot test of a personalized, interactive mobile health smoking cessation program. J. Health Commun. **17**(sup1), 44–53 (2012)
6. Beratarrechea, A., Lee, A.G., Willner, J.M., Jahangir, E., Ciapponi, A., Rubinstein, A.: The impact of mobile health interventions on chronic disease outcomes in developing countries: a systematic review. Telemed. e-Health **20**(1), 75–82 (2014)
7. Lorenz, A., Mielke, D., Oppermann, R., Zahl, L.: Personalized mobile health monitoring for elderly. In: Proceedings of the 9th International Conference on Human Computer Interaction with Mobile Devices and Services pp. 297–304. ACM, 9 September 2007
8. Chomutare, T., Fernandez-Luque, L., Årsand, E., Hartvigsen, G.: Features of mobile diabetes applications: review of the literature and analysis of current applications compared against evidence-based guidelines. J. Med. Internet Res. **13**(3) (2011)
9. Ricci, F.: Mobile recommender systems. Information Technology & Tourism. **12**(3), 205–231 (2010)
10. Share your calendar with someone - Calendar Help - Google Support. https://support.google.com/calendar/answer/37082?hl=en
11. Holy name Medical Center: Calendar of Events. http://www.holyname.org/events/March.aspx
12. Archive Team: The Twitter Stream Grab. https://archive.org/details/twitterstream
13. NLTK: WordNet Interface. http://www.nltk.org/howto/wordnet.html
14. Chang, C.C.: LIBSVM – A Library for Support Vector Machines. https://www.csie.ntu.edu.tw/~cjlin/libsvm/
15. Github. libsvm/java at master · cjlin1/libsvm · GitHub. https://github.com/cjlin1/libsvm/tree/master/java
16. GitHub - Java port of c++ version of facebook fasttext. https://github.com/ivanhk/fastText_java
17. Fasttext. https://fasttext.cc/
18. Jannach, D. and Lerche, L., Gdaniec, M.: Re-ranking recommendations based on predicted short-term interests – a protocol and first experiment. In: ITWP 2013: Proceedings of the Workshop Intelligent Techniques for Web Personalization and Recommender Systems at AAAI (2013)
19. Rendle, S., Freudenthaler, C., Gantner, Z., Schmidt-Thieme, L.: BPR: Bayesian personalized ranking from implicit feedback. In: Proceedings of the Twenty-Fifth Conference on Uncertainty in Artificial Intelligence (UAI 2009)
20. Wikipedia: Spearman's rank correlation coefficient. https://en.wikipedia.org/wiki/Spearman%27s_rank_correlation_coefficient

Testing a Model of Adoption and Continued Use of Personally Controlled Electronic Health Record (PCEHR) System Among Australian Consumers: A Preliminary Study

Jun Xu$^{(\boxtimes)}$, Xiangzhu Gao, Golam Sorwar, Nicky Antonius,
and John Hammond

Southern Cross University, Lismore, Australia
jun.xu@scu.edu.au

Abstract. This study aims to investigate factors influencing adoption and continued use of PCEHR system among consumers (individual users) in Australia. The data collected via online questionnaire survey were analysed via a Structural Equation Modelling (SEM) approach. The results indicate that: (1) "External Factors & Influences" and "Individual Differences" are significant factors that influence "Perceived Benefits" of the PCEHR system, which in turn influence adoption of the PCEHR system; (2) "External Factors & Influences", "Individual Differences", and "PCEHR System Characteristics" are significant factors that influence "Perceived User Friendliness" of the PCEHR system, which in turn influence adoption of PCEHR system; (3) "Facilitating Factors" are significant factors that influence both "Realized Benefits" and "Realized User Friendliness", which in turn influence continued use of PCEHR system; and (4) "Voluntariness of Adoption" and "Voluntariness of Continued Use" are significant factors that influence both adoption and continued use of the PCEHR system respectively.

Keywords: Electronic Health Records · PCEHR system · Adoption
Continued use · Structural equation modelling · Australia

1 Introduction

Electronic health records (EHRs) are electronic repositories of information regarding the health status of a subject of care. As a health information source, EHRs underpin all the other e-health initiatives, and EHRs can assist in managing health information in a consumer/patient-focused approach and in improving health service providers' ability to provide more effective and efficient services to consumers/patients with maximized benefits and minimized errors and re-admissions [34]. The current release of the PCEHR (including PCEHR being re-named My Health Record) system in Australia is far from mature and suffers criticisms from major stakeholders, and there is a lack of uptake and utilization [42]. The system is facing various challenges, and users are neither enthusiastic about registration nor in using the system [44, 48]. Participation in the PCEHR system is essential for adoption and use of the system. At this stage, consumers have not been active in participation for different reasons and various

© Springer International Publishing AG, part of Springer Nature 2018
M. Mokhtari et al. (Eds.): ICOST 2018, LNCS 10898, pp. 121–133, 2018.
https://doi.org/10.1007/978-3-319-94523-1_11

concerns. The interests of consumers have not been properly represented in the development and implementation of the PCEHR system (e.g., even in the recent PCEHR review ordered by the Coalition Government, not one review panel member really represented. Recently the opt-out model has been re-examined by the Australian government [17], and trials of the opt-out approach for the PCEHR system commenced in 2016 [13]. However even though the change to the opt-out model was intended to increase registrations for the PCEHR system, the long-term and sustainable success of the system requires far more incentives and efforts than initial registration for the system [16]. Australia has invested significantly in e-health [6, 29, 32]. Despite this investment, the system has not been well received by consumers. In addition, there is a lack of comprehensive empirical studies examining factors that influence the uptake and use of electronic health record systems, especially the PCEHR system. For example, Nguyen et al. [41] conducted a systematic review on electronic health record implementations by reviewing 56 peer-reviewed journals from various sources from 2001 to 2011. The review only found a small number of studies on consumers/patients (less than 12). Available research has focused on perspectives of healthcare professionals or providers [31, 38, 40, 46, 47, 53]. This study aims to address the gap via developing a model of adoption and continued use of the PCEHR system among Australian consumers by looking at two research questions:

- What are the factors influencing Australian consumers' decision to adopt the PCEHR system?
- What are the factors influencing Australian consumers' decision of their continued use of the PCEHR system?

The outcomes of this research will go some way to answering concerns and issues associated with the PCEHR system and offer some insights and recommendation for improving the efforts in deploying the system and improving the efficiency of resources required for the implementation.

2 Background

2.1 Demographic Information

Xu et al. [57] developed a model for the Adoption and Continued Use of the PCEHR system, which is illustrated in Fig. 1. In the pre-adoption stage, it is suggested that the external factors including external environment and influences, individual differences, and PCEHR system characteristics influence the adoption of the PCEHR system in an indirect way with their influence being mediated by the perceived benefits (usefulness) and perceived user-friendliness (usability) of the system. At the same time, the research model postulates that the perceived benefits, perceived user-friendliness, subject norms, and voluntariness have a direct effect on the adoption of the PCEHR system, and it also indicates that perceived user friendliness affects perceived usefulness. In the post-adoption stage, it is suggested that the facilitating factors influence the continued use of the PCEHR system in an indirect way with their influence being mediated by the realized benefits (usefulness) and realized user friendliness (usability) of the system [1, 2, 14, 15, 31, 39, 43]. At the same time, the research model postulates that realised benefits, realised user-friendliness, subject norms, and voluntariness have direct effect on the continued use of the PCEHR system, and it also suggests realised user-friendliness affects realised usefulness.

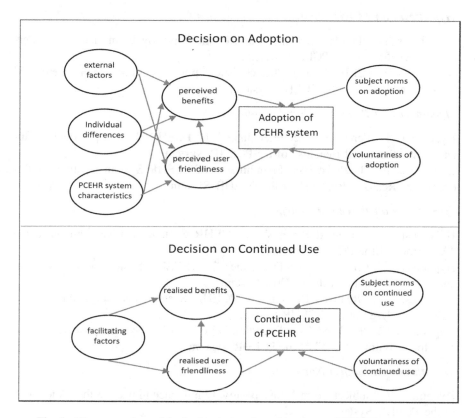

Fig. 1. The research model of adoption and continued use of PCEHR system [57]

2.2   Hypotheses

The hypotheses depicted in the research model in Fig. 1 to be tested in this research, are as follows:

Hypotheses on External Factors & Influences

Hypothesis 1a: "External Factors & Influences" positively influence the "Perceived Benefits" of the PCEHR System.
Hypothesis 1b: "External Factors & Influences" positively influence the "Perceived User Friendliness" of the PCEHR System.

Hypotheses on Individual Factors

Hypothesis 2a: "Individual factors" positively influence the "Perceived Benefits" of the PCEHR system.
Hypothesis 2b: "Individual factors" positively influence the "Perceived User Friendliness" of the PCEHR system.

Hypotheses on PCEHR System Characteristics

Hypothesis 3a: "PCEHR System Characteristics" positively influence the "Perceived Benefits" of the PCEHR System.
Hypothesis 3b: PCEHR System Characteristics" positively influence the "Perceived User Friendliness" of the PCEHR System.

Hypotheses on Perceived User Friendliness

Hypothesis 4: "Perceived User Friendliness" of PCEHR System positively influences the "Perceived Benefits" of the PCEHR System.
Hypothesis 10: "Realized User Friendliness" of PCEHR System positively influences the "Realized Benefits" of the PCEHR System.

Hypotheses on Perceived Benefits

Hypothesis 5: "Perceived Benefits" of PCEHR System positively influence the "Adoption" of the PCEHR System.
Hypothesis 6: "Perceived User Friendliness" of PCEHR System positively influence the "Adoption" of the PCEHR System.
Hypothesis 11: "Realized Benefits" of PCEHR System positively influence the "Continued Use" of the PCEHR System.
Hypothesis 12: "Realized User Friendliness" of PCEHR System positively influence the "Continued Use" of the PCEHR System.

Hypotheses on Subject Norms

Hypothesis 7: "Subject Norms" have positively influence impact on the "Adoption" of the PCEHR System.
Hypothesis 13: "Subject Norms" have positively influence impact on the "Continued Use" of the PCEHR System.

Hypotheses on Voluntary Use

Hypothesis 8: "Voluntary use" of PCEHR System negatively influences the "Adoption" of the PCEHR System.
Hypothesis 14: "Voluntary use" of PCEHR System negatively influences the "Continued Use" of the PCEHR System.

Hypotheses on Facilitating Factors

Hypothesis 10a: "Facilitating Factors" positively influence the "Realized Benefits" of the PCEHR System.
Hypothesis 10b: "Facilitating Factors" positively influence the "Realized User Friendliness" of the PCEHR System.

3   Research Methods

Staff and students in an Australian university, who are eligible for registering with and using the PCEHR system, were invited to take part in the online questionnaire survey, which asked questions about the participants' adoption and use of the PCEHR system. The message of "This questionnaire is designed for Australian Permanent Residents and Australian Citizens" was displayed at the top of the survey to ensure respondents were eligible to register for the PCEHR system. If respondents were not eligible, then the survey responses were not counted. Two rounds of e-mail invitations for participating in the research were sent to the two generic email lists of staff and students. Sending emails to these two email addresses required University approval from the university. The second email invitations were a follow-up after the first round. The survey questions were developed from literature on innovation diffusion and technology acceptance [43, 44, 54] and the authors' previous studies on PCERH system in Australia [55, 56]. In addition, the researchers sent the online survey invitation to their networks. In the end, 66 validly completed surveys, which had responses to all the questions on factors in the research model, were received.

Structural Equation Modelling (SEM) approach was employed to analyse the collected survey data. Having a sizeable sample population for the approach is critical to produce reliable results [23]. This study adopts the 'case-to-latent variable' ratio approach, which is a well-established approach accepted by many researchers [5, 7, 9, 11, 19, 25, 29]; and the suggested 5:1 ratio of sample cases to number of variables in the model [9, 50] was used to calculate the minimum sample size for running the SEM test in this study. Therefore the sample size of 66 in this research is well suited to the SEM analysis (i.e., it is bigger than the required 40 samples for the 8 composite variables in the adoption model and required 30 samples for the 6 composite variables in the continued use model). The model test by application of SEM consists of two parts: a measurement model and a structural model [3, 4, 26, 27]. The measurement model measures the relationships of observed variables with their underlying constructs. The structural model examines the casual relations between the constructs.

4   Results

4.1   Demographic Information

Among 66 received responses, 63.6% are female and 36.4% are male. In descending order, 25.8% of the respondents are in the 50–59 age group, 24.2% in the age group of 40–49, 19.7% in the age group of 30–39, 10.6% in age group of 60–65, 10.6% in other age groups (e.g., younger than 18 and older than 65), 7.6% in the age group of 21–29, and 1.5% in the age group of 18-20. 74.2% of respondents are from New South Wales, 21.2% from Queensland, and 4.6% from Victoria. 80.3% of the respondents have at least a Bachelor's degree, with 1.5% having Honour's Degree, 10.9% having Graduate Certificate or Graduate Diploma, 15.2% having a Master's degree, and 16.7% having a Doctorate's degree. The distribution of the respondents by occupation is as follows: 28.8% educational professionals, 10.5% administrators, 10.5% managers, 9% technology and engineering professionals, 7.5% students, 46% health care professionals,

6% company directors and business owners (including self-employed), 4.5% accounting, consulting and legal professionals, 3% sales staff, 3% community and personal services workers, 3% tourism and hospitality staff, 1.5% public servant, and 1.5% media professionals, and 3% librarians.

The respondents report varied e-health experience. 53% of the respondents state they don't have any e-health experience, 34.8% having experience of using electronic systems for healthcare supportive services (e.g., online appointment scheduling, checking in via kiosks, claiming expense online), 15.2% having experience of participating in online health programs (e.g., health and fitness through diet and exercise programs), 13.6% having experience of using telemedicine (i.e., enabling doctors and nurses to see and diagnose patients remotely), 9.1% having experience of online treatments and assessments, 18.2% having experience of using health-related phone/tablets apps, 24.2% having experience of using wearable health and fitness tracking technology, 1.5% gaining e-health experience via registering with PCEHR system, and 1.5% having e-health research experience. Only 10.6% of the participants have registered for the system (including for their dependent children) while another 28.8% suggest that they will register for the system in the future. Among those participants who have registered, 85% have registered for more than 12 months, 2.5% for more than 24 months, and 4.2% for less than 1 month. 71.4% of respondents have registered themselves and the remaining 28.6% registered with assistance from government agencies or while they are in hospital. 57.5% have registered for the system online, 14.2% at their GP's practice/clinic, 14.2% at a mobile station/booth, and 14.2% at the place of a health care provider (other than their GP). In addition, the majority (57.1%) of the registered participants have not used the system at all after their registration for the system (either don't want to use or don't know how to use).

4.2 Model Measurement

Model estimation is a critical step where the model's goodness-of-fit and parameters are assessed to determine how well the model explains the data [21, 24, 29]. Table 1 summarises the measures adopted in this research to estimate model fit, namely the $\chi 2$ goodness-of-fit statistic and its p score, CMIN/DF, CFI, GFI and RMSEA, and their respective threshold values [7–10, 12, 18, 23, 24, 28–30, 45, 49].

After the model estimate processes were completed (including required iterations to remove unfit variables), model saturation and perfect model fit for all the 14 composite factors is achieved, resulting in 69 variables for 14 composite factors.

4.3 Structural Model for Adoption

Table 2 presents the results of the structural model test of adoption of PCEHR system. The results are assessed based on the estimated path coefficient value (β) with a critical ratio (t) and probability (p). The absolute value of $t \geq 1.645$ and $p \leq 0.05$ are the thresholds used to accept the hypothesized relationships between the variables [12, 20, p.343]. Furthermore, β evaluates the relative influence of the predicting variable to the dependent variable [12]. For example, when Perceived Benefits increase by 1 standard deviation, Adoption Decision is estimated to increase by 0.693 standard deviation.

Table 1. Measures for estimate model fit

If χ2 and p values are...	If CMIN/DF value is...	If CFI value is...	If GFI value is...	If RMSEA value is...	The recommended assessment is...
Insignificant (p > = 0.05)	<= 3	> = 0.900	> = 0.900	< 0.100	Model is saturated and the fit is perfect
Significant (p < 0.05)	> 3	< 0.900	< 0.900	> = 0.100	Model is rejected and diagnostics undertaken to improve model fit

Table 2. SEM output for hypothesised path relationships in structural model for adoption decision

Hypothesis	Path	Standardised Estimate (β)	Standard Error (S.E.)	Critical Ratio (t)	Probability (p)	Result
H1(a)	EX → PB	0.387	0.139	2.788	0.005	Supported
H1(b)	EX → PU	0.357	0.161	2.220	0.026	Supported
H2(a)	ID → PB	0.484	0.198	2.447	0.014	Supported
H2(b)	ID → PU	0.585	0.266	2.198	0.028	Supported
H3(a)	PS → PB	0.028	0.064	0.435	0.663	Not Supported
H3(b)	PS → PU	0.778	0.211	3.687	< 0.001	Supported
H4	PU → PB	-0.020	0.170	-0.120	0.905	Not Supported
H5	PB → SA	0.693	0.100	6.944	< 0.001	Supported
H6	PU → SA	0.447	0.150	2.979	0.003	Supported
H7	SN → SA	0.287	0.188	1.524	0.127	Not Supported
H8	VA → SA	0.339	0.133	2.546	0.011	Supported

4.4 Structural Measurement for Continued Use

Table 3 reports the results of the structural model test of continued use of PCEHR system. Again the results are assessed based on the estimated path coefficient value (β) with a critical ratio (t) and probability (p). The absolute value of $t \geq 1.645$ and $p \leq 0.05$ are the thresholds used to accept the hypothesised relationships between the variables [12, 20, p.343]. Further, β evaluates the relative influence of the predicting variable to the dependent variable [5] For example, when Realised Benefits increase by 1 standard deviation, Continued Use is estimated to increase by 0.601 standard deviation.

Table 3. SEM output for hypothesised path relationships in structural model for continued use

Hypothesis	Path	Standardised Estimate (β)	Standard Error (S.E.)	Critical Ratio (t)	Probability (p)	Result
H9(a)	FF → RP	0.293	0.141	2.073	0.038	Supported
H9(b)	FF → RU	0.311	0.118	2.630	0.009	Supported
H10	RU → RP	0.489	0.125	3.924	<0.001	Supported
H11	RP → SC	0.601	0.097	6.226	<0.001	Supported
H12	RU → SC	0.626	0.120	5.207	<0.001	Supported
H13	SNP → SC	0.272	0.171	1.586	0.113	Not Supported
H14	VC → SC	0.362	0.115	3.157	0.002	Supported

5   Results

As seen in Table 2, all the hypotheses for the adoption part of the research model are supported except H3a, H4, and H7, which are not supported.

- *H3a:* The result of the non-significant influence of the PCEHR system character-istics on perceived benefits of the PCEHR system, indicates that while the users of the PCEHR system value the system characteristics (e.g., data accuracy, com-pleteness, and currency, accessibility, availability, information control, their attitude toward (or perceptions of) the system will not be influenced by these factors. Some possible reasons include: (1) their lack of engagement/involvement in the PCEHR system rollout/implementation (i.e., 74% respondents), (2) their lack of knowledge of the system (i.e., 68.2% respondents), (3) their lack of e-health experience (i.e., 53% respondents having no e-health experience), (4) low registration/adoption and use of the system (e.g., only 10.6% participants have registered for the system, and the majority (57.1%) of the registered users have not used the system at all after registration). In addition, the users' key concerns are security and privacy concerns, which are not covered/addressed by system features (but by the system user friendliness factor).
- *H4:* The proposed positive influence of user-friendliness on usefulness of the PCEHR system is not supported by the survey data. One possible explanation is that the usefulness of the PCEHR system is not an important determinant of adoption decision of the system. Users will not adopt the system until they can clearly see the benefits of the system, and they could view the use of the system as extra burden/work for them, which may (or may not) be necessary unless they can clearly realize the benefits of using the system (e.g., better and new health services, better management of their medical information, improving effectiveness and efficiency of health service systems, saving time and money). In addition, as mentioned earlier on, as a result of their lack of knowledge of the PCEHR system and engagement/involvement in the roll-out/implementation of the system, and low registration and use of the system, their understanding and experience of the system (including user friendliness of the system) is very limited.

- *H7:* It is seen from the results that Subject Norms don't influence users' adoption decision of the PCEHR system. This insignificant relationship is a surprise as past research [31, 33, 52] has found that Subject Norms are positively associated with the individual's acceptance of new technology, and past studies [22, 51] have suggested that Subject Norms are more important in early stages of innovation implementation, when users have limited direct experience from which to develop attitudes and perceptions. A possible explanation is that users/consumers will be more willing to accept and use the system when the use of the system is on the voluntary basis (e.g., opt-in approach) even though Subject Norms (e.g., influence from doctors and respected people) could have an impact on their acceptance and use of the system. Furthermore, while influence from their trusted people could influence users' decision of accepting and using the system, other issues such as benefits of the system, privacy and security concerns could have negative impacts on their willingness to try and adopt the system. In addition, even though users may view the system as being useful or/and user-friendly, they may not be confident enough to use the system themselves for reasons such as lack of knowledge and experience of e-health and PCEHR system, lack of engagement/involvement in the implementation/roll-out of the system, low registration and use of the system. It appears respondents want their doctors or/and health care providers to manage their patients' health/medical information.

Meanwhile Table-3 indicates that all the hypotheses of the continued use part of the research model are supported except **H13**. The results indicate that Subject Norms does not influence users' continued use of the PCEHR system. It can be argued that even though users may realize the benefits of using the system and like the functions of the system, for reasons mentioned in the previous discussion of the non-significant influence of Subject Norms on adoption of the PCEHR system, users could still like/want their doctors or/and their health care providers to continually manage the medical/health information of patients.

6   Conclusions and Future Directions

This research tested a model of adoption and continued use of the PCEHR system by surveying consumers/users in Australia. The model is unique in the sense that it includes both adoption and continued use of the PCEHR system in one model and many factors and variables are very specific to the PCEHR system adoption and continued use. The collected data were analysed using a structural equation modelling (SEM) approach. The results suggest that with only a few exceptions, most of the factors of the model were found to be important determination of users'/consumers' decision of adoption and continued use of the system. Significant factors for adoption of the PCEHR system include: External Factors and Influences, Individual Differences, PCEHR System Characteristics, Perceived Benefits, Perceived User Friendliness, and Voluntariness. Significant factors for continued use include Facilitating Factors, Realized Benefits, Realized User Friendliness, and Voluntariness. As far as the researchers are aware, the developed model of adoption and continued use of the

PCEHR system will be the first study on the implementation of the PCEHR system in Australia. Identified factors and variables of the model can assist in understanding challenges and issues associated with the continuous development and implementation of the system and serve as guidelines to the successful implementation of the system. In addition, the outcomes of this research can contribute to the improvement of the awareness of the system among Australian consumers.

An obvious limitation of the research is the small sample size. Although the invitation to participation was sent twice via email, which could reach thousands of the staff and students that were eligible to use the system, the participation rate is low since we were not allowed to send individual invitations as per the University's policy but rather only permitted to send blanket invitations via 2 generic email addresses (i.e., one to all staff in the University and the other to all students in the University). One reason for the low participation rate could be that likely respondents knew very little about the PCEHR system and possibly believed they could add little to a survey which may have included many responses of 'not applicable.' The immediate next step is to test the model using large scale studies (e.g., a national survey of consumers in Australia). This present study basically tested the whole model of adoption and continued use of the PCEHR system. In the future, parts of the model can be extracted and examined in detail. Future research also could look at developing and testing a model of adoption and continued use of the PCEHR system among health services providers.

References

1. Agarwal, R., Prased, J.: Are individual differences germane to the acceptance of new information technologies. Decis. Sci. **30**(2), 361–391 (1999)
2. Ajzen, I., Fishbein, M.: Understanding Attitudes and Predicting Social Behavior, vol. 07632. Prentice-Hall Inc, Englewood Cliffs (1980)
3. Anderson, J.C., Gerbing, D.W.: Some methods for respecifying measurement models to obtain unidimensional construct measurement. J. Mark. Res. **19**(4), 453–460 (1982)
4. Anderson, J.C., Gerbing, D.W.: Structural equation modelling in practice: A review and recommended two-stepped approach. Psychol. Bull. **103**(3), 411–423 (1988)
5. Arbuckle, J.: Amos 21 User's Guide, IBM (2012)
6. Australian Government: Budget 2017–2018: Budget Statements 2017–18 Budget Related Paper No. 1.10, Health Portfolio (2017), Accessed 14 May 2017. http://www.health.gov.au/internet/budget/publishing.nsf/Content/2017-2018_Health_PBS_sup4/$File/2017-18_Health_PBS_Complete.pdf
7. Bagozzi, R.P., Yi, Y.: Specification, evaluation, and interpretation of structural equation models. J. Acad. Mark. Sci. **40**(1), 8–34 (2012)
8. Barrett, P.: Structural equation modeling: adjusting model fit. Pers. Individ. Differ. **42**(5), 815–824 (2007)
9. Bentler, P.M., Chou, C.P.: Practical issues in Structural Modelling. Sociol. Methods Res. **16**(1), 78–117 (1999)
10. Browne, M.W., Cudeck, R.: Alternative ways of assessing model fit. In: Bollen, K.A., Long, J.S. (eds.) Testing structural equation models. Sage, Newbury Park, CA (1993)
11. Breckler, S.J.: Applications of covariance structure modeling in psychology: Cause for concern? Psychol. Bull. **107**(2), 260–273 (1990)

12. Byrne, B.M.: Structural Equation Modeling With Amos: Basic Concepts, Applications, and Programming. Lawrence Erlbaum Associates, New York (2001)
13. Coyne, A.: Australia's first opt-out e-health site to start trials this week, itnews, 27 January 2016. Accessed 22 Feb 2016. http://www.itnews.com.au/news/australias-first-opt-out-ehealth-site-to-start-trials-this-week-414099
14. Davis, F.D.: Perceived usefulness, perceived ease of use, and user acceptance of information technology. MIS Q. **13**(3), 319–340 (1989)
15. Davis, F.D., Bagozzi, R.P., Warshaw, P.R.: User acceptance of computer technology: a comparison of two theoretical models. Manag. Sci. **35**(8), 982–1002 (1989)
16. Department of Health and Aging: Expected Benefits of the National PCEHR System, May 2012
17. Department of Health: Patients to get new myHealth Record: $485 m 'rescue' package to reboot Labor's e-health failures, Media Release, 10 May 2015. Accessed. 18 Feb 2016. https://www.health.gov.au/internet/ministers/publishing.nsf/Content/health-mediarel-yr2015-ley050.htm
18. Garson, D.G.: Structural Equation Modeling. Statistical Associates Publishing, Asheboro (2012)
19. Goldstein, H., Bonnet, G., Rocher, T.: Multilevel structural equation models for the analysis of comparative data on educational performance. J. Educ. Behav. Stat. **32**(3), 252–286 (2007)
20. Hair, J.F., Black, W., Babin, B., Anderson, R.: Multivariate data analysis. Prentice Hall Inc, Upper Saddle River (2010)
21. Hair, J.F., Bush, R., Ortinau, D.: Marketing Research. McGraw-Hill Companies Incorporated, New York (2008)
22. Hartwick, J., Barki, H.: Explaining the role of user participation in information system use. Manag. Sci. **40**(4), 440–465 (1994)
23. Hox, J.J., Bechger, T.M.: An Introduction to Structural Equation Modeling. Fam. Sci. Rev. **11**, 354–373 (1998)
24. Hu, L., Bentler, P.M.: Cutoff criteria for fit indexes in covariance structure analysis: conventional criteria versus new alternatives. Struct. Equ. Model. **6**(1), 1–55 (1999)
25. Jackson, D.L.: Revisiting sample size and number of parameter estimates: some support for the N: q hypothesis. Struct. Equ. Model. **10**(1), 128–141 (2003)
26. Jöreskog, K.G.: Testing structural equation models. In: Bollen, K.A., Long, J.S. (eds.) Testing structural equation models, pp. 294–316. SAGE Publications, Newbury Park (1993)
27. Jöreskog, K.G., Sorbom, D.: LISREL VI: Analysis of Linear Structural Relationship by the Method of Maximum Likelihood. National Education Services, Chicago (1984)
28. Jöreskog, K.G.: On chi-squares for the independence model and fit measures in LISREL (2004). Accessed. 10 Jul 2017. http://www.ssicentral.com/lisrel/techdocs/ftb.pdf
29. Kerlin, J., Heath, J.: E-health scheme to be revived after panel review, The Australian Financial Review, 24 May 2014. Accessed 18 Feb 2016. http://www.afr.com/business/health/pharmaceuticals/ehealth-scheme-to-be-revived-after-panel-review-20140523-iupi8
30. Kline, R.B.: Principles and practice of structural equation modeling. The Guilford Press, New York (2001)
31. Liker, J.K., Sindi, A.: User acceptance of expert systems: a test of the theory of reasoned action. J. Eng. Tech. Manage. **14**(2), 147–173 (1997)
32. Lohman, T.: Australian e-health spending to top $2 billion in 2010, Computerworld, 15 April 2010. Accessed 30 Jun 2016. https://www.computerworld.com.au/article/634109/google-hangouts-chat-collaboration-app-hits-booming-market/
33. Lucas, H.C., Spitler, V.K.: Technology use and performance: a field study of broker workstations. Decis. Sci. **30**(2), 291–311 (1999)

34. McQuade-Jones, B., Murphy, J., Novak, T., Lisa-Nicole, S.: Nurse practitioners and meaningful use: transforming health care. J. Nurs. Pract. **10**(10), 763–768 (2014)
35. McQuitty, S.: Statistical power and structural equation models in business research. J. Bus. Res. **57**(2), 175–183 (2004)
36. Manning, M., Munro, D.: The Survey Researcher's SPSS Cookbook. Pearson Education Australia, Sydney (2007)
37. Mendelson, D., Wolf, G.: My electronic health record - Cui Bono: for whose benefit. J. Law Med. **24**, 283–296 (2016)
38. Mendelson, D., Wolf, G.: Health privacy and confidentiality. In: Freckelton, I., Petersen, K. (eds.) Tensions and Traumas in Health Law. Federation Press, Sydney (2017)
39. Moore, G.C.: End-user computing and office automation: a diffusion of innovation perspectives. INFOR **25**(3), 214–235 (1987)
40. Muhammad, I., Teoh, S.Y., Wickramasinghe, N.: The application of a sociotechnical analysis for the personally controlled electronic health record, In: Proceedings of PACIS 2012 (2012)
41. Nguyen, L., Bellucci, E., Nguyen, L.T.: Electronic health records implementation: an evaluation of information system impact and contingency factor. Int. J. Med. Inform. **83**, 779–796 (2014)
42. Partel, K.: Toward better implementation: Australia's My Health Record, Deeble Institute Issues Brief, No. 13, 30/10/2015, pp. 1–20 (2015)
43. Rogers, E.M.: Diffusion of Innovations, 4th edn. The Free Press, New York (1985)
44. Sansom, M.: My Health Record: Medics speak up, Government News, 15 August 2016. Accessed 15 Apr 2017. http://www.governmentnews.com.au/2016/08/24703/
45. Schumacker, R.E., Lomax, R.G.: A Beginner's Guide to Structural Equation Modeling. Routledge, New York (2010)
46. Smith, C., Ellis, I., Jaffray, L.: Nursing competencies needed for electronic advance care planning in community. GSTF Int. J. Nurs. Health Care **1**(1), 160–164 (2013)
47. Steininger, K., Stiglbauer, B.: EHR acceptance among Austrian resident doctors. Health Policy Technol. **2015**(4), 121–130 (2015)
48. Swinn, M., Weber, M.: My Health Record: The resuscitation of e-health, or a data placebo?, Image & Data Manager, 13 April 2017. Accessed 10 May 2017. https://idm.net.au/article/0011469-my-health-record-resuscitation-e-health-or-data-placebo
49. Tabachnick, B.G., Fidell, L.S.: Using multivariate statistics. Allyn and Bacon, Boston (2001)
50. Tanaka, J.S.: How big is big enough: sample size and goodness of fit in structural equation models with latent variables. Child Dev. **58**, 134–146 (1987)
51. Taylor, S., Todd, P.A.: Understanding information technology usage: a test of competing models. Inf. Syst. Res. **6**(2), 145–177 (1995)
52. Thompson, R.L., Higgins, C.A., Howell, J.M.: Personal computing: toward a conceptual model of utilization. MIS Q. **15**(1), 125–143 (1981)
53. Ward, M.J., Froehle, C.M., Hart, K.W., Collins, S.P., Lindsell, C.J.: Transient and sustained changes in operational performance, patient evaluation, and medication administration during electronic health record implementation in the emergency department. Ann. Emerg. Med. **63**(3), 320–328 (2014)
54. Xu, J., Quaddus, M.: Examining a model of knowledge management systems adoption and diffusion: a partial least square approach. J. Knowl.-Based Syst. **27**, 18–28 (2012)
55. Xu, J., Gao, X., Sorwar, G., Croll, P.: Current status, challenges, and outlook of E-Health record systems in Australia. In: Sun, F., Li, T., Li, H. (eds.) Knowledge Engineering and Management. AISC, vol. 214, pp. 683–692. Springer, Heidelberg (2014). https://doi.org/10.1007/978-3-642-37832-4_62

56. Xu, J., Gao, X.J., Sorwar, G., Croll, P.: Implementation of E-Health Record Systems in Australia. Int. Technol. Manag. Rev. **3**(2), 92–104 (2013)
57. Xu, J., Gao, X.J., Sorwar, G.: A research model of consumers' adoption and continued use of the Personally Controlled Electronic Health Record (PCEHR) system. Int. Technol. Manag. Rev. **4**(4), 187–200 (2014)

Creating Smarter Spaces to Unleash the Potential of Health Apps

Jean-Marie Bonnin[1]([✉]), Valérie Gay[2]([✉]), and Frédéric Weis[3]([✉])

[1] IMT Atlantique - IRISA, Rennes, France
jean-marie.bonnin@irisa.fr
[2] University of Technology Sydney, Broadway, NSW 2007, Australia
valerie.gay@uts.edu.au
[3] University Rennes 1 - IRISA, Rennes, France
frederic.weis@irisa.fr

Abstract. Technologies necessary for the development of pervasive health apps with intensive and seamless interactions with their environments are now widely available. Research studies and experimentations have demonstrated the real ability for health apps to interact with their environment. However, designing, testing and ensuring the maintenance and evolution of pervasive health apps remains very complex. In particular, there is a lack of tools to enable developers to design apps that can adapt to increasingly complex and changing environments (sensors added or removed, failures, mobility etc.). This paper reflects our vision to reduce this complexity and is based on our current research work on smart environment and personalized health monitoring apps. It uses SAM, a smart asthma monitoring app as an illustration to highlight the need for a comprehensive set of new interactions to help health app developers interact with the users' environment, and more specifically get a smarter access to the data. Some requirements can be on the minimum quality level of the data and the way to adapt to the diversity of the sources (data fusion/aggregation), on the network mechanisms used to collect the data (network/link level) and on the collection of the raw data (sensors). It discusses possible solutions to address these needs.

Keywords: Smart space · Ubiquitous applications
Edge/Fog computing · e-Health · Chronic disease management
Asthma management · IoT · Context awareness

1 Introduction

Smart space eco-systems are becoming a mass market reality. Large areas of our living spaces are now instrumented: short/long-range and low energy communications, a broad variety of visible (smart objects) or invisible (sensors and actuators) objects. The applications of the smart spaces are boundless. There is a real ability to adapt the smart space to the behaviors and needs of users, however mainstream applications are barely existent.

© Springer International Publishing AG, part of Springer Nature 2018
M. Mokhtari et al. (Eds.): ICOST 2018, LNCS 10898, pp. 134–145, 2018.
https://doi.org/10.1007/978-3-319-94523-1_12

In this paper we use the definition of [8] for smart space: *A smart space is a smart environment that has commuting embedded into it and can provide information that can be used to model the real world into the virtual computing world.*

This paper envisions smarter spaces with massive but scalable interactions between individuals and their everyday working and living environments such as residential housing, public buildings and vehicles. It focuses on the needs of app developers for better ways to interact with their environment and in particular use the opportunity of tapping into the vast amount of data collected from the physical environments for **health apps**. Today, this can only be done if the environment has especially been developed for it (for example "smart" hospital room). They are difficult to adapt to increasingly complex situations, even though environments in which they evolve are more open, or change over time (new sensors added, failures, mobility etc.)

Being able to develop health apps that are ready to deploy and evolve in everyday environments should allow significant cost reduction. Unfortunately, designing, testing and ensuring the maintenance as well as the evolution of such a pervasive application remains very complex. In our view, the lack of resources by which data issued from real environments are made available to health app developers is a major concern.

This paper is looking into this lack of data exposure and its objective is to explore how application development, setup and maintenance could be simplified in an open smarter space eco-system. Using an existing health app we developed as a basis, Sect. 2 presents an example on asthma management and shows how this chronic condition would benefit from access to the data issued by the smart space eco- systems. Section 3 gives our motivation for a new approach and focuses on one main challenge: providing health app developers with a better and smarter access to the environment data. The paper concludes with perspectives and future work.

2 Illustration: SAM - Smart Asthma Monitoring

One chronic condition that would benefit from getting better data from smart space eco-systems is **asthma**. According to GAN[1] in 2014, asthma may affect more than 334 million people worldwide. A few projects focusing on Asthma management exist [16] but they either use a tightly controlled environment or they do not adapt to their environment and rely mainly on personal area networks and specialized individual sensors (e.g. peakflows). Some cloud infrastructure solutions exist [7]. However they do not have the level of pervasiveness this paper envisions.

Figure 1 illustrates our vision. It features one citizen, Alex, an active middle age man that is prone to asthma attacks mostly triggered by pollen and pollution and a team of clinicians that help him managing his condition. Alex is using

---

[1] Global Asthma Network.

the app we developed. The app collects health and fitness data from different sources and gives Alex the possibility to aggregate data from different sources. The app interacts with a wide range of wireless devices and wearable health trackers and also aggregates data from third party apps. It offers Alex personalized exercise tracking and monitoring of biometric data such as heart rate, respiration, body temperature, weight, food intake, blood pressure, cholesterol, asthma, blood glucose and many more.

Fig. 1. Illustration of an asthma management scenario

Three important steps are involved in his asthma management in the smart space: Data collection, Data analysis and Nudge, feedback and service presentation.

2.1   Data Collection for Asthma

On a typical day, while Alex is living an active life, the smart space collects as much relevant data as possible in order to offer Alex the best overview on his asthmatic condition. His app collects data from wireless devices supporting open standard protocols such as the Google Android Wear smart watches and fitness trackers that allow third party developers to retrieve the data directly from the device (Fig. 2, box 1). It also collects data from devices (peakflow meter, pollution meter) paired with Alex's mobile device (Fig. 2, box 2) via Bluetooth or ANT+. Alex is in control of the data he wants to collect and how it is collected. He can enter data manually (Fig. 2, box 3) and annotate a reading by adding comments and contextual information, such as extra performed activities. For closed and proprietary wireless devices (Fig. 2, box 4 and 5), data is obtained via their server through an open API (e.g. Fitbit, Jawbone, Withings, myFitnessPal and Fatsecret).

Data is also collected from the smart space in order to offer more fine-grained analysis (Fig. 2, box 6). The context of Alex can be important and one of the challenges is to identify and collect the data that is important for a particular user in order to provide timely feedback. For Alex, our app captures location-based information about the Air Quality Index (AQI) and pollen levels. In the global scenario summarized in Fig. 1, our mobile application collects the data within Alex's smart space and in the cloud, for example, to get real-time data on the pollen and pollution levels in the different locations Alex intends to travel to today. Another example is to get forecast on air quality in Alex's smart home environment.

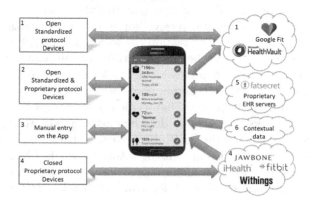

Fig. 2. Our app's eco system

2.2 Data Analysis and Data Storage for Asthma

Currently, the app stores all data locally on the mobile device, or on the cloud on a server chosen by the user. Alex opts for that in order to get more intelligent feedback based on his long-term history and possibly by comparing his data with the data of other citizens with similar conditions. Some of his sensors can also contribute to crowd sensing and help other asthma sufferers. Alex also opts for his clinicians to get access to his data and decide, for example, that there is a need to make adjustments to his asthma plan. This option gives Alex's clinicians an overall view on his health and fitness data and help them making a more accurate and personalized assessment. This could also allow hospital to estimate how many hospital beds they need to reserve for victims of asthma attack.

2.3 Nudge, Feedback and Service Presentation

For the feedback, we opted for a user-centred approach where Alex is in control of the way the data is presented to him. Triggers are personalised to Alex and the app provides threshold to trigger an alert. For example, the app would alert Alex when the air quality deteriorates and gets under his thresholds and raises an alarm if it gets hazardous for his condition. A similar approach will be taken for the pollen level. Alex can either see the data in real-time, or just get a notification or nudge when necessary or even ignore the data and get a phone call from his doctor if he needs to do something. Alex opted for a nudge when needed and an automatic reaction from his smart space when possible (automatic closing/opening of doors and windows at home or in the car, adjustment of the air conditioning). He selected to have real-time analysis and get warnings and references to his asthma plan based on his personal threshold levels on several parameters (including pollen and pollution level, peak flow readings). He may also be contacted by his clinicians to make an appointment or to adjust his asthma plan. Based on his calendar that contains the place and activities, he is planning to go to, he may also receive some advice to change plans (e.g.: work from home, exercise indoor) based on the location's current and forecasted data. Alex lives in Australia and he has an asthma action plan: a written plan, prepared for him by a healthcare professional. It allows him to reduce the severity of acute asthma flare-ups. Asthma action plans help recognize worsening asthma and advise what to do in response. They typically include: a list of prescribed medication, including dosage; what to do when asthma gets worse; what to do in an emergency; the name of the health professional predominantly responsible for treating the person and the date. In the future we would like Alex's asthma plan to be integrated in a health applications that would monitor the different triggers in the smart spaces and react according to the patient's asthma plan.

2.4   Challenges to Develop SAM to Support this Vision

Most of the vision presented in this example is feasible today but parts of it still bring interesting challenges. This section highlights some of the challenges developers have to be able make this vision possible.

Silos. There is an increasing amount of health- and fitness-related information that has been collected and stored in the cloud. However, the data usually resides in silos and in addition, in most cases health and fitness data is separated. According to Mandi et al. [11], these data streams will initially remain confined to their respective platforms and will have very limited ways to integrate with electronic health records (EHRs). To provide better health outcomes and better patient engagement, a complete picture is needed which combines informal health and fitness data collected by the user, together with official health records collected by health professionals. Combining these two streams, the data can be analyzed using data analytics and health professional expertise to offer better personalized advice and care. There is good evidence that the integration can improve therapeutic management [3].

For chronic disease patients, there is often a need to monitor several physiological parameters and not just their activity level or environmental data. The presence of data silos prevents these users from obtaining an overall view of their condition. To engage these users in active monitoring of their condition, it is important to have all health and fitness data in one place and give them a personalized overview and feedback on trends and progress. Moreover, device manufacturers develop their own protocol and data formats to retrieve data from the device or to send commands to the device. Some protocols are straightforward, using plain text to send or receive data. Many however, implemented complex protocols with numerous commands to control and exchange data. Without a detailed specification it is impossible to communicate with these devices.

Quality and privacy of the data. With the increase of data sources comes the need to be able to differentiate the sources based on their quality, security and trust levels. There is a need to express requirement on the network mechanisms used to collect the data (network/link level) security aspects in particular - and on the collection of the raw data (sensors). This would lead to a better service for asthma sufferer as their asthma management would be able to dynamically adjust itself to the status of the smart-space (e.g. change the air conditioning at home or in a personal car).

Abstraction level. Health app developers also need to get the right level of abstraction to trigger an action. To get to that level of abstraction (e.g. is the pollution level too high wrt the users thresholds) there is a need to combine data at different levels (e.g. raw or elaborated data).

Detection of unreliable sensors. The reliability of the sensors varies widely and reliability is very important for health apps like SAM and health professionals that need to make a diagnostic. In Alex's case, air pollution data comes from accurate and expensive sensors like the ones of his high tech building at work, but it also comes from the low cost gadget Alex is carrying. The gadget might be untested and therefore not be fit for purpose to justify, on its own, a change to his medication or his asthma plan. For example, devices made for the fitness market are not necessarily approved by the Food and Drug Administration (FDA) and as such even less reliable. If we are able to tags the source of the reading, it would be beneficial for a health professional in his/her assessment of the data quality. Many health professionals discard self-collected health. Fitness and environmental data due to the unreliability of the data and prefer to use their own data for diagnosis. We believe that over time more health professionals will accept the data if the source is properly tagged so that they know which device, or which application, generated the data.

3   Smarter Access to the Local Data

The technologies supporting the pervasive services presented in the asthma management example, with intensive and seamless interactions between individuals and their environments, are now widely available. Spaces in which Alex lives are increasingly enriched with these technologies. Alex's asthma can be monitored in his working and living environment: residential housing, public buildings, vehicles, etc. as illustrated on Fig. 3a. These environments are themselves organized in silos that do not interact with each other and do not coordinate well. In each environment, designing an application involves implementing one or more logical control loops which include four stages: (1) data collection in the real environment, (2) the (re)construction of information that is meaningful for the application and (3) for decision making, and finally, (4) action within the environment. While many decision-algorithms have been proposed, the **collection** and **construction** of a reliable and relevant perception of the environment still poses major challenges.

Developing Health apps that are ready to evolve in different environments and that overcome the existing silos would involve significant cost reduction. Unfortunately, as illustrated in Sect. 2, designing, testing and ensuring the maintenance as well as the evolution of a pervasive health application remains very complex. In our view, the lack of resources by which properties of the real environment are made to application developers is a major issue. Most current solutions are based on a massive collection of raw data from the environment, stored and processed on remote servers [12] and use specialized cloud services for delivering pervasive services. These solutions isolate the developer from the real environment that often needs to be depicted according to complex, heavy and expensive processes.

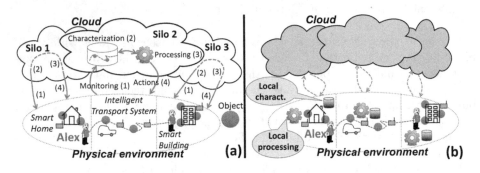

Fig. 3. Design of a pervasive app using cloud services/local data and local processing

However, new paradigms like edge or fog computing [14] offer alternative ways of bringing computing capabilities to the edge of the network. Objects and infrastructure integrated into user smart space often provide a more suitable support to pervasive applications. The objects can carry different kinds of data, like current smart space air quality. The description of the actual state of the environment can be richer, more accurate, and, meanwhile, easier to handle. The processing can be distributed by being built directly into the environment, facilitating scalability and resilience by the processing autonomy; and finally, moving the processing closer to the edge of the network avoids major concerns about data sovereignty and privacy encountered in cloud-based infrastructures. Figures 3b and 1 illustrated a plausible "distribution" of an asthma management scenario between Alex's local environment and cloud-based services. The best place to use the data depends partly on what kind of data is needed for making decision and trigger processing. Fine decisions can be made closer to the objects producing the data. **Local data characterization** and **local processing** reduce the computing and storage resources in the cloud. The latter can be always used to store selected or transformed data for global historical analysis or optimization, for example for health and fitness history.

There is a need for a comprehensive set of new models and architectures to help smart space designers making those distribution choices. We propose a design approaches that exposes local properties of the environment to pervasive applications. The developer must be able to manage and to enrich locally data produced in the environment. In return the application would then be able to build their knowledge about their environment (perception) in order to adjust their behavior (eg. level of automation) to the actual situation. In the following, we present three research directions to develop models of data-centric service architecture.

3.1 Characterizing Data Quality

Several studies have proposed data quality analysis [9] and methodologies for identifying data quality issues [5]. The quality of the raw data collected in the smart space (temperature, sound level, pollen level etc.) are of crucial importance to assess the quality of the perception of the environment and therefore to ensure correct behavior of a health pervasive app. Poor quality data is often a result of poor representation of the physical environment. Data quality can be characterized through several dimensions. Here the term dimension is defined as a "measurable extent of a particular kind": timeliness, accuracy, confidence, reliability, confidentiality, etc. For example, timeliness refers to time data should be available for use by an app within an acceptable time relative to its time of creation.

In an environment instrumented with smart objects and sensors interconnected with low energy communications, the way data is produced, consolidated, and aggregated has an impact on its quality dimensions. Moreover part of these quality dimensions requires gathering information from several communication layers (link and network layers) at several entities (the object itself, access point, router etc.) to be computed on the fly. **Lightweight cross-layer interactions** to collect relevant data have to be designed for this purpose, the goal is to expose "augmented" data (initial raw data + some pertinent dimensions selected by the app developer) to the pervasive app. Figure 4 illustrates these principles.

A **frugality** principle should guide the design, therefore it is not appropriate to build all imaginable attributes. It is necessary to identify attributes relevant to the application and to have mechanisms to activate or deactivate at run-time the process to collect them. A "frugal" service uses as few resources as possible, while having the possibility to use much more when it is required. This is quite a different approach than **best-effort services** where a networked application uses all the resources it can use and if there are not enough resources, it tries to mitigates the effects.

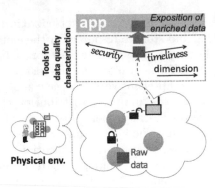

Fig. 4. Enriching data collected in smart environment using cross-layer interactions

3.2   Providing Pertinent Abstractions

Raw data should only be used directly to determine low-level abstractions. Further help in abstracting from low-level details can be provided by **data fusion**. The pervasive community increasingly understands that developing pervasive apps should be supported by such data fusion tools [15]. While many definitions exist for data fusion, we use the one in [10]: *Information fusion is the study of efficient methods for automatically or semi-automatically transforming information from different sources and different points in time into a representation that provides effective support for human or automated decision making.*

A good construction of a meaningful information (for example "air quality in the home", "level of activity in a room", "posture of a person" etc.) reduces the complexity and helps developers to concentrate on the application logic.

Moreover, the reactivity required in pervasive systems and the aggregation of large amounts of data (and its processing) in the cloud are antagonists. Fusion tools that can be deployed closer to the edge of the network are needed.

Traditional data fusion systems are often designed to use a set of dedicated sensors. Moreover, most approaches rely directly on sensor measures making them hard to deploy in many different environments and for different pervasive apps. They require an *ad hoc* tuning phase as the behavior of a sensor can change from one environment to another. Finally, the techniques to be used in our approach are guided by different criteria [13]: (1) the relevance of abstractions produced for pervasive applications, (2) the anonymization of exploited raw data, (3) the processing time and computing power required for processing, (4) the ignorance of the system (the system should be able to be indecisive when it does not have enough clue of what is going on) and (5) the no predetermined sensor configuration (the data fusion process should be if possible independent from the configuration of sensors).

We proved [13], through the use of dedicated algorithms and a layered architecture that data fusion tools can be deployed using the Belief Function Theory (BFT) [6]. Raw data collected in the environment can been seen as an "accumulation of evidence". BFT enables the use of multiple sources to infer a meaningful abstraction defined by app developers. In our approach, an abstraction used by pervasive app is computed by a chain of three tasks as illustrated in Fig. 5:

- **Model.** The transition between a raw sensor value and a model of the sensor is made through the use of a "belief function" which maps each sensor value to a possible state (state 1, state 2 etc.) of the abstraction. A belief function represents the "degree of belief" associated to each possible value of the abstraction.
- **Fusion.** Then a set of belief functions (corresponding to a set of sensors) can be combined (fused).
- **Decision.** Finally the system can decide what is the "best" value for the abstraction.

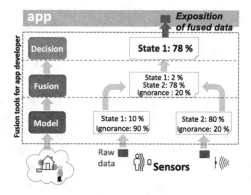

Fig. 5. Building high level abstraction with raw data collected in smart environment

3.3 Detecting New Sensors/Detecting Unreliable Sensors

One of the reasons why pervasive apps are not affordable for mainstream adoption comes from the necessity to control all the aspect of the environment to ensure the correctness of the decision-making. This is especially true for apps that move in various unknown and uncontrolled environment. Building a fit for purpose perception using available data from the environment is one way to simplify the deployment since it alleviates the need to know *a priori* the peers we need to communicate with. As stated in Sect. 3.2, it is not possible to use data as it is produced; it is then necessary to calibrate the raw data issued from a sensor to take into account its specificities. Such a calibration depends on the usage, this is why it is often done upon a complex installation phase on the field and not during the manufacturing process. Some solutions exist to solve this issue. As an application could not know *a priori* all sensors, if nobody does it before, it has to establish **knowledge** about sensors and the quality of the information they generate (eg. how to calibrate them) for a set of purposes. Such knowledge could be stored in the environment, then the information could be provided to other applications or instances when needed.

More generally to ease the design of new applications and to align the development of new products with the ever faster standard developments, continuous integration could be used in parallel with **continuous conformance** and **interoperability testing**. New shared platforms like [1] aim at facilitating this by providing remote testing tools. Unfortunately, from an application perspective it is not possible to be certain that all potential peers in the surrounding have a compliant behavior for the property it needs [4]. Moreover, upon failure or security breach, a piece of equipment could stop to operate properly and lead to global misbehavior. Testing devices at runtime is then necessary. As for calibration the result of such conformance or interoperability tests could be stored safely in the environment by authoritative testing entities. Applications could then interact with the device with a higher confidence. The confidence level of a device could be part of the quality attribute of the information it contributed to generate.

4   Conclusion

We highlighted some of the complexity and the challenges of designing, testing and maintaining pervasive health app that need a great deal of interactions with smart spaces. An illustration based on asthma management highlights the importance of the interactions with the smart space to offer better and more scalable health apps. It then discussed how we envision smarter space eco-systems with a focus on one challenge: providing health app developers with tools to access local environment data. Solving this first challenge would make health apps able to perceive their environment and dynamically adjust their behavior (e.g. level of automation, need for additional information/data) to the actual status of their environment. This, in turn, would create smarter spaces and enable more scalable and reliable health apps.

In this paper, we do not address explicitly the privacy issues. However, our approach is inspired by the fog computing principles and collecting pertinent information and tagging the environment close to the users lead us to consider several questions in relation with data sovereignty/residency: What is the nature of the stored data? Where is it stored? Who holds it? Who can access it? We may consider the models [2] in the design of our tools. In our study case, we partially solve the issues by using citizen participation: Sam, the asthma suffer has the option to choose where his data comes from, where he stores it and who has access to it.

This paper envisioned smarter spaces with massive but scalable interactions between individuals and their everyday working and living environments. The potential of the smarter space is huge and not limited to health app. Smart space could help support better housing facilities, better accessibility for disabled people, smart plant, automated cooperative vehicle or car-Infrastructure cooperation.

References

1. F-interop: Platform for online interoperability and performance test (2016). Accessed 1 Mar 2018. http://www.f-interop.eu/
2. Antignac, T., Le Métayer, D.: Privacy by design: from technologies to architectures. In: Preneel, B., Ikonomou, D. (eds.) APF 2014. LNCS, vol. 8450, pp. 1–17. Springer, Cham (2014). https://doi.org/10.1007/978-3-319-06749-0_1
3. Becker, S., Miron-Shatz, T., Schumacher, N., Krocza, J., Diamantidis, C., Albrecht, U.V.: mhealth 2.0: Experiences, possibilities, and perspectives. JMIR mHealth uHealth 2(2), May 2014
4. Calinescu, R., Ghezzi, C., Kwiatkowska, M., Mirandola, R.: Self-adaptive software needs quantitative verification at runtime. Commun. ACM 55(9), 69–77 (2012)
5. Challa, S., Gulrez, T., Chaczko, Z., Paranesha, T.: A data driven approach for discovering data quality requirements. In: IEEE 8th International Conference on Information Fusion. University of Auckland Business School, Auckland, New Zealand, December 2014
6. Dempster, A.: Upper and lower probabilities induced by a multivalued mapping. Ann. Math. Stat. 38, 325–339 (1967)
7. Huang, X., Matricardi, P.M.: Allergy and asthma care in the mobile phone era. Clin. Rev. Allergy Immunol, May 2016
8. Jayaraman, P.P., Zaslavsky, A., Delsing, J.: On-the-Fly Situation composition within smart spaces. In: Balandin, S., Moltchanov, D., Koucheryavy, Y. (eds.) NEW2AN/ruSMART -2009. LNCS, vol. 5764, pp. 52–65. Springer, Heidelberg (2009). https://doi.org/10.1007/978-3-642-04190-7_6
9. Jayawardene, V., Sadiq, S., Indulska, M.: An Analysis of Data Quality Dimensions. Technical report, The University of Queensland, February 2015
10. Khaleghi, B., Khamis, A., Karray, F.O., Razavi, S.N.: Multisensor data fusion: a review of the state-of-the-art. Inf. Fusion 14(1), 28–44 (2013)
11. Mandl, K., Mandel, J., Kohane, I.: Driving innovation in health systems through an apps-based information economy. Cell Syst. 1(1), 8–13 (2015)
12. Mun, M., Reddy, S., Shilton, K., Yau, N., Burke, J., Estrin, D., Hansen, M., Howard, E., West, R., Boda, P.: PEIR, The personal environmental impact report, as a platform for participatory sensing systems research. In: Proceedings of the 7th International Conference on Mobile Systems, Applications, and Services, MobiSys 2009, pp. 55–68. ACM, New York (2009)
13. Pietropaoli, B., Dominici, M., Weis, F.: Multi-sensor data fusion within the belief functions framework. In: Balandin, S., Koucheryavy, Y., Hu, H. (eds.) NEW2AN/ruSMART -2011. LNCS, vol. 6869, pp. 123–134. Springer, Heidelberg (2011). https://doi.org/10.1007/978-3-642-22875-9_11
14. Shi, W., Cao, J., Zhang, Q., Li, Y., Xu, L.: Edge computing: vision and challenges. IEEE Internet Things J. 3(5), 637–646 (2016)
15. TalebiFard, P., Leung, V.C.: A data fusion approach to context-aware service delivery in heterogeneous network environment. In: 2nd International Conference on Ambient Systems, Networks and Technologies (ANT-2011), Niagara Falls, Canada, pp. 312–319, September 2011
16. Votis, K., Lalos, A., Moustakas, K., Tzovaras, D.: Analysis, modelling and sensing of both physiological and environmental factors for the customized and predictive self-management of asthma. In: 6th Panhellenic Conference of Biomedical Technology. Athens, Greece, May 2015

A Dynamic Distributed Architecture for Preserving Privacy of Medical IoT Monitoring Measurements

Salaheddin Darwish[1]([⊠]), Ilia Nouretdinov[1], and Stephen Wolthusen[1,2]

[1] School of Mathematics and Information Security, Royal Holloway,
University of London, Egham, UK
{salaheddin.darwish,i.r.nouretdinov,stephen.wolthusen}@rhul.ac.uk
[2] Department of Information Security and Communication Technology, Norwegian
University of Science and Technology, Trondheim, Norway

Abstract. Medical and general health-related measurements can increasingly be performed via IoT components and protocols, whilst inexpensive sensors allow the capturing of a wider range of parameters in clinical, care, and general health monitoring domains. Measurements must typically be combined to allow e.g. differential diagnosis, and in many cases it is highly desirable to track progression over time or to detect anomalies in care and general monitoring contexts. However, the sensitive nature of such data requires safeguarding, particularly where data is retained by different third parties such as medical device manufacturers for extended periods. This appears to be very challenging especially when standards-based interoperability (i.e using IoT standards like HyperCAT or Web of Things-WoT) is to be achieved. This is because open meta-data of those standards can facilitate inference and source linkage if compiled or analysed by adversaries. Therefore, we propose an architecture of pseudonimyised distributed storage including a dynamic query analyser to protect the privacy of information being released.

Keywords: Medical IoT · Differential privacy · Pseudonymisation
Meta-data · Anonymisation

1 Introduction

Privacy has been identified as a major concern in the Internet of Things (IoT) [27], but earlier it was mostly concentrated on such aspects as identification of individuals and interactions, localisation and tracking, without paying much attention to the profiling of individuals and their behaviour based on data sources ranging from radio-frequency identification (RFID) tags via surveillance devices to wearable components. Nevertheless, there are few attempts to address this particular issue in IoT like in RFC-7744 [24]. However, despite the IoT potential for improved outcomes as well as cost savings identified in various domains including the health sector [7], individuals are subject to monitoring by diverse

© Springer International Publishing AG, part of Springer Nature 2018
M. Mokhtari et al. (Eds.): ICOST 2018, LNCS 10898, pp. 146–157, 2018.
https://doi.org/10.1007/978-3-319-94523-1_13

sensors over extendable time-periods, resulting in **linkage** of such different sources as a major risk for **re-identification** [10]. Measurements and observations not only limited to IoT environments may be linked together eventually as individual data sources become interchangeable and are no longer restricted to vertical application domains in which anonymisation can take place as required.

Current practice frequently relies on information being de-identified in a particular context, but without considering how such information may be linked with other sources or over longer time-periods as may become feasible for health monitoring and care where symptoms may be analysed algorithmically or are desirable for research purposes. It is, however, well known that merely anonymising a *pre-defined* subset of attributes will not prevent re-identification when combined with other attributes [17]. This, however, has severe implications for how such information arising in a medical context may be processed, stored, and presented. In the United Kingdom, common law and a number of laws including the UK Data Protection Act (1998), the NHS Act (2006), Social Care Act (2012), Human Rights Act (1998), and Data Protection (Processing of Sensitive Personal Data) Order (2000) impose bounds on handling of sensitive information, whilst EU General Data Protection Regulation (2016/679) coming into effect in 2018 imposes further constraints. Also, similar (less prescriptive) considerations apply in other jurisdictions where e.g. the U.S. Health Insurance Portability and Accountability Act (HIPAA) Privacy Rule defines health information as individually identifiable if (1) it identifies the individual; or (2) there is a reasonable basis to believe the information can be used to identify the individual.

In order to allow the flexible effective aggregation of diverse IoT data sets and measurements in a privacy-preserving and lawful manner, it is insufficient just to aggregate even de-identified sources, but rather must provide further control over processing and queries, *particularly where data sources may be aggregated over time or new sources added.* In this work, we specifically address the impact of involving *external sources (prior knowledge)* on the control of privacy protection via using e.g. a **meta-data** element in medical IoT (referring to Hyper-CAT [4] and W3C Web of Things-WoT [2] standards) which is typically used for describing IoT asset and attributes semantics for interoperability and discovery purposes. For this reason, we propose an architecture of pseudonimyised distributed storage incorporating dynamic query-based privacy protection relying on differential privacy models to ensure that constraints are honoured.

Section 2 reviews related work. Section 3 describes meta-data potentials in privacy. Section 4 addresses the proposed distributed storage model for protecting privacy. Section 5 analyses the problem of aggregation and proposes a query-based approach for selective release. Conclusions and future work are in Sect. 6.

2   Background

Emerging of various IoT-based and mobile health applications has offered an open and seamless way of tracking health of population such as HealthKit [1], Medical IoT monitoring [20,21,23,26], etc. However, using such complex systems poses more privacy concerns about how the sensitive information is being handled. Also, most IoT-related security works are focusing on securing communication rather than data at rest. Therefore, it is very demanding to expand the vision of how to effectively protect privacy of data in this system.

In order to protect the privacy of data records, some transformations need to be applied. They may involve reversible operations (such as encryption and pseudonymisation) and irreversible ones (anonymisation, deleting, obscuring the data [5]). According to [18,19], pseudonymisation is developed as an alternative for encryption as a privacy-enhancing technique in which identification data must be replaced with cryptographically generated pseudonyms to keep some form of secret association with original data. In this particular approach, original data or measurements are presumed to be held separately and securely from processed data. However, this technique appears to be insufficient alone for maintaining the privacy, because an attacker can make a data analysis of the open measurements when data from different IoT devices for the same patients are collected together.

As presented in [5], there are different types of obscuring anonymising strategies. They include: replacing data with synthetic one [8], data swapping [6], imputation of gaps [22] or noise [9], rounding, binning and suppression [12,13]. In our context, rounding (binning) is considered as a simple and 'fair' deterministic approach of data generalisation (i.e. refer to numerical discrete and continuous data type) that does not require imputing any wrong information into the data, such as artificial noise. These strategies have to be measured with some quantitative criterion to ensure that the privacy defence is kept at some satisfactory level. Two the most well-known criteria are *k-anonimity* [25] and *differential privacy* [9]. An example of privacy defence for time series MIoT data is shown in [16] based on differential privacy framework. In this certain work, data are collected from one sensor and the goal is to prevent identifying the small time changes by the attacker. In addition, we need to involve the prior knowledge about feature dependence into differential privacy as some different sensor measurements may be correlated. Necessity to modify the differential privacy approach [9] for dependent features is stated and partially addressed in [14].

On the other side, the meta-data aspect becomes very critical since the meta-data may possibly contain some information which can be linked to an individual or group resulting in privacy violation. Madaan et al. [15] discuss the impact of meta-data on the privacy goals. This work demonstrates the potential role of meta-data which can play in constructing prior information threatening privacy, and how to mitigate this risk by adopting a differential privacy framework.

3   Meta-data

For interoperability and integration purposes, most well known IoT standards incorporate meta-data to describe IoT devices and its interactions, for example, HyperCAT [4] and Web of Thing (WoT) - Thing Description (TD) [2]. Meta-data involved in the medical IoT system without mindful consideration appears to be intuitively harmless to data privacy. However, nowadays because of new technological innovations, meta-data can be easily compiled and analysed, leading to disclosure of sensitive information: device attributes, patient location, etc. Analysed meta-data of a given medical IoT system enables adversaries to establish a comprehensive profile of a patient's location, medical conditions, medical devices in use, etc. Also, some meta-data may contain some explicit and implicit potentials (e.g. some semantics) in drawing a picture about patient's patterns of behaviour, interactions, and associations, exposing even more about that patient than the content of his\her medical conditions. Therefore, meta-data becomes a significant source of knowledge which can be encoded and exploited by adversaries to threaten privacy and this element needs to be taken into account seriously when tackling privacy issues in the medical IoT system.

To realise the significance of meta-data privacy leakage, we rely in this work on two well-known IoT standards, HyperCAT [4] and W3C Web of Things (WoT) [2]. The HyperCAT standard introduces an extensible, lightweight JSON-based catalogue which facilitates description and discovery of IoT resources over the Web using REST APIs, meta-data, semantic annotations, and special URI conventions. This standard is proposed in order to enable distributed data sources (i.e. hubs) to be utilised collaboratively by applications in a uniform machine-readable format. While, Web of Things presents a versatile IoT standard refining the Internet of Things by integrating smart things not only into the Internet (the network) but into the Web (the application layer). This standard leverages platform-independent APIs for web developers and offers a means for different platforms to discover and inter-operate with each other. This depends on rich JSON-based meta-data, Thing Description (TD), to define the data and interaction models for

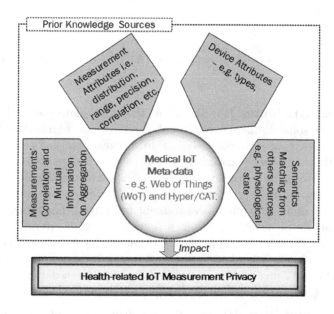

Fig. 1. Meta-data capabilities on privacy

applications, and the communications and security requirements for platforms to communicate seamlessly. Also, it is important to address that Web of Things is still in the early stage of fully incorporating semantics of things and the domain constraints associated with this semantics, seeking for building W3C's extensible RDF and Linked Data. Therefore, we propose an exhaustive set of related-measurement and device information which can be extracted from accessible meta-data and may be linked, causing a privacy risk to a given patient as shown in Fig. 1. To perceive meta-data capabilities, we use meta-data from HyperCAT or W3C Web of Things (WoT) as an illustrative example to support our claims. we identify four main properties: (1) device attributes, (2) measurement attributes, (3) measurement correlation/mutual information and (4) semantics matching from others sources.

```
{ ...                                          {
  "interaction": [                               "catalogue-metadata": [
    {                                            { ....
      "@id": "val",                                "items": [
      "@type": ["Property","Temperature"],         {
      "name": " Body Temperature",                   "href": "/cat/CompanyA/thremo ",
      "unit": "celsius",                             "item-metadata": [
      "outputData":{                                   { "rel": "urn:ReadingType",
          "@type": ["reading"],                          "val": "Body Temperature"
          "type": "number",                            },
          "min": 34,                                   {"rel": "urn:ReadingType:min",
          "max" : 40 },                                  "val": "34"
      "writable": false,                               }
      "observable": true,                              {"rel": "urn:ReadingType:max",
      "link": [{                                         "val": "40"
          "href" : "coap://example.com/temp",          }]
          "mediaType": "application/json"            ......
      }]                                           }
    ...                                        }
}              (A)                                            (B)
```

Fig. 2. Two simple meta-data samples for (A) TD-WoT and (B) HyperCAT

Measurement Attributes: It is noticeable that meta-data used in IoT context seems to enclose some useful information about attributes of individual measurement such as measurement prior distribution, ranges, precision (error rate) and correlation. However, these extracted attributes can be exploited and linked by adversaries resulting in a privacy violation of a patient associated with these measurement attributes. For example, learning about a range and probability density function of an individual measurement from meta-data along with incorporating a sample of measurement data reveals sensitive information about a patient medical status. Some types of measurements have the capability to show dependence which can be linked to the individual, for example, opening door, motion, etc. Figure 2 presents two simple examples of meta-data representations of thermometer sensor using Web of Things and HyperCAT.

Device Attributes: Meta-data may include device attributes which are unassociated with the measurement being generated, but likely to leak some sensitive information about the patient (e.g. location, portability, etc). Some attributes of a device like being wearable or using some communication medium and protocols (e.g. BLE, Zigbee, etc.) may indicate to the patient localisation.

Measurement Correlation/Mutual Information on Aggregation: In some cases in the system, measurements of different medical devices or sensors are usually aggregated or grouped in a gateway before sending them to the back-end storage. Knowing about this aggregation and some features of associated devices from meta-data, some information sensitive can be easily obtained or inferred (i.e. patient location, health condition). Also, some information about a possible influence of the physiological measurements on each other (e.g. having a certain blood pressure and heartbeat measurements can be connected with heart problems) can be a threat to the privacy see Sect. 5. For example, the W3C WoT standard, unlike the HyperCat standard, offers a structured and visible meta-data (i.e. TD of Gateway Servient) indicating where and how data is combined. Therefore, this particular information along with some extra information about some device attributes (e.g. TD for Bluetooth devices communicating to the same gateway) may reveal sensitive location properties. Being aware of aggregation of some certain types of medical measurements (e.g. ECG, body pressure, GPS, motion, etc.) may often expose some medical status or health problem.

Semantics Matching from Others Sources: Most meta-data models are typically enriched with semantics (using common vocabularies) for more machine and human readability and involve some semantic annotations for facilitating resource discovery and knowledge reasoning. This information of semantics may enable adversaries to find and learn a lot of extra related-measurement and -device information either manually or automatically and this particular prior knowledge can be exploited to breach privacy. However, the current Hyper-CAT and Web of Things standards only rely on statics approaches incorporating the semantics by using semantics annotation for some properties in the meta-data (e.g. using JSON-LD in Web of Things whereas using RDF-based Uniform Resource Identifiers (URIs) which typically identify data sources in HyperCAT). For example, some particular semantic queries for the meta-data in these standards can be requested in order to discover more details about medical devices in the system including related measurement attributes and constraints.

4 Pseudonymisation

The diverse and pervasive nature of the measurement data in a medical IoT system incites several privacy threats (e.g. identification and attribute disclosures including information linking [11,27]) as a result of subject (i.e. patients and devices) asset association, intermediate data aggregation and system meta-data being incorporated. Also, for the purpose of system control and data utilisation, individual measurements in this particular system unlike a typical health systems demonstrate a strong link with the device and patient information (e.g. patient and device records IDs) whether directly or indirectly as most IoT devices and sensors is normally bound to a certain patient or vicinity. Therefore, pseudonymisation offers a distinct approach to preserve privacy by anonymising data with the advantage of reversing this anonymisation if required. Pseudonymisation is a technique where all data identifiers should be changed by one or more artificial identifiers or pseudonyms [11]. Various approaches for patient pseudonymisation are proposed as shown in [3]. In this work, we adopt the simple approach of substituting real indentifiers with pseudorandom identifiers as some particular approaches in [3] appear to suffer from performance and management overheads because of heavily using crypto methods and intricate interactions. We propose a model of pseudonymised distributed storage offering an effective means to protect measurement privacy with keeping utility of measurement data competently, in medical IoT systems as shown in Fig. 3. This model mainly assumes there are multiple measurement providers (e.g. Third-party or IoT vendors) which typically store medical or health-related measurements collected from IoT sensors or gateways. Each measurement provider should keep measurements along with their own associated IoT devices' and patients' information in a pseudonymised form via using the pseudonymisation service provided by a resolution storage centre. In addition, all providers are assumed to share different pseudo-random identifiers with the resolution centre not the original identifiers associated with their patients for protection purposes in case a resolution centre is compromised. In other words, each provider must have a table for mapping between its real IDs and their random IDs generated for sharing with the centre. The resolution centre has twofold roles. The first one is to generate and store random pseudonyms for the different identifiers (i.e patient, device and measurement IDs) whereas the second role is to control and resolve analyst queries with preserving privacy. The resolution centre relies on a set of master tables for mapping between different generated pseudonyms with their corresponding provider identifiers. Important to stress that adopting this specific pseudonymisation approach is to impede any privacy breaches coming from device and patient levels. On the other side, the de-pseudonymised service in the resolution centre as a second level of privacy protection involves a query analyser to anonymise results of a query sufficiently before posting to the data analyst. Also, the query analyser is used to restrict some queries if releasing those queries may lead to re-identification by exploiting some prior knowledge extracted from meta-data and query history, the details will be discussed in the next section.

Finally, we argue that our distributed storage model with providing purely randomised (not derived) pseudonyms for patient, device and measurement identifiers does not guarantee unlinkability, but it makes the process of linking a pseudonym to an individual very cumbersome and demand a lot of effort and resources. In our architecture, the resolution data centre is only a map between different measurement data repositories and patient and device repositories, so any compromise which may occur to the resolution centre or other repositories, will arguably not compromise the whole system. In other words, the key privacy advantage of a distributed system is avoiding a central point of data aggregation. Important to

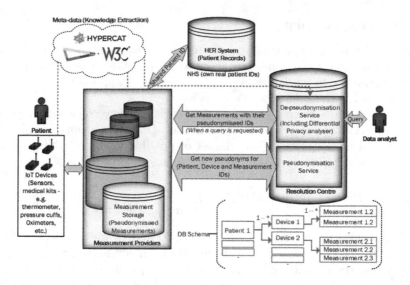

Fig. 3. The proposed distributed architecture: a pseudonymising system

mention that the proposed architecture is assumed to have a standard access control managing access of front-end and back-end parties (e.g. RBAC) and also establish a secure communication between different endpoints.

5   Differentially Private Query De-Pseudonymisation

Even if the data records are pseudonymised, there is still a chance for adversaries to identify a patient from data analysis, i.e. analysis of the measurements generated by different sensors for a certain patient (see DB Schema diagram at Fig. 3) collected at the resolution centre storage.

According to the scheme of data processing, we assume that the *Measurement Storage* (see Fig. 3) collects together only the records and strictly pseudonymised references to patients. They should not include any other information related to the patients such as their meta-data or history of illness.

We also expect some input in the form of *queries* from a user (i.e. *data analyst*). The system contains a *query analyser* block (*Differential Privacy analyser*) which uses *prior knowledge* for decisions.

We assume that the data record is collected for a patient in the form of $(t_1, s_1, d_1), \ldots, (t_m, s_m, d_m)$ where t_i is a time stamp, s_i is a reference to a sensor, d_i is the numerical value of a *measurement*.

The prior knowledge of the data comes from knowledge resources such as meta-data (obtained by HyperCat and Web Of Things), and domain-specific expertise. We assume that it comes in the form of restrictions on possible *joint* distribution of the observations coming from different sensors.

5.1   Privacy Constraint

The principal way of keeping the privacy is an *anomymising strategy* $\mathcal{A}$ transforming the original measurement sequence to a form observable to the user. We prefer this strategy to be deterministic, but assume it applied to the measurement values only, while the schedule is open.

We consider the following version of differential privacy constraint for deterministic strategies, under prior knowledge. Let $D \in R^m$ mean an individual data record, $\mathcal{A}$ be a strategy, $\mathcal{P}$ be the set of possible joint probability density functions P on R^m. The $(\varepsilon, \mathcal{P})$-*differential privacy constraint* for $\mathcal{A}$ is

$$\forall P \in \mathcal{P} : Prob_P \{\mathcal{A}(D) = \mathcal{A}(D')\} = \int_{D \in R^m \, s.t. \, \mathcal{A}(D) = \mathcal{A}(D')} P(dD) \geq e^{-\varepsilon}$$

where P generates m-dimensional data records D and D' independently of each other, $\mathcal{P}$ is the class of possible density functions on R^m according to the prior knowledge and the parameter ε (known as a *privacy budget*) quantifies strength of the constraint. This requirement means that the data record produced for a patient should be with high probability indistinguishable from another record generated for another patient with same (or similar) schedule of measurements.

The useful property of $(\varepsilon, \mathcal{P})$-differential privacy constraint is its decomposability, related to sharing the privacy budget over the queries. Assume that $q \leq m$ is the overall number of queries, $k_1, \ldots, k_q$ are the number of measurements addressed by the queries and

$$0 = \varepsilon_0 \leq \varepsilon_1 \leq \cdots \leq \varepsilon_{k-1} \leq \varepsilon_k \leq \cdots \leq \varepsilon_q \leq \varepsilon$$

where ε_k is a measure of the volume of information available for disclosure after first k queries. A way to satisfy the privacy constraint is dividing it into steps:

$$Prob_P \{\mathcal{A}(d_{q_1}, \ldots, d_{q_k}) = \mathcal{A}(d'_{q_1}, \ldots, d'_{q_k})$$

$$|\mathcal{A}(d_{q_1}, \ldots, d_{q_{k-1}}) = \mathcal{A}(d'_{q_1}, \ldots, d'_{q_{k-1}})\} \geq e^{-(\varepsilon_k - \varepsilon_{k-1})}.$$

5.2   Scheme of Differential Privacy Analyser

The central system has to include Differential Privacy analyser block for the queries in its Resolution Centre (see Fig. 3). We assume that this block contains the prior information available for the work. In order to give a safe answer to the next query, it stores the history of preceding queries (Fig. 4).

We introduce a anonymisation strategy of sequential binning (rounding) for the measurements in this architecture as most data are numerical:

$$\mathcal{A}_k : D = (d_{q_1}, \ldots, d_{q_k}) \rightarrow (b_1, \ldots, b_k) = B$$

where $b_j = \left[\frac{d_{q_j}}{r_j}\right] \times r_j$. Here square brackets mean eplacing a number with the closest integer. The values r_j is the *resolution level* (precision) for the j-th query.

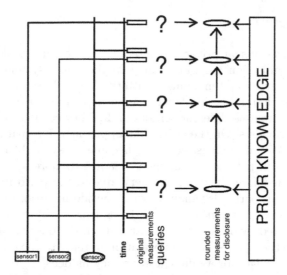

Fig. 4. Differential Privacy analyser for De-pseudonymisation service.

Calculation of the resolution coefficients is linked to the order of queries: r_k is a function of the previously observed feature values $(d_{q_1}, \ldots, d_{q_k})$ but not of the later ones. We can also assume that, up to fixed prior knowledge, r_j is a function of $b_1, \ldots, b_{k-1}$ and d_{q_k} only, as shown by the arrows on the Fig. 4. This way of binning means that classes of indistinguishable records are represented in the vector space of possible records as multi-dimensional parallelepipeds ('bricks') of possibly different sizes.

The exact way of calculation depends on the form of the prior knowledge $\mathcal{P}$. In the sequential setting done above, the estimation of r_i becomes a relatively easy task for empirical estimation in the most typical cases. Especially, if $\mathcal{P}$ consists of only one or several distributions P one can make simulation of the conditional distribution of d_{q_k} given $b_1, \ldots, b_{k-1}$, and decrease r_i as far as the conditional privacy constraint is not empirically broken for any P. If $\mathcal{P}$ is a parametric distribution with some range of parameters, then it can be reasonably approximated by scanning over a grid within the allowed parameter range. We recommend users to give a desirable resolution level $\hat{r}_i$ which is sufficient, so that attempts for further decreasing r_i can be stopped when $r_i = \hat{r}_i$ is reached.

It is also required to select a strategy of sharing privacy budgets. Possible examples may be as follows. *Equal share:* for an initially fixed positive number q, $\min\{\varepsilon/q, \varepsilon_r\}$ is considered as *upper bound* for $(\varepsilon_k - \varepsilon_{k-1})$, that is either spent totally at a step, or decreased if the reachable $\hat{r}_k$ is smaller than r_k required by the user. *Share in geometric progression:* for an initially fixed $h < 1$, $h\varepsilon_r$ is considered as *upper bound* for $(\varepsilon_k - \varepsilon_{k-1})$; all the rest is done the same way as above. Those strategies can be modified in various ways, e.g. higher weights may be given to more important sensors.

6   Conclusions

We propose a prototypical privacy architecture integrating both pseudonymisation and anonymisation techniques in a Medical IoT system for a sake of protecting data privacy and maximising utility. A distributed pseudonymisated storage using pseudo-random identifier generators is developed to suite the distributed MIoT system as different sensors or IoT devices may be provided by different MIoT providers. On the other side, apparently, medical IoT meta-data like HyperCAT, Web of Things, etc. may become a key enabler to directly or indirectly infer about patient measurements leading to more privacy breaches in such a system. Therefore, we design a query analyser to perform the anonymisation stage and this particular analyser with considering prior knowledge (from meta-data, domain experts, measurement dependence, etc.) must control releasing queries requested by data analysts. In addition, the query analyser may use a quantitative method of disclosing information in reply to the queries, based on a limited privacy budget for a differential privacy model.

One direction of the future work is to tackle different types of measurements, for example, textual or categorical. The differential privacy model can be developed further e.g. addressing the leakage of information through the schedule. The may involve elements of inter-feature binning suggested in [16].

Acknowledgments. This work was supported by Technology Integrated Health Management (TIHM) project awarded to the School of Mathematics and Information Security at Royal Holloway as part of an initiative by NHS England supported by InnovateUK.

References

1. HealthKit — Apple Developer Documentation. https://developer.apple.com/documentation/healthkit
2. W3C Web of Things Architecture. https://w3c.github.io/wot-architecture/#sec-building-blocks-thing-description
3. Aamot, H., Kohl, C.D., Richter, D., Knaup-Gregori, P.: Pseudonymization of patient identifiers for translational research. BMC Med. Inform. Decis. Mak. **13**(1), 75 (2013)
4. Beart, P., Jaffey, T., Davies, J.: Hypercat 3.00 Specification (2016). http://www.hypercat.io/standard.html
5. O'Keefe, C.M.: Protecting confidentiality while making data available for research and policy analysis. http://www.bioss.ac.uk/rsse/2016/15Nov2016RSS_Protecting.pdf
6. Dalenius, T., Reiss, S.P.: Data-swapping: a technique for disclosure control. J. Stat. Plan. Inference **6**(1), 73–85 (1982)
7. Dimitrov, D.V.: Medical internet of things and big data in healthcare. Healthc. Inf. Res. **22**(3), 156–163 (2016)
8. Duncan, G.: Statistical confidentiality: Is synthetic data the answer? (2006). http://slideplayer.com/slide/9374068/, in UCLA IDRE:UCLA
9. Dwork, C., Roth, A.: The algorithmic foundations of differential privacy. Found. Trends Theor. Comput. Sci. **9**(3/4), 211–407 (2014)

10. El Emam, K., Jonker, E., Arbuckle, L., Malin, B.: A systematic review of re-identification attacks on health data. PLOS One **6**(12), 1–12 (2011). Correction published in PLOS ONE 10(4)e0126772
11. Garfinkel, S.L.: NISTIR 8053. de-identification of personal information. Technical report, National Institute of Standards and Technology (NIST), Gaithersburg, MD, USA (2015)
12. HESA: Rounding and suppression to anonymise statistics. https://www.hesa.ac.uk/about/regulation/data-protection/rounding-and-suppression-anonymise-statistics
13. Lin, Z., Hewett, M., Altman, R.B.: Using binning to maintain confidentiality of medical data. In: Proceedings of the AMIA Symposium, pp. 454–458 (2002)
14. Liu, C., Chakraborty, S., Mittal, P.: Dependence makes you vulnerable: differential privacy under dependent tuples. In: Network and Distributed System Security Symposium (2016)
15. Madaan, N., Ahad, M.A., Sastry, S.M.: Data integration in IoT ecosystem: Information linkage as a privacy threat. Computer Law & Security Review (2017)
16. Hadian, M., Liang, X., Altuwaiyan, T., Mahmoud, M.M.E.A.: Privacy-Preserving mHealth data release with pattern consistency. In: IEEE Global Communications Conference, pp. 1–6 (2016)
17. Narayanan, A., Shmatikov, V.: Myths and fallacies of "Personally Identifiable Information". Commun. ACM **53**(6), 24–26 (2010)
18. Neubauer, T., Kolb, M.: An evaluation of technologies for the pseudonymization of medical data. Stud. Comput. Intell. **208**, 47–60 (2009)
19. NOMINET: Privacy guidelines for IoT: what you need to know. https://www.nominet.uk/researchblog/privacy-guidelines-iot-need-know-infographic/
20. Paré, G., Moqadem, K., Pineau, G., St-Hilaire, C.: Clinical effects of home tele-monitoring in the context of diabetes, asthma, heart failure and hypertension: a systematic review. J. Med. Internet Res. **12**(2), e21 (2010)
21. Rahmani, A.M., Gia, T.N., Negash, B., Anzanpour, A., Azimi, I., Jiang, M., Liljeberg, P.: Exploiting smart e-Health gateways at the edge of healthcare internet-of-things: a fog computing approach. Future Gener. Comput. Syst. **78**(2), 641–658 (2018)
22. Reiter, J.: Simultaneous use of multiple imputation for missing data and disclosure limitation. Survey Methodol. **30**, 235–242 (2004)
23. Riazul Islam, S.M., Kwak, D., Kabir, H., Hossain, M., Kwak, K.-S.: A comprehensive survey. IEEE Access **3**, 678–708 (2015)
24. Selander, G., Mani, M., Kumar, S.: RFC 7744 - Use Cases for Authentication and Authorization in Constrained Environments. Technical report, Internet Engineering Task Force (IETF), May 2016. https://tools.ietf.org/html/rfc7744
25. Sweeney, L., Samarati, P.: Protecting privacy when disclosing information: k-anonymity and its enforcement through generalization and suppression. Harvard Data Privacy Lab (1998)
26. Tarouco, L.M.R., Bertholdo, L.M., Granville, L.Z., Arbiza, L.M.R., Carbone, F., Marotta, M., de Santanna, J.J.C.: Internet of Things in healthcare: interoperatibility and security issues. In: 2012 IEEE International Conference on Communication, pp. 6121–6125. IEEE, Junuary 2012
27. Ziegeldorf, J.H., Morchon, O.G., Wehrle, K.: Privacy in the internet of things: threats and challenges. Secur. Commun. Netw. **7**(12), 2728–2742 (2014)

Biomedical and Health Informatics

Telemedicine Collaboration in Cancer Treatment: A Case Study at Brazilian National Cancer Institute

Antônio Augusto Gonçalves[1,2(✉)],
Carlos Henrique Fernandes Martins[1], José Geraldo Pereira Barbosa[2],
Sandro Luís Freire de Castro Silva[1], and Cezar Cheng[1]

[1] Instituto Nacional do Câncer - COAE Tecnologia da Informação,
Rua do Resende 195, Rio de Janeiro 20230-092, Brazil
augusto@inca.gov.br
[2] Universidade Estácio de Sá - MADE,
Avenida Presidente Vargas 642, Rio de Janeiro 200071-001, Brazil

Abstract. Brazil presents a complex scenario in cancer treatment. The occurrences have been growing around 600.000 new cases every year. The development of telemedicine has been a priority to INCA and its importance to the delivery of healthcare services in Brazil is huge. The PACS' deployment allied with the creation of a national network of cancer care institutions were the priorities of INCA's telemedicine project. This environment can remove communication barriers and ensure better collaboration among physicians across the country. The purpose of this article was to study the telemedicine adoption by physicians. The implementation of telemedicine can be considered as a type of disruptive innovation which changes radically the doctor-patient relationship.

Keywords: Telemedicine · Telemedicine collaboration

1 Introduction

Brazil presents a complex scenario in cancer treatment. The occurrences and rates of death have been increasing, around 600.000 cases every year: they are mainly increasing when it comes to prostate cancer in men and breast cancer in women. Research has found that waiting lines for treatment and diagnosis have turned into a routine in many regions of the country, resulting in patients being diagnosed at advanced stages of the disease.

National Cancer Institute (Instituto Nacional de Cancer [INCA]) is the federal agency in charge of setting and implementing assistance, education and cancer prevention policies, with a specific coordination team based in the city of Rio de Janeiro. Since 1997, INCA has made deep changes in its organization, with the purpose of converting its Research Center (RC) into a Technological Development Center (TDC) that is skilled of leading Brazilian efforts towards the development of diagnostic and treatment protocols in the oncology. From this background of improvement, Information and Communication Technologies (ICTs) have played a relevant role in supporting innovation processes in cancer care.

© Springer International Publishing AG, part of Springer Nature 2018
M. Mokhtari et al. (Eds.): ICOST 2018, LNCS 10898, pp. 161–170, 2018.
https://doi.org/10.1007/978-3-319-94523-1_14

Telemedicine is a new medical integrated tool to support medical professionals and healthcare services and will be a part of mainstream medicine, despite its challenges and complexity. It allows medical professionals to make decisions about treatment, prescription medication, diagnosis, and more on a shared basis [1].

The purpose of this research was to study the deployed telemedicine system and its adoption by physicians at Brazilian National Cancer Institute. The deployment of telemedicine can be considered as a type of disruptive innovation in health services. It is located at the border between process innovation and organizational innovation and may be viewed as a case of innovation adoption by INCA.

Telemedicine provides a powerful means to link healthcare specialists between geographically remote locations and to decrease the staff traveling time. Telemedicine use has been a priority to INCA and its importance to the delivery of healthcare services in Brazil is increasing through the consolidation of scientific networks among healthcare specialists.

It is crucial to highlight that cancer services are essentially multidisciplinary, involving primary care doctors, pathologists, oncologists and surgeons [2]. The quality of these services has been affected by the restricted number of qualified oncology professionals and by the scarce number of professional networks specialized in complex procedures that involve cancer treatment. The use of Information and Communication Technologies (ICTs) tools can contribute expressively to integrate these professionals and in the improvement of healthcare services [3].

2 Literature Review

Generally, Telemedicine can be defined as the use of Information and Communications Technologies by all healthcare professionals in order to deliver health care services, where distance is a critical factor [4]. The Federal Medical Council of Brazil defined telemedicine as "the exercise of medicine through the use of interactive methodologies of audiovisual communication and data, with the purpose of assistance, education, and research in Health".

Telemedicine is part of a broader process or chain of care and is not a unique technology. Telemedicine can improve this chain and thus increase the quality and efficiency of healthcare, increasing the fairness and equality of health service delivery, especially in remote areas [5].

The development of telemedicine has radically transformed the medical activities and the doctor-patient interactions with a great impact on the relationship between physicians and patients. Besides, the information exchanged between a physician and other medical specialists should support the decision making [6].

Telemedicine has the potential to take benefits to organizations and patients by enabling appropriate access to cost-effective and high-quality healthcare services. Telemedicine covers the following medical activities [7]:

- Teleconsultation - aims to allow a medical professional to give a remote consultation to a patient and, if necessary, a health professional may be present;

- Tele-expertise - aims at enabling a medical professional to solicit remotely the opinion of one or more other medical specialists who have the special training or skills;
- Telemonitoring - enable a medical professional to interpret at a distance the data necessary for the medical follow-up of a patient and, where appropriate, to take decisions relating to the care of the patient. The recording and transmission of data can be automated or carried out by the patient himself or by a health professional;
- Teleassistance - enable a medical professional to assist remotely another health professional during the performance of an act.

Different barriers continue to challenge widespread telemedicine adoption by healthcare organizations. These barriers include technology, financial, legal/standards, business strategy, and human resources issues. The first step for the development of a successful implementation is evaluating the needs of stakeholders and technical requirements. Telemedicine should be driven by the requests of patients and clinicians rather than technology. Each stakeholder has its specific requirements that should be addressed [8].

Innovation in healthcare is defined as those changes that help healthcare practitioners focus on the patient by helping healthcare professionals work smarter, faster, better and more cost-effectively [9]. According to the Organization for Economic Cooperation and Development, process innovations encompass new or substantially improved techniques, equipment, and software used in process activities. That is the case of the implementation of information and communication technologies (ICT) if they are intended to improve the efficiency and/or quality of the supported process. In turn, management innovations usually deal with people and the organization of work. Management innovations often affect the internal and external infrastructure and create new business models. By their very nature, they are more likely to be disruptive because they represent major changes in the way services are provided.

The processes of innovation generation and innovation adoption differ considerably. Adoption is generally a problem-solving process in which an existing idea is adapted to address the recognized needs and identified problems within an organization [10]. The adoption process emphasizes the integration of the innovation into the organization.

The organizational adoption decision is mainly determined by (i) the characteristics of the innovation as perceived by top management (relative vantage, compatibility, complexity, trialability, observability and uncertainty), (ii) characteristics of the adopting organization (size, structure, innovativeness), and (iii) environmental influences (network externalities, competitive pressures). In turn, the perceived innovation characteristics are influenced by (iv) the innovation supplier marketing efforts (targeting, communication, risk reduction), (v) social network (interconnectedness, network participation) and (iii) environmental influences (network externalities, competitive pressures) [11].

It is important to examine the acceptance of innovations within organizations because, if there is no acceptance among the target group, the desired consequences cannot be realized and the organization may eventually discontinue the intended adoption. At the individual level, innovation acceptance is influenced by (i) the individual attitude towards innovation (beliefs, effects), (ii) social usage (network externalities, peer usage), and (iii) personal dispositional innovativeness. In turn, the individual attitude towards innovation is influenced by social usage, personal dispositional innovativeness, and organizational factors (training, social persuasion, organizational support). Lastly, personal dispositional innovativeness is determined by personal characteristics (demographics, tenure, product experience, personal values) [11].

The efficient implementation of telemedicine depends on the right understanding of the impact of providing a telemedicine service to different areas. Other steps of the implementation plan such as developing a care services plan, developing a business plan and related technology must follow the valuation and prioritization of the intervention required, which must lead to improving the effectiveness, efficiency, and quality of care delivered by the healthcare system [12].

Despite the slow acceptance, the adoption of telemedicine into health services has been effective. The evaluation of successful cases may improve future applications. Inefficiency still exists in majority healthcare services and it is necessary to understand how to overcome those inefficiencies using innovation. The stakeholders' perceptions of the benefits of the innovation, the consensus among participants and their interactions can positively influence the innovative process [13].

Collaboration is essential for physicians and other healthcare professionals involved in telemedicine protocols so that everyone is responsible for his/her actions and decisions in accordance with their areas of complementary skills. Telemedicine is a new approach to decision support that has experienced continuous development and has shown its capacity to aggregate quality to medicine [7].

Telemedicine has played an important role in reducing costs in medicine and at the same time increasing accessibility to health care, particularly to remote and underserved areas. Furthermore, the results from a research conducted to compare telemedicine consultation and inpatient consultation suggest that patients were similarly satisfied with both types of consultation considering physician's competence and his skill in an interpersonal relationship [14].

Telemedicine is a reality and a prospect for chronic diseases and cancer, but require coordinated processes among participating healthcare providers, the training of the participating staff and the adjustment of organizational structures [15].

Telemedicine is projected to be used to facilitate the creation of a more integrated healthcare service, with the aim of increasing access, quality, patient satisfaction, and treatment efficiency in patients with cancer. Cancer-related research and treatment is a long, complex and high-risk process and involves a myriad of organizations [16].

3 Methodology

This study was developed through a qualitative research design to present a descriptive analysis of the deployed telemedicine system and its adoption by physicians at National Cancer Institute (Instituto Nacional de Cancer [INCA]). Telemedicine is expected to support both hospitals and the national oncology network, the implementation of which has been placed in the hands of the INCA. It is intended to facilitate the creation of a more integrated healthcare service, with the aim of increasing access, quality, patient satisfaction, and treatment efficiency in patients with cancer.

This holistic single-case study intends to contribute to the knowledge of organizational phenomena, presenting a contemporary description of the system implemented, through an empirical inquiry, within its context using a variety of data sources and answering the questions what, who, where and how [17]. Data were collected through participant observation, internal documents, and semi-structured interviews. Participant observation is considered an important source for conducting scientific research [18], particularly in health organizations [19]. Twenty semi-structured interviews were conducted with those responsible for the initiation and implementation phases of the telemedicine project. The INCA as a unit of analysis made possible to take advantage of the professional experience of the authors while working at its Information Technology Division. The first author is the INCA's Chief Information Office [CIO] and associate professor at the graduate program in Business Administration that has been conducting this study. The second is a coordinator of the Telemedicine University Network at INCA.

The participants selected for the interviews were physicians, nurses, teaching and research professionals, systems analysts and ICT infrastructure technicians. The data, collected has been analyzed by the categorical content investigation method, triangulating the frequency of terms present in the recorded answers with the observations and data obtained by the researchers. The deployment of telemedicine collaboration in cancer treatment was chosen as a case study in order to exploit the professional knowledge of the authors and due to the fact that INCA is reputably one of the most qualified healthcare organizations to conduct oncology research in Brazil.

4   INCA's Case Study

The proactive usage of telemedicine by physicians plays important role in its successful implementation. They may act as sponsors of telemedicine by deciding whether it is offered or not. Therefore, physicians must actively participate in the acceptance of telemedicine service. On the other hand, physician resistance is common when new information systems are implemented in healthcare organizations. Some professionals may identify innovation process as a risk to their skills and may be unwilling to adopt it [20]. Therefore, to influence professionals to adopt telemedicine, it is important to comprehend how physicians perceive the benefits of telemedicine.

In the course of recent years, INCA has spent approximately $ 1,500,000.00 in Picture Archiving and Communication System (PACS') implementation to make access to patients' radiology exams quicker, easier and safer anywhere in all hospital units. The system has become fully operational in less than one year, with low impact at the hospitals' routine. The high investment in planning and training of physicians and staff members, allied with the sponsorship of the top management, contributed substantially to the success of PACS' deployment.

Before PACS' implementation each imaging modality, like as magnetic resonance imaging (MRI), X-ray and computed tomography (CT) had its specific printer for printing images. The paper-based operation was subject to losses and wastage. The project managers were originally concerned about resistance by physicians and staff members. Hence, the rollout strategy was to start the new process in the radiology division and progressively implementing the modernization in other sectors. Physicians, staff members, and IT technicians were submitted to a training program. The fact that staff members are selected to attending in-company courses with external instructors has contributed to reducing barriers to innovation. The efforts to establish a cooperation environment were decisive. In the end, the resistance to PACS' deployment was small.

The elimination of the necessity for film provided savings of $ 650.0000/year in chemicals, water and film maintenance. All of these savings have resulted in 2.5 years for the investment payback. The new procedure also provided a reduction of 8 million liters of water, approximately 15 thousand liters of chemicals and 52 kg of silver, which has contributed hugely to decrease the adverse effects of the hospital's operation.

The PACS' deployment allied with the creation of a national network of cancer care institutions to provide complementary oncology treatment channels are the priorities of INCA's telemedicine project. This environment can remove communication barriers and ensure better interaction and collaboration among medical programs across country, continent or in the world. The telemedicine approach is vital because healthcare organizations are moving away from the perspective based on paper medical records to one that focuses on electronic medical records.

Telemedicine in Brazil offers considerable prospects for progress, with the potential for integrated remote regions to the major centers of reference in the prevention, diagnosis and treatment areas. The objective of Telemedicine project at INCA was born in face of the institution´s desire to actively engage in the development of policies of the Ministry of Health, especially in the use of Telemedicine in educational, qualification of healthcare professionals, knowledge management and networking initiatives in cancer. The project is to start the activities of telemedicine in INCA for the execution of technical and scientific activities aimed at the control and prevention of cancer that allows the training and the remote monitoring of technicians of the health secretariats and other partner institutions offering professionals support, whether in virtual meetings, discussion of cases or in continuing education. These activities aim to strengthen the qualification process of the professionals involved in national cancer control actions and improve the mechanisms for the management of national cancer control actions using information and communication technologies.

Telemedicine enables the improvement of professional networks where complementarity of knowledge is the bases for achieving efficiency, quality, and safety.

The sharing of information caused by the rollout of telemedicine project at INCA has created the following collaboration environments as shown in Fig. 1:

- Collaboration environment that enables professionals of INCA Prevention Department to share information, train and prepare health professionals from the Health Departments of the States and Municipalities of Brazil in the prevention of the breast and cervical cancers.
- Collaboration model in the analysis of radiology exams where a remotely located radiologist can search for a second opinion of INCA medical specialists. The exchanges of images are made by using PACS functionalities (Picture Archiving

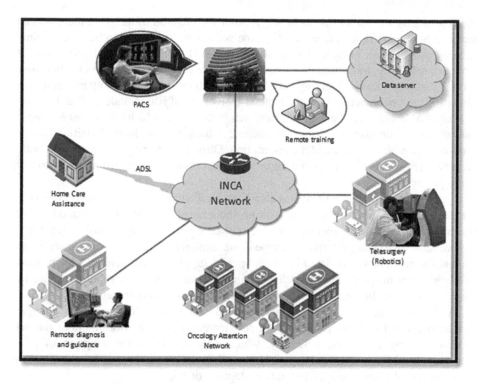

Fig. 1. INCA telemedicine environment

and Communication System) which provide economical storage and efficient access to images from multiple imaging diagnostic modalities such as X-ray, computed tomography (CT), endoscopic image and magnetic resonance imaging (MRI).

- Collaboration model where members of National Cancer Institute's Network have remote meetings which allow for shared decision-making, technical discourse and policy definitions to combat cancer in Latin America and strengthen regional integration.
- Collaboration model where members of INCA share the knowledge and expertise of the institution with those working directly with cancer care, like the live streaming of robotic surgery, with the possibility of interaction among the Inca professionals and other professionals and students.
- Collaboration environment in which robotic surgical procedures performed by professionals of the Inca is transmitted in real time. This environment allows the multidisciplinary discussion of the case, through the interaction of the Inca surgeon with the professionals of other teaching and research institutions.

For the acceptance of telemedicine at an organizational level, it was important to sign a cooperation agreement between INCA and RUTE (Telemedicine University Network), which culminated in the creation in 2011 of a hub of this network at INCA. The fact that the Inca is a member (pole) of RUTE has allowed its professionals to share information with the other 123 poles (Institutions) registered, which has increased the pressure for the use of this technology. After the creation of the polo, there was an increase in interest in telemedicine and some actions in this direction became routine, such as participation in Special Interest Group (GIS), such as cervical and multidisciplinary residency, transmissions of commemorative events such as The October Rose (breast cancer), Tobacco Fighting, etc. In 2017 the Inca was invited to participate in a pilot project in conjunction with the Federal University of Rio Grande do Sul, Bahiana School of Medicine and the National Research Network, in which a low-cost hardware and software solution are being developed, which allows high definition image transmission with low bandwidth consumption. During the testing phase, some robotic surgery transmissions in high-definition were successfully made from INCA to the participating institutions.

The adoption of telemedicine has also been facilitated by INCA's great propensity for innovation. However, within the institute, there are areas more prone than others. In this way, the adoption of telemedicine does not take place homogeneously. Regarding the pressure (marketing efforts) of telemedicine equipment suppliers, only recently an acquisition process was initiated in which several suppliers were invited. This process involved visits hospitals that use telemedicine in Brazil when the solutions could be seen in operation. In some cases, it was possible to test the equipment at INCA.

At the level of the individual, it is noticed that in a general way the younger professionals of INCA are more adept at new technologies. The Institute does not yet provide training in a systematic way, which does not favor the adoption of telemedicine. In addition, a critical mass of telemedicine users has not yet been reached in Brazil that could positively influence the adoption of this tool.

The functional requirements related to INCA telemedicine network are described in Table 1 as follows:

Table 1. Functionalities of INCA telemedicine environment

Process	Module	Description
Transmission of medical procedures like a robotic surgery (live streaming)	Videoconferencing embedded into a telemedicine tool (Multi presence Experimental Program) Telepresence and Tele education	Videoconference as a means of facilitating a comprehensive set of collaboration capabilities
Remote meetings with a share of information and knowledge	Video Conferencing/Web conference/Telepresence	Videoconference/Web conferencing as a means of facilitating a comprehensive set of collaboration capabilities
Sharing of medical data required for an analysis of radiology exams	Picture Archiving and Communication System (PACS) Viewer Digital Imaging and Communications in Medicine (DICOM)	Analysis of radiology exams where a remotely located radiologist can
Remote interaction and exchange (audio/video)	Video conferencing/Web conferencing/Audio conferencing	Means of facilitating a comprehensive set of collaboration capabilities

5   Conclusion

The purpose of this research was to study the deployed telemedicine system and its adoption by physicians at Brazilian National Cancer Institute. Telemedicine in the Brazilian National Cancer Institute has been evolving, mainly due to the adoption of innovative technologies, such as the one developed in conjunction with the National Research Network and the Federal University of Rio Grande do Sul, a low-cost solution that allows the institute to transmit image in 4 K and high definition with low bandwidth consumption. This technology is being tested with foreign institutions for transmission of robotic surgery in real time, with the possibility of interaction between the Inca surgeon and health professionals from other institutions.

Telemedicine, additionally, avoid the detachment of professionals and improves reduction cost with air tickets and communication between remote healthcare professionals and specialists. These are advantages that impact not only on the patient and caregivers but affect all the stakeholders.

Telemedicine will support the Oncologic Attention Network which is the strategic vehicle through which the Brazilian National Cancer Institute (INCA) bases its national integration plan on. Its purpose is to create a partnership between organizations in charge for research and services in the cancer area. This network leads into a cooperation environment which makes possible to congregate doctors, administrators and society segments that represent patients. Its goals are the following: (i) to make the access to information and knowledge easy on all spheres – doctors, hospital administrators and patients; (ii) to establish a community for the practice of research and treatment; (iii) to deploy an integrated *collaboration environment* with easy access to useful information to support clinical and executive decision-making processes.

Telemedicine as a tool of remote patient-physician interaction is growing and virtual consultations with specialists are possible. Potential benefits of telemedicine include improved access to health care, reduced waiting time for appointments, and increased adherence to treatment protocols. In this context, collaboration is very important to physicians and other healthcare specialists. There are also new research challenges and opportunities in the development of collaborative knowledge modeling using telemedicine services.

Nowadays when telemedicine services are becoming widespread and huge amounts of personal data are being available, confidence becomes one of the most important issues in telemedicine services deployment. Familiarity with the technology can help. On the other hand, incidents such as hackers breaking into the system or technological problems may have a deep effect on users' confidence in telemedicine services.

Telemedicine has changed radically the doctor-patient relationship. For that reason, physicians and patients should trust in telemedicine services. Confidence is an important requirement for adoption of innovation and may, thus, be critical to physicians in the decision making about using telemedicine or not.

References

1. Doumbouya, M.B., Kamsu-Foguem, B., Kenfack, H., Foguem, C.: A framework for decision making on teleexpertise with traceability of the reasoning. IRBM **36**(1), 40–51 (2015)
2. O'Brien, D.M., Kaluzny, D.A., Sheps, G.C.: The role of a public-private partnership: translating science to improve cancer care in the community. J. Healthc. Manag. **59**(1), 17–29 (2014)
3. Bardhan, I.R., Thouin, M.F.: Health information technology and its impact on the quality and cost of healthcare delivery. Decis. Support Syst. **55**(2), 438–449 (2013)
4. WHO, a health telematics policy – Report 11–16 December Geneva (1997)
5. Risto, R., Arto, O., David, H.: Assessing telemedicine: a systematic review of the literature. CMAJ **165**(6), 765–771 (2001)
6. Kamsu-Foguem, B.K., Tiako, P., Tiako, F., Fotso, L.P., Foguem, C.: Modeling for effective collaboration in telemedicine. Telemat. Inf. **32**(4), 776–786 (2015)
7. Simon, P., Pellitteri, W.: Le décret français de télémédecine: une garantie pour les médecins. Eur. Res. Telemed. **1**(2), 70–75 (2012)
8. Vlmarlund, V., Le Rouge, C.: Barriers and opportunities to the widespread adoption of telemedicine: a big-country evaluation. Stud. Health Technol. Inf. **192**, 933 (2013)
9. Thakur, R., Hsu, S.H.Y., Fontenot, G.: Innovation in healthcare: issues and future trends. J. Bus. Res. **65**(4), 562–569 (2012)
10. Damanpour, F.: 270 J. Daniel Wischnevsky. J. Eng. Technol. Manag. **23**, 269–291 (2006)
11. Frambach, R.T., Schillewaert, N.: J. Bus. Res. **55**, 163–176 (2002)
12. Armfield, N.R., Edirippulige, S.K., Bradford, N., Smitha, C.: Telemedicine is the cart being put before the horse? Med. J. Aust. **200**(9), 530–533 (2014)
13. Thakur, et al.: J. Bus. Res. **65** 562–569 (2012)
14. Agha, Z., Schapira, R.M., Laud, P.W., Mcnutt, G., Roter, D.L.: Patient satisfaction with physician-patient communication during telemedicine. Telemed. J. EHealth Off. J. Am. Telemed. Assoc. **15**(9), 830e839 (2009)
15. den Berg, Van, Schumann, M., Kraft, K., Hoffmann, W.: Telemedicine and telecare for older patients—a systematic review. Maturitas **73**(2), 94–114 (2012)
16. Goldblatt, E.M., Lee, W.-H.: From bench to bedside: the growing use of translational research in cancer medicine. Am. J. Trans. Res. **2**(1), 1–18 (2010)
17. Cooper, D.R., Schindler, P.S.: Métodos de pesquisa em administração, 7a edn. Bookman, Porto Alegre (2003)
18. Argyris, C., Putnam, R., Smith, D.M.: Action science: action science concepts, methods and skills for research and intervention. Jossey Bass, Nova York (1985)
19. Queiroz, D.T., Vall, J., Souza, J.M.A., Vieira, N.F.C.: Observação participante na pesquisa qualitativa: Conceitos e aplicações na área de saúde. Revista de Enfermagem da UERJ **15**(2), 276–283 (2007)
20. Rho, M.J., Choi, I.Y., Lee, J.: Predictive factors of telemedicine service acceptance and behavioral intention of physicians. Int. J. Med. Inf. **83**, 559–571 (2014)

Evaluating Iris Scanning Technology to Link Data Related to Homelessness and Other Disadvantaged Populations with Mental Illness and Addiction

Cheryl Forchuk[1,2($\boxtimes$)], Lorie Donelle[2], Miriam Capretz[2],
Fatima Bukair[2], and John Kok[2]

[1] Lawson Health Research Institute, London, ON, Canada
cforchuk@uwo.ca
[2] Western University, London, ON, Canada

Abstract. The overall objectives of this research were to assess the functionality of iris scanning technology in a community setting and to evaluate the acceptability to shelter clients of using iris scanning as a form of identification. In order to assess the feasibility of implementing iris scanners in a shelter setting, the research team documented the number of people who agreed to be scanned, the number of people who declined, and the number of successful scans completed. The research team collected 200 scans over the course of 3 visits. A second iris scan was requested of 50 individuals to allow the research team to assess whether the technology accurately identifies someone over a period of time. The results indicate that most people found the technology acceptable, and that the number identifier was consistent over repeated scans.

Keywords: Iris scanning · Biometrics · Public acceptability · Mental illness
Addiction · Homelessness · Identification

1 Introduction

On any given night, there are approximately 35,000 Canadians experiencing homelessness [1]. A conservative estimate of nearly 235,000 Canadians access emergency shelters or sleep on the streets every year [1]. The transient and unstable nature of homelessness makes maintaining belongings challenging, thus, it is common for individuals who are homeless and/or have mental illnesses to lose pieces of identification, such as health cards, birth certificates or social insurance cards. Loss of identification can leave individuals stranded without any access to continued non-urgent care or services such as rehabilitation facilities. Without access to these services, individuals rely on emergency services causing an increasing strain on healthcare dollars. Loss of identification is a barrier faced by homeless people that impair their access to health care [2]. Although Canada has universal healthcare, the majority of homeless people do not possess proof of coverage due to stolen or loss of identification [3]. This loss of identification therefore impedes equitable access to healthcare services and can result in denial of healthcare services. A survey conducted in Toronto stated that 7% of homeless

© Springer International Publishing AG, part of Springer Nature 2018
M. Mokhtari et al. (Eds.): ICOST 2018, LNCS 10898, pp. 171–178, 2018.
https://doi.org/10.1007/978-3-319-94523-1_15

individuals reported having been refused health care services at least once due to loss of their health card [4].

This project aims to explore another means of identification, iris scanning, in hopes of finding an identification strategy that is independent of an individual's ability to recall from memory or need to carry identification, and thus improve their access to care. The overall objectives of the proposed research are:

- To assess the functionality of the iris scanning technology in a community setting and
- To evaluate the acceptability to clients and staff of using iris scanning for client identification.

2   Materials and Methods

Description of the Setting

Staff at a homeless shelter coordinated with the research staff to strategically set up a table and a few chairs in the open foyer to allow for visibility of the research staff and project. Signs asking for volunteers to participate in this project were placed at both door entrances of the homeless shelter. In addition, volunteers spoke to potential participants and directed them to the main table. The foyer was the most ideal place for the research staff to recruit individuals as it was used as the common area to socialize. This allowed curious participants to approach the table and ask questions about the project.

Recruitment

The research team was at the site from 8:00AM to 6:00PM to collect data for three days. This allowed the research team to approach individuals staying at or coming into the shelter at breakfast, lunch and dinner. Individuals at the shelter were either staying there for the month or accessing its services such as the food bank. Individuals entering and exiting the building were approached and informed about the study; 200 participants were recruited by research staff upon full disclosure of the project's objective. Verbal consent was obtained to participate in the study. Of the total participants, 191 agreed to be scanned and interview once, while nine participants agreed for interview only.

The qualitative approach used for this research was hypothesis generating rather than hypothesis testing. This pilot study investigating the use of iris scanning technology among individuals living homeless and with mental illness was exploratory in nature. The research questions guiding this exploratory research include:

1. What are the implementation issues related to deploying iris scanners in a homeless shelter?
2. What are the staff perceptions related to acceptability of the technology?
3. What are the client perceptions related to acceptability of the technology?
4. What ethical issues are identified related to the use of iris scanning?
5. What policy issues are identified related to the use of iris scanning?

Instruments

A researcher-developed questionnaire was generated that inquired about participants' gender, previous use or not of the scan, their perception of iris scan and whether they prefer iris scan or ID card like health card for service delivery. Iris scanning was performed using equipment called Seek Avenger from Crossmatch Technologies and was used during the three days' study on site at the homeless shelter.

Data Analysis A research assistant entered the raw data into a Microsoft Excel spreadsheet on a desktop computer for analysis. For quantitative analysis, the research team used SPSS Statistics Software to generate descriptive statistics. Another research assistant conducted qualitative analyses by applying a thematic grouping of responses, that is, identifying recurrent themes and opinions expressed by the participants.

3   Results

The findings yielded an overall greater degree of acceptability of iris scanning as a form of identification. As established in the research plan, 200 participants were successfully recruited; 154 males and 54 of those were female; 73% and 27%, respectively. Of the total participants, 191 agreed to be scanned and interviewed while 9 participants agreed to an interview only (Table 1). Of the 191 who agreed to a scan, 50 agreed to complete a second scan. Reasons for agreeing to scanning included pursuit of safe reliable ID, curiosity/inclination for new technology, support research and good cause, or merely being approached by research assistants. Those not scanned but interviewed provided the following reasons; not having enough information to decide, suspicious and untrusting of the capacity of the system to safeguard and manage the information being collected.

One hundred and sixty-seven (87%) of the 191 (Table 1) scanned also answered the question on their preferred form of identification. Of the total 167, 146 (87%) preferred Iris Scanning while 21 (13%) preferred an ID card for identification. Those that enrolled for a second scan had the same reason for agreeing as those scanned first time. The purpose of the second scan was to authenticate the first scan. As a result, 49 out of 50 first and second scans were matched; that is 98% accuracy while the remaining 2% was due to the participant's eye becoming watery. It was noted in the fieldnotes that when participants' eyes got teary, the scanner was not able to generate the same code as the first scan. This was fixed by requesting the participants to blink between scans to allow for a better authentication. Iris scan authentication was successful in 182 participants out of 188 (Table 1).

Table 1. Iris scanning – descriptive statistics (n = 200)

	Frequency (%)
Gender	
Male	146 (73.0%)
Female	54 (27.0%)
Previously used iris scanner	

(continued)

Table 1. (*continued*)

	Frequency (%)
Yes	2 (1.0%)
No	198 (99.0%)
Agreed to scan	
Yes	191 (95.5%)
No	9 (4.5%)
Prefer iris scan or ID card for service (n = 167)	
Iris scan	146 (87.4%)
ID card	21 (12.6%)
Had second scan (n = 187)	
Yes	50 (26.7%)
No	137 (73.3%)
Iris scan worked (n = 188)	
Yes	182 (96.8%)
No	6 (3.2%)

Source: SPSS Data analysis tool,
Lawson Health Research Institute

To arrive at the encompassing themes identified below, the research team analysed the participants' responses from the qualitative questionnaire (Table 2). Those who agreed because of money provided or a free coffee card were grouped under "Incentive". Responses that indicated acceptance because they were asked, peer/self-motivated, helping a good cause, or supported the research were grouped under "Help research/good cause". Participants that indicated that because they kept losing ID cards, think that Iris Scanning is a safe form of identification, can't lose it or because of health services and housing were group under "Safe and fast identification".

Table 2. Acceptability and functionality of iris scanning ID method

Question	Answer	#	%
1. Did you use the iris scanner just now?	Yes	191	95.5
	No	9	4.5
2. Reason for agreeing to scanning	Curiosity	50	26.2
	Told to do it/Just because/Don't know	40	20.9
	Free coffee card	38	19.9
	Research/Want to help	18	9.4
	Heard about it/Wanted to do it	16	8.4
	Identification/Security	15	7.9
	Eye problems	7	3.7
	Other	7	3.7

(*continued*)

Table 2. (*continued*)

Question	Answer	#	%
3. Would you prefer an iris scan or an ID card like a health card for service?	Iris Scan	146	87.4
	ID Card	21	12.6
	Missing	33	
4. Why would you prefer an iris scan?	ID cards get lost/Don't need to carry ID card around	25	32.1
	Fast and easy	22	28.2
	Interesting/Cool	12	15.4
	Better security	8	10.3
	Don't know	1	1.3
	Other	10	12.8
	Missing	68	

4 Discussion

The high percentage of participants preferring Iris Scanning as a form of identification (87%) is consistent with their status of homelessness, mental health or substance abuse. Participants want a reliable way of identification as it is required to access services such as healthcare, housing and related utilities and a sense of societal belonging. The 13% that objected to iris scanning was due to either fear of being tracked by government agencies (police or security), information falling in criminal hands for misuse, or simply for the lack of system capacity to manage the data. These concerns are not unique to the demographics targeted by this pilot study but also reflected in other international studies [5, 6].

A 98% accuracy rate for second scan authentication of the participants' identity points to the evidence echoed in the literature indicating that Iris Scanning is a reliable method of Biometric identification. The results of our study were almost identical to a study conducted by Latman & Herb [7]. In that study, an iris recognition system was evaluated in a sample of 277 participants in the United States for accuracy and reliability. The system was able to enroll, match 1:1 and verify individuals often within 3 s in the first round [7]. The demographic characteristics, room lighting conditions and eye conditions did not modify the results. Although eye condition did not modify the results in other studies, it was noted in this study that teary eyes did in fact influence the code generated by the scanner. Participants who had teary eyes between first and second scan had a different code generated for them, this was due to the tears forming a layer on the iris and thus not scanning properly. To confirm that teary eyes were in fact the reason behind the mismatched code, participants were asked to blink a few times and had their iris scanned again. The third code matched the first code, thus, enabling us to recommend to participants to blink a few times between scans.

The implication of this evidence is that if a reliable and sustainable identification system were to be implemented in this group of demographics, Iris scanning could be a viable and potentially successful option. In addition, implementation of iris scanning could be cost effective within this population given the frequency of ID card loss at a rate of 10% a year and the running of weekly ID clinics held at an intercommunity health centre and at an Ontario Works location. Of course, public fears and perception of surveillance, inability of the system and safety of information must be addressed before implementation. According to Jain et al. [8] "by using biometrics, it is possible to confirm or establish an individual's identity based on "who she is," rather than by "what she possesses" (e.g., an ID card) or "what she remembers" (e.g., a password)" (p.4). In addition, biometric identification has to meet four requirements: universal, distinctive, invariant with time and be measured quantitatively. For it to be used, it must be acceptable to the client, fast and accurate, and cannot succumb to fraudulent means [8].

Challenges

In conducting a further literature review, we looked at peer-reviewed journal articles published from year 2000 to the present date. We used the following terms "Iris scanning Technology, identification and public acceptance". We found 150 peer reviewed journal articles from which we selected 10 relevant articles to our research.

According to Martin and Donovan [5], when the UK Government tried to implement a nationwide National Identification Scheme based on biometric technology (iris scanning, finger printing, face recognition), they assumed that the public would accept the proposal because the technology was straightforward. Nevertheless, it emerged that the term public was not a unitary one but one of diversity, where there were a group of intended users who were accepting, while other members of the public who were knowledgeable of the proposed technology were a vocal opponent. The key factor that led to the UK Government ID plan failure was the charged political environment in which the discourse took place as the technology would appear to pervade the government's relationship with the public, in addition to opposition from a knowledgeable research team at the London School of Economics and a pressure group known as No2ID [5]. Further, the authors note that the discourses in enacting public acceptability were problematic due to intertwined issues such as rights, autonomy and citizenship, and that biometric technology was confusing which limited the ability to discuss the Scheme in great detail.

Moody [6] tried to shed light on public perception and acceptance of biometric identification by first comparing the types that are currently in use by many organizations for different purposes. Fingerprint Scanning is either performed by silicone or ultrasound scanners but results can be affected by skin dryness or dirt and grime build up on the reader. Nevertheless, it was the most accepted by the respondent as form of identification to access an Automated Teller Machine (ATM), computer log on, and office access [8]. On the other hand, Moody [6] reported that Iris scanning technology, though more accurate, was the least understood and least accepted. The public feared invasion of privacy and identity theft. Moody [6] concluded by recommending that, regardless of the use, the public should be involved in the process through education and information dissemination about biometric technology.

As recurring themes in the literature, as well as this study's findings, the public perceived that biometric technology could be used for unintended purposes. Participants noted that they feared being watched by security or police, information falling into the wrong hands and lack of technological capacity to for data management and integrity. Brown [9] examined comparative policy research of United States and China on Healthcare Data Protection and Technology acceptance. In both countries, despite differing political cultures, their governments were keen supporters of using Health Information Technology to improve quality of care. In addition, support for sharing information to address public health matters by authorized health personnel was accomplished through enacting laws such as the Patient Protection and Affordable Care Act of 2010 in the United States and the passing of personal data guidelines (although not enforceable) in China [9].

According to Brown [9] the type of biometric technology used varied according to the end user situation; per example in a South Bronx clinic, they preferred iris scanning ID for identification because many of their clients had the same first and last name, and because finger printing was associated with criminal activity and police [9]. A medical insurer in Florida introduced iris scanning to prevent fraud, whilst in China iris scanning is frequently used in miners' identification because fingerprint scanning was not suitable in the mining environment [9].

5 Conclusions

Based on current qualitative and descriptive statistics as well as a literature review, Iris scanning is a safe and reliable form of identification that can withstand fraudulent activity among a group of community-based participants accessing homeless shelters. It was acceptable for most of the participants studied in this pilot. In addition, if implemented it can be cost-effective within the homeless population given the frequency of ID card replacement and the lack of access to non-emergency health care services, the latter of which leads to an increase in emergency department usage and therefore funding. In providing a quality-assured iris recognition program, individuals experiencing homelessness can gain access to services that they may not have been able to access previously. Full acceptability of biometrics technology within health care could support quality of care and act on public health matters. This can happen by combining enforceable legislation with public awareness to allay fears of their personally identifiable data falling into criminal hands, and assure the public that third parties will not have access to their information and the system is capable of managing electronic medical records.

Acknowledgments. Would like to acknowledge the Salvation Army for facilitating the research environment. Also, we appreciate the commitment of the research assistants for data collection and auditing to make sure the quality of research is assured. Finally, we would like to thank the participants for their voluntary participation. We would also like to acknowledge the granting agency for making the funding available.

Conflicts of Interest: The authors declare no conflict of interest.

References

1. Gaetz, S., Dej, E., Richter, T., Redman, M.: The State of Homelessness in Canada 2016. Canadian Observatory on Homelessness Press, Toronto (2016)
2. Stark, L.R.: Barriers to health care for homeless people. In: Jahiel, R.I. (ed.) Homelessness: a Prevention-Oriented Approach. Johns Hopkins University Press, Baltimore (1992)
3. Hwang, S.W., Windrim, P.M., Svoboda, T.J., Sullivan, W.F.: Physician payment for the care of homeless people. CMAJ **163**, 170–171 (2000)
4. Crowe, C., Hardill, K.: Nursing research and political change: the street health report. Can Nurse. **89**, 21–24 (1993)
5. Martin, A.K., Donovan, K.P.: New surveillance technologies and their publics: a case of biometrics. Public Underst. Sci. **24**, 842–857 (2015)
6. Moody, J.: Public perceptions of biometric devices: the effect of misinformation on acceptance and use. IISIT. **1**, 753–761 (2004)
7. Latman, N.S., Herb, E.: A field study of the accuracy and reliability of a biometric iris recognition system. Sci. Justice **53**, 98–102 (2013)
8. Jain, A.K., Ross, A., Prabhakar, S.: An introduction to biometric recognition. IEEE Trans. Circuits Syst. Video Technol. **14**, 4–20 (2004)
9. Brown, C.L.: Health-care data protection and biometric authentication policies: comparative culture and technology acceptance in china and in the united states. Rev. Policy Res. **29**, 141–159 (2012)

Missing Information Prediction in Ripple Down Rule Based Clinical Decision Support System

Musarrat Hussain[1], Anees Ul Hassan[1], Muhammad Sadiq[1],
Byeong Ho Kang[2], and Sungyoung Lee[1(✉)]

[1] Ubiquitous Computing Lab, Department of Computer Science and Engineering,
Kyung Hee University, Seoul, South Korea
{musarrat.hussain,anees,sadiq,sylee}@oslab.khu.ac.kr
[2] School of Engineering and ICT, University of Tasmania, Hobart, Australia
byeong.kang@utas.edu.au

Abstract. Clinical Decision Support System (CDSS) plays an indispensable role in decision making and solving complex problems in the medical domain. However, CDSS expects complete information to deliver an appropriate recommendation. In real scenarios, the user may not be able to provide complete information while interacting with CDSS. Therefore, the CDSS may fail to deliver accurate recommendations. The system needs to predict and complete missing information for generating appropriate recommendations. In this research, we extended Ripple Down Rules (RDR) methodology that identifies the missing information in terms of key facts by analyzing similar previous patient cases. Based on identified similar cases, the system requests the user about the existence of missing facts. According to the user's response, the system resumes current case and infers the most appropriate recommendation. Alternatively, the system generates an initial recommendation based on provided partial information.

Keywords: Information prediction · Ripple down rules
Clinical decision support system

1 Introduction

1.1 Background

Clinical Decision Support System (CDSS) are extensively used in healthcare to provide domain-specific decisions about the patient at the required time. It has an imperative role in improving patient care and reducing the chances of error in decision making by assisting physicians in the decision [1]. Domain experts' knowledge is transformed into a computer interpretable format, which is utilized by the system for taking intelligent decisions. Most of existing CDSS [2, 3] model experts' knowledge in if-then-else rules format which is an effective method of knowledge representation.

Existing CDSS generate recommendations based on input symptoms by reasoning over the available rules in the knowledge base [4, 5]. System's decision rely relies on users' provided information and complete information results in the appropriate recommendation. However, users may not be able to provide complete information while

© Springer International Publishing AG, part of Springer Nature 2018
M. Mokhtari et al. (Eds.): ICOST 2018, LNCS 10898, pp. 179–188, 2018.
https://doi.org/10.1007/978-3-319-94523-1_16

interacting with the system. The user may consider some information as irrelevant while that may play an imperative role in decision making. Therefore, the system needs to be smart enough to facilitate users for providing complete information. In order to provide a most appropriate decision, the system should predict missing information and ask the user to provide that information. Alternatively, the system generates an initial recommendation based on provided information.

Apart from the user input, knowledge base also has a pivotal role in recommendation generation. The systems' intelligence usually depends on the knowledge evolution. The knowledge evolves with the passage of time because of new research and findings. The new knowledge needs to be adopted by CDSS to generate right decisions. Most of the existing systems are one-shot systems and uses machine learning approaches for generating knowledge base. The primary drawback of these systems is this that a human expert cannot update the knowledge base. For knowledge evolution, one-shot systems need to rebuild the model with a complete cycle of verification and validation process. Furthermore, it cannot guarantee preservance of model accuracy.

In this study, we used Ripple Down Rules (RDR) for knowledge storing and as a validation methodology, which stores experts' knowledge in a form of tree structure consists of nodes and branches [6, 7]. Each node in RDR tree stores a complete if-then rule and represents a particular classification class. While branches of the tree represent parent-child relations in the RDR tree. The sequence of rules (nodes) matched with a case in RDR tree is known as path of the case. RDR model stores experts' knowledge in comprehensible format (tree-structured), understandable by machine and human experts [7]. Human experts can add their knowledge to the system without the involvement of knowledge engineers. RDR adapts new knowledge by extending existing knowledge (add a new child or new branch to the RDR tree) without affecting the previous one which preserves the previous accuracy. It works as a real-time verification and validation process. All the knowledge is verified at the time of updating the knowledge base. RDR uses forward chaining inference mechanism that matches the current case/input facts with the root node and traverse child nodes of all matched rules at each level until no match is found. Finally, the last matched rule result is presented to the user as a recommendation. RDR has many benefits as compared to other models including real-time knowledge validation and verification. However, it also completely relies on user input. If a user misses some of the key information during interaction with the system, it may generate an inappropriate recommendation.

1.2 Proposed System Overview

The proposed system extends the RDR mechanism to facilitate users for providing complete information by prediction of missing information in the user's input. Extended RDR identifies and predict missing information by analyzing similar previous patient cases. The system compared facts and attributes of the similar previos patient cases with the current case and find the missing facts in the input case. The system asks questions for identified missing information from the user to get the final decision. However, if the user is unable to provide the system identified missing information the system generates an initial recommendation for provided partial information. The complete detail of the proposed mechanism and its benefit will be described in the upcoming sections.

The rest of the paper is structured as follows. In Sect. 2, we describe the existing work related to Question/Answer based RDR systems. In Sect. 3, we describe the proposed methodology. Section 4 describes a case study. Section 5 describes results and Sect. 6 concludes the study.

2 Related Work

The history of CDSS begins from 1960 and have made colossal progression with the ascent of innovation [8]. It still needs to fulfill day-to-day requirements and expectations. The proposed approach is motivated by conversational systems; therefore, the related work described below is with the domain of general-purpose conversational system rather than CDSS. The commonalities and differences of proposed technique and techniques of existing systems are depicted in Table 1.

E.M. Glina et al. [9] proposed a conversational system, which constructs an arbitrary search tree from parts of the active database and searches node incrementally based on user interaction with the system. The last node returns the result of each step as the conversation response and it logged the complete path followed by the conversation. On users' new request, the system matches current node's children, if no child matched, the system traverses the tree in the backward direction and search in other child nodes. If the system is not able to answer a query, it records that query and later asks domain expert to provide a response. In this way, the system evolves the knowledge base by domain experts' continuous input. The primary drawback of this system is, it totally relies on users' input. The system has no capability to predict the missed information during the user interaction.

Table 1. Comparison of the proposed approach with existing approaches.

Approaches	Interactive	Path tracking	Case preservance	Predict missing information
E.M. Glina	No	Yes	Yes	No
D.Q. Nguyen (KBQAS)	Yes	No	No	No
Q.T. Gia (IRDR)	Yes	No	No	No
Proposed	Yes	Yes	Yes	Yes

D.Q. Nguyen et al. [10] proposed a question answering system named KBQAS having answer retrieval mechanism for asked questions, which are mapped with ontological rules. If the system does not match a concept, then it provides the extracted concept to the user for its clarification. After clarification of concepts, the system maps those concepts with the question format to get an appropriate answer. The limitation of this system is, it processes each question in isolation and extracts concepts from a single question, which may not be beneficial and may lose contextual information. Therefore, the system should consider, all other related questions to extract related concepts for high accuracy in rules mapping to give an appropriate answer.

Q.T. Gia [11] proposed an Interactive RDR (IRDR) that enhanced the RDR capabilities by asking questions for more information and the users each response is considered as a new case. Existing IRDR simulation studies have been done, however, due to the poor results of the technique it has not been published. The main reason for poor results of IRDR is the lack of case status preservation. In each iteration, the system considers the input case as a new case, which increases the computational cost and gives answers with low accuracy.

Mostly the existing systems focus on accurate mapping of current case with the rules of the knowledge bases. These existing systems except IRDR are considered as a one-shot learning and execution systems. One shot system needs to be trained on huge data before using. In execution, the user query from the system and the system responses accordingly. These systems have limited capability to deal with the input queries having incomplete information. If the users miss some information during an interaction, the existing systems are not able to detect the missing information and to generate new questions on the fly to ask the user. Therefore, the existing systems generate results based on provided information, which may cause produced poor results.

3   Proposed Methodology

This work is the part of our current ongoing project so-called Intelligent Medical Platform (IMP)[1]. IMP aims to utilize artificial intelligence and Big Data technologies for providing proactive and predictive healthcare services to improve public health. In this research, we focused on two major issues of the existing CDSS and recommender systems. First, the proposed system predicts missing information by analyzing similar cases and ask users to provide them for delivering most appropriate recommendation. Secondly, it preserves the current status of the user case, and resumes it on new information to generate a recommendation in the appropriate context and reduces the recommendation generation time. To achieve the aforementioned goals, the proposed system is conceived with three major components: *Case Analyzer*, *Question Moderator*, and *Frequent Path Miner* as depicted in Fig. 1. The system has two repositories *RDR Rules Base* and *Frequent Paths* repository. The details of these components are described in following subsections.

---

[1] http://imprc.cafe24.com/.

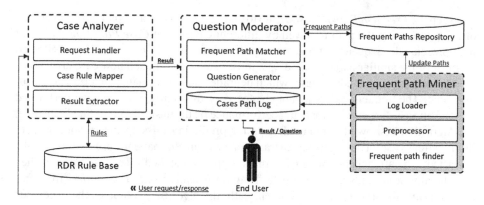

Fig. 1. Proposed system architecture

3.1 Case Analyzer

Case Analyzer is devised for effective manipulation of user request considered as a new case. It consists of three subcomponents. The subcomponent *Request Handler* formulates the case and extracts available facts from the case. *Case Rule Mapper* module starts mapping extracted facts from the root node of RDR tree with the rule condition at each node. If rule condition is matched with the case facts, then it checks the child nodes of that node until no further rule matched. The *Result Extractor* extracts last matched rule result, considered as candidate recommendation. The candidate recommendation of the matched rule along with the case information is sent to *Question Moderator* to find missing information in the current case.

3.2 Question Moderator

Question Moderator is needed to increase the system accuracy by considering similar cases to generate a final recommendation. *Question Moderator* matches the current case path followed in RDR tree with similar cases path known as *Frequent Path*. The objective of this path matching is to find missing information based on a most used path from *Frequent Path Repository* and to generate an appropriate recommendation. If the frequent path is different from the current case path, then *Question Moderator* asks questions for the information required to follow the same path as a frequent path. On the users' response to the question, the current case state is resumed to process the case in the appropriate context and reduced the execution time. Additionally, it tracks the path followed by each case and logs the path information in the *Cases Path Log* repository for finding a frequent path in RDR tree.

3.3 Frequent Path Miner

Different cases follow diverse branches of RDR tree based on associated facts. Therefore, *Frequent Path Miner* module is devised to find path followed pattern in RDR tree and keep the *Frequent Path Repository* up to date. It finds a frequent path for each branch of RDR tree using the path followed by different cases from *Case Path Log*. Frequent path presents the sequence of node in a specific branch of RDR tree that are followed by most of the similar patients. Finding a most used path for each new case arrival is a time consuming and a tedious task, which degrades the performance in terms of execution time. The frequent path may not change very frequently, therefore we performed this task in an offline manner for better performance on the basis of a predefined schedule.

Algorithm 1 shows the required steps for predicting missing information in user input/patient case. The algorithm extracts facts from the patient case at line 1. The extracted facts are matched with RDR rules to find a matched rule. Based on matched rule the algorithm finds a frequent path from the *Frequent Path Repository* (frequent-Paths). Using the information of frequent path, the algorithm computes the difference between provided facts and facts from the matched rule and considers as missing information. The missing facts are added to the patient case according to users' acknowledgment, which leads to the most appropriate result. The advantages of our approach are interpreting user query in the given context, considering other similar cases, asking for missing information and preserving the current case status.

Algorithm 1. Missing Information Prediction

Input: *patientCase, FrequentPaths*

Output: *facts #input + resolved missing facts*

1.   *facts ← extractFacts(patientCase);*

2.   *mappedRule ← relatedRule(facts);*

3.   *frequentPath←frequentPath(mappedRule, frequentPaths);*

4.   *predictedRule ← frequentPath.getRule();*

5.   *missingFacts ← difference (predictedRule.Facts, facts);*

6.   **for each** *fact* **in** *missingFacts* **do**

7.   *acknowledged ← forwardToUser(fact);*

8.   **if** *acknowledge, do* **then**

9.   *facts.add(fact);*

10. **end if**

11. **end**

---

4   Realization of the Proposed Methodology

To realize the proposed methodology, a diabetes diagnosis scenario is described. The example scenario consists of 7 rules, as shown in Fig. 2. We consider a patient case with facts Hyperursis, Thirst, Unexplained Weight Loss and HbA1c = 6.7. The steps required for the methodology are given as follows.

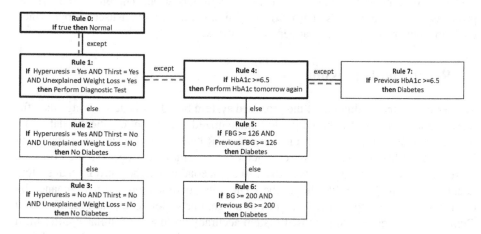

Fig. 2. Partial diabetes knowledge representation using RDR

4.1 Initial Recommendation Generation

The initial recommendation will be generated based on the aforementioned provided input. *Case Analyzer* starts matching the given facts with the rules stored in *RDR Rule Base*. First, it would check the Rule 0 stored at the root node, known as a default rule of the RDR tree. The condition of the rule satisfied therefore, it checks the next level i.e. Rule 1 and continue checking until no further rules' conditions satisfied. For the provided facts, Rule 4 is the last satisfied rule represented by bold boxes in Fig. 2. The system generates "Perform HbA1c tomorrow again" as the initial recommendation. This information is passed to *Question Moderator* for analysis and finding missing information.

4.2 Question Moderation

Question Moderator uses the generated initial recommendation matched rule path and *Frequent Path* to predict missing information. The frequent path for Rule 4 is up to Rule 7 as shown by dotted line in Fig. 2. The *Question Moderator* finds required facts for Rule 7 that are not provided as an initial input. In this example, "Previous HbA1c" is detected as a missing fact. Therefore, the system asks the user about the existence of "Previous HbA1c" and would expect a response from the user. Users' subsequent response would facilitate the system in order to generate a final recommendation.

4.3 Final Recommendation Generation

Starting from the previously fired rule (Rule 4) the users' response is mapped with child rules of Rule 4. As depicted in Fig. 2, most of the patients have "Previous HbA1c" value, but the user was not considering it as important fact but only rely on "Current HbA1c" value. While taking an appropriate decision "Previous HbA1c" value has a key role. If the user provides Pervious HbA1c value greater than 6.5, Rule 7 will be fired and the system will respond "Diabetes" as a final recommendation. Therefore, the system produces a more accurate result by predicting missing information in users' input, which leads to a better decision for treatment and diagnosis.

5   Result and Discussion

We performed the evaluation of the proposed system based on systems' usage data for three weeks. The result is based on 300 anonymized real diabetic patients' data. The results achieved compared with conventional RDR based CDSS system, as depicted in Fig. 3. At the first week, both systems achieved accuracy 86% because the proposed system does not have *Frequent Path* data. At the second week, the conventional system accuracy increased to 86.7% due to the RDR rules modification and maintenance by domain experts. Based on the first week of usage, our system calculates the *Frequent Path*, which increased the proposed system accuracy up to 87%. Similarly, after third week the accuracy of the conventional system increased to 87% due to rules modifications. However, our proposed system accuracy increased to 87.5% because of *Frequent Path* updation which leads to accurate prediction of missing facts and increased overall system accuracy.

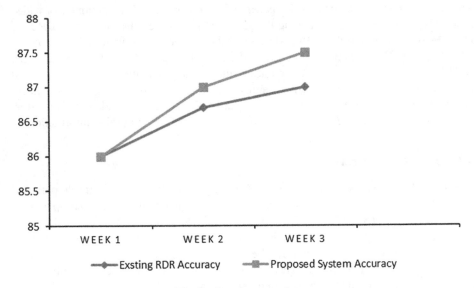

Fig. 3. Result comparison

The preliminary result of three weeks concluded that the proposed system will have greater effects and achievement in improving system accuracy with the systems' usage and passage of time.

One of the major challenge faced is long waiting time for getting user response. The system waits for the answer of the query until user response. If a user doesn't respond for a long time, the system will remain in waiting state. To overcome this issue, we set 2 min waiting time as a threshold time. When the user is not able to answer in 2 min, the system gives a primitive result based on the initial values.

6 Conclusion and Future Work

The proposed system considers similar cases to give the appropriate recommendation with better performance and accuracy. Additionally, it is capable of generating primitive recommendations based on the initial incomplete information. The similar cases help in finding missing information and the system asks questions for those missing information to reach the appropriate recommendation. The advantages of the proposed technique include accurately predicting missing information by considering similar cases, interacting with the user for missing information, delivering most appropriate recommendations and reducing execution time. In the future, we will evaluate and enhance the proposed system to deploy in different hospitals for timely decision making in diagnosis and treatment.

Acknowledgments. This research was supported by Basic Science Research Program through the National Research Foundation of Korea (NRF) funded by the Ministry of Science, ICT & Future Planning (2011-0030079) and by Institute for Information & communications Technology Promotion (IITP) grant funded by the Korea government (MSIT) (No. 2017-0-00655).

References

1. Wright, A., Sittig, D.F., Ash, J.S., Sharma, S., Pang, J.E., Middleton, B.: Clinical decision support capabilities of commercially-available clinical information systems. J. Am. Med. Inform. Assoc. **16**, 637–644 (2009)
2. Caballero-Ruiz, E., García-Sáez, G., Rigla, M., Villaplana, M., Pons, B., Hernando, M.E.: A web-based clinical decision support system for gestational diabetes: automatic diet prescription and detection of insulin needs. Int. J. Med. Inf. **102**, 35–49 (2017)
3. Jung, H., Yang, J., Woo, J.-I., Lee, B.-M., Ouyang, J., Chung, K., Lee, Y.: Evolutionary rule decision using similarity based associative chronic disease patients. Clust. Comput. **18**, 279–291 (2015)
4. Kemppinen, J., Korpela, J., Elfvengren, K., Polkko, J.: Clinical decision support system for opioid substitution therapy. In: 2015 48th Hawaii International Conference on System Sciences (HICSS), pp. 3054–3063. IEEE (2015)
5. Zhou, Q.: A clinical decision support system for metabolism synthesis. In: International Conference on Computational Intelligence and Natural Computing, 2009, CINC 2009, pp. 323–325. IEEE (2009)
6. Gaines, B.: Induction of ripple-down rules. In: Proceedings of the 5th Australian Joint Conference on Artificial Intelligence. World Scientific (1992)
7. Hyeon, J., Oh, K.-J., Kim, Y.J., Chung, H., Kang, B.H., Choi, H.-J.: Constructing an initial knowledge base for medical domain expert system using induct RDR. In: 2016 International Conference on Big Data and Smart Computing (BigComp), pp. 408–410. IEEE (2016)

8. Hussain, M., Khattak, A.M., Khan, W.A., Fatima, I., Amin, M.B., Pervez, Z., Batool, R., Saleem, M.A., Afzal, M., Faheem, M.: Cloud-based Smart CDSS for chronic diseases. Health Technol. **3**, 153–175 (2013)
9. Glina, E.M., Kang, B.H.: Conversation system with state information. University of Tasmania (2009)
10. Nguyen, D.Q., Nguyen, D.Q., Pham, S.B.: Ripple Down Rules for question answering. Semantic Web, pp. 1–22 (2015)
11. Richards, D.: Two decades of ripple down rules research. Knowl. Eng. Rev. **24**, 159–184 (2009)

Study of Annotations in e-health Domain

Khalil Chehab[1]([⊠]), Anis Kalboussi[2,3], and Ahmed Hadj Kacem[1]

[1] ReDCAD Research Laboratory and Faculty of Economics and Management,
University of Sfax, Sfax, Tunisia
khalilisig@gmail.com, ahmed.hadjkacem@fsegs.rnu.tn
[2] Higher Institute of Computer Science and Management,
University of Kairouan, Kairouan, Tunisia
anis.kalboussi@isigk.rnu.tn
[3] ReDCAD Research Laboratory, University of Sfax, Sfax, Tunisia

Abstract. The efforts to computerize the medical record of a patient began in 1990. In the documents of this record, the healthcare professional practices the annotation activity. Most medical annotation systems are made to perform a specific task. As a result, we have dozens of medical annotation system that we sneak a fragmented image in the absence of generic classification for these. In this article, we try to present a unified image by classifying 30 medical annotation systems based on 5 generic criteria and the features offered by them. From these two classifications, we present our observation and the limits of these systems.

Keywords: e-heath · Annotation · Classification · Health record
Annotation system · Healthcare professionals

1 Introduction

The paper annotation practice is very common. Indeed, during our reading we are all accustomed to scribble our comments in a margin of document, to highlight, to circle sections, to paste post-it…, which aims to enrich and add value to information [40, 43]. Annotation is a central practice in many professions: teachers annotate copies of students; professors exchange annotated documents during their work; Engineers co build engines by annotating sketches of plans to make them evolve, doctors comment on patient folder, etc. [39, 44].

Annotations, thus, take various forms and are used for different functions [28]. Moreover, computerization of documents offers us new perspectives to use these annotations (indexation, creation, document, assistance, etc.) which do not exist on paper [41].

In this article, we focus on the annotations and annotative activities of healthcare professionals (**hp**) and we focus on annotations produced either in public hospitals or in private sector.

Since the majority of documents of the hospitalized patient's document are standardized forms, and as they are different from one specialized physician to another, the creators of this document impose rules of reading and writing which; favor a good

© Springer International Publishing AG, part of Springer Nature 2018
M. Mokhtari et al. (Eds.): ICOST 2018, LNCS 10898, pp. 189–199, 2018.
https://doi.org/10.1007/978-3-319-94523-1_17

resolution of the health problems, enable the improvement of the quality of healthcare and the collaboration between healthcare professionals. Integration of informal information, which does not exist on the structured paper document, is widely used. These annotations can be a potential source of information.

The digital annotative activity is carried out by systems that are specially developed to annotate medical documents and which are reserved to the healthcare professionals. The development of these systems appeared since 1998 with the hospitexte [32] system. There are dozens of medical annotation systems but most of them focus on the field of bioinformatics and medical imaging.

The purpose of the article is to provide a unified idea about the annotation systems used by healthcare professionals. This panoramic view is based on a classification of thirty (30) annotation systems developed in literature over the past twelve years by industry and researchers. This organization of annotation systems is built firstly on the basis of five generic criteria [31]: standard annotation (computational/cognitive); category of annotation system (application/plug-in/website); type of annotative activity (manual/semi-automatic/automatic); annotated resource type (text/webpage/video/audio/image/database/web service/doc/html/pdf) and practitioner. A second comparison is made based on the functionalities offered by the medical annotation systems.

This paper is organized as follows: Sect. 2 gives a general presentation of the annotation systems and a classification of these tools based on several criteria; Sect. 3 draws some key observations and a discussion of open research problems on annotation systems. Finally Sect. 4 concludes this article.

2   Health Record Annotations and Medical Annotation Systems

2.1   Definition of Medical and Record Annotation Systems

There are several definitions of the medical annotation. According to [28] health record annotation "is a particular note related to a target. The target can be a collection of documents, a document, a segment of the document (a paragraph, a group of words, an image, part of an image, etc.) or an annotation. Each annotation has content, materialized by an inscription. This is the trace of a mental representation elaborated by the annotator about the target, resulting from a cognitive process located, reading the annotated document. The content of the annotation may be interpreted by another reader. The anchor links the annotation to the target (an arrow, a circled sentence, etc.)."

In [31] biomedical annotation is: "a biological interpretation, an enrichment of knowledge sharing in the life sciences. We divide protein sequence information into inflexible data called basic data and data that characterize sequences called annotation".

These Definitions of annotation can be classified according to elements that make up the annotation [33]: Each person has his or her own method of annotation that can be called an annotative footprint which is a written presentation of the mental state of a document reader in a specific context. This fragmentation even at the level of definition of the annotation, gives us from the beginning a vision on the fragmented image of the medical annotation systems.

2.2 Features of Medical Annotation Systems

2.2.1 Type of Medical Annotation Object (Cognitive/Computational)

- **Cognitive:** this annotation is created to be used by a human agent. In this case, the annotation requires a cognitive and intellectual effort to be interpreted. This annotation has a visible visual form on the document [34].
- **Computational:** this annotation is intended to be processed and manipulated by software agents. These annotations are also called meta-data. They allow us to annotate computer resources to facilitate their exploitation by machines.

2.2.2 The Medical Annotation Activity (Manual, Automatic, Semi-automatic)

Annotation activity begins with the choice of anchor and annotation form in the annotation toolbar related to the annotation software. Then, the annotation must complete the properties of the annotation; this process ends with the attachment of the annotation to a well-defined target. Based on this process we can classify the annotative activity as: manual, semi-automatic or automatic [35, 38].

- **Manual:** the process already mentioned will be carried out totally by the user himself, who selects the form of the annotation, selects the anchor and creates the annotation. This process is similar to the process of annotation when a paper support is available.
- **Automatic:** the annotation process already mentioned is carried out totally by the machine. These annotations are based on either context sensors or pattern recognition techniques, etc.
- **Semi-automatic:** in this case, the process will be done from the start by the user. After a while, the system acquires and understands the way the user annotates. It moves to a suggestion of annotations that are automated, based on an annotation model built with rules under development. At this stage, human intervention remains just to validate or not validate and to refine the annotation rules created at a certain level, where there are no corrections and there is complete acceptance of the suggested rules, human intervention is canceled and the process becomes totally automated.

2.2.3 Healthcare Professional (Practitioner)

It is the annotator that is equipped with an annotation system to use all the functionalities offered by the latter. In our case, the practitioners are healthcare professionals (doctor, nurse, biologist, and radiologist). The healthcare cycle is composed of four phases (diagnostic, treatment, advice, follow up and observation). Each practitioner, with a medical annotation system, intervenes in one or many phases, according to their role, to accomplish a specific task in which annotation is made.

2.2.4　Type of Annotation System

- **Application:** an application is created to annotate the resources already consulted. These applications offer several functionalities as the types below.
- **Plug-in:** these are the expansion modules, an external module that is added to a website or software and which will make it possible to provide annotation functionalities to the latter.
- **Website:** these are specialized websites to annotate consulted resources by registered users on the web.

Knowing the type of annotation system facilitates the development of a patient record model which will be proposed in future research. This model allows communicating with different types of medicals annotations systems.

2.2.5　Type of Annotated Resource

Annotated resources can be: word document, pdf, image, text, video, html, audio, etc.

Table 1 presents a comparative study of the medical annotation systems seen in the bibliographical study using the 5 criteria already explained.

Table 1. Classification of medical annotation system based on five criteria

Name of annotation system	Year	healthcare professional (Practitioner)	Annotated Resource type	Category of Annotation					Type of annotation		
				Application	Plug-in	Web	Cognitive	Computational	Manual	Automatic	Semi-automatic
ODMSummary[1]	2017	Doctor	HTML								
3dBionote [2]	2017	Biologist	Image								
Verdant [3]	2017	Biologist	Text								
Med3D [4]	2016	Doctor	Image								
GIDAC [5]	2016	Radiologist	Image								
Vcf-miner[6]	2016	Biologist	Text								
SemAnatomy3D [7]	2015	Radiologist	Image								
Icare [8]	2015	Nurse	Document								

(*continued*)

Table 1. *(continued)*

Name of annotation system	Year	healthcare professional (Practitioner)	Annotated Resource type	Category of Annotation					Type of annotation		
				Application	Plug-in	Web	Cognitive	Computational	Manual	Automatic	Non-automatic
Cart [9]	2015	Biologist	Image								
Domeo Annotation [10]	2014	Biologist	HTML								
BioR [11]	2014	Biologist	Text								
3dmarkup radiologist [12]	2014	Biologist	Image								
Vita [13]	2014	Radiologist	Image, video								
Marky [14]	2014	Radiologist	All type								
Medetect [15]	2013	Doctor	HTML								
Bioannote [16]	2013	Biologist	Image								
Biocat [17]	2013	Biologist	Image								
Ratsnake [18]	2012	Radiologist	Image								
Flersa [19]	2012	Radiologist	Image								
SMItag [20]	2012	Radiologist	Image								
Mammoapplet [21]	2012	Radiologist	Image								
MedAt [22]	2011	Doctor	Document								
DoctorEye [23]	2010	Radiologist	Image								
Radsem [24]	2009	Doctor, Nurse, Radiologist	Image, text, video								
@note [25]	2009	Biologist	text								
Ipad [26]	2008	Radiologist	Image								
Arthemis [27]	2007	Radiologist	Video								
DocAnnot [28]	2006	Doctor, nurse	Document								
DSS-meda [29]	2006	Doctor	Video								
Annoteimage [30]	2005	Radiologist	Image								

2.3 Functionalities of Medical Annotation Systems

– Manage annotation: each medical annotation system studied can be dealt with through at least one of these functionalities:
  • Creating annotation: creating annotation can be automatic, manually or semi-automatic however in the healthcare field the automatic annotation is much used.
  • Modifying annotation: with this function we can modify the anchor, the shape, the annotating content and the annotated content.
  • Saving annotation: this function offer the possibilities to record this annotation in a form specified by the constructor of the system.

- Deleting annotation: deleting annotation without archiving.
- Viewing annotation: many systems offer a specific view manner. These viewing methods include an ordering algorithm that offer the prioritization view, Gantt view, etc.
- Sharing an annotation: sharing an annotation with healthcare professionals, the share can help health professional.
- Sending a message that contains an annotated document: the hp sends a message document or record that contains annotation. This function assures asynchronous communication between healthcare professionals.
- Filtering annotations: (automatic, manual):
  - Manual: the health professional can choose to view only a collection of annotation chosen according to criteria.
  - Automatic: the healthcare professional visualizes only the annotations for which he has the right to see.
- Searching annotation: searching an annotation based on several criteria.
- Fusing annotated documents: creating an annotation report with annotated documents. Fusing can offer a summary of the state of patient based on annotation, also this function facilitates to paramedic practitioner the preparation of deposit report that is exchanged between paramedic healthcares which contains the state of all hospitalized patient.
- Comparing annotations: to see whether annotation has the same significance or not.
- Refining annotation: the practitioner trace a manual shape of an annotation object, the computer intervenes automatically to re-trace the shape drawn manually. This function used a lot in medical image annotation.
- Extracting annotation: extracting an annotation from annotated document. This annotation, already created, is extracted to be stored in a specific form (text, xml, etc....) or to be analyzed.
- Linking annotation to external source: the annotated content is a link to an external source.
- Localizing annotation and area calculation of annotated zone: this function offer the coordinates of the shape used in the annotation of the resource, and calculate the area of this shape. Medical image which has already been annotated can be reused with this function that has the ability to localize the annotation. Generally speaking, the annotated zone in the image is an abnormal zone (sick zone) and the calculation of area can offer additional information.

Table 2 presents a comparative study of the medical annotation systems seen in the literature review using the functionalities offered by each system as a criterion for comparison. This technical study helps us, in future works, at the design of record annotation model.

Table 2. Classification of medical annotation based on functionalities

Name of annotation system	Managing	Sharing	Sending annotated Doc	Filtering	Searching	fusing	comparing	refining	Extracting	Linking to external source	Localizing and calculating annotated zone
ODMSummary	X						X				
3dBionote			X		X						
Verdant	X										
Med3D	X							X	X		X
GIDAC	X								X		X
Vcf-miner				X							
SemAnatomy3D	X										
Icare	X			X	X						
Cart	X										
Domeo Annotation	X										
BioR	X				X				X		
3dmarkup radiologist	X										X
Vita	X								X		
Marky	X		X		X						
Medetect	X		X								
Bioannote	X		X		X						
Biocat	X										
Ratsnake	X								X		
Flersa	X										
SMltag	X										
Mammoapplet	X	X			X						X
MedAt	X										
DoctorEye	X										
Radsem	X	X								X	
@note	X		X								
Ipad	X										
Arthemis	X				X				X		
DocAnnot	X	X	X	X		X					
DSS-meda	X										
Annoteimage	X										

3 Observation and Limitation

Based on Tables 1 and 2 we have determined these limits:

- **Annotating a patient record**
  Most of the applications already seen are from the field of medical biology specifically they are specialized to annotate genomes. The annotation applications of the documents of the patient record are almost limited. This record contains medical document which is annotated.
- **Annotation model of a patient's record**
  The patient's record goes through different stages to complete its final state. Throughout this process, several interveners make their mark on this record.
  The synchronous or asynchronous cooperation requires a specific model to manage these steps.
- **No health care cycles have been developed**
  Every healthcare professional is involved in one or more phases of care, and in this phase every healthcare professional uses a process to achieve the objectives of the care phase. For example: The nurse intervenes in the phase of care cycle follow-up to achieve the objectives of this phase.
  He has his own cycle that is developed (through supervision and observation). In this context, the medical annotation is produced and this context is the real one.
  It is necessary to take into consideration this context and to try to computerize it to understand the annotation in its context and not to lose its semantics.
  Also if we propose an assistance of health care professional, the developments of health care cycle make the task of assistance easy. Each step of this cycle has a specific assistance.
- **Delete and edit an annotation**
  In a hospitalized patient record, and with medical annotation systems we cannot speak of "delete an annotation" function, we are only talking about a visual deletion of the annotation whereas actually this annotation must be archived for future needs. Edit annotation: we must create a modification history of each action even in case of drafting error, this action must be archived.
- **Problem of genericity and interoperability**
  The platform structure is a solution to organize health care process and to facilitate communication with each system that execute sub-task. The absence of a generic annotation model of a patient's record favors the fragmentation of existing medical systems. This problem aggravates with this absence if we talk about the cooperation between the annotation systems. To overcome this problem it is necessary to use standard model of annotation. We have two famous standards those are annotea [37] standard and Dublin core [36] model. Also we can focus on generic model proposed in many research works [42] that can help to inspire a record patient model. Standards and generic model can provide a bridging mechanism and an interface that allow heterogeneous resources that can be linked to this model and collaborate to share annotations.

4   Conclusion and Future Work

In this article, we studied 30 medical annotation systems based firstly on 5 criteria which are: standard annotation (computational/cognitive); category of annotation system (application/plug-in/website); type of annotative activity (manual/semi-automatic/automatic); annotated resource type (text/webpage/video/audio/image/database/web service/doc/html/pdf) and practitioner.

In a second time we studied these systems by detailing the functionalities offered by the systems, and other features already seen in the literature. We ended this article by listing the observations and limitations of these systems.

In future research, we will focus on the representation of an annotation model for the hospitalized patient's record that overcomes the problems already mentioned.

References

1. Storck, M., Krumm, R., Dugas, M.: ODMSummary: a tool for automatic structured comparison of multiple medical forms based on semantic annotation with the unified medical language system. PLoS One 11(10), e0164569 (2017)
2. Segura, J., Sanchez-Garcia, R., Martinez, M., Cuenca-Alba, J., Tabas-Madrid, D., Sorzano, C.O.S., Carazo, J.M.: 3DBIONOTES v2. 0: a web server for the automatic annotation of macromolecular structures. Bioinformatics 33(22), 3655–3657 (2017)
3. McKain, M.R., Hartsock, R.H., Wohl, M.M., Kellogg, E.A.: Verdant: automated annotation, alignment and phylogenetic analysis of whole chloroplast genomes. Bioinformatics 33(1), 130–132 (2016)
4. Lavrič, P., Bohak, C., Marolt, M.: Collaborative view-aligned annotations in web-based 3D medical data visualization. In: 2017 40th International Convention on Information and Communication Technology, Electronics and Microelectronics (MIPRO), pp. 259–263. IEEE, May 2017
5. Vizza, P., Guzzi, P.H., Veltri, P., Cascini, G.L., Curia, R., Sisca, L.: GIDAC: a prototype for bioimages annotation and clinical data integration. In: 2016 IEEE International Conference on Bioinformatics and Biomedicine (BIBM), pp. 1028–1031. IEEE, December 2016
6. Hart, S.N., Duffy, P., Quest, D.J., Hossain, A., Meiners, M.A., Kocher, J.P.: VCF-Miner: GUI-based application for mining variants and annotations stored in VCF files. Brief. Bioinform. 17(2), 346–351 (2016)
7. Banerjee, I., Patanè, G., Spagnuolo, M.: SemAnatomy3D: annotation of patient-specific anatomy (2015)
8. Marrast, P.: Equipement informatique des annotations et des pratiques d'écriture professionnelles: une étude ancrée pour l'organisation des soins en cancérologie. Doctoral dissertation, Université de Toulouse, Université Toulouse III-Paul Sabatier (2015)
9. Deghou, S., Zeller, G., Iskar, M., Driessen, M., Castillo, M., van Noort, V., Bork, P.: CART—a chemical annotation retrieval toolkit. Bioinformatics 32(18), 2869–2871 (2016)
10. Clark, T., Ciccarese, P.N., Goble, C.A.: Micropublications: a semantic model for claims, evidence, arguments and annotations in biomedical communications. J. Biomed. Semant. 5(1), 28 (2014)
11. Kocher, J.P.A., Quest, D.J., Duffy, P., Meiners, M.A., Moore, R.M., Rider, D., Dinu, V.: The Biological Reference Repository (BioR): a rapid and flexible system for genomics annotation. Bioinformatics 30(13), 1920–1922 (2014)

12. Moreira, D.A., Hage, C., Luque, E.F., Willrett, D., Rubin, D.L.: 3D markup of radiological images in ePAD, a web-based image annotation tool. In: 2015 IEEE 28th International Symposium on Computer-Based Medical Systems (CBMS), pp. 97–102. IEEE, June 2015

13. Roy, S., Brown, M.S., Shih, G.L.: Visual interpretation with three-dimensional annotations (VITA): three-dimensional image interpretation tool for radiological reporting. J. Digit. Imaging **27**(1), 49–57 (2014)

14. Pérez-Pérez, M., Glez-Peña, D., Fdez-Riverola, F., Lourenço, A.: Marky: a lightweight web tracking tool for document annotation. In: Saez-Rodriguez, J., Rocha, M., Fdez-Riverola, F., De Paz Santana, J. (eds.) PACBB 2014, pp. 269–276. Springer, Cham (2014). https://doi.org/10.1007/978-3-319-07581-5_32

15. Tian, L., Zhang, W., Bikakis, A., Wang, H., Yu, Y., Ni, Y., Cao, F.: MeDetect: a LOD-based system for collective entity annotation in biomedicine. In: IEEE/WIC/ACM International Joint Conferences on Web Intelligence (WI) and Intelligent Agent Technologies (IAT), 2013, vol. 1, pp. 233–240. IEEE, November 2013

16. López-Fernández, H., Reboiro-Jato, M., Glez-Peña, D., Aparicio, F., Gachet, D., Buenaga, M., Fdez-Riverola, F.: BioAnnote: a software platform for annotating biomedical documents with application in medical learning environments. Comput. Methods Prog. Biomed. **111**(1), 139–147 (2013)

17. Zhou, J., Lamichhane, S., Sterne, G., Ye, B., Peng, H.: BIOCAT: a pattern recognition platform for customizable biological image classification and annotation. BMC Bioinform. **14**(1), 291 (2013)

18. Iakovidis, D.K., Goudas, T., Smailis, C., Maglogiannis, I.: Ratsnake: a versatile image annotation tool with application to computer-aided diagnosis. Sci. World J. (2014)

19. Navarro-Galindo, J.L., Samos, J.: The FLERSA tool: adding semantics to a web content management system. Int. J. Web Inf. Syst. **8**(1), 73–126 (2012)

20. Federico, L., Néstor, D., Oscar, C.: Smitag: a social network for semantic annotation of medical images. In: 2012 XXXVIII Conferencia Latinoamericana En Informatica (CLEI), pp. 1–7. IEEE, October 2012

21. Mata, C., Oliver, A., Torrent, A., Marti, J.: MammoApplet: an interactive Java applet tool for manual annotation in medical imaging. In: 2012 IEEE 12th International Conference on Bioinformatics and Bioengineering (BIBE), pp. 34–39. IEEE, November 2012

22. https://nit.felk.cvut.cz/drupal/projects/medical-annotation-tool-medat

23. David, R., Graf, N., Karatzanis, I., Stenzhorn, H., Manikis, G.C., Sakkalis, V., et al.: Clinical evaluation of DoctorEye platform in nephroblastoma. In: 2012 5th International Advanced Research Workshop on In Silico Oncology and Cancer Investigation-The TUMOR Project Workshop (IARWISOCI), pp. 1–4. IEEE, October 2012

24. Möller, M., Regel, S., Sintek, M.: RadSem: semantic annotation and retrieval for medical images. In: Aroyo, L., et al. (eds.) ESWC 2009. LNCS, vol. 5554, pp. 21–35. Springer, Heidelberg (2009). https://doi.org/10.1007/978-3-642-02121-3_6

25. http://anote-project.org

26. Rubin, D.L., Rodriguez, C., Shah, P., Beaulieu, C.: iPad: semantic annotation and markup of radiological images. In: AMIA Annual Symposium Proceedings, vol. 2008, p. 626. American Medical Informatics Association (2008)

27. Liu, D., Cao, Y., Kim, K.H., Stanek, S., Doungratanaex-Chai, B., Lin, K., et al.: Arthemis: annotation software in an integrated capturing and analysis system for colonoscopy. Comput. Methods Progr. Biomed. **88**(2), 152–163 (2007)

28. Bringay, S.: Les annotations pour supporter la collaboration dans le dossier patient électronique

29. Mrozowski, P., Kononowicz, A.A.: DSS-MEDA a web-based framework for video annotation in medical e-learning. Bio-Algorithms Med-Systems **2**(4), 51–56 (2006)

30. http://www.si.washington.edu/content/annoteimage
31. Kalboussi, A., Omheni, N., Mazhoud, O., Kacem, A.H.: How to organize the annotation systems in human-computer environment: study, classification and observations. In: Abascal, J., Barbosa, S., Fetter, M., Gross, T., Palanque, P., Winckler, M. (eds.) INTERACT 2015. LNCS, vol. 9297, pp. 115–133. Springer, Cham (2015). https://doi.org/10.1007/978-3-319-22668-2_11
32. Charlet, J., Bachimont, B., Brunie, V., El Kassar, S., Zweigenbaum, P., Boisvieux, J.F.: Hospitexte: towards a document-based hypertextual electronic medical record. In: Proceedings of the AMIA Symposium, p. 713. American Medical Informatics Association (1998)
33. Mille, D.: Modèles et outils logiciels pour l'annotation sémantiquede documentspédagogiques. Doctoral dissertation, Université Joseph-Fourier-Grenoble I (2005)
34. Caussanel, J., Cahier, J.P., Zacklad, M., Charlet, J.: Les Topic Maps sont-ils un bon candidat pour l'ingénierie du Web Sémantique? In: Actes des 13e journées francophones d'ingénierie des connaissances (IC). Prix AFIA de la meilleure présentation (2002)
35. Azouaou, F.: Modèles et outils d'annotations pour une mémoire personnelle de l'enseignant. Doctoral dissertation, Université Joseph-Fourier-Grenoble I (2006)
36. Dublin Core Metadata Initiative: Dublin core metadata element set, version 1.1 (2012)
37. Kahan, J., Koivunen, M.R., Prud'Hommeaux, E., Swick, R.R.: Annotea: an open RDF infrastructure for shared web annotations. Comput. Netw. **39**(5), 589–608 (2002)
38. Kalboussi, A., Mazhoud, O., Kacem, A.H.: Comparative study of web annotation systems used by learners to enhance educational practices: features and services. Int. J. Technol. Enhanced Learn. (IJTEL) **8**(2), 129–150 (2016)
39. Kalboussi, A., Mazhoud, O., Kacem, A.H.: Functionalities provided by annotation systems for learners in educational context: an overview. Int. J. Emerg. Technol. Learn. (IJET) **11**(2), 4–11 (2016)
40. Kalboussi, A., Mazhoud, O., Omheni, N., Kacem, A.H.: A new annotation system based on a semantic analysis of learner's annotative activity to invoke web services. Int. J. Metadata Semant. Ontol. **9**(4), 350–370 (2014)
41. Kalboussi, A., Mazhoud, O., Kacem, A.H.: Annotative activity as a potential source of web service invocation. In: Proceedings of the 9th International Conference on Web Information Systems and Technologies (WEBIST 2013), pp. 288–292. SciTePress (2013)
42. https://www.w3.org/TR/mediaont-10/
43. Kalboussi, A., Omheni, N., Mazhoud, O., Kacem, A.H.: An interactive annotation system to support the learner with web services assistance. In: Proceedings of the 15th IEEE International Conference on Advanced Learning Technologies (ICALT 2015), pp. 409–410. IEEE (2015)
44. Kalboussi, A., Mazhoud, O., Hadj Kacem, A., Omheni, N.: A formal model of learner's annotations dedicated to web services invocation. In: Proceedings of the 21st International Conference on Computers in Education (ICCE 2013), pp. 166–169. APSCE (2013)

Smart Environment Technology

Users' Perceptions and Attitudes Towards Smart Home Technologies

Deepika Singh[1,3(✉)], Ismini Psychoula[2], Johannes Kropf[1], Sten Hanke[1], and Andreas Holzinger[3]

[1] AIT Austrian Institute of Technology, Wiener Neustadt, Austria
deepika.singh@ait.ac.at
[2] School of Computer Science and Informatics, De Montfort University, Leicester, UK
ismini.psychoula@dmu.ac.uk
[3] Holzinger Group, HCI-KDD, Institute for Medical Informatics/Statistics, Medical University Graz, Graz, Austria

Abstract. The concept of smart home is a promising and efficient way of maintaining good health, providing comfort and safety thus helps in enhancing the quality of life. Acceptability of smart homes relies on the users' perceptions towards its benefits and their concerns related to monitoring and data sharing. Within this study, an online survey with 234 participants has been conducted to understand the attitudes and perceptions of future smart home users, followed by detailed analysis of their responses. In general, the users agree that the smart home technology would improve the quality of life to a greater extent and enhance the safety and security of residents. On the contrary, they raise several concerns such as the increased dependence on technology and the monitoring of private activities, which may be seen as perceived drawbacks. The obtained results show that the older adults (ages from 36 to 70 years) are more open to monitoring and sharing data especially if it useful for their doctors and caregivers while the young adults (ages up to 35 years) are somewhat reluctant to share information.

Keywords: Smart home · Users' perspective · Acceptability
Data sharing

1 Introduction

In recent years, the concept of assistive technology has been developed tremendously to facilitate self-care, enhance independence, provide comfort and improve the quality of life of the individuals. With the rapid increase in aging population around the world, smart home technology has gained a lot of attention due to its versatile applications in the area of Internet of Things (IoT). It is defined as a living environment where all the devices in the home have the capability to interact with each other and also with the occupants living inside [1]. These devices include smart appliances (refrigerators, washers, TVs etc.), security and

© Springer International Publishing AG, part of Springer Nature 2018
M. Mokhtari et al. (Eds.): ICOST 2018, LNCS 10898, pp. 203–214, 2018.
https://doi.org/10.1007/978-3-319-94523-1_18

safety systems (sensors, monitors, cameras and alarms) and smart energy equipment (thermostats and smart lighting) which are interconnected using standardized communication protocols [2]. There has been major growth in the market of smart home devices owing to the growing aging population, rising demand for home health care, assisted living and energy consumption [3]. According to the report in [4], the global market of smart homes is expected to reach USD 53.45 billion by 2022 and industry analysis shows compound annual growth rate (CAGR) of 14.5% between 2017 and 2022.

Despite many applications and the variety of features, smart homes are still not capable of fully incorporating the demands of the users. High costs and long device replacing cycles are the potential market barriers in the complete adoption of smart homes. Furthermore, privacy and trust related issues with the data collected by the smart home devices are the major challenges [5]. Along with the privacy protection, the actual needs and concerns of future smart home inhabitants need to be considered. Various studies have been conducted with older adults to know their requirements, concerns and perceptions for smart homes [6]. The results of the surveys showed the interest of the participants in the assistive technologies and the necessity of smart home technology for independent living, safety and better quality of life [7,8]. However, in another study [9] participants expressed a variety of concerns including usability, reliability, accessibility and absence of public policy at the state or federal level promoting smart home technology adoption for aging population. According to the national survey of UK homeowners [10], policymakers can play an important role in mitigating perceived risks of smart home technologies by supporting design and operating standards, guidelines on data security and privacy, quality control and energy management in future smart homes. Users' attitudes have also been analyzed towards different type of assisted living services [11]; the study reports that people with many social contacts and high interest in technology showed acceptance for electronic services at home. The results for the different applications were insensitive to gender and age. The wide acceptance of smart homes depends on the way it serves the needs and demands of the user to the best possible extent. In order to do so, opinions of the end users irrespective of their demographics are of great importance. Within the current study, an online survey with a detailed questionnaire was conducted. The questionnaire focuses on identification of needs in performing daily living activities; users' attitudes towards monitoring inside and outside the home and their views regarding robots or personal assistant. There were also questions related to data sharing e.g. which data they would like to share with their doctor. The main aim of the survey was to find out the users' attitudes and their concerns in adopting a smart home.

The paper is structured into four sections. First section introduces the topic and the aim of the study and second section presents the methodology and performed analysis of the responses obtained from the participants. Third section reports the results and discussions and the last section concludes the study and highlights the major findings.

2   Methodology

In this section, the questionnaire design, employed statistical procedures, and demographics of the sample are explained. An online survey was used for this study and data was collected during the period of January - February 2018. The aim was to understand the individuals' attitude towards smart home technologies (their benefits and drawbacks) as well as opinions towards data sharing. The study was approved by the Ethics Committee of De Montfort University in accordance with the Code of the British Computer Science Society and the Chartered Institute for IT. Individuals were asked to participate on a voluntarily basis and the average time taken to complete the survey was approximately 15 min. Full anonymity of the participants was maintained during the study.

In the survey, the questionnaire was divided into six different sections. The first section contained socio-demographic questions (participants' age, gender, location, education and computer or IoT knowledge). The second section of the survey consisted of questions related to the users' ease of performance in daily living activities and their thoughts regarding smart home features. The third section was related to social engagement and devices for outdoor monitoring. The fourth section comprised of questions related to a personal assistant (such as an avatar) and views regarding user interfaces. Benefits, concerns and drawbacks of smart home technologies were asked in the fifth section. The last section of the survey included questions related to users' perception towards monitoring daily living activities and health related data.

2.1   Data Collection

The survey was distributed through e-mails, social media and university groups with an aim of reaching as many respondents as possible (convenience sampling). A sample size of N = 234 was chosen for the analysis; which includes individuals of various backgrounds spread across the globe as shown in Table 1.

The sociodemographic variables used are described as follows:

– Gender: We included gender as a demographic variable to see if there are differences in the perception and acceptance of smart home technologies and data sharing between male and female. The gender breakdown achieved in the study is 58.1% male and 41.9% female. However, the ratio may differ from the real world demographics but the aim was to have significant number of participants from each gender.
– Age: Age is usually negatively correlated with acceptance of technologies thus it was included as a factor to indicate if there is an interest on the adoption of smart home technologies from the upcoming generations. During the survey, we have classified participants into five age groups (as shown in Table 1), which we have classified further on a broader level for the analysis as young adults (ages up to 35 years) and older adults (ages from 36 to 70 years).
– Location: Location was included at the level of continent to show if there are differences in the perception of people from different parts of the world.

- Education: In the previous years, there has been an assumption that educated people who are exposed to advanced technology on a regular basis might accept technology more eagerly than less educated people. However, recent trends indicate that this assumption might no longer be valid due to ease and increased user-friendliness of new technology.
- Computer and IoT Devices: Comfortability and acceptance of technology in daily life varies from person to person, therefore, the participants were asked to classify themselves on their level of computer knowledge and list the IoT devices they already own, if any.
- Familiarity with smart homes: The familiarity with smart homes factor was added to show if the participants are already aware of this technology and if they are familiar with its operation and functions in real life.

Table 1. Demographic breakdown of the participants (N = 234)

		Count	Table N%
Gender	Male	136	58.1%
	Female	98	41.9%
Age	Under 18	5	2.1%
	18–24	58	24.8%
	25–35	100	42.7%
	36–55	48	20.5%
	56–70	23	9.8%
Which of these best describes your location?	Asia	100	42.7%
	Africa	2	0.9%
	North America	24	10.3%
	South America	3	1.3%
	Europe	101	43.2%
	Australia/Oceania	4	1.7%
What is the level of your highest education?	Not completed school	7	3.0%
	Completed school	35	15.0%
	University degree	99	42.3%
	Postgraduate degree	93	39.7%
How would you classify yourself as a computer user?	Beginner	1	0.4%
	Basic Knowledge	22	9.4%
	Moderate	88	37.6%
	Expert	123	52.6%

2.2   Statistical Analysis

For the analysis, Microsoft Excel and IBM SPSS Statistics were used to generate the descriptive statistics of the data and the item-level results of each question of the survey. In addition, Cronbach's alpha value is calculated to test the reliability of the survey with $\alpha = 0.740$. A significance level of 5% is used for all the analyses.

3   Results and Discussion

In the beginning of the survey, participants were asked about familiarity with the concept of smart homes and IoT devices used by them. The data obtained showed that the participants from Europe, Americas (South America and North America) and Australia are more familiar with smart home technologies (Europe = 63%, Americas = 66.6% and Australia = 75%) as compared to participants from Asia (43%). The familiarity with smart homes could also be related with the use of various IoT devices by the participants. As can be seen from Table 2, participants from Europe, Americas and Australia use presence sensors, voice assistant and thermostats comparatively more than that of the participants from Asia and Africa; whereas Asians prefer Fitbit and smart blood pressure cuffs. Other popular IoT devices owned by all the participants include smart phones (94.4%), tablets (59.8%) and smart TVs (57.7%).

Table 2. Smart home familiarity and IoT devices owned by the participants based on location

	Location					
	Asia (N = 100)	Europe (N = 101)	America (N = 27)	Australia (N = 4)	Africa (N = 2)	Total (N = 234)
Smart Home familiarity						
Yes	43%	63.3%	66.6%	75%	50%	55.1%
No	20%	11%	7.4%	25%	None	29.9%
Kind of	37%	24.7%	25.9%	None	50%	15%
IoT Devices owned						
Smart Phone	95%	94%	92.5%	100%	100%	94.4%
Smart Watch	25%	27.7%	40.7%	50%	None	28.2%
Smart TV	55%	60.3%	59.2%	40%	50%	57.7%
FitBit	32%	26.7%	33.3%	50%	None	29.9%
Tablet	47%	66.3%	81.4%	50%	50%	59.8%
Presence sensors	8%	15.8%	25.9%	25%	None	13.7%
Sleep monitors	16%	10.8%	18.5%	50%	None	14.1%
Monitoring cameras	20%	23.7%	33.3%	25%	None	23.1%
Smart Blood pressure cuffs	17%	9.9%	3.7%	50%	None	12.8%
Voice Assistant	16%	20.7%	55.5%	50%	None	23.1%
Thermostat	18%	45.5%	48.1%	50%	50%	34.2%

In order to know the participants' ability in performing routine activities and their preferences in monitoring camera installation, a 5-point Likert scale (1 = Strongly Disagree to 5 = Strongly Agree) was used. Majority of the participants (upto 75%) agreed or strongly agreed that they "feel safe even when they are alone", "can perform their daily activities" and "are physically active inside the home"; which can be attributed to the age factor. Safety and security are clearly perceived as important aspects in smart homes as 60% of all participants either agreed or strongly agreed on the point of home security system and cameras outside the home, as depicted in Fig. 1. A two-way analysis of variance (ANOVA) test is performed to analyze preferences about cameras outside the home with respect to the different locations and age of the participants.

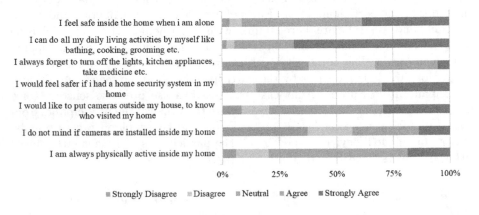

Fig. 1. Attitudes towards home activities

The test result showed that age is not a significant factor while location exhibits a high significance (p = 0.000); Asian and American participants agreed or strongly agreed with camera installation outside the home whereas Europeans and Australians disagreed. A similar trend is noticeable with cameras installed inside the home, where only North Americans agreed and the rest disagreed.

In concern to social engagement and outside home activities of the participants, we tried to understand their attitudes towards monitoring of outdoors activities (Fig. 2). Over 50% of all the participants agreed or strongly agreed on the point of "going outside daily for exercise". Most of the participants (70%) disagreed on "not feeling comfortable going outside alone", this is an expected result given the average age of the participants. With respect to the statement "I would not mind if I was monitored when outside the home", 59.4% of all the participants strongly disagreed or disagreed whereas 22.7% agreed or strongly agreed. It was expected that the participants who agreed or strongly agreed should be from the group of older adults but there was no significant contrast observed among the age groups.

Next, the opinions of the participants about personal Artificial Intelligence (AI) assistants are analyzed. As can be seen from Fig. 3, the opinions are quite

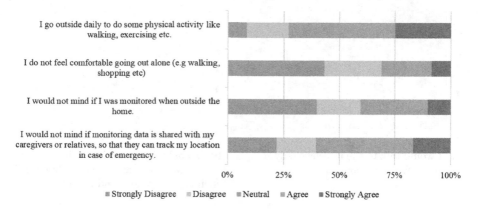

Fig. 2. Attitudes towards outdoors activities

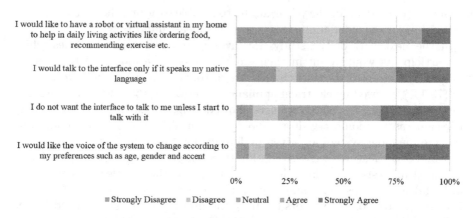

Fig. 3. Attitudes towards personal Artificial Intelligence assistants

balanced in general e.g. almost equal number of participants were either in agreement or disagreement on having a robot or virtual assistant. In the following question with regards to the behavior and abilities of the personal AI assistant, most of participants agreed or strongly agreed that "they would talk to the interface only if it speaks their native language". Also, the majority does not want the interface to start talking with them on its own, they prefer to initiate the conversation and finally, they would like to be able to adjust the speech settings such as gender, age and accent.

A more in-depth analysis was performed to examine if the demographic variables affect the preferences of the participants in context to the capabilities and settings of the personal AI assistant. In Fig. 4, it can be noticed that the effect of gender is not important while there is a trend for age mainly between the age groups of 25–35 years and 56–70 years. For the older adults, it is important ($p = 0.005$) that the system speaks their native language, as seen in Fig. 4a. In contrast, it is quite the opposite from the perspective of young adults (Fig. 4b). Furthermore, it is

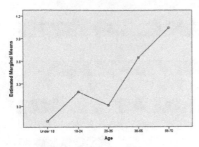
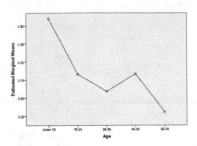

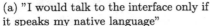

(a) "I would talk to the interface only if it speaks my native language"

(b) "I would like the voice of the system to change according to my preferences (such as age, gender and accent)"

Fig. 4. Effect of age on personal assistant settings

important (p = 0.026) for the young adults to be able to adjust the speaking/voice settings but for the older adults this feature is of least importance.

In the next part of the study, we investigated about the facilities which the participants would want in their smart homes. The most widely accepted facilities according to the participants are automatic lighting and heating control (79.1%) followed by electrical appliances controlling (68.4%) and emergency alarm system (67.9%). The responses showed (Fig. 5) that security and safety with cameras to monitor visitors, monitoring health status inside home and medicine reminder system are given preference by Asians in comparison to others, while other features were given almost equal preferences. Subsequently, we performed analysis to explore the effect of age on their preferences based on the broad age groups i.e. young adults and older adults. Safety and security with cameras to monitor visitors (74.6%), monitoring health status inside home (50.7%) and medicine reminder system (52%) are preferred by the older adults. More young adults are interested in automation in lighting and heating control (82.2%) as compared to older adults (73.2%).

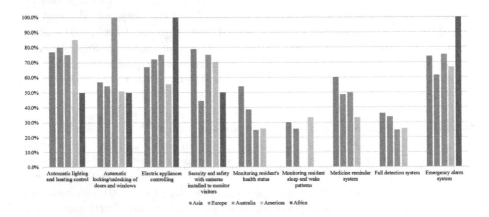

Fig. 5. Facilities the participants would want their smart home to have

The majority of participants perceive the potential benefits as improved quality of life (73.1%), safety (72.6%) and comfort (70.1%), which can be seen in Fig. 6. On the other hand, the drawbacks of smart homes (Fig. 7) are perceived as the increased dependence on technology (76.1 %), the monitoring of private activities (64.5%) and the increased physical idleness (45.3%). This is a general observation of the participants about the perceived benefits and concerns, however, some of the participants expressed their concerns in form of free text as well, e.g. *"Security measures on appliances is lacking and their connectivity to the internet is increasing. This immensely increases the risk of abuse of these appliances. For example a voice activated appliance serving as microphone for spying. Even for transmitting medical data their should be strict guidelines"*.

"In my point of view living in a smart home would decrease person's efficiency of doing physical work and increase dependency on machines and technologies".

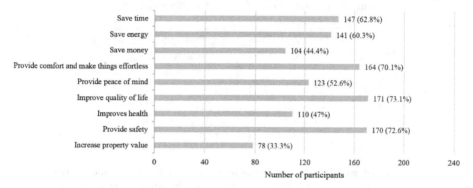

Fig. 6. Perceived smart home benefits

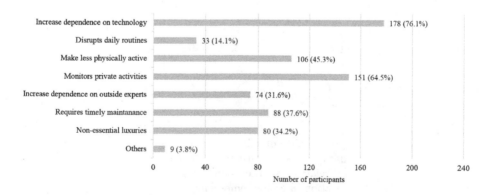

Fig. 7. Perceived smart home drawbacks

From the analyses, it has been observed that Europeans are more concerned towards privacy (74%) in comparison with Asians (54%), whereas older adults group of Asians prefers safety and security (77%) over privacy.

Further analysis of the individual questions in the section about attitudes towards smart home monitoring (Fig. 8) shows that age plays an important role

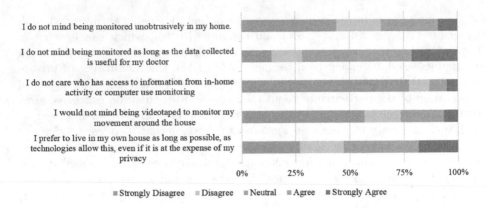

Fig. 8. Attitudes towards smart home monitoring

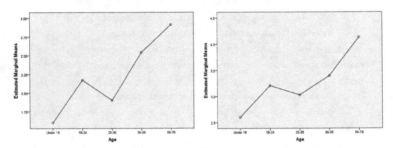

(a) I do not mind being unobtru-(b) I do not mind being monitored
sively monitored in my home   as long as the data collected is use-
                               ful for my doctor

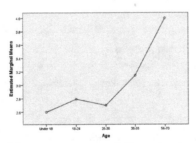

(c) I would not mind if monitoring
data is shared with my caregivers
or relatives so they can track my
location in case of emergency

Fig. 9. Effect of age on monitoring attitudes

in the attitude of the participants. More specifically in the context to the statement "I do not mind being monitored unobtrusively in my home", a significant difference (p = 0.003) can be observed (Fig. 9a) in the opinions, especially between the age groups 23–35 years and 56–70 years. There is also an effect of age on the statement "I do not mind being monitored as long as the data collected is useful for my doctor" (Fig. 9b). The young adults disagree with the statement while the older adults agree (p = 0.004). In context to the statement "I would not mind if monitoring data is shared with my caregivers or relatives so they can track my location in case of emergency" the responses were quite equally distributed on the Likert scale. It was further investigated using a two-way ANOVA test to see the effect of age on the responses. In Fig. 9c, it is visible that age has a significant effect (p = 0.004) on the willingness of people to share their location data with their relatives or caregivers in case of emergency.

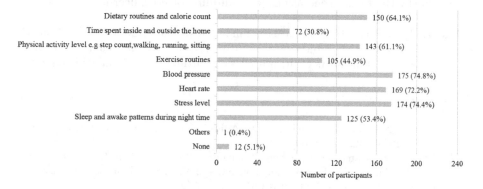

Fig. 10. Smart home data the participants would want to share with their doctor

The last section of this study focuses on data sharing concerns and the kind of data which participants would like to share with their doctors (Fig. 10). Most of the participants agreed with sharing their health related data such as blood pressure (74.8%), stress level (74.4%) and heart rate (72.2%). Also, they do not mind sharing dietary regimes and calorie count (64%) and physical activity level (61%). It is also important to note that 5.1% of the total participants mentioned that they do not want to share any data with their doctor; interestingly all these participants are from Europe and North America.

4 Conclusion

The vision of smart homes can only be realized when the people get interested in adopting these technologies in their daily lives; and the interest can be raised when the developers incorporate their specific needs and concerns into it. This study gives an insight about those needs and concerns for the upcoming smart home users. We investigated the various aspects of usual indoor and outdoor activities to know their ease and activity level. Most of participants irrespective of their location are physically active which could be related to the age (approx. 90% are below 55 years). On having a personal AI assistant to help in daily living activities, around 30% of the participants agreed, majority of them are over 35 years. The most widely accepted facilities according to the participants are automatic lighting and heating control (79.1%) followed by electrical appliances controlling

(68.4%) and emergency alarm system (67.9%). The prospective users of smart home technology perceive the benefits as comfort, safety and improved quality of life but show concerns over the increased dependence on technology and the monitoring of private activities, which may be seen as perceived drawbacks. The older adults are more open to monitoring and data sharing compared to the young adults, especially in cases where the data are beneficial for their doctors and caregivers. The reluctance of the young adults towards smart home technologies and monitoring needs to be further assessed with dedicated studies to understand their concerns and needs. It will help in making the smart home technologies more acceptable by the future generations with minimal or no concern.

Acknowledgement. This work has been funded by the European Union Horizon2020 MSCA ITN ACROSSING project (GA no. 616757). The authors would like to thank the participants and members of the project's consortium for their valuable inputs.

References

1. Cheek, P., Nikpour, L., Nowlin, H.D.: Aging well with smart technology. Nurs. Adm. Q. **29**(4), 329–338 (2005)
2. Cook, D.J.: How smart is your home? Science **335**(6076), 1579–1581 (2012)
3. Chan, M., Campo, E., Estéeve, D., Fourniols, J.Y.: Smart homescurrent features and future perspectives. Maturitas **64**(2), 90–97 (2009)
4. Zion Market Research: Smart Home Market 2016. www.globenewswire.com/news-release/2018/01/03/1281338/0/en/Global-Smart-Home-Market-to-Exceed-53-45-Billion-by-2022-Zion-Market-Research.html/. Accessed 23 Feb 2018
5. AlAbdulkarim, L., Lukszo, Z.: Impact of privacy concerns on consumers' acceptance of smart metering in the Netherlands. In: 2011 IEEE International Conference on Networking, Sensing and Control (ICNSC), pp. 287–292. IEEE (2011)
6. Demiris, G., Oliver, D.P., Dickey, G., Skubic, M., Rantz, M.: Findings from a participatory evaluation of a smart home application for older adults. Technol. Health Care **16**(2), 111–118 (2008)
7. Visutsak, P., Daoudi, M.: The smart home for the elderly: perceptions, technologies and psychological accessibilities: the requirements analysis for the elderly in Thailand. In: 2017 XXVI International Conference on Information, Communication and Automation Technologies (ICAT), pp. 1–6. IEEE (2017)
8. Singh, D., Kropf, J., Hanke, S., Holzinger, A.: Ambient assisted living technologies from the perspectives of older people and professionals. In: Holzinger, A., Kieseberg, P., Tjoa, A.M., Weippl, E. (eds.) CD-MAKE 2017. LNCS, vol. 10410, pp. 255–266. Springer, Cham (2017). https://doi.org/10.1007/978-3-319-66808-6_17
9. Coughlin, J.F., D'Ambrosio, L.A., Reimer, B., Pratt, M.R.: Older adult perceptions of smart home technologies: implications for research, policy & market innovations in healthcare. In: 29th Annual International Conference of the IEEE on Engineering in Medicine and Biology Society, EMBS 2007, pp. 1810–1815. IEEE (2007)
10. Wilson, C., Hargreaves, T., Hauxwell-Baldwin, R.: Benefits and risks of smart home technologies. Energy Policy **103**, 72–83 (2017)
11. Ziefle, M., Rocker, C., Holzinger, A.: Perceived usefulness of assistive technologies and electronic services for ambient assisted living. In: 2011 5th International Conference on Pervasive Computing Technologies for Healthcare (PervasiveHealth), pp. 585–592. IEEE (2011)

USHEr: User Separation in Home Environment

Sumeet Ranka$^{(\boxtimes)}$, Vishal Singh$^{(\boxtimes)}$, and Mainak Choudhury$^{(\boxtimes)}$

Samsung Research Institute, Bangalore, India
{sumeet.ranka,vishal.singh,m.choudhury}@samsung.com

Abstract. With the increase in presence of smart devices in our daily life, it is an important problem for these devices to be more intelligent. The most sought after problems in this area are activity recommendation and prediction. Researchers have proposed solutions for this problem, however, most of them are based on single-user home space. In this paper, we propose an unsupervised approach to separate the logs of multi-user home space into buckets equal to the number of users. With a minimal set of assumptions, the aim of the method is to transform the multi-user problem to a single-user problem. It is achieved by estimating the layout of the house and then tracking the users at room-level. We achieved empirically-determined high precision in estimating the layout and 74% accuracy in separating the multi-user stream.

Keywords: Smart environment · Smart home · User personalization
Context-aware computing · Multi-user home space · Layout generation

1 Introduction

A smart environment has been defined as an environment that can acquire and apply knowledge to adapt to the lifestyle of its inhabitants in order to improve their experience in the environment [1]. With the increase in the interaction of the human beings with various devices, the requirement to draw out inferences in a smart environment have come up in various application areas such as security, health care, and automation. The main objective of a smart environment is to achieve a simpler, more productive, and a comfortable life for its inhabitant. Needs ranging from turning the air conditioner on automatically to reminding an Alzheimer's patient to take medicine can be served by a smart environment. A large number of such needs can be solved using activity recognition and indoor tracking of the inhabitants. For instance, meal activity can be predicted/recognized which might strongly correlate with medicine intake time as well and can be used to remind the inhabitant about the medicine.

The idea of activity prediction and recommendation can be described at broad scale of Activities of Daily Living (ADLs) such as eating and sleeping, and can also be scaled down to the individual settings of a device. The main factor that needs to be considered while designing a solution is that it should

© Springer International Publishing AG, part of Springer Nature 2018
M. Mokhtari et al. (Eds.): ICOST 2018, LNCS 10898, pp. 215–224, 2018.
https://doi.org/10.1007/978-3-319-94523-1_19

not be obtrusive for the user. Frequent notifications for annotations or use of visual data can defeat the important purpose of making the life simpler and safer. Researchers have applied methods from sequence mining [4,5], Bayesian networks [3], and neural networks [6,11], and achieved good results in user activity recognition and prediction. However, most of them have been proposed and analyzed in a single-user environment. The real world settings are mainly multiuser based and the characteristics of these two scenarios differ significantly. The device logs generated in multi-user scenario are interleaved and may not contain user information tagged along with the log. This case mainly arises when the user physically interacts with the device, e.g. switching on the air conditioner using a remote. Moreover, there are cases when the users are performing a joint activity, e.g. watching a television. This event will not portray a behavior specific to a user but will include joint characteristics. As a result, for application-oriented research, it is vital to come up with methodologies that understand and incorporate the characteristics of multi-user settings.

In this paper, we have made an attempt to separate the event log stream generated from the sensors into n different buckets at the room level, where n denotes the number of users in the house. The analysis of the behavior of a specific user is a simpler task when the data contains information related to a single user alone. The proposed method is an unsupervised approach and assumes the information of the number of users staying in the house. From the sensor log data, the algorithm first estimates the layout of the house at room level and using the obtained layout, it tracks the user inside the home at room level. This tracking results in the separation of the multi-user log stream into individual streams. This processing of multi-user stream, apart from activity prediction and recognition, can be useful in other application areas such as:

- Propagating personalized settings across rooms over devices such as an air conditioner. When a person moves from one room to another, we can track the user and apply the same setting across devices in the current room.
- Indoor localization can help in voice command systems, wherein location of the user can be used to single out the device for which the command is uttered. For instance, "Turn on the light", command will turn on the light nearest to the person uttering the command.
- Tracking the residents in a home can help in detecting the anomalies or undesired motions inside the house.
- Generic notifications or delivery of service can be achieved at a specific location. We can deliver the message regarding events like the arrival of a person at the doorstep at a specific location instead of broadcasting it across the house.

1.1   Related Work

For the applications involving activity prediction and recognition, methods have been proposed in both single-user and multi-user home space. Active-LeZi [4] based on sequence mining shows 86% accuracy. It considers the triggering of each sensor as a term in the sequence and mines out patterns in it. The patterns are identified by creating a trie structure of the contexts obtained. Another approach, SPEED [5] is based on the frequency of the windows formed using *START* and *STOP* state. It obtained 88.3% accuracy when evaluated on CASAS dataset. Though they have high accuracies, the main problem with these approaches is that the results are based on single resident data. In the case of multiple residents both the approaches, Active-LeZi and SPEED, fail to mine out the patterns due to close interleaving of individual user's logs.

Another approach, CRAFFT [3], uses Bayesian networks and is fast enough for real world deployment. They obtained an average accuracy of 66% over three different apartments. The hypothesis is that an activity is conditionally dependent on the following three attributes: location, time of the day, the day of the week. Based on current activity and its attributes, the next set of attributes are predicted. After predicting the attributes, they are used along with the current activity to predict the next activity that is likely to be performed. For this approach as well, the analysis was based on single resident environment.

A hybrid approach [2] was proposed using CRAFFT [3] and SPEED [5]. Though this method obtained an accuracy of 91% and the dataset used for the analysis consisted of the daily activities of multiple residents, the approach assumes that the event log data is initially annotated with the user information. As discussed before, the annotation is difficult in a real-life setting.

In another paper, LSTM [6] was used specifically to tackle multi-user home space. It considers activities as words and maps them to 3-dimensional vectors. The next word (activity) vector is predicted using LSTM and a set of words (activities) that are close to the predicted vector are considered the possible activities that will be performed in the next time interval. They achieved 82% accuracy using this method. However, LSTM is a supervised approach. The activities that will be performed is to be known beforehand and the set of activities has to be fixed. As a result, this method takes in initial assumptions that are difficult in a real-life setting.

Occupancy detection was looked upon using classification algorithm [7]. In a lab setup, they analyzed and compared Bayesian network, decision trees, and linear regression. Their proposed method achieved an accuracy of 83% over classes of occupancies (0, 1, 2, 3). However, some of the parameters, such as number of computers running and number of people in the lab, based on which their model is designed does not portray general characteristics of a house or requires annotation which again raises the inconvenience issue.

In-house tracking of the user was looked upon by Yang et al. [8]. They predicted the number of people in-house and identified the persons based on the history of the usage. The analysis was done at the house level. However, to give the user a more personalized experience, room-level granularity is more important. The advent of AI speakers, such as Google Home and Alexa, can be used for in-house tracking as well. However, as the user is not expected to speak continuously, the significance of sensors increases in such cases.

The above mentioned methods either lack the characteristics of a multi-user setting or require annotation on the side of the inhabitants of the house. In this paper, we aim to propose a method that addresses these issues and converts a multi-user problem to a single-user problem by tracking the users.

2   Methodology

There are two main phases of separating the multi-user log stream into multiple single-user log stream.

1. Layout Estimation: The main purpose of this phase is to deduce the layout of the house from the log stream by estimating the relative placement of the sensors present in the house. This clustered group of sensors will represent a room in the house which will then be used in tracking the user.
2. In-house Tracking: Based on the layout obtained in the first phase, the users are tracked and the logs are tagged with the user information. This results in the separation of the log stream.

2.1   Layout Estimation

This phase involves estimating the layout of the house. The objective is to come up with a directed graph, $G = (V, E)$ where the node set V in G represent the sensors present in the house and the edge set E depicts the pair of sensors which are spatially immediate neighbors. In addition to the target graph, the sensors are clustered to represent a room in the house.

The target graph is obtained using multiple approaches which are described below:

– Room Transition Point Based Approach: In this approach, a weighted graph is generated with sensors as nodes. An edge from sensor M_i to M_j exists if there is a finite probability of the recording of excitation of M_j after M_i by any user. This probability is approximated using counts of ordered pair (M_i, M_j). For apartments with multiple residents, ordered pairs of the type (M_a, M_b) will exist even when the sensors are not spatially placed together. These cases arise due to simultaneous activities performed by multiple users in spatially separate locations. Such erroneous edges are removed using empirically obtained threshold T. The threshold T is calculated using the Eq. 1. The edges with weights above the threshold are retained and the rest are dropped.

$$T = \mu_i + 1.5\sigma \tag{1}$$

where:
$$\mu_i = \frac{\sum_j E_{ij}}{\sum_j 1}$$
$$\sigma = \sqrt{\sum \frac{(E_{ij} - \mu_{ij})^2}{\sum_j 1}}$$
E_{ij} denotes the edge weight between sensor M_i and M_j,

Depth First Search (DFS) algorithm is then applied on this graph to obtain different clusters representing different rooms in the house. A concept of an absorbing node is also introduced to get better set of clusters. An absorbing node is defined as a node which can act as an entry or an exit point for a room represented by a cluster. These nodes are obtained using Hidden Markov Model (HMM). The HMM is used to create a separate set of clusters for the same data. After that, for every two clusters, the inter-cluster edge with the highest number of ordered-pair is selected and the nodes attached are marked as the absorbing state for the DFS. This step considerably improves the clusters obtained.

- The second approach involves finding the cross-correlation between the sequences of sensor activation obtained over time to determine the spatial closeness of the two sensors. If any pair of sensors is relatively placed together then the motion of the user makes the sensors activate in a similar manner. This leads to a high similarity in their time-shifted sequences. The following equation is used to calculate the edge weight between a pair of sensor nodes:

$$E_{ij} = \frac{CC(M_i, M_j)}{CC(M_i, M_i) \cdot CC(M_j, M_j)} \tag{2}$$

where $CC(M_i, M_j)$ is the cross-correlation between the activation pulse of sensor M_i and sensor M_j. It is given by the following equation:

$$CC(M_1, M_2) = max\{\sum_{\tau} \sum_{k} m_{1k}\delta[n - k] \sum_{l} m_{2l}\delta[\tau - n - l]\} \tag{3}$$

where m_{1k} represents the value for the kth sensor. Its value is 1 if sensor M_1 is triggered and 0 otherwise.

After obtaining this graph, a force directed representation is created in a higher dimension (4 in our case) using the Fruchterman-Reingold algorithm [9] and then spatial clustering is done in this space using K-means clustering. To carry out K-Means clustering, the optimal cluster count is calculated using silhouette score. After obtaining the clusters, the edge weights are replaced with the Euclidean distance in the newly projected space. For every cluster, all the intra-cluster edges are retained, and for every pair of clusters, the inter-cluster edge with the least distance value is retained and the rest are dropped. This approach yielded much better results compared to the first approach.

2.2 In-House Tracking

After layout estimation, residents are tracked using the shortest path algorithm. For this, the distance between the two sensors is obtained by taking the Euclidean distance between the two corresponding vectors obtained in the first phase. We start with some initial estimated position for every resident. As the event log for a sensor is obtained, the resident which is nearest to the triggered sensor is tracked to that location. In this manner, the users get tracked and the interleaved log gets separated into n different streams, where n is the number of inhabitants in the house.

The tracking was performed at two different levels of granularity: Room Level and Sensor Level. The dataset used for the analysis, did not have annotations specifying the identity of the user responsible for triggering the sensor. As a result, the ground truth was not available to test our method. For the generation of ground truth, a reference graph of the layout was manually created, and shortest path algorithm was run on this graph. The trace result obtained served as the ground truth for our analysis. This trace was manually checked up and the few inconsistencies found were corrected. The inconsistencies mainly arised at time instances when the two users were either performing a joint activity or passed through a corridor at the same time.

3   Experiments

In this section, we first describe the dataset which has been used for the analysis and then we discuss the performance of the algorithm for layout inference and the in-house tracking.

3.1   Dataset

The datasets used are openly accessible[1] and were collected as part of the CASAS smart home project [10] of Washington State University. For the analysis, we have used five different datasets collected on different setups. They were chosen on the basis of the different collection time, type of layout, and the relationship between the residents. Table 1 describes the details for each dataset.

Table 1. Details of each dataset used

Name of the setup	Number of motion sensors	Duration	Relationship
Tulum	31	6 months	Couple
Kyoto	51	9 months	Independent residents
Cairo	27	2 months	Couple + Pet
Paris	29	4 months	Couple + Pet
HH121	28	11 days	Independent residents

Some of the datasets contain other sensors such as door sensors and item sensors. However, these sensors are user controlled and do not reflect the static behavior of the layout of the house. For e.g., a door may remain open as a result

---

[1] Can be accessed using the URL: http://casas.wsu.edu/datasets/.

of which the state of the corresponding sensor may not change its state when the user passes through that area. A motion sensor always changes its state whenever user passes over it and hence its change in state is not affected by the dynamic behavior of the user. As a result, we only consider motion sensors for inferring the layout of the house.

The motion sensors used for these datasets have two states: ON and OFF. For inferring the layout, we considered both the states. On the other hand, for in-house tracking, we considered only ON values. OFF value does not contribute to the path of the user. They timeout after a fixed duration. As a result, log stream consisting of ON values for the motion sensors is used for in-house tracking.

3.2 Results

The performance of the room layout estimation is empirically determined and evaluated qualitatively by comparing it with the actual layout.

The accuracy of the in-house tracking is calculated for four different cases taking two parameters in consideration. First parameter is about the granularity level of the tracking. The user is tracked at two levels: Room-level and Sensor-level. The second parameter is whether the positions of every user at a particular time instance is considered an ordered pair (preserving user identities) or an unordered pair (not preserving user identities). The accuracy is determined as follows:

$$Accuracy = \frac{\sum_t result_t}{Total\ no.\ of\ time\ points} \tag{4}$$

where

$$result_t = \begin{cases} 1, & \text{Actual Positions of Users} = \text{Obtained Positions of Users.} \\ 0, & \text{otherwise.} \end{cases}$$

Layout Generation. Based on the rooms obtained, the sensors grouped together are marked on the layout of the house. Figures in Fig. 1 indicate that the layouts have been estimated accurately.

In setups of Cairo (Fig. 1c) and Paris (Fig. 1d), a room with single sensor falls in the group of the sensors present in the adjacent room or the adjoining corridor. For e.g., in Cairo setup, the sensors M025, M026 and M027 fall in the group. It is so because it is most likely that M026 or M027 get triggered before or after M025. As a result of such behavior, the cross-correlation values of these sensors are high and hence they belong to the same group.

Motion Tracking. The results of the motion tracking are mentioned in the Table 2.

One of the challenges in tracking was to resolve the identity of the users when they come close to each other, this is evident from the fact that when identities are not resolved the accuracy increases significantly in both room level and sensor level granularity (Fig. 2).

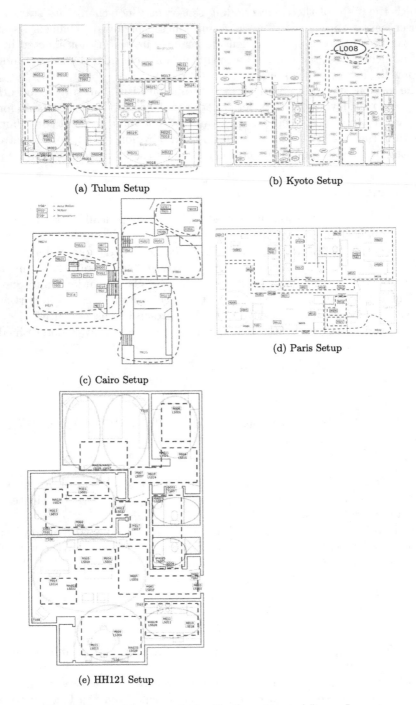

(a) Tulum Setup

(b) Kyoto Setup

(c) Cairo Setup

(d) Paris Setup

(e) HH121 Setup

Fig. 1. Sensor Maps overlaid with the estimated Room Layout

Table 2. Results of resident tracking performed on Kyoto setup

Granularity	Accuracy (in %)
Sensor level (with identity)	34
Room level (with identity)	42
Sensor level	65
Room level	74

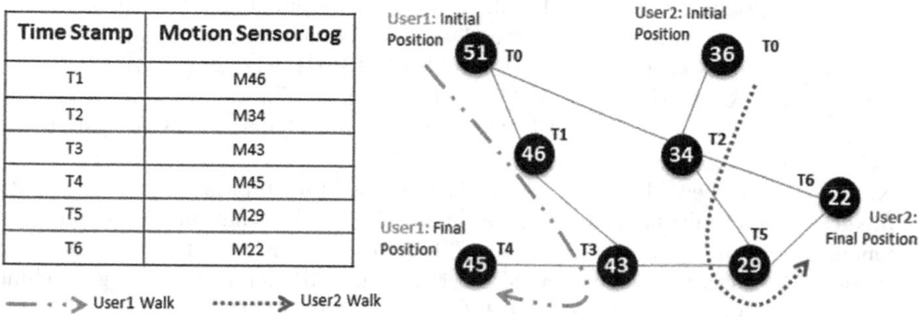

Time Stamp	Motion Sensor Log
T1	M46
T2	M34
T3	M43
T4	M45
T5	M29
T6	M22

Fig. 2. Excerpt of in-house tracking

4   Conclusion

In this paper, an attempt to convert a multi-user setting problem to a single-user setting problem was made which involved estimating the layout of the house and to track the inhabitants of the smart environment. The current approaches lack incorporating the characteristics of the multi-user settings and some of them require frequent annotations which could be obtrusive to the user. The proposed method addresses this issue with its unsupervised approach and tracks every individual user inside the house with an accuracy of 74%. As a result, the obtained single-user streams can be used to solve more complex problems such as activity recognition and prediction, which can bring a great amount of personalization to the smart environment for all its inhabitants.

A strong challenge appears when users are frequently performing joint activities resulting in highly interleaved activity trails. The current solution gives 42% accuracy for identifying users for each trail. These errors mainly arise after the users perform any joint activity and needs refinement to eliminate them. In our future work, we will focus on this aspect of the problem and also tag users to location trails. We will also look into putting AI speakers along with motion sensors for estimating location of users using ambient sounds. The amalgamation of inferences obtained from the speakers and the sensors present can help in obtaining better results.

References

1. Cook, D., Das, S.K.: Smart Environments: Technology, Protocols and Applications. John Wiley & Sons, 28 October 2004
2. Wu, Z.H., Liu, A., Zhou, P.C., Su, Y.F.: A Bayesian network based method for activity prediction in a smart home system. In: 2016 IEEE International Conference on Systems, Man, and Cybernetics (SMC), pp. 001496–001501. IEEE, 9 October 2016
3. Nazerfard, E., Cook, D.J.: CRAFFT: an activity prediction model based on Bayesian networks. J. Ambient Intell. Humaniz. Comput. **6**(2), 193–205 (2015)
4. Gopalratnam, K., Cook, D.J.: Active lezi: an incremental parsing algorithm for sequential prediction. Int. J. Artif. Intell. Tools **13**(04), 917–29 (2004)
5. Alam, M.R., Reaz, M.B., Ali, M.M.: SPEED: an inhabitant activity prediction algorithm for smart homes. IEEE Trans. Syst. Man Cybern.-Part A Syst. Hum. **42**(4), 985–90 (2012)
6. Kim, Y., An, J., Lee, M., Lee, Y.: An activity-embedding approach for next-activity prediction in a multi-user smart space. In: 2017 IEEE International Conference on Smart Computing (SMARTCOMP), pp. 1–6. IEEE, 29 May 2017
7. Moraru, A., Pesko, M., Porcius, M., Fortuna, C., Mladenic, D.: Using machine learning on sensor data. J. Comput. Inf. Technol. **18**(4), 341–347 (2010)
8. Yang, L., Ting, K., Srivastava, M.B.: Inferring occupancy from opportunistically available sensor data. In: 2014 IEEE International Conference on Pervasive Computing and Communications (PerCom), pp. 60–68. IEEE, 24 March 2014
9. Fruchterman, T.M., Reingold, E.M.: Graph drawing by force-directed placement. Soft. Pract. Exp. **21**(11), 1129–1164 (1991)
10. Cook, D.J., Crandall, A.S., Thomas, B.L., Krishnan, N.C.: CASAS: a smart home in a box. Computer **46**(7), 62–69 (2013)
11. Bourobou, S.T., Yoo, Y.: User activity recognition in smart homes using pattern clustering applied to temporal ANN algorithm. Sensors **15**(5), 11953–11971 (2015)

An Indoor Navigation System for the Visually Impaired Based on RSS Lateration and RF Fingerprint

Lalita Narupiyakul[2,3], Snit Sanghlao[1], and Boonsit Yimwadsana[1,3(✉)]

[1] Faculty of Information and Communication Technology, Mahidol University,
999 Phuttamonthon 4 Road, Salaya, Phuttamonthon, Nakhonpathom 73170, Thailand
{snit.san,boonsit.yim}@mahidol.ac.th
[2] Faculty of Engineering, Mahidol University, 999 Phuttamonthon 4 Road, Salaya,
Phuttamonthon, Nakhonpathom 73170, Thailand
lalita.nar@mahidol.ac.th
[3] Integrative Computational BioScience Center, Office of the President, Mahidol University,
999 Phuttamonthon 4 Road, Salaya, Phuttamonthon, Nakhonpathom 73170, Thailand

Abstract. Indoor positioning and navigation have recently gained a significant increase in interest in academia due to the proliferation of smart phones, mobile devices and network services in buildings. Various techniques were introduced to achieve high performance of indoor positioning and navigation. In addition, the inventions of creative location-based service applications for mobile and Internet of Things devices for business purpose have helped push the demand for indoor positioning and navigation system to an unprecedented level. However, currently, unlike outdoor positioning system which commonly uses GPS, there is no de facto standard for indoor positioning technique and technology. Furthermore, even though there are already a number of various location-based service applications, a few of them target visually impaired users who would gain significant benefits from this technology. We propose our indoor navigation system based on RSS lateration and RF Fingerprint using Wi-Fi and Bluetooth Low Energy. The user interface is tailor-made to be suitable to the visually impaired.

Keywords: Indoor location-based positioning · Navigation · Visually impaired
RF fingerprint · RSS lateration

1 Introduction

The abundance and adoption of smart phones and the availability of the Internet have introduced and popularized in a wide range of location-based positioning applications, especially in navigation and supply chain management. In the past 20 years, outdoor navigation technology has matured thanks to the abundant deployment of GPS satellites and enjoyed various supporting applications such as location-based marketing, location-based health and emergency services, supply-chain management and logistics, disaster management and recovery, and the Internet of Things-related applications. However, the GPS-based positioning and navigating systems do not work indoor because of the

© Springer International Publishing AG, part of Springer Nature 2018
M. Mokhtari et al. (Eds.): ICOST 2018, LNCS 10898, pp. 225–235, 2018.
https://doi.org/10.1007/978-3-319-94523-1_20

lack of line of sight between mobile device and GPS satellite. Indoor navigation system has been developed and researched with a lot of attention in the recent years. However, there are still rooms for further improvement of indoor navigation performance including accuracy, precision and detection delay. Path loss, shadow fading, and interference are considered major problems of indoor positioning and navigation.

A number of indoor positioning and navigating application has been introduced recently. However, a few of them are developed to support the visually impaired who would gain a lot of benefits from this system. Most visually impaired cannot grasp the sense of direction when they are in a building. Importantly, they cannot understand or use the map like the sighted people. In order to support the visually impaired when they are inside a building, to help them go to their destined location by themselves, and to help them gain confidence in living in the society on their own, we developed our indoor navigation system for the visually impaired and tested it at Ratchasuda College, Mahidol University, Thailand which is the place where they will first learn how to live their life with disabilities. We also discuss remaining challenges and future work on improving the performance of indoor navigation system.

2 Background

Location-based positioning technologies are often associated with the Global Positioning System (GPS) [1]. For the indoor area, location-based positioning cannot effectively use GPS because the RF signals supporting GPS cannot go through walls and ceiling of buildings well. The line-of-sight requirement of GPS signals cannot be achieved. Many indoor location-based positioning (localization) systems were proposed using different techniques such as Cell of Origin, Distance-Based (Lateration), Angle-based (Angulation) and Location Patterning (pattern recognition) based on various RF technologies that could be used indoor such as Wi-Fi, Bluetooth, Zigbee, RFID, UWB, Visible Light, Acoustic signals and ultrasound [2]. Despite various efforts for over 20 years, indoor positioning remains an open challenge, especially when smart phones should be supported for indoor positioning system.

Most indoor location-based positioning systems [13] are usually implemented using one or several techniques as a real-time system which only estimate the location of the user based on the most current timestamps, registered access point, signal strength readings, or angle-of-incidence measurements. Cell of Origin is one of the simplest mechanisms of estimating location position of the user in any system based on RF 'cells' that the user's mobile device (e.g., smart phone) is registered to. The location of the mobile device is assumed to be the location of the associated cell.

Distance-based (lateration) techniques commonly consist of 3 popular strategies: Time of Arrival (ToA), Time Difference of Arrival (TDoA) and Received Signal Strength (RSS). The ToA technique [3] is based on the precise measurement of the arrival time of a signal transmitted from a mobile device to several receiving sensors. Since the speed of signals in the air and the distance between the receiving sensors are known, the arrival timestamp to several sensors (e.g., access points) could be used to estimate the distance between the mobile device and the sensor which one can draw a circle around the sensor. The location position of the mobile device is determined by the intersection point of the circles around sensors. A major drawback of the ToA technique is that the system requires all clocks of all sensors and mobile device to be synchronized which is very difficult to do in practice.

Lateration using Time Difference of Arrival (TDoA) [4] technique uses relative time measurements at each receiving sensor instead of absolute time measurements used in ToA technique so that TDoA only require the time of sensors to be syncrhonized. The distance and time difference between each sensor could be used to construct a hyperbola with foci at the locations of both sensors. The intersection of several hyperbola curves estimates the location position of the mobile device.

Lateration using Received Signal Strength (RSS) [5] estimated the distance between a mobile device and a sensor by first estimating the distance between the mobile device and a sensor based on a general power loss model which assumes the relationship between power loss and distance between the model device and sensor. Circles could be drawn to estimate the location of the mobile device. The RSS lateration technique could be performed on either network-side or client-side. In order to avoid inconsistent metrics of power measurement, most implementations use network-side estimation and this technique has been widely used in practice.

Angle-based (Angulation), Angle of Arrival (AoA), [6] sometimes called Direction of Arrival (DoA), determines the angle of incidence, that each receiving sensors received signals from mobile device. The direction of arrival could be used to draw straight lines going out of each receiving sensor in the direction of arrival. The intersection of the lines going out of receiving sensors provide the estimation of the location position of the mobile device.

Location Patterning, RF Fingerprinting, [7] is based on the pattern recognition of RF signals received by various sensors based on the matching between the measured RF signal strengths from various sensors and the record RF signal strengths from various sensors pre-recorded in a database (calibration) giving the assumption that there should be no two positions in any area that have the same RF signal profile. Since a mobile device can detect signals from various access points at any position, the matching of the received signal strengths against the stored signal strength profile in the database is usually conducted using classification techniques such as deterministic distance estimation algorithm (such as Euclidean and Manhattan distance), Probabilistic algorithms (such as maximum likelihood estimation, and naïve Bayes) and machine learning algorithms (such as support vector machine, neural networks, or random forest). Due to the usually unpredictability of path loss and shadow fading in buildings, RF fingerprinting technique is considered one of the most accurate methods for location-based positioning because the actual RF signal strength profiles are pre-recorded. However, any change in the condition of the indoor environment will result in the inaccurate location position estimation. In addition, this technique cannot effectively provide high resolution of location position estimation because the classification will have to be overly complexed as it has to classify the received signal strength patterns into too many classes.

Due to the popularity of the indoor positioning system in the recent years, several applications were introduced including location-based marketing, location-based health services, asset management/tracking, supply-chain management, disaster management and recovery, and the Internet of Things-related applications [2]. However, few applications have focused on indoor navigation system for the visually impaired. According to some interviews with several visually impaired people and their instructors, indoor navigation system will be highly beneficial to them because the system will help them quickly learn about the building they are in. Without the assistance from indoor navigation system, the visually impaired may need at least a few months to familiarize themselves with the building. In addition to the positioning aspect of the system, navigating or guiding the visually impaired is different from guiding sighted people. The visually impaired are not able to realize direction easily. The indoor navigating system must not only provide high accuracy and precision for location positioning, but must also be a user-friendly navigation tool.

In terms of performance, in order to practically deploy indoor location-based positioning system, the system requires higher accuracy and precision than outdoor positioning system due to the granularity of objects in indoor environment. Obtaining high accuracy and precision remains a challenge due to the different path-loss model involving attenuation and shadow fading effects in different indoor environment [12]. The performance of current indoor positioning techniques are shown in [13], however they are subject to different testing site.

3   System Design

According to our objectives, our indoor navigation system must be able to not only provide accurate and precise location position of the user's client device like other indoor navigation systems do, but also provide indoor navigation user interface suitable to the users who are visually impaired. Sighted users can observe the surrounding environment and interact with the indoor map using their own sense of direction at the same time. They can usually recognize where each room or wall are located in the map and the direction of their walking. Unfortunately, the visually impaired users cannot visually deduce any information. In real life, most of them have some sense of direction after they get used to the place for some time (this could take months or years to get used to the location and direction of walkways, rooms and objects). After some interview sessions with visually impaired people, we have been informed that they usually pictured locations and rooms as connected blocks of rectangles whose sizes and dimensions correspond to the actual sizes of each room or walk way. We observed that, even though, they could walk without any problem, they still need to use canes in order to make sure that they are walking in the right direction and to avoid objects that may appear accidentally.

The design of the indoor navigation system for the visually impaired consists of two components as follows:

I. Interactive map interface for the visually impaired

The interactive map interface allows the visually impaired user to know the current location position, find information about a specific place or room, and navigate the user to a room selected by the user. This interface system has to support how the visually impaired understand positions and locations of a map. Conventional 2D maps which are a scale-down version of the actual map are not suitable for the visually impaired since each object is too small for the visually impaired to select and remember the location of the object on the screen.

Simple rectangular-based blocks are suggested by the visually impaired to be used as rooms or sections on a floor (Fig. 1). The visually impaired can tap and hold a block in order to listen to the room or place's information represented by the block. The visually impaired can hold and drag his/her finger to nearby block in order to listen to the information about the nearby rectangles in the direction of the finger. In addition to the interactive map, standard user interface for the visually impaired is used. Users input information using gestures such as swiping (linear navigation – swipe with two fingers until a desired item is found and then select using double taps), dragging (touch exploration) and external keyboard. The output is usually provided as voice. TalkBack [8] and VoiceOver [9] are popular vision accessibility utilities for Android and iOS respectively. All user interface inputs (such as buttons and textboxes) are added with object description order to allow the screen reader to read the input names. The output will be provided to the user in the form of voice.

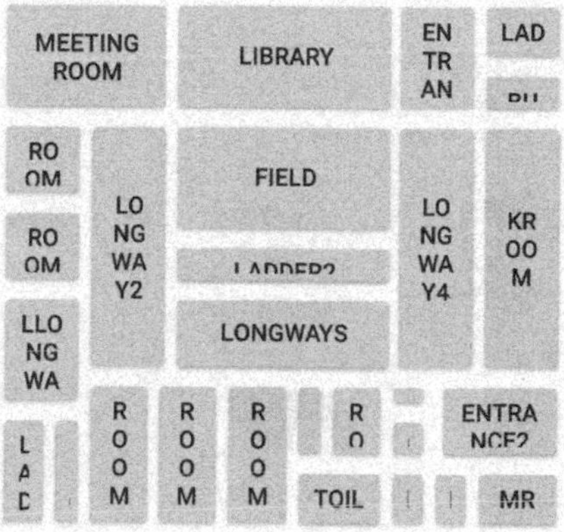

Fig. 1. The display of interactive map suggested by visually impaired testers.

II. Indoor navigation system for the visually impaired

The indoor navigation system for the visually impaired consist of two major components which are indoor location-based positioning system and navigation system.

Indoor location-based positioning system is the heart of the entire system. One of the key issues that visually impaired have when they are inside a building is that they are unable to locate themselves in the building. Our indoor location-based positioning system is an integration of a hardware and software system designed mainly to use two strategies including RSS-based lateration with RF propagation and RF Fingerprinting of Wi-Fi signal. This is because of the abundant availability and wide adoption of Wi-Fi technology and smart phones. Since most people nowadays carry a Wi-Fi enabled smart phone, detecting location of a smart phone users inside a building using Wi-Fi signals is a natural choice. In order to provide convenient access to client's location for all clients using different smart devices, the calculation for estimating the clients' locations is performed by a location-based service (LBS) server in the network rather than by the clients due to different clients' computing performance and RF hardware. Our RSS-based lateration techniques utilize ToA, TDoA and RSS to estimate the most probable location of a smart phone client. All access points are therefore connected to a single time server via Wi-Fi controller to make sure that all access points are synchronous. The RF Fingerprinting of Wi-Fi signal is designed to take into accounts possible changes in RF environment. In addition to the accuracy provided by RF signal calibration, the attenuation, multipath and shadow fading effects of Wi-Fi signals emitting from access points are predicted for the entire floor in order to create a path-loss model which is used in conjunction with the result from RF calibration in order to improve accuracy and precision. We set our calibration resolution to be 3×3 square meters.

When a mobile client would like to know its current location, the mobile client will send a location request to a LBS server which takes the client's RSS information from multiple access points via Wi-Fi controller to calculate its most probable location based on the lateration result and map information and RF fingerprint with path-loss model in the location server's database [10].

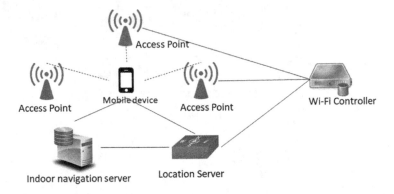

Fig. 2. Hardware Architecture of the Indoor location-based positioning system

The system hardware and software designs are shown in Figs. 2 and 3. Navigation system consists of client application and server applications as shown in Fig [3]. The client application consists of position tracking module that tracks user location, path finding module which calculates the least-cost path between the destination entered by the user and the users' current location, and interactive map which allows sighted and visually impaired user to navigate the map interactively on smart phone. The server application consists of location-based positioning system which estimates the location of the client using RSS Lateration and RF Fingerprinting techniques. The Map and Wi-Fi Management system manages and provides Wi-Fi access point services to the Wi-Fi access points, location-based positioning systems. The report engine provides statistical and visual information to the administrator of the system.

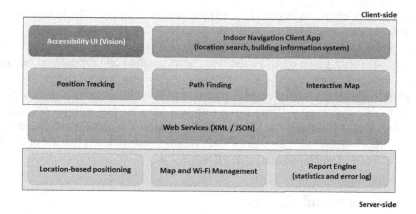

Fig. 3. Software Architecture of the Indoor location-based navigation system

Each room or location is represented by the nodes and the cost (e.g. distance) between any two nodes are represented by the edges of a graph which is used as input to a least-cost path finding algorithm (e.g. Dijkstra or Floyd-Warshall). We designate the exact location position of a room by its door or a designated location.

Once the least-cost path is found, the path will be translated into a set of instructions that will help guide the visually impaired from the current position.

The calculation of the current user location position and the least cost path from the user location position to a destination is performed periodically both in hardware and software in order to provide up-to-date navigation information to the user.

4 Implementation

We installed 13 Cisco 3702 access points with hyperlocation tracking modules which added more directional antennas (for AoA) and Bluetooth Low Energy (BLE) function to improve location tracking capability of the sensors.

The access points were connected to the Cisco UCS C220 M4 server (2.30 GHz E5-2650 with 32 GB of PC4-17000 RAM) via Cisco 2504 Wireless Controller and Catalyst 2960-X 24-port 1 GB switch. VMWare vSphere 6 was installed as platforms for Cisco Prime Infrastructure and CMX server appliance which provides backend map service and location service interface to client's indoor navigation application. The network devices and server are installed in an isolated network.

In order to deploy the access points, we have to consider the placement of the access points in order to ensure that any location positions used in navigation must be able to receive adequate signals from at least 3 access points. This placemen principle is significantly different from installation of access point for network access service which requires a least one highest signal strengths for best connectivity performance. For location-based positioning, we used Cisco's predictive path-loss model to generate RSS heat maps of Wi-Fi signals based on simulated access point installation location to ensure the coverage of at least 3 access points for any location position. We input the locations of walls and other obstacles into the Cisco Prime Infrastructure in order to help improve the path-loss model prediction for heat map generation. After we are satisfied with the simulation results, we calibrated the location-based positioning system by walking around the area with Cisco CMX calibration client installed and running on our smart phones for several times.

We implemented the mobile client application as standalone application on Android and iOS mobile operating systems using standard libraries and utilities provided by Google and Apple (TalkBack and VoiceOver respectively), especially for vision accessibility in order to make sure that sighted and visually impaired users can use our system with low difficulty level and installation effort.

5   Experiments and Results

We installed our system at Ratchasuda College, Mahidol University which is an academic institution for teaching the disabled how to live their lives with disabilities. All 13 access points are installed at the ceiling on the first floor of the main building of Ratchasuda College. Figure 4 shows the installation and the heat map of Wi-Fi signals covering our test area. We tested our system in two aspects: technical testing, usability testing.

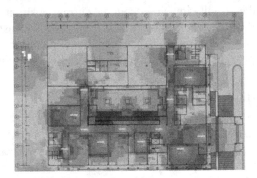

Fig. 4. Simulated heat map of the signal strength of our system installed at Ratchasuda College, Mahidol University. The blue area represents the location of the access points.(Color figure online)

5.1   Technical Testing

We divided our technical testing phase into two sub-phases, hardware testing and software unit testing, to ensure that our hardware and software system could operate correctly. The hardware testing consists of two parts: network test and location-based positioning test. The network test was conducted to ensure that all connections allowed the flows of the data to follow our hardware and network design (Figs. 2 and 3). After testing, we found that all connections performed correctly as we expected and the average delay performance between access points to location server was measured to be 28.72 ms. The delay between a mobile device (smart phone) and location server was measured to be 37.31 ms.

After the hardware system was ready, the software packages were installed and tested. We tested the location-based positioning capability of the hardware and software system using Cisco's web-based testing tools and found that the positions were detected with accuracy error of 1.22 m on average, and the detection delay was measured to be 8 s on average.

We implemented our indoor navigation system for Android and iOS using Cisco CMX API for location-based services and tested it with Samsung Galaxy S7, Samsung Galaxy Note 8, Huawei P9, Apple iPhone 7, and Apple iPhone 7 Plus. The accuracy of location position was measured to be 1.12 m, and the detection delay was measured to be 137 ms on average. We believe that the detection performance of Cisco's web-based testing tools was affected by the web interface of the system. We also found that the accuracy performance of the system dropped significantly in the area around the edge of the system coverage. The least-cost path calculation, navigation and the text-to-speech system was tested and the accuracy performance was satisfactory.

In order to improve the accuracy, precision and delay performance of our system, we tried different approaches such as reducing the RF channel scanning time, adjusting directions of access points' antennas, relocating the access points, and avoiding possible RF interference from other devices in the environment. We observed that if a user waited for at least 1 min, the accuracy error will be less than 1 m with the precision error at 3.05% on average in the dense-AP area and 7.6% on average in the sparse-AP area usually around the edge of the coverage area.

5.2 Usability Testing

We tested our systems with 3 visually impaired and 5 sighted. The sighted people will have their eyes covered to simulate the visually impaired condition. We separated our testing into 2 major functionalities:

5.2.1 Interactive Map

At the beginning, our visually impaired testers tested our system with conventional map system which is a scale-down version of actual map. All of them had problems with the conventional map system since the text-to-speech system could not read the direction and position of the map and the objects on the map were too small. The interactive map as large blocks of rooms or areas was suggested. We revised our interactive map system to be a block-based map only for the selection of room destination. The navigation part used the conventional map concept in the backend since the least-cost finding function still requires a connected graph to operate.

Table 1 shows that all users were quite satisfied with the selection interface of room for origin and destination using visual accessibility utilities such as swiping and text-to-speech (TalkBack and VoiceOver).

Table 1. Usability test results

Test	Average satisfaction level 1 (lowest) to 5 (highest)	
	Visually-impaired	Sighted (eyes closed)
Navigation	3.3	3.1
Interactive map	3.9	3.3
Overall user interface	4.4	3.5
Overall application performance	5	3.3

5.2.2   Navigation

Table 1 shows that all users were satisfied with the guided directions provided by the system. However, during the navigation, the detected location positions did not follow the movement of the users smoothly due to the delay in finding the actual current user position. Occasionally, the detected location positions of user randomly jumped to a different position far away from the average actual user positions.

6   Discussion

The results from the usability tests show that the visually-impaired are slightly more satisfied with our system more than the sighted. This is because the visually-impaired are more familiar with the sound-based non-graphic systems. In technical aspects, even though our indoor navigation for visually impaired system could function correctly and better than several current techniques [13] as we expected, there is still some room for improving the detection performance in accuracy, precision and detection delay. We learnt from our test results that the complexity of walls, hallways and barriers significantly affect accuracy due to shadowing fading and multipath effect. Placing access points by following best practices [10] is recommended.

In order to deal with precision error of the system which could be caused by some fluctuation in the Wi-Fi frequency signals from interference or environment conditions, we compare the last updated client position with prior location and the map. If the last updated client position is too far from prior location and not in a possible area in the map, the client system will send a request to a server to update its position again. According to our experiments, it took at least 60 s for the system to update a client position. Constantly sending requests for client current position by the client to the location server does not always give most current location of the client because the server does not update its client position database quickly. The period for each update is approximately 4 s which is approximately the time required for an access point to scan all Wi-Fi channels in all Wi-Fi frequency spectrum of 2.4 and 5 GHz and calculate client positions [10]. This is not an issue for GPS location positioning because GPS uses only fixed frequency spectrums [1]. We could turn off the scanning of some channels in order to speed up the channel scanning process. In the future, we could improve position and orientation estimation capability using built-in inertial sensors and accelerometer of smart phones to improve location positioning and tracking of our system [11].

7 Conclusion

This work presents an indoor positioning systems for the visually impaired based on RSS Lateration and RF fingerprinting with a special UI designed for the visually impaired. The system achieves accuracy performance of 1.12 m with precision error of 3.05%. This may not be practical because a user has to wait for at least 60 s to get an up-to-date position due to Wi-Fi scanning. Even though our visually impaired testers expressed satisfaction in using our system, other distance estimation strategies such as position and orientation estimation with smartphone's inertial sensor and accelerometer should be used to improve accuracy and delay performance.

Acknowledgments. This research project was supported by the Broadcasting and Telecommunications Research and Development Fund for Public Interest, Office of the National Broadcasting and Telecommunications Commission (Thailand) and partially supported by Faculty of Information and Communication Technology, Mahidol University.

References

1. Parkinson, B.W., Spilker J., Axelrad, P., Enge, P.: Progress in Astronautics and Aeronautics: Global Positioning System: Theory and Applications, vol. 2. AIAA (1996)
2. Liu, H., Darabi, H., Banerjee, P., Liu, J.: Survey of wireless indoor positioning techniques and systems. IEEE Trans. Syst. Man Cybernet. Part C (Appl. Rev.) **37**, 1067–1080 (2007)
3. Ali, A.A., Omar, A.S.: Time of arrival estimation for WLAN indoor positioning systems using matrix pencil super resolution algorithm. In: Proceedings of the 2nd Workshop on Positioning, Navigation and Communication (WPNC), pp. 11–20 (2005)
4. Young, D.P., Keller, C.M., Bliss, D.W., Forsythe, K.W.: Ultra-wideband (UWB) transmitter location using time difference of arrival (TDoA) techniques. In: 37th Asilomar Conference on Signals, Systems and Computers, vol. 2, pp. 1225–1229 (2003)
5. Kumar, P., Reddy, L., Varma, S.: Distance measurement and error estimation scheme for RSSI based localization in wireless sensor networks. In: 5th IEEE Conference on Wireless Communication and Sensor Networks (WCSN), pp. 1–4 (2009)
6. Rong, P., Sichitiu, M.L.: Angle of arrival localization for wireless sensor networks. In: 3rd Annual IEEE Communications Society on Sensor and Ad Hoc Communications and Networks, pp. 374–382 (2006)
7. Chan, S., Sohn, G.: Indoor localization using Wi-Fi based fingerprinting and trilateration techniques for LBS applications. In: International Archives of the Photogrammetry, Remote Sensing and Spatial Information Sciences, XXXVIII-4/C26, pp. 1–5 (2012)
8. Get started on Android with TalkBack. https://support.google.com/accessibility/android
9. Accessibility on iOS – Apple Developer. https://developer.apple.com/accessibility/ios/
10. Cisco Unified Wireless Location Based Services – Cisco Systems. https://www.cisco.com/en/US/docs/solutions/Enterprise/Mobility/emob30dg/Locatn.html
11. Dabove, P., Ghinamo, G., Lingua, A.M.: Inertial Sensors for Smartphones Navigation, Springerplus, PMC, 4:834. https://doi.org/10.1186/s40064-015-1572-8
12. Basiri, A., et al.: Indoor location based services challenges, requirements and usability of current solutions. Comput. Sci. Rev. **24**, 1–12 (2017)
13. Karnik, J., Strelt, J.: Summary of available indoor location techniques. IFAC-PapersOnlione **49**(25), 311–317 (2016)

Specifying an MQTT Tree
for a Connected Smart Home

Adrien van den Bossche[1]([✉]), Nicolas Gonzalez[1], Thierry Val[1], Damien Brulin[2], Frédéric Vella[1], Nadine Vigouroux[1], and Eric Campo[2]

[1] IRIT, CNRS, UPS, UT1, UT2J, Université de Toulouse, Toulouse, France
{Adrien.van-den-Bossche,Nicolas.Gonzalez,Thierry.Val,Frederic.Vella,
Nadine.Vigouroux}@irit.fr
[2] LAAS-CNRS, Université de Toulouse, CNRS, UT2J, Toulouse, France
{Damien.Brulin,Eric.Campo}@laas.fr

Abstract. Ambient Assisted Living (AAL) represents one of the most promising Internet of Things applications due to its influence on the quality of life and health of the elderly people. However, the interoperability is one of the major issues that needs to be addressed to promote the adoption of AAL solutions in real environments, and to find a way of common exchange between the available connected tools to share the data exchanged. This article will present software buses needs and specify an API based on a MQTT software bus treelike architecture. An example is given to illustrate the efficiency of the API developed in a smart home.

Keywords: Ambiant assisted living · Software bus · MQTT
Connected devices · Elderly people · Smart home

1 Introduction

Ambient Assisted Living (AAL) represents one of the most promising Internet of Things (IoT) applications due to its influence on the quality of life and health of the elderly people [1]. AAL can be used for preventing, curing, and improving wellness and health conditions of older adults [2]. IoT consists of connected smart objects capable of identifying, locating, sensing and assisting. [3] gives a survey on the emergence of AAL tools for older adults based on an ambient intelligence paradigm. The technologies mentioned include smart homes (ambient sensors), wearable and mobile sensors, mobile devices, assistive devices, automated systems of processing, and so on, which require a common exchange protocol to share their real time data [4]. However, the interoperability is one of the major issues to be addressed to promote the adoption of AAL solutions in real environments.

In the context of the connected smart homes, the software buses establish a simple and effective way to transfer these data. Due to their open nature, the software buses facilitate this information sharing and allow real time exchanges.

© Springer International Publishing AG, part of Springer Nature 2018
M. Mokhtari et al. (Eds.): ICOST 2018, LNCS 10898, pp. 236–246, 2018.
https://doi.org/10.1007/978-3-319-94523-1_21

However, to allow a reliable, effective and secured access to the sensors, the actuators, the connected objects and the assistive tools of the AAL, an Application Program Interface (API) is needed. For instance, this API allows the interaction devices and processing algorithms to create easily and safely the digital environment. This article specifies such an API based on a MQTT software bus treelike architecture.

After introducing the context of the study, the authors of the article propose a brief state of the art of the software buses and discuss the equivalent proposals found in the literature. The chosen bus, as well as the designed hierarchical model are then detailed. An application of the model in a living lab (smart home of Blagnac) to control ambient sensors is presented, before concluding with a conclusion and perspectives.

2   Context and Problematic

2.1   Messaging Protocols

Messaging Protocols enable simplification of real-time exchanges between connected agents. These information exchanges are done via message notifications instead of polling, which is more efficient for the network. Each message is received by each connected agent, so a high number of messages can be exchanged, which implies an important quantity of resources (Central Processing Unit, memory, bandwith, etc.) on embedded devices that are generally energy constrained. To limit messages, Messaging Protocols provide some filtering mechanisms. Filtering is a key element for the deployment of messaging protocols since it provides selection criteria to select useful messages.

2.2   Need of an API Dedicated to Smart Homes

Intelligent and connected smart home consists of heterogeneous sets of technologies. The high diversity of the current standardised communication technologies (LoRa, Zigbee, KNX, Z-Wave, Bluetooth, etc.) or proprietary substantially increases the complexity of the networking of sensors, actuators, assistive tools and interaction devices deployed in AAL. In addition, one of the propriety needed in the AAL is the high level of reconfigurability.

Instead of sensors and actuators cabling into an electrical panel, it should be preferable to create a logical separation by an erasable programmable element. Moreover, this problem is accentuated by the multiplication of connected devices in the smart home that are not directly interoperable. To solve this problem, the solution is to create a hardware and/or software component that can interact with a device and transcribe its data in a standardised form. This operation can be greatly facilitated by a software bus to unify all the objects deployed with various network technologies; to do this, intermediate gateway nodes must be deployed to help the convergence of data on a common bus.

To be complete and allow good reconfigurability, the software bus can also be used as an API dedicated to smart homes. This API makes it possible to create a logical limit between access to all the physical devices of the house and the software defining the communication. This API must make it possible to activate an actuator of the ambient environment (such as light, shutter, door, etc.) and read the data coming from a sensor, etc. Thus, it will simplify the design and the evaluation of innovative technological components.

This API must be specified by making best use of the features of the selected software bus. The next section details the different software buses used in the field of AAL.

3   Related Works

As previously described, the efficiency of a solution based on a software bus depends strongly on the implemented sharpness of the filtering rules. In the literature, we meet generally three types of filtering [5]:

- Filtering based on the contents: the agents have to subscribe to a message content; to do this, they have to know the message or a part of it. A specification of contents by regular expression, for example, can be used. It is the case of the Ivy bus [6];
- Filtering based on the type: messages are typified by the emitting agent; the receiving agents have to subscribe to a type of particular message to receive it, it is the case of the KNX home automation bus which associates with every transmitted telegram a service identifier type destination;
- Filtering based on the subject: the agents have to subscribe to a shape of subject or topic. From then on, they receive all the subjects published with this subject. MQTT [7] is from this category.

Numerous protocols share the Internet of Things market, particularly CoAP (Constrained Application Protocol), MQTT (Message Queuing Telemetry Transport), AMQP (Advanced Message Queuing Protocol) and HTTP (HyperText Transfer Protocol). MQTT, by its publisher/subscriber paradigm and low protocol footprint, is a very interesting choice for a wide range of small objects [8]. The well-known HTTP protocol is not a binary protocol but a textual protocol, resulting in very large message sizes. It is mainly and historically dedicated to the IP world rather than IoT sensor networks and other connected objects world.

AMQP is a fairly complete protocol in terms of queue management algorithm, which allows it to be the asynchronous complement of HTTP while being able to interface easily with MQTT. AMQP stands out as an interesting choice for backends and gateways but not for constrained embedded systems [9]. CoAP and MQTT are two protocols that meet the same needs. They are more difficult to differentiate for our application [10]. CoAP is based on the User Datagram Protocol (UDP) and therefore it allows less restrictive embedded implementation than MQTT. However, MQTT has a topic filtering with a hierarchical tree organisation which makes it possible to consider very interesting filtering strategies thanks to the relationships between the nodes. In addition, if no queuing mechanism like AMQP is proposed, MQTT provides an option that allows the last message to be retained by the server and sent to any new connection from a client. Finally, MQTT has an extension called MQTT-SN (MQTT For Sensor Networks) that allows the use of the protocol on very constrained networks.

Furthermore, in order to make application software relatively portable and independent from the hardware, it is necessary to create an object abstraction layer by modelling their capabilities and characteristics. This modelling is a major challenge of AAL and Internet of Things (IoT). The purpose of our work, presented in this article, is not to propose a new abstraction layer of IoT, but to demonstrate that MQTT, by means of the structure of topics, makes it possible to implement this representation of flows [11].

With its advanced filtering capabilities, the MQTT bus is thus an excellent candidate to manage data transfer in a connected smart home where many heterogeneous data coexist.

4 Specifying an MQTT Tree for a Connected Smart Home

4.1 Technical Background: MQTT

MQTT is currently popular in the field of IoT, itself very busy in the field of connected smart home. To take full advantage of its advanced filtering by topic, to facilitate the scalability and efficiency of connected objects, and in order to easily analyse the amount of data generated, it is necessary to devote an in depth reflection on the hierarchical organisation of topics.

MQTT is based on a client/server message transport protocol. The agents connected to the bus are the clients and the server is designated by the term "broker". The filtering by topic is provided by this broker. An agent wishing to deposit a message on the bus is a publisher whereas an agent which has subscribed to one or more topic is a subscriber. This principle is illustrated in Fig. 1. An object can be both publisher and subscriber.

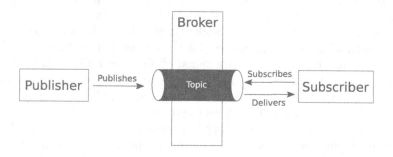

Fig. 1. Broker, suscriber, publisher with MQTT

An MQTT topic is the subject of the published message: it allows to filter messages. An MQTT topic is based on a tree structure where nodes are characters strings and where each level is separated by a slash.

Example: `house/bedroom/light/ceiling`.

MQTT topics are always absolute and noted from the root, which is implicit. To subscribe to a topic, it is possible to combine two wildcards: plus (+) and hash (#). Thus, an agent can subscribe to several subjects at the same time. Below two topics:

`house/bedroom/lamp/ceiling`
`house/bedroom/temperature/bed`

The wildcard + allows to consider the non-filtering and non-hierarchical case "Whatever the value of this topic level". For example, a subscription to `home/+/lamp/ceiling` will allow the agent to receive all ceiling lights in the house. The # wildcard allows you to consider the hierarchical non-filtering case "No matter what is below this topic level". For example, a subscription to `home/bedroom/#` will allow the agent to receive all messages related to the room: temperatures, lamps, etc. The topic tree-structure is free and chosen by the agent; nevertheless a specific configuration on the broker can introduce access rules on the tree (read-only, write-only, access denied) for each authenticated agent.

The MQTT broker does not provide for storing old messages; it is therefore generally necessary to associate the deployment of an MQTT bus to that of a database. However, MQTT proposes the retained mechanism which, if it is activated on a topic, forces the broker to retain the last message on this topic and also to communicate this last message from any new subscription to this topic. This storing is limited to a single previous message.

From this point of view, MQTT is a bus with very interesting features for AAL:

- It is based on TCP/IP: it is not dependent on a particular physical technology, and can be implemented on objects when an IP interface is available (smartphone, tactile tablet, embedded computing device such as Arduino/Raspberry, server...).
- It is based on a standard of IETF (Internet Engineering Task Forces) which is an open standard and recognised by the Internet standardisation agency.
- It is authenticated/encrypted: it makes it possible to initiate a thinking on the security of data and the respect for their retention to the users.
- It is deployable locally and is operational off-line: the broker can be deployed locally in a smart home and can be temporarily or permanently disconnected from the Internet without disruption. It is also possible to deploy a public broker, this makes it easier to share the data.
- MQTT works in real time and keeps in memory the last message: the messages are broadcast with a very low latency which allows the instantaneous processing of messages by automated systems. Moreover, by the retained option described above, the last message can be sent back to the connection, without soliciting the sending agent, which contributes to reducing the connection processing time of the intermittent or ephemeral agents (tablets in sleep mode for example).

However MQTT has some limitations. Because MQTT is based on the principle of flooding unicast messages to different subscribers it then can quickly overload the connected agents if the filtering is not done properly and, then, present a risk of no passage at scale. For example, some solutions minimise the description of the message in the topic and promote a rich content in the payload of the message by using a JavaScript Object Notation. This solution involves the reception and analysis of any message by the agent, whereas this analysis could be done by the broker. Indeed, as previously mentioned, the filtering by topic minimises the number of messages received by an agent. If the agent is an embedded device with few hardware resources (Central Processing Unit, memory, network channel) and energy (because battery power), an optimal filtering permit to maximise the performance of the agent and facilitates the transition to the scale of the entire system.

In a first trial, the housing environment is considered as known and relatively fixed. It can be thus described in a almost exhaustive way with a relatively weak modification frequency. The tree can thus take advantage of this quasi-exhaustive description to facilitate the filtering of messages. The proposed tree has to allow to maximise the possibilities of sorting by the topic specific for MQTT. We shall thus try to maximise the description of the environment to allow a very fine filtering. So, the broker can request the agent as little as possible, by transmitting only the necessary messages and to limit so the network overhead.

Some objects may also be natively MQTT compatible.

4.2   Contribution

As justified above, it is essential to take advantage intelligently of the flows filtering at the broker level to limit the number of messages. It is so necessary to create the most specific possible communication channels by using precise, explicit and hierarchical topics.

The second rule of design is being easily able to take advantage of the subscription in several topics via the use of wildcards. It is necessary to define for it an exhaustive treelike structure the root of which concerns general elements and sheets of which describe very precise elements. However, the design of this treelike structure need to have a complete representation of the ambient assistive tools available in AAL.

The tree proposed here allows to organise and to filter the transfers of messages on the MQTT bus. Its role is to interact with the connected house environment. This API which can evolve over time to propose a new organisation can have different versions. The next section presents the first version of this tree designed for research project on well being for elderly in a Living Lab.

The general format of the tree for the API #1 is represented by Fig. 2.

In this tree, the levels are to be considered by pair, with a first level (odd, n) allowing to interpret the second level (even, $n+1$). For example, at the first level, "api" allows to interpret the identifier "id" at the level 2 as being the version number of the API.

1	2	3	4	5	6	7	8	9
api	<id api>	room	<piece>	device	<device type>	id	<id>	<request/response/indication>

Fig. 2. Generic tree-representation

Levels 3, 5 and 7 are "free levels" where the fields are used to specify the place, the nature and to identify the equipment concerned by the message. Without being exhaustive, the Table 1 gives some examples of possible values by level.

Table 1. Examples of values of level 3, 5 and 7, with corresponding values 4, 6 and 8.

Level n	Content n	Content $n + 1$	Example
3	room	Name of room at level 4	kitchen
3	device	Name of object at level 4	smartphone
5	sensor	Physical parameter at level 6	temperature
5	light	Type of light at level 6	roof
7	id	Identification at level 8	1
7	localisation	Description of localisation at level 8	top door

The last level of the tree indicates the nature of the message, which can be:

- request: that is, a message intended to transport an order for an actuator or a request to interrogate a sensor;
- response: that is, a message in response to a request message, intended to carry the request processing confirmation for an actuator, or the data of a sensor;
- indication: that is, a message intended to carry the data from an actuator or a sensor on its initiative, either in case of change, or in case of regular sending.

Some topics, such as the on-off state of a lamp will be able to take advantage of the *retained* option of MQTT. At the subscription, the agent then automatically receives by the broker the last known value transported over the bus, without requesting the publisher again. This option makes it possible, for example, for a touch pad leaving a standby mode, to update the state of its interaction components without having to query the agents responsible for control of sensors and actuators linked to them.

5   Example of Deployment and Feedback

5.1   Test Platform

A first deployment of the contribution has been done on the *Smart home of Blagnac* living-lab (MIB) [12], dedicated to the elderly. The platform is a "real" house with several rooms: kitchen, bathroom, bedroom, living-room...

Fig. 3. The Smart Home of Blagnac

The MIB living-lab implements several heterogeneous networks and home-automation technologies. The main infrastructure is made of a KNX network for typical home-automation devices: lamps, rolling shutters, motion sensors, mobile furniture. Some others devices implement proprietary IP-based (WiFi, Ethernet) or Zigbee protocols (temperature sensors, other motion sensors, television remote control...). A Text-To-Speech system is also deployed (Fig. 3).

A simple middleware MiCOM [13] has been initially developed and deployed in the MIB living lab. This very simple middleware, based on the HTTP protocol has enabled several studies on usability and acceptability of Information Communication Technologies (tactile and speech interaction) to control an intelligent smart home. For more information, see [14,15]. However the HTTP protocol needs frequent polling for detecting sensors and actuators changes, which is not optimal.

5.2 Deployment on the Platform

The API has been deployed in the MIB Living Lab, in respect for the specification presented in Sect. 4. Several MQTT topics have been used for movement sensors, lamps, rolling shutters and Text-To-Speech system.

The movement sensors are available by room. If multiple sensors are available in a single room, the sensors are identified by the `id`. The deeper level of the tree is `indication`, since the data are published by the sensor; the *retained* option is activated: the broker memorises the last data and automatically sends it on each agent new connection, without need to explicitly request the data to the sensor. Topics are given on Fig. 4.

The lamps are also available by room. The lamp type (*ceiling, bedside...*) is given in the topic. If multiple lamps are available in a single room (such as in the kitchen) the lamps are identified by the `id`. The deeper level of the tree can be either `request` for a modification request or `indication` for a status request.

```
api/1/room/bathroom/sensor/movement/id/1/indication
api/1/room/bedroom/sensor/movement/id/1/indication
api/1/room/livingroom/sensor/movement/id/1/indication
api/1/room/livingroom/sensor/movement/id/2/indication
api/1/room/wc/sensor/movement/id/1/indication
```

Fig. 4. Topics used with movement sensors

The MQTT *retained* option is activated on the indication topic, as well as sensors. Topics are given on Fig. 5.

```
api/1/room/bathroom/lamp/ceiling/id/1/[request|indication]
api/1/room/bedroom/lamp/ceiling/id/1/[request|indication]
api/1/room/bedroom/lamp/bedside/id/1/[request|indication]
api/1/room/kitchen/lamp/ceiling/id/1/[request|indication]
api/1/room/kitchen/lamp/ceiling/id/2/[request|indication]
api/1/room/kitchen/lamp/ceiling/id/3/[request|indication]
api/1/room/livingroom/lamp/ceiling/id/1/[request|indication]
api/1/room/livingroom/lamp/ceiling/id/2/[request|indication]
```

Fig. 5. Topics used with lamps

As well as the lamps, the rolling shutters commands are available for each shutter with a request-type topic; the status (open/closed) is available with the indication topic. Topics are given on Fig. 6.

```
api/1/room/bedroom/window/shutter/id/1/[request|indication]
api/1/room/kitchen/window/shutter/id/1/[request|indication]
api/1/room/livingroom/window/shutter/id/1/[request|indication]
```

Fig. 6. Topics used with rolling shutters

At last, the Text-To-Speech system can be ordered by room or globally with the request topic. Topics are given on Fig. 7.

5.3   Using the API

This section proposes two examples (scenarios) that use the proposed API.

In a first scenario, the resident leaves the home and want to check if one or several lamps of the house are switched on. To proceed, the single following topic can be subscribed: api/1/room/+/lamp/+/id/+/indication. The state of each lamp (whatever the room, the lamp type and for all lamps in each room) is returned by the broker. Thanks to the retained option on these topics, the last state is returned, without need of requesting the current state.

```
api/1/room/bedroom/voice/say/id/1/request
api/1/room/kitchen/voice/say/id/1/request
api/1/room/livingroom/voice/say/id/1/request
```

Fig. 7. Topics used with the speech synthesis

In a second scenario, the resident wants to open all the rolling shutters of the house. As the jokers + and # cannot be used for publication, an exhaustive list of topics should be used to request the opening of the shutters:

```
api/1/room/bedroom/window/shutter/id/1/request
api/1/room/kitchen/window/shutter/id/1/request
api/1/room/livingroom/window/shutter/id/1/request
```

This example thus illustrates one of the limitations of the current (3.1.1) MQTT specification.

6   Conclusion and Perspectives

This paper has introduced the needs of a generic API to connect and share messages of connected objects via heterogeneous networking technologies in the AAL context. This paper has reported the importance and the principles of the MQTT bus. It also demonstrates the pertinence to accurately represent the tree of connected objects of AAL to take benefits of the features of the MQTT bus. In the prototyping of assistive tools for AAL applications, MQTT allows fast-prototyping and rapid deployment. The description syntax is simple and can be used by everyone, including researchers in human-computer interaction to test new control modes as well as engineers in home automation. The deployment on the MIB platform confirms the relevance of the accuracy of the tree-representation.

One of the next challenges concerns the self-adaptation of the API, taking into account the automatic discovery of new connected objects thanks to networking auto-configuration protocols. This automatic discovery mechanism should improve the scalabilty of the services provided by assistive tools of AAL.

References

1. Hammi, B., Khatoun, R., Zeadally, S., Fayad, A., Khoukhi, L.: Internet of Things (IoT) technologies for smart cities. IET Netw. J. **7**(1), 1 (2018)
2. Vergaard Hansen, F.O.: Ambient assisted living healthcare frameworks, platforms, standards, and quality attributes. Sensors (Basel) **14**(3), 4312–4341 (2014)
3. Rashidi, P., Mihailidis, A.: A survey on ambient assisted living tools for older adults. Biomed. Heal. Inform. IEEE J. **17**(3), 579–590 (2013)
4. Yacchirema, D.C., Palau, C.E., Esteve, M.: Enable IoT interoperability in ambient assisted living: active and healthy aging scenarios. In: 2017 14th IEEE Annual Consumer Communications & Networking Conference (CCNC), Las Vegas, NV, 2017, pp. 53–58 (2017)

5. Mühl, G., Fiege, L., Pietzuch, P.R.: Distributed Event-Based Systems. Chap. 2.3 Notification Filtering Mechanisms. Springer, Heidelberg (2006). https://doi.org/10.1007/3-540-32653-7

6. Buisson, M., Bustico, A., Chatty, S., Colin, F-R., Jestin, Y., Maury, S., Mertz, C., Truillet, P.: Ivy : Un bus logiciel au service du développement de prototypes de systémes interactifs, In: ACM IHM 2002, Poitiers, Novembre 2002, pp. 223–226 . ACM Press (2002). (in French)

7. MQTT Specification v3.1.1. http://docs.oasis-open.org/mqtt/mqtt/v3.1.1/os/mqtt-v3.1.1-os.html

8. Naik, N.: Choice of effective messaging protocols for IoT systems: MQTT, CoAP, AMQP and HTTP. In: 2017 IEEE International Systems Engineering Symposium (ISSE), Vienna (2017)

9. Cohn, R.: A Comparison of AMQP and MQTT. White Paper, StormMQ (2011)

10. Thangavel, D., Ma, X., Valera, A., Tan, H.X., Tan, C.K.Y.: Performance evaluation of MQTT and CoAP via a common middleware. In: 2014 IEEE Ninth International Conference on Intelligent Sensors, Sensor Networks and Information Processing (ISSNIP), Singapore (2014)

11. Mainetti, L., Manco, L., Patrono, L., Sergi, I., Vergallo, R.: Web of topics: an IoT-aware model-driven designing approach. In: 2nd IEEE World Forum on Internet of Things (IEEE WF-IoT). IEEE (2015)

12. The "Maison Intelligente de Blagnac" (Blagnac City's Smart Home) living lab website. http://mib.iut-blagnac.fr. (in French)

13. Vella, F., Blanc Machado, M., Vigouroux, N., van den Bossche, A., Val, T.: Connexion du Middleware MiCom avec l'interface tactile InTacS pour le contrôle d'une smart home. Journées francophones Mobilité et Ubiquité, Lorient, France (2016). (in French)

14. Bougeois, E., Duchier, J., Vella, F., Machado, M.B., Van den Bossche, A., Val, T., Brulin, D., Vigouroux, N., Campo, E.: Post-test perceptions of digital tools by the elderly in an ambient environment. In: Chang, C.K., Chiari, L., Cao, Y., Jin, H., Mokhtari, M., Aloulou, H. (eds.) ICOST 2016. LNCS, vol. 9677, pp. 356–367. Springer, Cham (2016). https://doi.org/10.1007/978-3-319-39601-9_32

15. Van den Bossche, A., Campo, E., Duchier, J., Bougeois, E., Machado, M.B., Val, T., Vella, F., Vigouroux, N.: Multidimensional observation methodology for the elderly in an ambient digital environment. In: Miesenberger, K., Bühler, C., Penaz, P. (eds.) ICCHP 2016. LNCS, vol. 9758, pp. 285–292. Springer, Cham (2016). https://doi.org/10.1007/978-3-319-41264-1_39

Short Contributions

Deep Learning Model for Detection of Pain Intensity from Facial Expression

Jeffrey Soar[1(✉)], Ghazal Bargshady[1], Xujuan Zhou[1], and Frank Whittaker[2]

[1] University of Southern Queensland, Queensland, Australia
soar@usq.edu.au
[2] Nexus eCare, Melbourne, Australia

Abstract. Many people who are suffering from a chronic pain face periods of acute pain and resulting problems during their illness and adequate reporting of symptoms is necessary for treatment. Some patients have difficulties in adequately alerting caregivers to their pain or describing the intensity which can impact on effective treatment. Pain and its intensity can be noticeable in ones face. Movements in facial muscles can depict ones current emotional state. Machine learning algorithms can detect pain intensity from facial expressions. The algorithm can extract and classify facial expression of pain among patients. In this paper, we propose a new deep learning model for detection of pain intensity from facial expressions. This automatic pain detection system may help clinicians to detect pain and its intensity in patients and by doing this healthcare organizations may have access to more complete and more regular information of patients regarding their pain.

1   Introduction

Painful conditions are one of the most common reasons that patients seek health care [1]; some patients may have difficulty providing accurate recall of pain or may be unwilling to disclose their pain. Assessment can be invasive and inconvenient [2].

The needs of the large number of people in chronic pain overwhelms health- care systems, and continues to worsen [3]. Healthcare providers may be less able to help patients who have chronic pain if there is not a complete understanding of symptoms and some patients such as the very young, or those with particular disabilities or conditions, may not be able to articulate their experiences. Automatic pain management systems have been demonstrated to better help clinicians to detect the level of pain of patients [2].

Faces have evolved to convey rich information for social interaction, including the expression of emotions and pain [4]. Researchers have applied machine learning to the task of automatic pain detection in a real-world clinical setting involving patients suffering pain [5].

In this study, we proposed a new deep learning model for detection of pain intensity from facial expressions. This automatic pain detection model can be used as a smart technology to detect pain level and can help patients and their careers to monitor and manage chronic pain.

© Springer International Publishing AG, part of Springer Nature 2018
M. Mokhtari et al. (Eds.): ICOST 2018, LNCS 10898, pp. 249–254, 2018.
https://doi.org/10.1007/978-3-319-94523-1_22

2 Related Work

2.1 Deep Learning

In the last few years, deep neural networks have become the classifier of choice for many machine learning tasks. Simply put, deep neural networks (DNNs) are a group of models that perform nonlinear function approximation. Suppose there is a function f that relates input x to some label y, a neural network learns a function f ($y = f(x; \theta)$) that approximates f, the true mapping from x to y, using parameters θ [6]. A deep neural network is usually represented as the composition of multiple nonlinear functions. Therefore, $f(x)$ can be expressed in the following manner:

$$f(x) = f^{(N)}\left(\left(f^{(3)}\left(f^{(2)}\left(f^{(1)}(x)\right)\right)\right)\right) \tag{1}$$

Equation 1 defines a feed-forward network or multilayer perceptron (MLP). It is called feed-forward because the output of each function $f^{(i)}$ is passed as input to the next function $f^{(i+1)}$. Each function $f^{(i)}$ represents a layer in the neural network and is typically composed of an affine operation followed by an element-wise nonlinearity: sigmoid, hyperbolic tangent (tanh), or rectified linear unit (ReLU). Consider some input $x \varepsilon R^N$ and its corresponding output $z \varepsilon R^M$, a simple exam- ple of a neural network layer is given in Eq. 2, where $W \varepsilon R^{M \times N}$ and $b \varepsilon R^M$ are the parameters to be learned and h is a user-selected nonlinear function. Each element of x is called an input unit and each element of z is an output unit. The depth of a neural network is defined as the number of layers. A neural network is usually classified as deep if it has a depth of three or more layers [6]:

$$z = h(W_x + b) \tag{2}$$

Convolutional Neural Networks (CNNs). One common modification to MLPs, which makes the network more suitable for tasks specific to computer vision, is to make the affine transformation in each layer a convolution operation. These networks are called Convolutional Neural Networks (CNNs) [7]. In an MLP, each output unit in z is dependent on all input units in x. This design, however, does not allow the network to model the local structures commonly found in images. With CNNs, each output unit in z is instead connected to a reduced number of input units, specifically a small contiguous region in the input. The reduction in the number of connections also means that CNNs have considerably fewer parameters to learn than MLPs [7].

Recurrent Neural Networks (RNNs). Despite being powerful tools for function approximation, MLPs and CNNs have one main drawback. They are both have difficulty modelling sequential data. This can be particularly problematic when dealing with speech or video data. In these instances, it would be advantageous to have a model whose feature representation can capture information from all the previous time steps but can also update its representation with what it sees in the future. Recurrent Neural Networks (RNNs) [8] present one way to create such a model. Consider a sequence of inputs of length $T(x1, ..., xt)$. RNNs have a state at each time point t, h_t, which captures all information of previous inputs $(x1, \ldots, xt)$. Then, when considering the input at the next time point, x_{t+1}, a new state, h_{t+1}, is computed using the new input x_{t+1} and the previous state h_t. At each time point t, the hidden state h_t can be used to compute an output O_t, typically a class label for classification or a continuous number for regression [9].

2.2   CNN Models for Facial Expression Analysis

Deep models such as deep belief and deep convolutional networks have allowed us to have an insight into the effect on extracting robust and abstract features [10] and some deep models are used for facial expression [11]. Susskind et al. [11] learned deep belief nets without supervision for recognizing facial action units and they showed features extracted by learned belief nets could easily accommodate different constraints in a real expressive environment. Differently, Xu et al. [12] used transfer features from deep convolutional networks to recognize facial expression, and they showed deep convolutional networks are more suitable for classification than deep belief nets. They used a facial expression recognition model on transfer features from deep convolutional networks (ConvNets) for face identification.

Liu et al. [13] introduced an AU (Action Unit) aware receptive field layer in a deep network, designed to search subsets of the over-complete representation, each of which aims at best simulating the combination of AUs. Its output is then passed through additional layers aimed at the expression classification, showing a large improvement over the traditional hand-crafted image features such as LBPs, SIFT and Gabors. Another example occurs where a CNN is jointly trained for detection and intensity estimation of multiple AUs. The authors pro- posed a network architecture composed of 3 convolutional and 1 max-pooling layers [14]. Zhao et al. [15] introduced an intermediate region layer that can learn region specific weights of CNNs. The region layer returns an importance map for each input image and the network is trained for joint AU detection. All these methods focus solely on feature extraction while the network output remains unstructured. Walecki et al. [16] introduced model structures and estimate complex feature representations simultaneously by combining conditional random field (CRF) encoded AU dependencies with deep learning. They designed a novel Copula CNN deep learning approach for modelling multivariate ordinal variables. Their model accounts for ordinal structure in output variables and their non-linear dependencies via copula functions modelled as cliques of a CRF.

3   Proposed Model

Based on the previous studies, the proposed model to detect patients pain intensity from facial expressions effectively was designed as BiLSTM-CNN-VSL-CRF framework. Figure 1 illustrates the architecture of our network in detail.

3.1   Long Short-Term Memory Networks (LSTM)

LSTM is a type of RNN which is capable of learning long-term dependencies present on sequential data. Standard RNNs are theoretically capable of learning long term

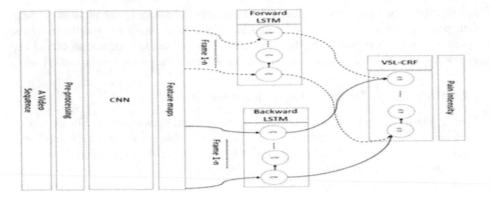

Fig. 1. The proposed model for pain intensity estimation from facial expression

dependencies, but in practice, it is difficult to train them because the gradients tend to either explode or vanish. LSTM differs from standard RNN because it has a cell state controlled by three gates, which decide how much information should be let through. These gates are known as forget, input and output gates. The amount of information that is let through each gate is controlled by a point-wise multiplication and sigmoid function, as the sigmoid function output is between 0 and 1, indicating how much of the information should let through the gate. At each time-step, the input gate is computed depending on the input to the LSTM for that time-step and the previously hidden state.

3.2   Bidirectional Long Short-Term Memory (BiLSTM)

For many sequences labeling tasks it is beneficial to have access to both past (left) and future (right) frames. However, the LSTM's hidden state h_t takes information only from past, knowing nothing about the future. An elegant solution whose effectiveness has been proven by previous work is bidirectional LSTM (BiLSTM). The basic idea is to present each sequence forwards and backwards as two separate hidden states to capture past and future information, respectively. Then the two hidden states are concatenated to form the final output.

3.3   VSL-CRF (Variable-State Latent Conditional Random Field)

CRFs are a class of log-linear models that represent the conditional distribution $P(h|x)$ as the Gibbs form clamped on the observation x [17]:

$$P(h|x, \theta) = \frac{1}{Z(x; \theta)} e^{s(x,h;\theta)} \tag{3}$$

Here, $Z(x; \theta) = h \in H e^{s(x,h;\theta)}$ is the normalizing partition function (H is a set of all possible output configurations), and θ are the parameters of the score function (or the negative energy) $s(x, h; \theta)$. Note that in this model, the states h is observed, and they represent the frame labels.

In VSL-CRF $v = (v1, ..., vk)$ be a vector of symbolic states or labels encoding the nature of the latent states h^v of the $i - th$ sequence, $i = 1, ..., N_y$ from class $y = (1, ..., K)$, either as nominal ($v_y = 0$) or ordinal ($v_y = 1$). The score function for class y in the VSL-CRF model is then defined as:

$$
s(y, x, h, v; \partial) =
\begin{cases}
\sum_{k=1}^{k} I(k = y) \cdot s\left(x, h; \theta_y^n\right), & \text{if } v_y = 0 \\
\sum_{k=1}^{k} I(k = y) \cdot s\left(x, h; \theta_y^o\right), & \text{if } v_y = 1
\end{cases}
\tag{4}
$$

where the nominal ($s(x, h; \theta^n)$) and ordinal ($s(x, h; \theta^o)$) score functions represent the sum of the node and edge potentials, respectively. Then, the full conditional probability of the VSL-CRF model is given by:

$$
P(y|x) = \sum_{h,v} P(y, h, v|x) = \frac{\sum_{h,v} exp(s(y, x, h, v))}{Z(x)}
\tag{5}
$$

where $Z(x) = \sum_{k,h,v} exp(s(k, x, h, v))$.

The VSL-CRF also performs integration over the latent variable m, the state of which (ordinal or nominal) defines the type of the latent states for each sequence of facial expressions [16]. The definition of the VSL-CRF in Eq. 5 allows it to simultaneously fit both ordinal and nominal latent states to each sequence, which may result in the model overfitting [16].

4 Conclusion and Future Work

There is interest in automatic pain intensity estimation in healthcare and medical fields. In the past decade, many approaches have been proposed for automatic pain intensity estimation. Early researchers tended to focus on estimating whether the subject is in pain or not, and thus, conduct pain intensity estimation as a classification problem by using deep learning. While the effectiveness of these models has been demonstrated on many general vision problems, in the facial data domain obtaining accurate and comprehensive labels is typically difficult. The model proposed in this paper has advantages over previous work offering significant potential for pain sufferers, their families and their careers.

For future work, we will develop a prototype system based on our new model. This automatic pain detection system will be tested using real work dataset.

References

1. Bicket, M.C., Mao, J.: Chronic pain in older adults. Anesthesiol. Clin. **33**, 577–590 (2015)
2. Kharghanian, R.; Peiravi, A., Moradi, F.: Pain detection from facial images using unsupervised feature learning approach. In: 2016 IEEE 38th Annual International Conference of the Engineering in Medicine and Biology Society (EMBC), pp. 419–422 (2016)
3. Thomas, D., Frascella, J., Hall, T., Smith, W., Compton, W., Koroshetz, W., Briggs, J., Grady, P., Somerman, M., Volkow, N.: Reflections on the role of opioids in the treatment of chronic pain: a shared solution for prescription opioid abuse and pain. J. Intern. Med. **278**, 92–94 (2015)
4. Frank, M.G., Ekman, P., Friesen, W.V.: Behavioral markers and recognizability of the smile of enjoyment. J. Pers. Soc. Psychol. **64**, 83 (1993)
5. Fasel, B., Luettin, J.: Automatic facial expression analysis: a survey. Pattern Recogn. **36**, 259–275 (2003)
6. LeCun, Y., Bengio, Y., Hinton, G.: Deep learning. Nature **521**, 436 (2015)
7. LeCun, Y., Bottou, L., Bengio, Y., Haffner, P.: Gradient-based learning applied to document recognition. Proc. IEEE **86**, 2278–2324 (1998)
8. Rumelhart, D.E., Hinton, G.E., Williams, R.J.: Learning representations by back-propagating errors. Nature **323**, 533 (1986)
9. Zhou, J.; Hong, X.; Su, F., Zhao, G.: Recurrent convolutional neural network regression for continuous pain intensity estimation in video. In: Proceedings of the IEEE Conference on Computer Vision and Pattern Recognition Workshops, pp. 84–92 (2016)
10. Krizhevsky, A.; Sutskever, I., Hinton, G.E.: Imagenet classification with deep convolutional neural networks. In: Advances in Neural Information Processing Systems, pp. 1097–1105 (2012)
11. Susskind, J.M., Hinton, G.E., Movellan, J.R., Anderson, A.K.: Generating facial expressions with deep belief nets. In: Affective Computing. InTech (2008)
12. Xu, M., Cheng, W., Zhao, Q., Ma, L., Xu, F.: Facial expression recognition based on transfer learning from deep convolutional networks. In: 2015 11th International Conference on Natural Computation (ICNC), pp. 702–708 (2015)
13. Liu, M., Li, S., Shan, S., Chen, X.: AU-aware deep networks for facial expression recognition. In: 2013 10th IEEE International Conference and Workshops on Automatic Face and Gesture Recognition (FG), pp. 1–6 (2013)
14. Gudi, A., Tasli, H.E., Den Uyl, T.M., Maroulis, A.: Deep learning based facs action unit occurrence and intensity estimation. In: 2015 11th IEEE International Conference and Workshops on Automatic Face and Gesture Recognition (FG), vol. 6, pp. 1–5 (2015)
15. Zhao, K., Chu, W.-S., Zhang, H.: Deep region and multi-label learning for facial action unit detection. In: Proceedings of the IEEE Conference on Computer Vision and Pattern Recognition, pp. 3391–3399 (2016)
16. Walecki, R., Rudovic, O., Pavlovic, V., Pantic, M.: Variable-state latent conditional random field models for facial expression analysis. Image Vis. Comput. **58**, 25–37 (2017)
17. Lafferty, J., McCallum, A., Pereira, F.C.N.: Conditional random fields: probabilistic models for segmenting and labeling sequence data. In: Proceeding of the 18th International Conference on Machine Learning 2001 (ICML 2001), pp. 282–289 (2001)

Study of Critical Vital Signs Using Deep Learning

Diego Felipe Rodríguez Chaparro[1],
Octavio José Salcedo Parra[1,2(✉)], and Erika Upegui[3]

[1] Department of Systems and Industrial Engineering, Faculty of Engineering,
Universidad Nacional de Colombia, Bogotá D.C., Colombia
{diefrodriguezcha,ojsalcedop}@unal.edu.co
[2] Faculty of Engineering, Intelligent Internet Research Group,
Universidad Distrital "Francisco José de Caldas", Bogotá D.C., Colombia
osalcedo@udistrital.edu.co
[3] Faculty of Engineering, GRSS-IEEE/UD & GEFEM Research Group,
Universidad Distrital "Francisco José de Caldas", Bogotá D.C., Colombia
esupeguic@udistrital.edu.co

Abstract. As the popularity of Deep Learning grows in the Science field, it is hard to avoid experiencing and discovering the scope of this powerful tool and all it has to offer. This work explores the possibility of using Deep Learning methodologies in the Medicine framework, oriented specifically to the study of vital signs from critical patients in the ER. Using a public domain dataset taken from Massachusetts General Hospital as well as the learning modules from Python, the objective is to use Deep Learning to calculate a patient's chances of survival based on his vital signs.

Keywords: Deep learning · Emergency room · Keras · Python
Vital signs introduction

1 Introduction

Nowadays, Machine Learning has gained popularity through several research fields, especially those that deal with large volumes of information for task automation and pattern modeling. Since the 1970s, researchers have been working in the study, creation and refinement of techniques that allow a computer to learn from observational data which led to the appearance of neural networks. A standard neural network consists of various interrelated processes called neurons which generate specific activations depending on the received stimuli, their interconnections or the actions caused by the stimuli [1].

As years went by and the techniques were polished, Deep Learning became popular due to this computation paradigm's scope. Its applications go from the advertising field with the analysis of search patterns to determine the type of advertising that would be the most attractive up to the Physics field with the study of large amounts of data to make predictions of future cosmic events. Its applications seem limitless.

Nevertheless, there is no doubt that the Medicine sector has the most attractive applications; doctors are able of getting more precise diagnostics and therefore prevent

© Springer International Publishing AG, part of Springer Nature 2018
M. Mokhtari et al. (Eds.): ICOST 2018, LNCS 10898, pp. 255–260, 2018.
https://doi.org/10.1007/978-3-319-94523-1_23

diseases during the early stages. In the emergency room (ER) where every second counts it is not only important to rapidly move and care for the patient but it is also crucial for the patient's survival to give a fast assessment and proper diagnosis [2].

2 Background

As was previously stated, the deep learning subject has become more appealing due to its never-ending multidisciplinary scope of application. The use of this model has contributed to the creation of various fields such as neural networks, graphic models, feature learning, unsupervised learning, pattern recognition and signal processing [3]. In image processing and its classification is where our focus lies, specifically in the medical field with the analysis of biomedical images which began in 1865 with the discovery of X-rays. This allowed a better understanding of how diseases manifested themselves inside the body [4] and paved the way for new advances.

The combination of Deep Learning and Medicine has enabled the use of precise diagnosis that can save lives. Although it shows great advances, the implementation of these technologies is still in its early stages and is not error-free. In B. Gerazov and R Conceicao's work this can be evidenced; in the study of X-ray mammography, there is an issue where the breast's natural tissue shows a dielectric contrast which is very similar to the one located on malign tumors. This leads to higher error rates in the detection [5]. The purpose of this work is to improve the classification percentage of tumors through Deep Learning which was possible with a hybrid approach known as a Deep Neural Network which was given not only images of mammograms but also classification results from conventional Machine Learning implementations.

Promising results were obtained with the previous research taking into account the existing limitations in terms of the reduced volume of the available information. This is only one of the aspects that affect this complex problem since this is a classification task that seeks optimal balance between the accuracy of the obtained classifications and the computational cost [6]. It can be approached in two different ways since the dataset provides two types of information: it provides visual readings from the patient's vital signs that show the states of the body's various systems. Since these signals are so complex, it is necessary to train the system to recognize the current situation of the patient based on those images. In Yudin and Zeno's work [7], two previously trained convolutional neural networks (CNN) were used and the machine managed a success rate of 83.2% when trying to classify images in 10 special categories: "ceremony", "concert", "demonstration", "football", "picnic", "race cars", "reunion", "swimming", "tennis", "traffic".

The other type of information that the dataset provides is a logbook that contains the records from the performed procedures to stabilize the patient. In previous work, where it is sought to predict future results by studying only the present that changes, a statistical analysis has been proposed in order to deliver success or failure rates [8]. This is only being explored up to now.

3   Methodology

The Keras library for Python and the MGH/MF waveform dataset from the physio.net website [9] were used as main tools to carry out this project. This dataset contains 250 records from patients that entered the Massachusetts General Hospital ER where the patient's entire information is stored as well as a digital form of his vital signs.

Some of these records include a logbook of the procedures performed on patients during their stay in the emergency room. Most of the data is qualitative so the parameters that are not decisive for the model will be ignored and a numeric value will be implemented for those that satisfy a descriptive function leaving the list of data as follows:

Patient data:

- Age: Numerical value of the patient's age
- Gender: 0 for male, 1 for female
- Pertinent medical record: 1 if the patient has one, 0 if not

Hemodynamic data

- Blood pressure: Numerical value
- Pulmonary blood pressure: Numerical value
- Right auricular pressure: Numerical value
- Rhythm: Numerical value
- Ventilation mode: This variable will have a value from 0 to 12, a unique value for every different value found in this description.

All this information corresponds to the input data for the Deep Learning model which will be organized in a .csv file so that the model accepts it without problems.

Since the dataset is small, the model will be trained by dividing the 250 registers into groups and they will go through the model one at a time in order to optimize and adjust it. This is known as the Stochastic Descending Gradient. This approach has proven to be useful when the amount of information is limited as in this case.

The model will obey to a disposition similar to the one shown in Fig. 1. The model will have dense connections to every node of the next layer which is recommended to have better results. In the output layer, two nodes will represent whether the patient will live or die seen as a classification problem.

As the experiments progress, the number of hidden layers and their nodes will be varied in order to minimize the error value and obtain more accurate predictions.

The activation function to be used in the hidden layers will be the ReLU (Rectified Linear Function) function that is included in the Keras library to capture nonlinear behavior. In the output layer, the *softmax* function will be used which is the most suitable in classification cases such as this one.

In the adjustment and optimization part, to achieve reverse propagation, the '*adam*' optimization function and 'categorical_crossentropy' loss function will be used. They are both included in Keras and are a suitable recommendation for these types of problems. To facilitate the interpretation of the model in terms of training progress, we will

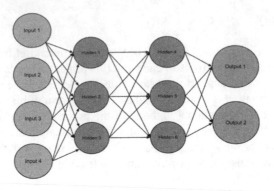

Fig. 1. Sequential model

add that the metrics are given in terms of accuracy during compilation. This will deliver a success rate of classification in their respective category.

The 'fitting' part of the model will be performed with the results thrown by the model and the real results. They will be obtained by interpreting the procedure logbooks to know if the patient lived or died after staying at the ER.

4 Design and Implementation

The focus of the Project is to prove the viability that a Deep Learning system can predict the survival capacity of an individual that is hospitalized in the ER. Since this work has a more experimental emphasis, it was decided to work on the Keras library from Python that enables to swiftly implement the solution and test it; it is necessary to have a Python version between 2.7 and 3.6 and have a smart learning library such as Tensorflow, CNTK or Theano. This experiment will use the Tensorflow at version r1.4 for Linux along with Python 2.7.

The initial model has a simple disposition; starting from a three hidden layer model without including the output layer, the hidden layers will have 50 nodes and the result layer will have 2 corresponding to the possible outcomes of this binary classification. Afterwards, the amount of nodes per layer will be varied and then the number of layers in the model with the purpose of reducing the loss function's value and increasing the prediction's success rate.

As previously mentioned, given the limited number of records in the dataset, it was chosen to train the model following the Stochastic Descending Gradient. After depurating the dataset and creating a new .csv file from the initial 250 registers, only 233 were usable as input. Most of them do not include complete data. The reasons behind this are mentioned in the records per se: system errors led to loss of information, the described situation was so extreme that there was no time to keep track of the records.

The records will be divided into batches of 50 records for the 'fitting' section of the model.

5   Evaluation of Results

After various tests with the model and performing the necessary adjustments, the results were improved with the following disposition:

A model with 4 hidden layers with 60 nodes each and the activation function 'ReLU'

- The output layer with 2 nodes and 'softmax' activation.
- In the compilation part, the 'adam' optimization function was used as well as the loss function 'categorical_crossentropy'
- The callback 'Early Stopping' was used with a 3 period patient value
- In the 'fitting' part, a lot size of 64 was used and in the end it was decided to use 30% of the data for validation and another 70% for training.

With this configuration, the following result was obtained:
60.12% accuracy was achieved in terms of prediction which is a good result that supports even further the idea of deep learning especially in classification tasks.

Fig. 2. Construction of the model

6   Discussion of Results

At the beginning, the results obtained seem promising with an accuracy of over 50% but if observed carefully many flaws can be detected. The dataset showed missing data which greatly affected the value of the loss function which can be seen in Fig. 2. The value of 'Nan' (not available) shows up and this is due to the explosive gradient issue that occurs because of two reasons: the first one is when the learning pace in the optimization function is too large and the results of the operation are not correct and propagate the error. In this experiment, this is not the case since the 'adam' function calculates the best pace to avoid such issue. The second reason happens when the loss function has very high values or very low values and the program detects the abnormal values so it gives the function an undefined or 'Nan' value. This happened in our case since there was data missing when training the model.

7   Conclusions

The use of Deep Learning in the Medicine field has proven to be a tool with great potential that promises to help improve the condition of the human being. This experiment only gives a glance at the potential of studying vital signs with machine learning. In future experiments, the multidisciplinary nature of projects such as this one need the help of experts that can offer advice on important aspects of the field. The possibility of using a different library than Keras must also be explored to enable the use of non-numerical data. Ana accurate numerical scale that represents a qualitative data is not always attainable. The results can be improved in various ways such as using a dataset with complete data depending on the final goal and choosing optimization, loss and activation functions that are suitable for the analyzed data. In this way, future investigations will offer better results in this medical research field.

References

1. Schmidhuber, J.: Deep learning in neural networks: an overview. Neural Netw **61**, 85–117 (2015). https://doi.org/10.1016/j.neunet.2014.09.003. http://www.sciencedirect.com/science/article/pii/S0893608014002135, ISSN 0893-6080
2. Webb, G.L., McSwain, N.E., Webb, W.R., Rodriguez, C.: Emergency department deaths. Am. J. Surg. **159**(4), 377–379 (1990). https://doi.org/10.1016/S00029610(05)81275-9. http://www.sciencedirect.com/science/article/pii/S0002961005812759, ISSN 0002-9610
3. Bengio, S., Deng, L., Larochelle, H., Lee, H., Salakhutdinov, R.: Guest editors' introduction: special section on learning deep architectures. IEEE Trans. Pattern Anal. Mach. Intell. **35**(8), 1795–1797 (2013)
4. Bradley, W.G.: History of medical imaging. In: Proceedings of the American Philosophical Society, vol. 152, No. 3, pp. 349–361 (2008)
5. Gerazov, B., Conceicao, R. C.: Deep learning for tumour classification in homogeneous breast tissue in medical microwave imaging. In: IEEE EUROCON 2017 (2017)
6. Affonso, C., Rossi, A.L.D., Vieira, F.H.A., de Carvalho, A.C.P.D.L.F.: Deep learning for biological image classification. Expert Syst. Appl. **85**, 114122 (2017). https://doi.org/10.1016/j.eswa.2017.05.039
7. Yudin, D., Zeno, B.: Event recognition on images by fine-tuning of deep neural networks. In: Abraham, A., Kovalev, S., Tarassov, V., Snasel, V., Vasileva, M., Sukhanov, A. (eds.) IITI 2017. AISC, vol. 679, pp. 479–487. Springer, Cham (2018). https://doi.org/10.1007/978-3-319-68321-8_49
8. Khan, S.H., Hayat, M., Bennamoun, M., Sohel, F.A., Togneri, R.: Cost-sensitive learning of deep feature representations from imbalanced data (2017)

Generation of Pure Trajectories for Continuous Movements in the Rehabilitation of Lower Member Using Exoskeletons

María Camila Sierra Herrera[1], Octavio José Salcedo Parra[1,2(✉)], and Javier Medina[3]

[1] Department of Systems and Industrial Engineering, Faculty of Engineering, Universidad Nacional de Colombia, Bogotá D.C, Colombia
{macsierrahe, ojsalcedop}@unal.edu.co
[2] Faculty of Engineering, Intelligent Internet Research Group, Universidad Distrital "Francisco José de Caldas", Bogotá D.C, Colombia
osalcedo@udistrital.edu.co
[3] Faculty of Engineering, GEFEM Research Group, Universidad Distrital "Francisco José de Caldas", Bogotá D.C, Colombia
rmedina@udistrital.edu.co

Abstract. In this article, the analysis of pure movements of the lower limb of the human being applied to the design of exoskeletons is explained, in order to be able to obtain bases for the selection of which meet the appropriate torque requirements that can move the robot and help perform continuous trajectories. These values are based on the trajectories that are obtained by measuring the orientation of the lower limb while the patient performs pure rehabilitation movements.

Having these movements fully developed, a communication can be applied by Bluetooth protocol, in such a way that signals are sent between the two parts of the exoskeleton of the lower limb to generate a successive walk clearly necessary in the rehabilitation.

Keywords: Lower limb · Bluetooth communication · Maximum torques Dynamic analysis · Orientations

1 Introduction

Actually, the medical robotic industry is booming, as well as limb injuries inferior [1], this is why it is important to exoskeleton that helps generate facilities in the realization of rehabilitation therapies. The medical professionals value positively [2] this type of robotic systems due to the fact that they finally end up injured in their back to the continued high efforts that should perform, which are most affected with the influence of a greater weight of the patient or a very serious injury since the effort of the subject is minimal and that of the physiotherapist should be maximum to obtain a satisfactory therapy.

© Springer International Publishing AG, part of Springer Nature 2018
M. Mokhtari et al. (Eds.): ICOST 2018, LNCS 10898, pp. 261–269, 2018.
https://doi.org/10.1007/978-3-319-94523-1_24

For an exoskeleton to be effective it must be designed with adequate material, but still more important the engines that provide the movement space should be able to withstand the high torques exerted, which can be produced by different factors, between them: high weight of a patient, or very serious injury.

Thus, there are many jobs that have been focused on the design of robots that help the lower limb rehabilitation [3, 4], but still there are more works that focus on the analysis dynamic of robots for engine selection [5, 6]. In others, the focus is on construction of interfaces for obtaining movements in healthy patients, who act as a reference [7, 8].

This paper introduces an analysis of the pure trajectory planning model for be able to generate continuous movements with a lower limb exoskeleton.

2   Background

In the world of medicine it is a challenge guarantee a person after an accident that the recovery process is quick and, also, provide the possibilities to eliminate all the physical consequences of the accident. In this way, Engineering intends to join this world for a long time generating the possibility of carrying out the rehabilitation processes of a more efficient and effective way, generating in the patient compliance with the results obtained after a tragedy.

Thus, many engineers focused on medical robotics seek to make exoskeletons that streamline these methods by helping both patients as health professionals involved in these processes. The fact of making an exoskeleton brings back many studies, from selection of materials, dynamic analysis, kinematic analysis, modeling, testing and so on, and thus being the interest of each one can focus on different stages of the general design of an exoskeleton.

There are works that show the general design of exoskeletons, in this case, for lower member as shown in [9, 10]. For other part, it is essential to establish the requirements necessary for the realization of an exoskeleton of lower limb in [11, 12] are shown developments that exoskeletons have had lower limb together with the bases that give rise to the improvement of these.

3   Methodology

For the development of this project the same in 4 parts:

- Modeling the exoskeleton,
- Realization of an interface where they will visualize the results,
- Analysis and realization of movement's cigars for the member exoskeleton lower,
- Combination of movements for generate a walk simulation.

4 Design

4.1 Analysis of Components

Taking into account, the member's parts lower views in Fig. 1, a recognition of the parts that make up the inferior member of the human being, in such a way that you can create a scaled version of it and be able to replicate the movement in a real test.

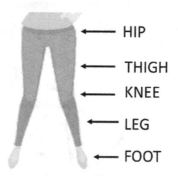

Fig. 1. Parts of the lower limb.

The exoskeleton parts were made up of the following way: the hip from the sacred region to the greater trochanter, the thigh from the trochanter greater to the kneecap, the leg from the kneecap to the ankle and the foot from the ankle to the tip of the fat finger of this one.

4.2 Rehabilitation Movements

Rehabilitation movements change according to the affected area in the lower limb, as well that many of these could be analyzed. In this case, the movements of interest are those where the joint must make the greatest effort, what refers to pure movements.

For the case of the hip, abduction would be and adduction shown in Fig. 2, for the thigh and the leg has flexion and extension movements seen in Figs. 3 and 4, respectively, and for the foot you have the dorsiflexion and plantarflexion, Fig. 5.

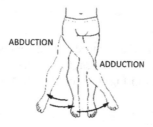

Fig. 2. Pure movements of the hip.

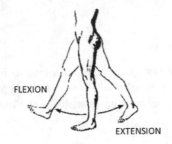

Fig. 3. Pure movements of the thigh.

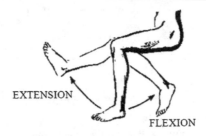

Fig. 4. Pure movements of the leg.

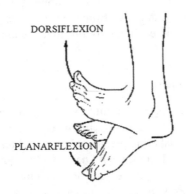

Fig. 5. Pure movements of the foot.

4.3   Modeling in Inventor

A model was designed in Inventor based on the parts already mentioned above, maintaining a synchrony between the lengths of each of the parties, so the result obtained was the next, as seen in Fig. 6. Modeling in Inventor.

Fig. 6. Modeling in Inventor.

4.4 Dynamic Model Assignment in Adams

The inventor model was exported to a file CAD which could be read in Adams, assigning after the movement restrictions Suitable: 6 rotational joints each of these established to the boards that make up the exoskeleton.

In search of obtaining the dynamic model, it created variables that could be sent from the Matlab software to generate movement in the joints and through the simulations get results of angular velocities and pairs in each one of them.

In Fig. 7 you can see the model in Adams.

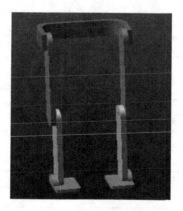

Fig. 7. Model in Adams.

4.5 Matlab Interface Design

In Matlab, pure trajectories were programmed that help simulate the movement of the legs based on the investigation of the movements existing rehabilitation, then show the graphs of the movement profiles created (Fig. 8).

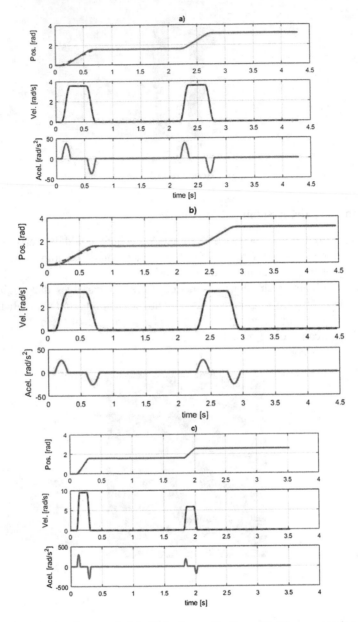

Fig. 8. Trajectories implemented. (a) Abduction adduction. (b) Flexo extension of the leg. (c) Flexo extension of the foot

5 Implementation

Having the trajectories, previously, shown, a model was made in the software of Matlab simulink that would allow you to send them trajectories to the CAD model of the exoskeleton in Adams, which through a dynamic analysis, allowed to obtain maximum speed values angular and even, like (Fig. 9):

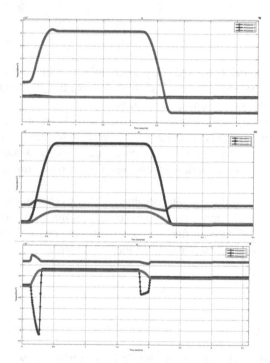

Fig. 9. Torque graphs for each pure movement. (a) Abduction-adduction. (b) Flexo leg extension. (c) Flexo extension of foot. Green - joint 1, Blue - joint 2, Red - articulation 3. (Color figure online)

Finally, the RMS or effective torque value is obtained and the maximum per articulation, having thus, respectively: for joint 1, a pair efficient of 36.57 Nm and maximum of 52.9 Nm; for the joint 2, an effective torque of 35.92 Nm and maximum of 51.60 Nm and for joint 3, a effective torque of 6 Nm and maximum of 7.58 Nm.

6 Discussion of Results

The design of exoskeletons requires many fields to be developed in an efficient way from medicine to engineering, is just as it becomes convenient to be clear many factors and requirements necessary for an efficient result.

The main thing in an exoskeleton is power implement rehabilitation trajectories that help speed up and improve the performance of therapies of each of the patients, that's how they also intervene in the proper selection of the engines that exert the greatest effort during the treatment.

Usually, as you have seen the trajectories have to perform are pure, because they facilitate concentration of the rehabilitation stage in a specific place of the member, as well as the combination of them can achieve a better result in the whole leg.

7 Conclusions

With the trajectory model presented, they were able to achieve pure trajectories for each of the joints of the exoskeleton, in addition to have the possibility to combine, in search of the generation of complex movements.

Having developed a model in Inventor of the exoskeleton, it was possible to carry out an implementation of this in Adams that being a Multibody dynamic analysis software helped in obtaining key values, such as: pairs and maximum angular speeds that help obviously to the selection of engines for a proper implementation of the exoskeleton.

With the combination of the results obtained in this work you can proceed to make Bluetooth communication with help from software Arduino and an Arduino NANO card that will allow to send the profiles of movements obtained at the appropriate times, obtaining a continuous and smooth walk of the exoskeleton.

References

1. Albán, O.A.V.: Aplicaciones de la Robótica al Campo de la Medicina. Universidad del Cauca (2007)
2. Galeano, D.: Robótica Médica. Universidad Católica Nuestra Señora de la Asunción (2016)
3. Mera, I.L.L., Daza, M.M.: Exoesqueleto para Reeducación en Pacientes con IMOC Tipo Diplejía Espástica Moderada. Universidad del Cauca (2010)
4. Sierra, H.A.: Control de un Exoesqueleto para Asistir en la Bipedestación y la Marcha de una Persona. Centro de Investigación y de Estudios Avanzados del Instituto Politécnico Nacional, David Martínez Alberto., "Análisis Cinemático y Dinámico del Robot Pasibot"., Universidad Carlos III de Madrid (2008)
5. Giraldo, A.F.M.: Caracterización Mecánica y Dinámica del Robot SCARA UV-CERMA (2014)
6. Instituto de Biomecánica de Valencia. GAIT Ortesis Inteligente para Rodilla y Tobillo (2006)
7. Burgos, P.S.J.: Desarrollo de un interfaz de usuario para guante de datos 5DT Data Glove. Universidad de Valladolid (2017)
8. Lajeunesse, V., Vincent, C., Routhier, F., Careau, E., Michaud, F.: Exoskeletons' design and usefulness evidence according to a systematic review of lower limb exoskeletons used for functional mobility by people with spinal cord injury. J. Disabil. Rehabil. Assist. Technol. **11** (7), 535–547 (2016)

9. Huo, W., et al.: Lower limb wearable robots for assistance and rehabilitation: a state of the art. IEEE Syst. J. **10**(3), 1068–1081 (2014)
10. Baluch., T.H., et al.: Kinematic and dynamic analysis of a lower limb exoskeleton. International Science Index (2012)
11. Chen, B., et al.: Recent developments and challenges of lower extremity exoskeletons. J. Orthop. Transl. **5**, 26–37 (2016)
12. Kwak, N.S., Müller, K.R., Lee, S.W.: A lower limb exoskeleton control system based on steady state visual evoked potentia. J. Neural Eng. **12**, 056009 (2015)

Integration of Complex IoT Data with Case-Specific Interactive Expert Knowledge Feedback, for Elderly Frailty Prevention

Vladimir Urošević[1][(⊠)], Paolo Paolini[2], and Christos Tatsiopoulos[1]

[1] Belit d.o.o. Beograd, Trg Nikole Pašića 9, 11000 Belgrade, Serbia
vladimir.urosevic@belit.co.rs
[2] Fondazione Politecnico di Milano,
Piazza Leonardo da Vinci 32, 20133 Milano, Italy

Abstract. This paper describes an environment based on rich interactive diagrams, allowing the geriatricians and caregivers to access, analyze and precisely annotate or label specific granular cases of interest in a variety of heterogeneous data collected, to identify "behaviour changes" through Smart City IoT and Open Data infrastructures. The overall goal is to detect and contextualize, as early and precisely as possible, negative changes that may lead to onset of MCI/frailty in the elderly population. The environment is being developed and piloted within the City4Age project, partially funded by the EU.

Keywords: Behaviour recognition · Ambient-assisted · Active healthy ageing
Unobtrusive · Data labelling · Semi-supervised · Interactive dashboard
Data assessments

1 Introduction

Numerous recent and ongoing projects, deployed systems and research initiatives in AAL (Ambient Assisted Living) and AHA (Active and Healthy Aging) are acquiring and processing growing volumes and variety of heterogeneous health personal data, particularly from Smart Cities. The ICT and institutional infrastructures are becoming established, sustainable, and practically ubiquitous, with steadily growing inflow and increased reliability of monitoring, surveillance, and citizen feedback data. New and/or improved sensors are continuously integrated in IoT networks (wearable/mobile devices, sensors in public spaces – cultural, shopping, commuting, etc.), available Open/Linked datasets are getting larger, more comprehensive and refined, shifting the challenge focus towards added value services based on acquired Big Data, predictive analytics, interpretation, contextualization, and deployment of intelligent systems. In the area of health, wellbeing and ageing, the urban public health and prevention are transforming from reactive to a predictive and eventually risk-mitigating system.

© Springer International Publishing AG, part of Springer Nature 2018
M. Mokhtari et al. (Eds.): ICOST 2018, LNCS 10898, pp. 270–276, 2018.
https://doi.org/10.1007/978-3-319-94523-1_25

2   Data Complexity and Heterogeneity Factors

Along with advances in technology infrastructures, socio-technological factors are additionally increasing the complexity and heterogeneity of acquired personal data:

- the globally upcoming ageing population in metropolitan areas [1] is mostly the generation of baby boomers - more active, skilled, and tech-savvier than previous generations of seniors [2], with increased online "footprint", providing more and more diverse personal data to be discerned and integrated, leading to richer profiles.
- increasingly adopted holistic policy management approach on city level, integrating and processing data from various city administration sectors - health, environment, planning, transport, and causing an increased number of correlations in the data used by the health/social services administrations, and geriatricians/physicians in everyday monitoring of geriatric care recipients (CRs).

The City4Age research project leverages unobtrusive "sensing" systems for early detection of risks and precursors of physical & cognitive frailty, to enable fully ambient-assisted Age-friendly Cities. The main "detection" challenge is identifying or reconstructing relevant behaviours of persons from input data streams and assessing frailty risks from relevant behaviour changes. The project is breaking new ground in expanding the Ambient-Assisted Environments from currently predominant indoor spaces (homes, elderly care centres, etc.) to outdoor and public environments, and in data-driven geriatrics in integration with domain knowledge.

3   Hybrid Detection Approach

Human behaviours are complex, commonly represented via multi-level hierarchical structured models, with human activities as fundamental decomposition units, consisting further of sequences of human actions as simplest units, mostly associated with unitary events captured by a sensor or reported through external input [3]. Recognition and synthesis is performed on multiple model structure and aggregation levels (activities from actions, behaviours from activities etc.), using different analytic techniques and algorithms. Higher-level variation Measures, Geriatric Factors and Subfactors in the model quantify the changes in specific behavioural domains relevant for active and healthy aged life and onset of physical and cognitive frailty [7].

Empirical evidence indicates that the integration of various sensory data of high temporal resolution practically introduces additional uncertainty into traditional geriatric and behavioural models and notably higher variations of behaviour on individual level. Similar or same behaviour variation pattern may denote high risk for one person but low or no risk for another. As unobtrusive sensory layer is constantly ubiquitously capturing (nearly) all activity and behaviour changes that occur, it becomes crucial to resolve and filter out the "false positives" - transient variations caused by external environmental factors (unobservable heterogeneity, model "frailty" [4]) or sensor imprecision, not by actual onsets of physical frailty or mild cognitive impairment (MCI) targeted for recognition. Currently prevalently used knowledge-based models that generalize contextual real-world observations into formal knowledge structures (computational rules, schemas or networks) therefore need mechanisms for refinement and increased robustness, to integrate newly acquired and/or more granular case-specific expert knowledge into model structures.

The City4Age project adopts a hybrid combined knowledge-driven and data-driven approach on all detection/recognition levels, aiming to integrate data mining and machine learning to obtain most value from collected data, supported and refined by ontology-based knowledge-driven recognition to associate contexts, overcome pattern granularity problems and boost performance [5]. Most successful data-driven recognition solutions mainly rely on supervised learning techniques, requiring significant sets of annotated or labelled cases/patterns to be used for training different kinds of classifiers in ML techniques. Manual input of the required amount of labels by the experts is not feasible for envisioned scale of City4Age scenarios in the long-term, with thousands of elderly persons potentially monitored in subsequent city-wide deployments after the project piloting on limited numbers (50–80 people in each of the 6 testbed cities) - and the increase of heterogeneity of acquired data and observed unrecognized behaviours is likely to be superlinear [6]. A combination of unsupervised learning techniques and knowledge-based models is therefore chosen as optimal, and new mechanisms for semi-automatic labelling of characterized behaviour patterns that denote "risk" are explored and developed.

4   Collaborative Dashboards for Knowledge Integration

Main developed components of the City4Age system exposed to the end-users, Individual Monitoring Dashboards (IMDs) provide the primary functionalities of interactive visualization of behavioural data of a single selected CR, and the collaborative environment for expert assessments/annotations of data in detection, supporting also the input of various indications for City4Age digital interventions, and of incentives and feedback on the effects and results of the interventions. Targeted expert users are primarily health-care professionals (geriatricians, general practitioners, intervention staff, etc.), assisted to fully detect, contextualize and annotate behavioural changes of the elderly people subject to their care.

Main visualization elements are rich composite diagrams – combined multi-line and stacked bar diagrams, showing aggregated time-series data, as optimally understandable and intuitive for the geriatrician experts. Once the desired CR is selected through list/search in preceding screens, the diagrams present the data acquired on the person in a selected or predefined time period in a general top-down flow, from high-level normalized aggregated model features (overall frailty status, geriatric domains, factor groups), supporting the drilling down to show specific granular data (sub-factor values, variation measures, activities). Primarily showing the decomposed influence of the underlying constituting "child" variable values on each of the detected variables (geriatric factor, sub-factor, variation measure) over time, the composite multi-line + bar diagrams can also show data on multiple model/aggregation levels at once on a single diagram, as exemplified by the top diagram on Fig. 1 – timeline changes of traditionally assessed frailty status (by a geriatrician) are rendered, expressed in 3-level

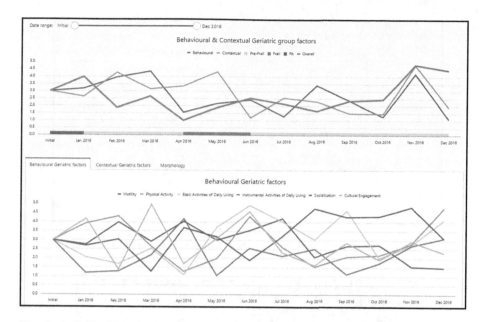

Fig. 1. Individual Monitoring Dashboards - combined multi-line and stacked bar diagrams

Fried Index notation, as additional stacked bar below the multiple lines for the main geriatric domains (factor groups).

The innovative advanced interaction is provided by the custom component for interactive data assessments/annotations on graphs. An assessment can be assigned to each point on a diagram, or any set of points selected by multiple-click or window selection, via a modal popup panel for assessment input, launched by the "Add" command from the informative pop-up panel shown on hover over selection (Fig. 2).

Each annotated data point or dataset can have one or a thread of multiple assessments assigned to it in different times. In common use cases of collaborative daily practice of caregivers, this provides the functionalities of:

- accurately selecting specific points, or sets of points, on the diagram, likely to denote significantly anomalous behaviour (on one or different series on the graph).
- storing the input assessments, and reading stored annotations (in freeform comments) provided by other colleague caregivers or different user roles.
- most importantly – **annotating the selected data point or dataset with structured categorized or quantifiable attributes**, interpretable as labelled data for training/refining the analytics. Primary is the basic risk assessment categorization (Warning - potential risk, Alert – evident risk), and the detection confidence label. In case a caregiver finds the specific value(s) inconsistent, or evidently wrong (determined by examining/interviewing the actual CR), the problematic data can be marked questionable or faulty by the assessment (Fig. 3, on the right). This data validity rating figures in the calculation of eventual risk ratios, modes and priorities.

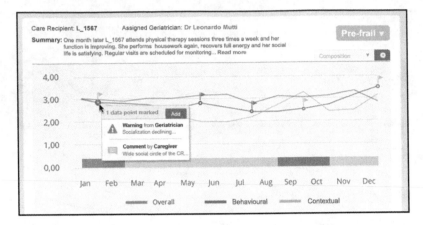

Fig. 2. Adding assessment on a selected data point or dataset on diagram

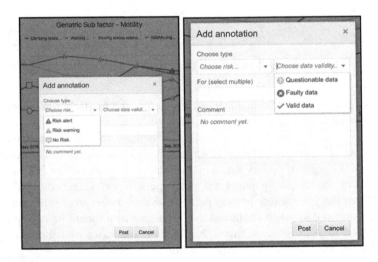

Fig. 3. Assessment/annotation input panel controls and fields

The categorized labelling attributes feature additional data marker icons for each of the categories. These markers are rendered on the source diagrams, so the annotated points can be seen immediately on the graph.

The risk categorization markers are plotted by default, being of highest interest, but parameterization allows optional different categorization as well. For points that have assigned multiple assessments with different risk, the marker denoting highest criticality in the set is shown (criticality order: ⚠ >> ⚠ >> 🗩, Fig. 4).

Overall dataset annotation process performed this way via the IMDs is still essentially manual, but leveraged and accelerated by the optimized UX and the workflow. When a significant number of input annotations is reached, the categorical Multi-Criteria Decision Making (MCDM) methods in the analytics layer will be able to semi-automatically infer annotations for classes of similar cases.

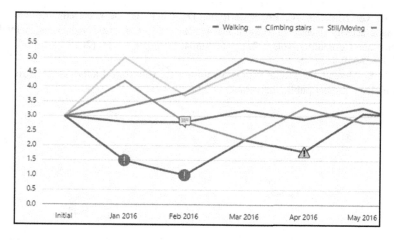

Fig. 4. Markers on points with assigned assessments/annotations on diagram

5   Conclusions and Further Work

Integrating complex detection data with interactive case-specific expert knowledge feedback through "Detection" Dashboard front-end components has been presented, as additional mechanism for advancing dataset annotation/labelling in knowledge-based support to unsupervised learning for human behaviour recognition. The development is performed in the scope of the City4Age project, aiming for the establishment of Age-friendly Smart Cities. Overall hybrid data- and knowledge-driven detection approach has been presented, as well as the primary functionalities of interactive visualization of behaviour data, and collaborative-interactive environment for geriatric care provision.

Further work continues in the development of Group Analytics Dashboards for identifying and annotating particular subgroups or clusters of elderly individuals of interest in the population, as well as in augmenting the data-driven analytic algorithms with annotations obtained from dashboards.

References

1. Genoe, M.R., Liechty, T., Marston, H.R., Sutherland, V.: Blogging into retirement: using qualitative online research methods to understand leisure among baby boomers. J. Leisure Res. **48**(1), 15 (2016)
2. Tiago, M.T., de Almeida Couto, J.P., Tiago, F.G.B., Faria, S.M.C.D.: Baby boomers turning grey. Eur. Profiles **54**, 13–22 (2016)
3. Díaz Rodríguez, N.: Semantic and fuzzy modelling for human behaviour recognition in smart spaces. In: Studies on the Semantic Web, vol. 23. IOS Press Amsterdam (2016)
4. Ayyagari, P.: Preventive Health Behaviors among the Elderly. Duke University (2008)
5. Azkune, G., Almeida, A.: A scalable hybrid activity recognition approach for intelligent environments. J. LaTeX Class Files **14**(8), 2015 (2015)

6. Azkune, G., Almeida, A., López-de-Ipiña, D., Chen, L.: A knowledge-driven tool for automatic activity dataset annotation. In: Angelov, P., et al. (eds.) Advances in Intelligent Systems and Computing, vol. 322, pp. 593–604. Springer, Cham (2015). https://doi.org/10.1007/978-3-319-11313-5_52
7. Copelli, S., Mercalli, M., Ricevuti, G., Venturini, L.: City4Age frailty and MCI risk model, v2, City4Age project public deliverable D 2.06 (2017)

The Affective Respiration Device
Towards Embodied Bio-feedforward in Healthcare

Idowu Ayoola[1,2]($\boxtimes$), Jelle Stienstra[1], and Loe Feijs[1]

[1] Department of Industrial Design, Eindhoven University of Technology,
LaPlace 32, 5612AZ Eindhoven, Netherlands
i.b.i.ayoola@tue.nl
[2] Onmi B.V., Eindhoven, The Netherlands

Abstract. In this paper, we discuss the Affective Respiration Device, its rationale and elaborate a few lessons learned from our attempt to embed this technology in the flow of everyday life. The device captures the respiratory behaviour of its viewer and provides bio-feedback and feedforward that enables people to come to terms with their breathing and activity in an engaging manner. After briefly discussing the theory, related work, and the system design we provide a use-scenario to highlight the experiential consequences of using the affective device. We further reflect on few learning points derived from a walk-through. This work aims to inspire design-thinking for patient's home monitoring to shift from the cognitive approach towards an embodied bio-feedback.

Keywords: Interaction design · Behaviour change
Action-perception loop · Respiration

1 Background

The Shift in Healthcare. To support self-management, hospitals and other care services began to consider the home settings as a source of inspiration. In effect, they—in their traditionally clinical setting—aim to create spaces and engagements in which people can feel at ease and to possibly improve the comfort and the perceived attractiveness of the hospital environment [7]. A conventional method for informing health professionals as well as patients about health indicators is by displaying measured values [2]. While these numbers, figures, graphs and so forth are insightful for the trained professional, these representations are not natural, with little to no inherent meaning to the patient from whom the data is derived, i.e., they have difficulty understanding these values and translating them to be actionable. With the expansion of professional healthcare towards self-management of health (i.e., quantified self), health technologies and devices are used in lifestyle applications. Many of these devices follow this conventional approach to presenting information to the patients. For the patients, it remains essential that they receive their diagnoses from their health professional, as they would not be able to study themselves to become experts that can grasp the

© Springer International Publishing AG, part of Springer Nature 2018
M. Mokhtari et al. (Eds.): ICOST 2018, LNCS 10898, pp. 277–284, 2018.
https://doi.org/10.1007/978-3-319-94523-1_26

subtleties in the presented data in a way the health professional with years of training does. As such in the home context where care services focus on quantifying physiological, behavioural or symptomatic signs, patients remain to rely on their health professionals when they are facing the numbers, figures, graphs and so forth that they would not be able to respond adequately due to a lack of actionable results. Providing patients with data that does not resonate with how they feel, or find useful, to rightfully change their behaviour does not benefit the patients progress and potentially undermines the continuous utilization of the solutions offered.

Respiration as an Early Indicator. The quality of breathing can give early signs of chronic health deterioration [2,15] and, therefore, is one of the key markers for spot-check [6]. Various sensor technologies that make it possible to integrate the sensors in daily living are fairly accessible for day-to-day use. Shortness of breath can induce stress and is common amongst heart patients. Breathing therapy is a common intervention to reduce stress. A known phenomenon in breathing therapy is resonant breathing. Resonant breathing training works by teaching people to recognize their involuntary heart rate variability and to control patterns of the physiological response [10,19,28]. Resonant breathing is slower than normal breathing averaging at about 5.5 breaths per minute. When this breathing frequency is reached, the person enters a relaxed state [19]. By controlling breathing pattern, it is possible to improve the quality of respiration which can lead to positive effects on the underlying processes that are associated with breathing and health.

2   State-of-the-Art

Since ancient times, breathing is studied and is used to develop methods and therapies for improving health matters. For example, breathing exercise [14] is used to achieve deep relaxation and reduce stress, Pranayama, is focused on deepening breathing [22]. In the area of voluntary breath regulation and respiratory based biofeedback, several systems have been built. Some methods attempt to control respiration sub-consciously through peripheral paced respiration [16], while other methods subject breathing to an external stimulus such as visual animation—using discrete light representations (that is, on or off), ambient light or sound animations [26,28]. The approaches try to provide feedback as instructions to be followed by the patients. However, most biofeedback methods are somewhat disembodied and out of context. The peripheral paced respiration in [16], and the design of direct audio feedback for heartbeat and heartbeat variability presented in [9] have attempted to make the feedback as natural as possible using light or sound. Breathesync (www.breathesync.com) is also similar to our approach but utilizes a disembodied approach. As a means to explore, the affective respiration device builds forth on similar approaches using physically embodied concept and aims to lure the user to breathe more slowly (perhaps more deeply) and consequently moderate their respiration rate. This approach describes our notion of bio-feedforward.

3   Towards a Natural Interaction

In general, designing for natural interaction aims to create artifacts, systems, and services that feel natural and require a limited amount of people's effort to be used. In line with alternative interfaces and interaction styles that have users dominantly rely on their thinking capabilities, *natural* and *intuitive* interaction paradigms [17] have found their way into the realm of human-computer interaction [11]. Approaches such as affective computing [18], experience design [13], embodied interaction [8], expressive and continuous interaction [20,23] and a few more were put forward to enable people in dealing with information in ways that rely less on their thinking skills [10,21].

In effect, the aim is to lower the need for contemplation (i.e., using our cognitive skills) through directly engaging the user with their data. In the attempt to create an alternative method of engaging with respiration data that redresses the balance to the embodied (perceptual-motor and emotional) skills, let us turn to the work of Bruns Alonso et al. [4,5,23]. With their Affective Pen [5], they showed that it was possible to take a physical movement of someone fiddling with a Pen and directly (counter-)map it to a Pen's movement behaviour so to stop the user from fiddling and consequently calming down.

The main idea embodied in the Affective Pen [5] is the action-perception loop. It departs from the idea that people adjust their behaviour at the moment. That is, at this time, while engaging with artifacts, people change their actions as the meaning of the actions emerge in interaction. The Affective Pen utilizes this idea in that it takes the actions (and thereby perceptions) of the user's movement and gently manipulates it while the user is in interaction with the Pen (i.e., the user is tricked). Crucial for this to work is a continuous interaction between person and pen that has to be taken into account.

The Interaction Frogger Framework [27], can be used to develop mappings between input and output that feel as direct couplings between action and perception leading to interactions that feel natural. The framework focuses on six aspects of coupling (e.g., time, location, direction, dynamics, modality, and expression) input and output. By rule of thumb, the more direct the aspects are mapped, the more natural the designed-for interactions are experienced. For example, by mapping the input and output timing closely, a continuous interaction can be achieved. By focusing on the very nuances of the aspects, movement behaviours can be inviting, persuading, inhibiting or coercing [23,25]. This framework and the above-mentioned approach to transforming behaviour through creating dynamic and interactive materiality has been successfully applied in the Affective Pen [5], a toothbrush [1], a smart-cup for specifying drinking [3] and a movement-sonification device for speed-skaters [24].

There is an opportunity to capture the "ungraspable respiration data" and to bring it in a loop of engagement. We propose to design for an action-perception loop in which the user dwells in synchronicity with own respiration data. The directedness of the action-perception as described by the Interaction Frogger Framework in [27], enables the person to reach a resonance state with his own body. Once this synchronicity is achieved, bio-feedforward is initiated as the action-perception loop adjusts dynamically (and highly subtle) adjust to invite or inhibit the respiration pace. This happens in a non-obtrusive manner, relying little on people's contemplation, and to bring this into the flow of everyday life.

The bio-feedforward approach creates new opportunities in the area of changing behaviour through an embodied interaction for healthcare. In the case of the Affective Respiration device, we like to respect the individuals respiratory state and to create a natural transition between the current state and the "clinically" recommended state. This has clinical importance as mentioned earlier. Such a natural or smooth transition may also help to reduce complications from occurring (e.g., a sudden change in blood-pressure). The bio-feedforward approach also presents the opportunity for automated or unsupervised personalization for respiratory training that is useful for remote care through remote settings.

4 Design Contribution

Concept. The Affective Respiration device consists of (a) a respiration capturing part, i.e., input, and (b) a feedback mechanism, i.e., output. The input is a camera that is used to detect breathing. The output manifests itself in the actual shape of the camera that can grow and shrink in size according to the breathing signal.

Interaction with the device is in three phases.

1. spot-check (the user situates him or herself in front of the device and breathe normally),
2. feedback (the user becomes aware of own breathing pattern), and,
3. feedforward (breathing is lured to a target rhythm).

Periodically or in cases where the patient experiences shortness of breath- or like to undergo a breathing therapy, he or she will stand in front of the device (Fig. 1a). The device then acquires the respiration pattern. This happens without providing any feedback. Afterward, direct feedback is given through movement that mimics the actual breathing pattern. When the user inhales the chest expands, consequently, the device also exhibits an outwards movement and vice-versa. Meaning, the faster the person breaths, the faster the device actuates and in effect co-breaths. The form allows the user to see own breathing pattern physically and engage with it directly. As soon as the user is in sync with the motion, the bio-feedforward mechanism is initiated. The Affective Respiration device gradually re-adjust its movement (out of sync) to persuade the user also to change the breathing as programmed.

Physical Prototype. A first prototype was carved out of foam in a rounded form, Fig. 1c, giving room in the middle for a flexible material with a projecting structure. The design details were further defined in the succeeding prototypes. Figure 1d shows the mechanical implementation of the final version. The flexible material was riveted in-between the outer shell, which allowed it to flex inwards and outwards from the center. The projecting structure coalesced when

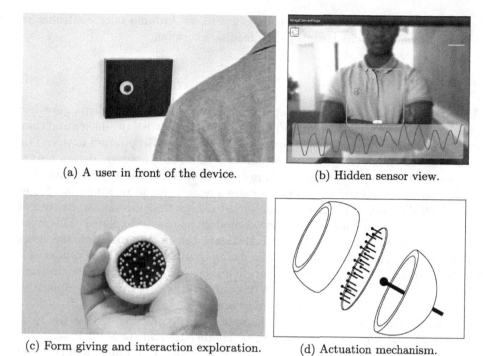

(a) A user in front of the device.   (b) Hidden sensor view.

(c) Form giving and interaction exploration.   (d) Actuation mechanism.

Fig. 1. Explorative prototype. (Color figure online)

the flexible material was in place. When pushed outwards from the center, the projecting structure also moved outwards in an intricate way. The projecting structure had limited space when pushed outwards; hence they slide and shove along each other. The outward movements left a black space in the middle, with an impression of something opening up and later closing like a living organism.

Integrated Technology. Respiration is captured via an integrated camera that scans at 15 frames per second for respiratory motion using advanced image processing algorithms running in C language. The algorithm uses motion magnification, a technique that acts like a microscope for visual motion [12]. The working distance between the camera and the person is dependent on the image quality. We used a 1.3 megapixel VGA CMOS camera with a view angle of 55 degrees. In daylight, the subject can stand between 0.5–2 m from the camera with good results. Figure 1b shows the camera view and the respiration analysis results, which is not visible to the user. A region of interest—the green box—is automatically detected in the sequence of images where the respiratory motion is pronounced. Within three seconds, a sinusoidal signal similar to a respiratory signal is obtained. After the initial delay, the respiratory movements are detected in real-time without any noticeable delay. The initial delay is due to the time to calibrate the input signal and identify the region of interest. The analysis program communicates via serial connection to an Arduino microcontroller to actuate the motors, which controls the feedback motion.

5   Discussion

A simple walk-through with a heart-failure patient and five students gave few insights. It was straight-forward for them to get in sync with the device and they were positive about the luring concept of the Affective Respiration device. The movement of the device was also fascinating to them. However, it was uncertain to what extent the luring effect may work for them. The physical modality of the concept at a fixed location may cause engagement to be somewhat forceful, which does not support mobile usage at events that necessitate the use of the device. Therefore, alternative digital modalities can be explored. This work will benefit from a clinical trial to investigate the extent to which the users breathing pattern may be affected. This helps to substantiate the notion of biofeedforward as described in this paper. The new study should utilize the data obtained from the respiratory sensor to compare the users normal respiratory rate to that obtained after feedforward is applied.

A significant difference with for example the Affective Pen is that the feedforward mechanism not only takes the engaging user in its loop. Potentially, other people can witness the pattern as it is provided in a public manner, and consequently, be influenced by the breathing pattern of the user as well. While breathing is considered a mostly private exercise, the Affective Respiration device makes it public. As it was rather easy for both the user and device to get in sync with each other, it is not unlikely to consider that people will get in sync with each other either, once they pick up the behaviour of others. This might have implications for the good and the bad; that should also be further investigated.

6   Concluding Remarks

This design case study presents the Affective Respiration device, a design that engages the traditionally represented physiological data in the interaction. We believe that the given approach has a potential value to (a) spot-check respiration as a health indicator, (b) provide biofeedback that makes bodily sense to patients allowing them to reflect on their breathing, and (c) administer a guided breathing exercise that can potentially reduce stress or blood pressure. We consider this approach to be of an embodied bio-forward nature rather than providing biofeedback. In effect, we propose to lure patients into changed behaviour. We speak of bio-feedforward because we coincidentally apply the biofeedback and bio-feedforward in such a manner that it is a directive for future use.

Acknowledgement. Thanks to the patient, students and everyone that were involved in this work.

References

1. Alonso, M.B., Stienstra, J., Dijkstra, R.: Brush and learn: transforming tooth brushing behavior through interactive materiality, a design exploration. In: Proceedings of the 8th International Conference on Tangible, Embedded and Embodied Interaction, TEI 2014, pp. 113–120. ACM (2014)
2. Andrews, T., Waterman, H.: Packaging: a grounded theory of how to report physiological deterioration effectively. J. Adv. Nurs. **52**(5), 473–481 (2005)
3. Ayoola, I.B.I., Ansems, K.E., Chen, W., Feijs, L.M.G.: Design of a smart cup - a tele-medical system for behavioral intervention through interactive materiality. In: Zhang, Y.-T. (ed.) The International Conference on Health Informatics. IP, vol. 42, pp. 96–99. Springer, Cham (2014). https://doi.org/10.1007/978-3-319-03005-0_25
4. Alonso, M.B., Hummels, C.C.M., Keyson, D.V., Hekkert, P.P.M.: Measuring and adapting behavior during product interaction to influence affect. Pers. Ubiquit. Comput. **17**(1), 81–91 (2013)
5. Bruns Alonso, M., Keyson, D.V., Hummels, C.C.M.: Squeeze, rock, and roll; can tangible interaction with affective products support stress reduction? In: Proceedings of the 2nd International Conference on Tangible and Embedded Interaction, TEI 2008, pp. 105–108. ACM (2008)
6. Butler-Williams, C., Cantrill, N., Maton, S.: Increasing staff awareness of respiratory rate significance. Resuscitation **62**(2), 137–141 (2005)
7. Dijkstra, K., Pieterse, M., Pruyn, A.: Stress-reducing effects of indoor plants in the built healthcare environment: the mediating role of perceived attractiveness. Prev. Med. **47**(3), 279–283 (2008)
8. Dourish, P.: Seeking a foundation for context-aware computing. Hum. Comput. Inter. **16**(2–4), 229–241 (2001)
9. Feijs, L.L., Funk, M.M., Yu, B.B.: Design of direct audio feedback for heart beat and heart beat variability. Appl. Psychophysiol. Biofeedback **39**(2), 147 (2014)
10. Feijs, L.M.G., Langereis, G.R., Van Boxtel, G.J.M.: Designing for heart rate and breathing movements. In: Design and semantics of form and movement, DeSForM 2010, vol. 6, p. 57 (2010)
11. Klemmer, S.R., Hartmann, B., Takayama, L.: How bodies matter: five themes for interaction design. In: Proceedings of the 6th Conference on Designing Interactive Systems, pp. 140–149. ACM (2006)
12. Liu, C., Torralba, A., Freeman, W.T., Durand, F., Adelson, E.H.: Motion magnification. ACM Trans. Graph. **24**(3), 519–526 (2005)
13. Marzano, S.: The New Everyday: Views on Ambient Intelligence. 010 Publishers, Rotterdam (2003)
14. Matsumoto, M., Smith, J.C.: Progressive muscle relaxation, breathing exercises, and ABC relaxation theory. J. Clin. Psychol. **57**(12), 1551–1557 (2001)
15. McMurray, J.J., Adamopoulos, S., Anker, S.D., Auricchio, A., Böhm, M., Dickstein, K., Falk, V., Filippatos, G., Fonseca, C., Gomez-Sanchez, M.A., et al.: ESC guidelines for the diagnosis and treatment of acute and chronic heart failure 2012. Eur. J. Heart Fail. **14**(8), 803–869 (2012)
16. Moraveji, N., Olson, B., Nguyen, T., Saadat, M., Khalighi, Y., Pea, R., Heer, J.: Peripheral paced respiration: influencing user physiology during information work. In: Proceedings of the 24th Annual ACM Symposium on User Interface Software and Technology, pp. 423–428. ACM (2011)
17. Norman, D.A.: The Psychology of Everyday Things. Basic books, New York (1988)

18. Picard, R.W., Picard, R.: Affective Computing, vol. 252. MIT press, Cambridge (1997)
19. Purwandini Sutarto, A., Abdul Wahab, M.N., Mat Zin, N.: Resonant breathing biofeedback training for stress reduction among manufacturing operators. Int. J. Occup. Saf. Ergon. 18(4), 549–561 (2012)
20. Ross, P.R., Wensveen, S.A.: Designing aesthetics of behavior in interaction: using aesthetic experience as a mechanism for design. Int. J. Des. 4(2), 3–13 (2010)
21. Rovers, A., Feijs, L., Van Boxtel, G., Cluitmans, P.: Flanker shooting game; model-based design of biofeedback games. In: Proceedings of DPPI 2009, pp. 483–494 (2009)
22. Singh, V., Wisniewski, A., Britton, J., Tattersfield, A.: Effect of yoga breathing exercises (pranayama) on airway reactivity in subjects with asthma. Lancet 335(8702), 1381–1383 (1990)
23. Stienstra, J., Bruns Alonso, M., Wensveen, S., Kuenen, S.: How to design for transformation of behavior through interactive materiality. In: Proceedings of the 7th Nordic Conference on Human-Computer Interaction: Making Sense Through Design, NordiCHI 2012, pp. 21–30. ACM, New York, NY, USA (2012)
24. Stienstra, J., Overbeeke, K., Wensveen, S.: Embodying complexity through movement sonification: Case study on empowering the speed-skater. In: Proceedings of the 9th ACM SIGCHI Italian Chapter International Conference on Computer-Human Interaction: Facing Complexity, CHItaly, pp. 39–44. ACM (2011)
25. Tromp, N., Hekkert, P., Verbeek, P.P.: Design for socially responsible behavior: a classification of influence based on intended user experience. Des. Issues 27(3), 3–19 (2011)
26. Vidyarthi, J., Riecke, B.E., Gromala, D.: Sonic cradle: designing for an immersive experience of meditation by connecting respiration to music. In: Proceedings of the Designing Interactive Systems Conference, pp. 408–417. ACM (2012)
27. Wensveen, S.A., Djajadiningrat, J.P., Overbeeke, C.: Interaction frogger: a design framework to couple action and function through feedback and feedforward. In: Proceedings of the 5th conference on Designing Interactive Systems: Processes, Practices, Methods, and Techniques, pp. 177–184. ACM (2004)
28. Yu, B., Hu, J., Feijs, L.: Design and evaluation of an ambient lighting interface of HRV biofeedback system in home setting. In: Hervás, R., Lee, S., Nugent, C., Bravo, J. (eds.) UCAmI 2014. LNCS, vol. 8867, pp. 88–91. Springer, Cham (2014). https://doi.org/10.1007/978-3-319-13102-3_17

Exploring Individuals' Perceptions on Personally Controlled Electronic Health Record System

Jun Xu(✉), Xiangzhu Gao, Golam Sorwar, Nicky Antonius,
and John Hammond

Southern Cross University, Lismore, Australia
jun.xu@scu.edu.au

Abstract. This research explores enablers for and obstacles to the acceptance and use of the Australian Government Personally Controlled Electronic Health Record (PCEHR) system and provides recommendations drawn from surveys from existing and potential individual users of the system. The results of the study indicate that the participants' major concerns are data security and information privacy. Participants value the importance of governance. They expect more benefits from the PCEHR system than traditional health records. They also expect a quality system that operates normally, a simple system that they can register and learn, and a usable system that they can use easily. The system needs efforts from stakeholders including individuals, health care providers, the Australian Government, legal professionals and system developers to satisfy individuals' expectations, and resolve the issues of the concerns.

Keywords: E-health record · PCEHR system · Acceptance and use
Individual users · Benefits · Software quality

1 Introduction

The Australian Government has invested A\$467 million in the national PCEHR system during the period of 2010 to 2012 [12]. This system allows doctors, hospitals and other healthcare providers to share individuals' health information to provide the best possible health care [7]. Although more than A\$1 billion has been invested for deploying the PCEHR system and its associated infrastructure [9], the system has not been widely accepted by individuals. This paper explores individuals' perceptions by identifying factors or variables affecting the acceptance and the continued use of the PCEHR system. Recommendations are provided to address the expectations of and issues perceived by the individuals.

2 Research Design

The research model consists of two parts: pre-adoption stage and post adoption stage [1, 6, 10, 12, 13, 15, 18]. In the pre-adoption stage, it is suggested that the external factors including external environment and influences, individual differences, and

© Springer International Publishing AG, part of Springer Nature 2018
M. Mokhtari et al. (Eds.): ICOST 2018, LNCS 10898, pp. 285–291, 2018.
https://doi.org/10.1007/978-3-319-94523-1_27

PCEHR system characteristics influence the adoption of the PCEHR system in an indirect way with their influence being mediated by the perceived benefits (usefulness) and perceived user-friendliness (usability) of the system. At the same time, the research model postulates that the perceived benefits, perceived user-friendliness, subject norms, and voluntariness have direct effect on the adoption of the PCEHR system, and also indicates that perceived user friendliness affects perceived usefulness. In the post-adoption stage, it is suggested that the facilitating factors influence the continued use of the PCEHR system in an indirect way with their influence being mediated by the realized benefits (usefulness) and realized user friendliness (usability) of the system At the same time, the research model postulates that realised benefits, realised user-friendliness, subject norms, and voluntariness have direct effect on the continued use of the PCEHR system, and also suggests that realised user-friendliness affects realised usefulness. Staff and students of Southern Cross University in Australia were invited to participate in an online questionnaire survey. It was also encouraged to distribute the invitation to their friends, neighbours and others beyond the University. Two rounds of e-mail invitations were sent to two generic email lists of staff and students. Frequency distribution is analysed and percentages are used to present the results. The results attempt to draw out major factors of enablers for and barriers to the acceptance and continued use of the PCEHR system. The higher the percentage of the respondents is, the more important the factor is. In this research, a factor is considerably more important when the percentage is equal to or greater than 50%.

3   Feedback Analysis

Surveys were examined initially and only those which had responses to all questions were accepted. The final number of fully completed surveys is 66. 63.6% are female and 36.4% are male. In descending order, 25.8% of the respondents are in the 50–59 age group, 24.2% in the age group of 40–49, 19.7% in the age group of 30–39, 10.6% in age group of 60–65, 10.6% in other age groups (e.g., younger than 18 and older than 65), 7.6% in the age group of 21–29, and 1.5% in the age group of 18–20. The majority of the survey respondents (68.2%) lack knowledge of the PCEHR system, and either have no knowledge/understanding of the PCEHR system or don't know much about the system. 74.2% of the respondents have not been involved in the implementation/roll-out of the PCEHR system, and 77.3% are happy to let health care providers (other than their GP) to access (either on a regular basis or case-by-case manner) their medical information in the system (either full access or partial access). Tables 1 and 2 presents factors influencing user's decision of adoption (mediated by perceptions) and continued use (mediated by realisations) of the PCEHR system. It can be seen that most of the factors are perceived to be important by the respondents.

Table 1. Factors influencing adoption decision

External factors & influences	Percentage of respondents	Individual differences	Percentage of respondents
Regulations and Policies	72.7%	Involvement	42.4%
ICT Infrastructure Development	56.1%	Experience/Skill	77.3%
Mobility	84.8%	Personal Innovativeness	68.2%
Availability of Computing Equipment and Popularity of Mobile Devices	71.2%	Computer Skills	75.8%
Affordability and Accessibility of Internet Services	63.6%	Attitude	68.2%
Economic Uncertainty	43.9%		
Continuity of the Government	59.1%		
Unified Approach	65.2%		
Transparency and Communication of The Operations of the PCEHR System	87.9%		
Governance	89.4%		
PCEHR system characteristics		Perceived/Expected benefits	
Trialability	89.4%	Personal Medical Information Management	89.9%
Accuracy, Completeness and Currency of the Information	93.9%	Better and New Services	78.8%
Access Control	97%	Efficiency/Productivity	87.9%
Information Control	90.9%	Effectiveness	87.9%
Children Information Control	87.9%	Quality	78.8%
Accessibility	92.4%	Safety	81.8%
Availability	93.9%	Time and Cost Reduction	83.3%
Regional/District Integration	93.9%	Continuity of Health Services	84.8%
Cross-state Integration	92.4%	Health and Well-Being	62.1%
Cross-border/International Integration	66.7%	Saving Lives	77.3%
Maintenance and Updates	93.9%	Equitable Access to Health Services	65.2%
Delegation	89.4%	Continuity of Health Services	83.3%
Perceived/Expected user friendliness		Subject norms	
Simple to Learn and Use	93.9%	Peer Pressure/Influence	36.4%
Easy to Register	92.4%	Following Early Users' Lead	34.8%
Affordable to Learn and Use	92.4%	Doctor's Lead	69.7%
Speed	90.9%	Respected People's Influence	57.6%
Easy to Contribute Information	90.9%	Doctor's Recommendation	72.7%
Privacy	95.5%	Media Influence	25.8%
Security	98.5%		
Human Assistance and Interaction	93.9%		

(*continued*)

Table 1. (*continued*)

Perceived/Expected user friendliness		Subject norms	
Multi-Channels Communication and Multiple Touch Points	90.9%		
Communities	50%		
Voluntariness		System adoption	
Opt-in Model	68.2%	Uploading and Storing Information	83.3%
Opt-out Model	57.6%	Disseminating and Sharing Information with Healthcare Providers	83.3%
Mandatory Use	37.8%	Disseminating and Sharing Information with Government Agencies	48.5%
Linking to Benefits	74.2%	Linking with Other Government Services	48.5%
Benefit Realization	84.8%	Managing Health Information	81.5%
		Better Understanding of Health Conditions	69.7%

Table 2. Factors influencing continued use decision

Facilitating Factors	Percentage of respondents	Realized benefits	Percentage of respondents
Incentives	62.1%	Personal Medical Information Management	87.9%
Imperatives	62.1%	Better and New Services	83.3%
Policy Updates	68.2%	Efficiency/Productivity	84.8%
System Improvements	84.8%	Effectiveness	86.4%
Promotion of Success Stories and Best Practices	66.7%	Quality	83.3%
Promotion of Benefits	68.2%	Safety	89.4%
Satisfying Needs Continuously	83.3%	Time and Cost Reduction	87.8%
Encouragement	54.5%	Continuity of Health Services	89.4%
Good Governance	77.3%	Health and Well-Being	81.8%
Funding	89.4%	Saving Lives	83.3%
Better Training	78.8%	Equitable Access to Health Services	86.4%
		Continuity of Health Services	86.4%

(*continued*)

Table 2. (*continued*)

Realized user friendliness		Subject norms on continued use	
Realized user friendliness		Subject norms on continued use	
Simple to Learn and Use	75.8%	Peer Pressure/Influence	31.8%
Easy to Register	74.2%	Following Early Users' Lead	39.4%
Affordable to Learn and Use	75.8%	Doctor's Lead	68.2%
Speed	74.2%	Respected People's Influence	50%
Easy to Contribute Information	75.8%	Doctor's Recommendation	71.2%
Privacy	78.8%	Media Influence	28.8%
Security	78.8%		
Human Assistance and Interaction	75.8%		
Multi-Channels Communication and Multiple Touch Points	71.2%		
Communities	37.9%		
Voluntariness of continued use		Continued use	
Opt-in Model	71.2%	Uploading and Storing Information	84.8%
Opt-out Model	53%	Disseminating and Sharing Information with Healthcare Providers	80.3%
Mandatory Use	37.8%	Disseminating and Sharing Information with Government Agencies	45.5%
Linking to Benefits	66.7%	Linking with Other Government Services	57.6%
Benefit Realization	77.3%	Managing Health Information	86.4%
		Better Understanding of Health Conditions	75.8%

4 Conclusions and Recommendations

The opt-out policy would register all eligible Australian residents in the PCEHR system however there is a long way to go to gain the acceptance and continued use of the system, especially by individual users. It needs the efforts of all stakeholders to resolve the issues of governance, meaningful use of the system, transparency, privacy, system security, quality and usability, education and promotion of the system's benefits.

- Registration: It is recommended that government should distribute promotion materials through doctors and provide bonus for doctors' effort in the recommendation and/or guidance according to complete entries of individual health records, as did in China [8].
- Privacy and security: It is recommended that the government should develop a policy of meaningful use of the PCEHR system, which determines that right users use the right data for the right purposes in the right circumstances, by integrating advices from healthcare providers, legal workers, system operators and other possible users. Meanwhile effective measures to identify threats to health data security, conduct risk analysis, and provide technical solutions to the threats as well as clear

security policy should be developed. Such measures should ensure appropriate secrecy, integrity and necessity [16] so that sensitive data are unintelligible by unauthorised people or organisations, critical data cannot be changed by unautho- rised people or organisations, and emergently needed data are instantly accessible.

- Benefits and technology: Individuals expect all the benefits from the PCEHR project (e.g., indicated in Review Panel [14]). Currently individuals are defined as consumers [4]. This definition is a barrier to the acceptance and use of the system. It is recom- mended that individuals are defined as 'citizens' with respect to the PCEHR system. While enjoying privileges, a citizen must also comply with legal requirements. Information should highlight that using the system results in savings, whilst in contrast, not using the system takes more welfare. Australia may introduce 'PCEHR Levy', which may be a part of the Medicare Levy or similar as the Flood Levy imposed in 2011 and 2012 [3]. It is also recommended that the government, healthcare providers, software developers and relevant device manufacturers carryout research on potential benefits from the PCEHR system. The Industry 4.0 [5] intro- duces the concept of 'smart' process control. The PCEHR system, as a 'Thing' in the Internet, will bring unpredictable benefits for individuals, as smart phone does [9, 17].
- System usability and quality attributes: It is recommended that system developers should interview the main users of individuals and healthcare providers, to understand their human and technical aspects for using the system. Different ver- sions of interfaces may be needed for different users according to such factors as: users' roles in the system, their age, their approaches and ways of accessing health records, their computing skills and Internet usage, and their health conditions. Some users may need special aids.

One major limitation of this study is the sample size not being large. Future work will look at increasing the scope and number of participants and conducting associated analysis to understand dependence among the influencing factors and difference among individuals.

References

1. Agarwal, R., Prased, J.: Are individual differences germane to the acceptance of new information technologies? Decis. Sci. **30**(2), 361–391 (1999)
2. Ajzen, I., Fishbein, M.: Understanding Attitudes and Predicting Social Behavior. Prentice-Hall, Englewood Cliffs (1980)
3. Australia Taxation Office: Flood levy (2015). Accessed 14 Jul 2016. https://www.ato.gov.au/Individuals/Dealing-with-disasters/Previous-years/Flood-levy/Flood-levy/
4. Australian Government: Personally Controlled Electronic Health Records Act 2012. Accessed 14 Dec 2014. https://www.legislation.gov.au/Details/C2012A00063
5. Brettel, M., Friederichsen, N., Keller, M., Rosenberg, M.: How virtualization, decentral- ization and network building change the manufacturing landscape: an industry 4.0 perspective. Int. J. Mech. Aerosp. Ind. Mechatron. Manuf. Eng. **8**(1), 37–44 (2014)
6. Davis, F.D., Bagozzi, P.B., Warshaw, P.R.: User acceptance of computer technology: a comparison of two models. Manage. Sci. **35**(8), 982–1003 (1989)

7. Department of Health: My Health Record (2016). Accessed 21 Jun 2016. http://health.gov. au/internet/main/publishing.nsf/Content/ehealth-record
8. Gao, X., Xu, J., Sorwar, S., Croll, P.: Implementation of E-Health record systems and E-Medical record systems in China. Int. Technol. Manag. Rev. 3(2), 127–139 (2013)
9. Gubbi, J., Buyya, R., Marusic, S., Palaniswami, M.: Internet of Things (IoT): A vision, architectural elements, and future directions. Future Gener. Comput. Syst. 29, 1645–1660 (2013)
10. Kerlin, J., Heath, J.: E-health scheme to be revived after panel review, The Australian Financial Review, 24 May 2014. Accessed 18 Feb 2016. http://www.afr.com/business/ health/pharmaceuticals/ehealth-scheme-to-be-revived-after-panel-review-20140523-iupi8
11. Liker, J.K., Sindi, A.A.: User acceptance of expert systems: a test of the theory of reasoned action. J. Eng. Tech. Manag. 14(2), 147–173 (1997)
12. Moore, G.C.: End-user computing and office automation: a diffusion of innovation perspectives. INFOR 25(3), 214–235 (1987)
13. NEHTA: Concept of Operations: Relating to the introduction of a Personally Controlled Electronic Health Record System (2011). Accessed 26 Sep 2012. http://www.yourhealth. gov.au/internet/yourhealth/publishing.nsf/Content/PCEHRS-Intro-toc/$File/Concept%20of %20Operations%20-%20Final.pdf
14. Review Panel: Review of the Personally Controlled Electronic Health Record (2014). Accessed 14 Dec 2014. http://www.health.gov.au/internet/main/publishing.nsf/Content/ PCEHR-Review
15. Rogers, E.M.: Diffusion of Innovations, 4th edn. The Free Press, New York (1995)
16. Schneider, G.P.: Electronic Commerce, 11th edn. Cengage Learning, Stamford (2015)
17. Ventola, C.L.: Mobile devices and Apps for health care professionals: uses and benefits. PubMed Central 39(5), 356–364 (2014)
18. Xu, J., Gao, X.J., Sorwar, G.: A research model of consumers' adoption and continued use of the Personally Controlled Electronic Health Record (PCEHR) system. Int. Technol. Manag. Rev. 4(4), 187–200 (2014)

Understanding Individual Users' Perspectives on the Personally Controlled Electronic Health Record (PCEHR) System: Results of Field Study

Jun Xu[✉], Xiangzhu Gao, John Hammond, Nicky Antonius, and Golam Sorwar

Southern Cross University, Lismore, Australia
jun.xu@scu.edu.au

Abstract. This study explores the understanding of and the current status of adoption and use of the personally controlled electronic health record (PCEHR) system among Australian consumers and aims to identify concerns/issues associated with the PCEHR system and factors influencing their decision regarding adoption and use of the PCEHR system. A qualitative field study was undertaken, in which 30 individuals/consumers were interviewed. The outcomes of this study have both theoretical and practical implications to the Australian Government's ongoing implementation of the PCEHR system.

Keywords: PCEHR system · Adoption & use · Consumers · Australia
Field study

1 Introduction

Apart from necessary personal data, health records include such information as individuals' prescribed medications, test results, care plans, immunisation records, health alerts, event summaries, hospital discharge summaries, and Medicare data. As a health information source, electronic health records (EHRs) underpin all other e-health initiatives [7]. The current release of the PCEHR system in Australia is far from mature and suffers criticisms from major stakeholders, and there is a lack of uptake and utilization [3]. The system faces various challenges, and users are neither enthusiastic in registering with nor in using the system [5, 6]. Consumers have not been active in participation for different reasons and various concerns. The interests of consumers have not been properly represented in the development and implementation of the PCEHR system. This study fills this gap by exploring the factors influencing the adoption and use of the PCEHR system by individual users via qualitative field studies.

2 Research Methods

Data were collected by means of semi-structured interview. 30 selected eligible individual users were interviewed in the Gold Coast and Brisbane areas of Queensland, Australia. The interview plan followed the guidelines of Whiteley et al. [9] and Patton [4].

© Springer International Publishing AG, part of Springer Nature 2018
M. Mokhtari et al. (Eds.): ICOST 2018, LNCS 10898, pp. 292–297, 2018.
https://doi.org/10.1007/978-3-319-94523-1_28

The high level perspective of external factors and internal factors in a model for adoption and use of the PCEHR system developed by Xu et al. [8] guided the entire interview process. Interview questions based on this perspective were first developed and tested by a third person. The interview questions focused on: (i) the general perceptions and understanding of the PCEHR system; (ii) the current status of adoption and use of the system; (iii) concerns and issues associated with system; (iv) obstacles to adopt the system; and (v) motivating factors for adopting and use the system. A pre-interview session was first conducted through telephone, which provided each participant with an idea about the interview process. Content analysis [1] was chosen for analysing the interview transcripts. Content analyses were carried out in two stages. According to Miles & Huberman [2], stage one dealt with single interview transcripts and developing tables of factors, variables and their links for each interview, while stage two dealt with cross-interview transcripts and aimed at integrating all the individual factors, variables and their relationships to compile a final list of factors and variables and their links.

3   Results

Of the 30 interview participants, 16 are female and 14 are male. 3 participants are in the 21–29 age group, 8 in the age group of 30–39, 5 in the age group of 40–49, 4 in age group of 50–59, 5 in the age group of 60–64, and 5 over 65. Two participants are Aboriginal Australian or Torres Strait Islander. 24 participants have at least a Bachelor's degree, with 13 having Bachelor's Degree, 5 having Graduate Certificate or Graduate Diploma, 5 having a Master's degree, and 1 having a Doctorate's degree. The distribution of the participants by occupation/profession is as follows: 5 retired, 2 IT professionals, 2 nurses, 1 pharmacist, 1 teacher, 1 self-employed, 1 mortician, 1 student, 1 marketing professional, 1 consultant, 1 home duties, 1 travel agent, 1 public servant, 1 fulltime carer, 1 bus driver, 1 executive legal secretary, 1 trainer and assessor, 1 HRM professional, 1 accountant, 1 draftsperson, 1 office manager/secretary, 1 carpenter, 1 unemployed, and 1 transport industry employee. A wide spectrum of occupations is therefore represented. The reported averages of weekly household income in 2015–2016 financial year are: 5 more than $1,800, 5 in the range of $1,501 to $1,800, 2 in the range of $1,101 to $1,500, 3 in the range of $901 to $1,100, 3 in the range of $701 to $900, 4 in the range of $401 to 700, 2 less than $401, and 6 not answered. The participants reported the following household compositions: (a) am the only person: 9; (b) more than one person in household:10; (c) household with child(ren) under 14 years: 4; (d) household with child(ren) 14–18 years: 5; (e) household with child(ren) over 18 years: 2; (f) household with member(s) over 65 years: 1; (g) household with members having a chronic condition: 6. 18 participants indicate they have private health insurance. 3 participants have registered with the PCEHR system, 3 have e-health experience, and 25 have experience with other government systems (e.g., Census and MyGov). Meanwhile only 3 participants have obtained information about the PCEHR system (i.e., having seen/read writing in the newspaper, having seen advertising in the doctor's office, and/or having been provided with brochures by the doctor's receptionist). Four interview participants reported that they did not know what the

PCEHR system is about, whilst the remaining participants all have some (although varied) understanding of the PCEHR system.

Views on PCEHR System Characteristics/Features

- Option to test the system before registration: 21 participants would like to have the opportunity to test the system before registering with the system. The reasons include: (1) "Any good system should be fully tested, e.g., testing privacy and security so why use dummy data to learn the system; (2) Just to see how it works; (3) That would be great."
- Option to see the full reports or just summary data: Participants' responses to the option to see the full reports or just summary data in the system vary: 16 participants want to see full reports (including 1 participant who wants to have the search function for summary data); 8 participants want to see summary data only (including 1 participant only wants to see summary data for last 2 years); 3 participants want to see summary data but with the option to view full reports; 1 participant wants to have the both options of full reports and summary data (for last 2 years); 1 participant wants to see either full report or summary data; 1 participant is only interested in current year's data.
- Link the PCEHR system worldwide: 18 participants think the Australian PCEHR system should link worldwide while 10 participants don't think it is necessary. Some of their views or concerns include: (1) "Just Australia. Could have opt-in as part of travel/health insurance; (2) Yes. Also travel insurance need to access/view to determine pre-existing conditions; (3) No. What happens in Australia stays in Australia; (4) Yes for a hospital only; (5) It would be a useful benefit or desirable.
- Trust GP and other healthcare providers to update information: 27 participants trust their GP to update their medical information in the PCEHR system. Some of their comments are: (1) "Yes. I trust the GP but not trust the Government system; (2) GPs already complain about doing unfunded work. They want to be reimbursed for this duty; (3) Yes but only important information required (to be put into the system)." Meanwhile 24 participants also trust other healthcare providers to update information in the PCEHR system.
- Option of Delegation/Health directive in special conditions: 21 participants agree that they will delegate the functionality or use to other people in special conditions or emergency situations (e.g., a person who can no longer make decisions for themselves), and another 6 participants will do so under a health directive or power of attorney for special conditions or emergency situations.
- Public sector work with Private sector for the greater good of the system: 16 participants believe that the public sector should work with the private sector for the greater good of the PCEHR system while 14 participants are sceptical about co-operation. Some of their concerns consist of: (1) "I would like to think so. Not sure about efficiencies, there is room for improvement; (2) Theoretically great but unlikely; (3) Depends on the cost. If private sector paid to use system, then they should work together; (4) All control and access so they probably need to work together.

Users' Expected Benefits

When asked about the expected/perceived benefits of the PCEHR systems, the participants mention many perspectives: (1) Better medical/health information management:

"Know that records kept electronically secure. Accurate data"; (2) Faster and better access to the medical/health information: "One central body holding all the information. All relevant health issues available to the GP. Distance is no problem especially for the traveler. Speed of access of information if records are categorized properly"; "Being able to access any time if needed. Being able to view updates from other parties. Used for follow-up of conditions"; (3) Better healthcare services and system: "Improve patient care and speed"; "Holistic approach to healthcare. Treating professionals have complete health record. More efficient diagnosis and less bed time which leads to critical diagnosis and targeted treatments quicker"; (4) More streamlined processes: "Stop doctor shopping. No getting drugs from more than one doctor"; "Ease in transferring GPs"; (5) Better health awareness: "More awareness of your health. Get alerts"; "Stop multiple visits and have an audit trail of visits"; (6) Cost reduction and time saving: "Reduced costs., Getting medical history faster, Should save time and doctor should run on time as all information presented"; (7) Economic benefits: "Economic benefit leading to lower cost of delivery leading to cost efficiencies"; (8) Mobility: "Mobility. Able to look up dates (of conditions) as system accessible"; (9) Research and Trend Identification and Disease Prevention: "Ability to develop trends"; "Disease prevention and tracking"; (10) Mistake Reduction: "Help save mistakes e.g. wrong drugs given"; (11) Better Communication between Healthcare Providers: "Communication between all healthcare providers. Deliver health benefits leads to economic benefits to the Australian community".

System Management Issues

- Rules for managing data change in the system: Participants suggest protocols and rules should be established to manage all data changes in the PCEHR system. Comments for general protocols of data change include: (1) "There should be protocols for any change for everyone who can access; (2) Approval by third party or the GP for all changes made by all who access; (3) There should be strict guidelines in place for complete privacy; (3) Rules should be approved by Board of Practitioners; (4) All changes should be approved by patient. Changes by YOU (need to be) approved by GP.
- Who should control the system?: 23 interview participants believe that relevant federal or state governments should take control of the operation of the PCEHR system while 5 participants argue that the system should be controlled by non-government entities outside of the government (e.g., private enterprise, independent governing body and regulator).
- Who should maintain the system?: 19 interview participants have the view that relevant federal or state governments should be responsible for maintaining the PCEHR system while 9 participants argue that the system should be controlled by non-government entities outside of the government (e.g., private enterprise, independent governing body and regulator, most efficient and secure organization, an organization with good computer skills, a separate system to Medicare).
- Who should pay for maintaining the system?: All interview participants point out that the government should pay for maintaining the PCEHR system.
- Should be a fee to view the information?: 29 interview participants believe that no fees should be charged for viewing the information in the PCEHR system, 4

participants suggest that fees should be charged for excessive viewing, 1 participant believes third parties should pay for viewing, and 1 participant suggests there should be a limit on free viewing (e.g., 20 times per annum).

- Concerns over the ability to access and save information in the system: Some concerns over the ability to access and save information in the PCEHR system include: (1) "Major concern as to the saving of data to mobile devices; (2) Should have read only access and should have no ability to save; (3) No concerns except download to personal devices.

Reasons for Not Registering with the System

Some reasons for not registering with the PCEHR system mentioned by interview participants include: (1) Lack of information and knowledge about the system: "Not seen any information and therefore not registered. Did not know about the system"; "Government fraud. Not trust government. Information may end up in the wrong hands"; "Not know much about it. Need more information before making a decision"; "Don't read material in mail that was not addressed to me. (If not addressed to me, I think of it as junk mail and throw it out.). Hate reading screens of information": "The great unknown - know nothing about the system"; "No knowledge about it"; (2) Lack of awareness; (3) Apathy/Lack of interest; (4) Lack of required computer skills; (5) Aversion to computer systems or Don't trust computers; (6) Lack of established access protocols; (6) Time poor or being lazy: "No time"; "Too lazy - not enough time and effort"; (7) Lack of opportunity: "Not really have any medical issues"; "Don't go the GP often"; (8) Lack of necessity: "My GP already has enough information regarding my health"; (9) General ignorance of the users by the government; (10) Privacy concerns and security of system: "Seen many cases when information leaked. Concerns over who can access. Concerns over ability to save data"; (11) No trust towards the government: "Sceptical. No confidence in the Government to pull this off. If they cannot run the country successfully, then how can they pull this off?"; "Government fraud. Not trust government. Information may end up in the wrong hands".

Compulsory Registration

16 interview participants support the notion of compulsory registration in the PCEHR system while 14 participants have different views. Meanwhile 24 interview participants believe if the compulsory registration is the way to go in the future, then an opt-out option should be provided.

4   Conclusions

Of the 30 participants, only 3 have voluntarily registered with the PCEHR system. Some participants do not know the system well, some do not know if the system has been launched, and most had not seen any printed material about the system. They indicated that they would register after reading printed material, such as an information pack for individual users. The information pack could be similar to the Tax Pack which assisted taxpayers to complete their individual tax returns. The Tax Pack was widely accepted as it contained all information about tax matters for individuals in one complete book and was written in simple English for all readers to understand. Furthermore it is preferable for individual users to have an information pack which also sets out how to communicate with the system operator, technical support help desks and healthcare providers. Privacy of medical information is a concern. Those with chronic conditions were very guarded as to what their condition was during the interview and did not want others having access to their records. Security of data is another concern based on their experience of using other information systems, such as bank systems. There is a lack of trust in technology: if banks cannot keep the data secure, then what are the chances that health records would not be leaked? There is also an issue of trust in government. Although the government does issue regulations for the control and use of individual information, it is not transparent to the individual as to what the information would be used for in the operation phase. Some participants cannot see the wide merits for all individual users, limiting the benefits to emergency use or remote use. The jury was out on whether the system should be linked to other countries. The field studies reported in this paper were conducted only in the Gold Coast and Brisbane areas. Future research could look at collecting more qualitative data by interviewing more PCEHR users and conducting focus group studies in various cities and regions, and the outcomes of such qualitative studies would lay a solid foundation for subsequent quantitative studies (e.g., national surveys). The researchers will also look at pursuing the option of seeking funding to develop a very comprehensive Information Pack which will address all concerns and benefits in a balanced way.

References

1. Berg, B.L.: Qualitative Research Methods for the Social Sciences. Allyn and Bacon, Boston (2001)
2. Miles, M.B., Huberman, M.A.: An Expanded Sourcebook: Qualitative Data Analysis, 2nd edn. SAGE Publications Thousands Oaks, California (1994)
3. Partel, K.: Toward better implementation: Australia's My Health Record, Deeble Institute Issues Brief, No. 13, 30/10/2015, pp. 1–20 (2015)
4. Patton, Q.M.: Qualitative Evaluation and Research Methods, 2nd edn. SAGE Publications, Newbury Park (1990)
5. Sansom, M.: My Health Record: Medics speak up, Government News, 15 August 2016. Accessed. 15 Apr 2017. http://www.governmentnews.com.au/2016/08/24703/
6. Smith, C., Ellis, I., Jaffray, L.: Nursing competencies needed for electronic advance care planning in community. GSTF Int. J. Nurs. Health Care 1(1), 160–164 (2013)
7. Xu, J., Gao, X.J., Sorwar, G., Croll, P.: Implementation of E-Health record systems in Australia. Int. Technol. Manag. Rev. 3(2), 92–104 (2013)
8. Xu, J., Gao, X., Sorwar, G.: A research model of consumers' adoption and continued use of the Personally Controlled Electronic Health Record (PCEHR) system. Int. Technol. Manag. Rev. 4(4), 187–200 (2014)
9. Whiteley, A., McCabe, M., Buoy, L., Howie, F., Klass, D., Latham, J., Bickley, M., Luckheenariam, L.: Planning the qualitative research interview, Working Paper Series 98.01, Graduate School of Business, Curtin University of Technology, Australia (1998)

Context-Based Lifelog Monitoring for Just-in-Time Wellness Intervention

Hafiz Syed Muhammad Bilal[1,2], Muhammad Asif Razzaq[1],
Muhammad Bilal Amin[1], and Sungyoung Lee[1(✉)]

[1] Department of Computer Engineering, Kyung Hee University,
Seocheon-dong, Giheung-gu, Yongin-si, Gyeonggi-do 446-701, Korea
{bilalrizvi,asif.razzaq,sylee}@oslab.khu.ac.kr,
m.b.amin@ieee.org
[2] National University of Sciences and Technology, Islamabad, Pakistan
bilal.ali@seecs.edu.pk

Abstract. These days adoption of healthy behavior can be quantified through Ubiquitous computing and smart gadgets. This digital technology has revolutionized the self-quantification to monitor activities for improving lifestyle. Context based lifelog monitoring is among the processes of tracking individual's lifestyle in an effective manner. We have proposed a methodology for context-based monitoring of an individual's prolonged sedentary physical activity and unhealthy dietary behavior in the domain of wellness and give just-in-time intervention to adapt healthy behavior. It detects multiple unhealthy activities of its users and verifies the context for intervention generation. The results depict that the average response of the context-based just-in-time interventions is about 75%.

Keywords: Lifelog · Context-based · Just-in-time · Unhealthy behavior
Wellness services · Sedentary lifestyle · Unbalanced diet

1 Introduction

Innovative and smart gadgets have supported the wellness domain to enhance individual health and improve socio-economic situations by quantifying the human activities and daily routine. In 1990s, wellness was introduced as *Wheel of Wellness* [1, 2] with categorization of nutritional knowledge, physical fitness, stress management, environmental and social awareness [4]. Today, wellness domain requires innovative user centric platforms which should digitize wellness and health parameters to provide precise recommendations and wellness services [3]. The change in behavior requires a just-in-time (JIT) intervention which meets the constraints and conditions of the environment. The intervention should adapt according to the individual's dynamic status, the goals to target and the changes required for improvement [5].

© Springer International Publishing AG, part of Springer Nature 2018
M. Mokhtari et al. (Eds.): ICOST 2018, LNCS 10898, pp. 298–303, 2018.
https://doi.org/10.1007/978-3-319-94523-1_29

1.1   Behavior's Concerns and Wellness Applications

Wellness literature shows that unhealthy behavior includes smoking, sedentary lifestyle, higher alcohol intake, and unhealthy diet. The unhealthy diet may increase the risk of chronic diseases like cardiovascular disease, hypertension, diabetes, and premature mortality [6]. The mortality rate is the indication of population's health status which is linked with the higher risk of lifestyle based diseases [13]. The unhealthy lifestyle is an influential cause of chronic diseases and premature death [9]. The regular interrupts in sedentary activities enhance metabolic profile of individual as compared to sedentary ones [8].

The design and development of wellness and health care applications are focusing to track the individual's activity log to identify lifestyle pattern [14]. The identified patterns support proactively to diagnose the cause of undesired fitness and health issues. There are multiple wellness applications are available [6] i.e. GoogleFit, Noom Coach, Apple Healthkit, Google Fit, and etc. These applications quantify user activities, step counts, calories consumption, and provide visualization of user status.

1.2   Context-Based Adaptive Intervention

The design of intervention plays a vital role to adopt the changes in behavior. The retention or abandonment of intervention requires to consider the constraints, status and context of the user. The effectiveness of intervention needs to specify the extent and duration of engagement for targeted behavior. The JIT adaptive intervention is an emerging way to promote the healthy behavior adoption with the usage of powerful mobile and sensing technologies [5].

2   Context-Based Just-in-Time Lifelog Monitor Architecture

Most of the wellness applications recognizes the user activities and provide interactive visualization to the users on demands [14]. Self-quantification and managing log provide foundation to take proactive action to avoid bad impact of unhealthy lifestyle pattern. The proactive demands in wellness domain lead us to propose context-based JIT lifelog monitor for appropriate intervention generation. According to the JIT philosophy "produce right item, at the right time, in right quantity" [7] supports us to monitor the right person, at right time, for right behavior.

The proposed context-based JIT lifelog monitor as shown in Fig. 1, consists of four components. These components manage the guidelines-based rules related to unhealthy patterns, monitor the lifelog, verify the context and constraints, and notify the wellness stakeholders instantly. The main components are *Monitor Event Configurator, Constraints Configurator, Situation Event Detector,* and *Intervention Manager.*

Monitor event manages the information of the monitor-able activities along with respective quantities in configuration database. The constraints define the situation of a specific monitor-able event and is responsible to manage the multiple constraint conditions related to the monitor-able events. Constraints configurator verifies the situation by checking all constraint conditions related to that monitor-able event. Situation event detector continuously monitors the event to verify the state where it crosses the threshold quantity defined by expert. The information of micro-nutrients is extracted from the food database of United States Department of Agriculture [17] and consumption of micro-nutrients are obtained with the help of serving quantity [18]. The physical activity behavior is categorized into sedentary or active on the basis of Canadian Physical Activity guidelines [16]. If context supports the intervention, then Intervention Notifier is activated otherwise Intervention Adapter modifies the intervention time by delaying until the context become favorable for the intervention or otherwise ignores it.

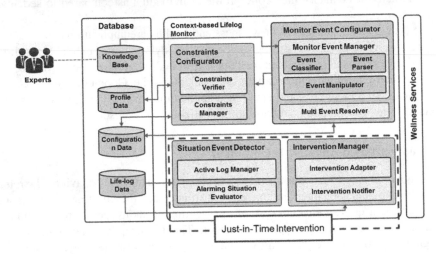

Fig. 1. Architecture of context-based JIT lifelog monitor

3   Integration of Context-Based Lifelog Monitor with Wellness Platform

We have integrated the proposed lifelog monitor with an open source Mining Minds (MM) platform [11, 14]. The individual's context is identified through key attributes location, time, physiological factors, preferences, and activity to generate personalized wellness recommendations [10]. The complexity of the platform is managed through *Supporting Layer (SL), Knowledge Curation Layer (KCL), Information Curation Layer (ICL), Service Curation Layer (SCL),* and *Data Curation Layer (DCL)* respectively as shown in Fig. 2.

The *SL* provides multidimensional view of the activities' pattern and analytical reports. It classifies the stakeholders on the basis of access rights and demands [12]. The *SCL* manages personalized recommendation services to provide support either in push or pull mode on the basis of the user requirements [15]. The *KCL* helps an expert to express the knowledge into rules to define the unhealthy behavior using knowledge authoring environment [12].

The *ICL* recognizes individual's activities and context through sensory data of emotion, movement, and location. The lifestyle patterns are recognized through the low and high level contexts [11]. The *DCL* continuously gathers and manages the raw multi-modal sensory data into lifelog and big data storage [3].

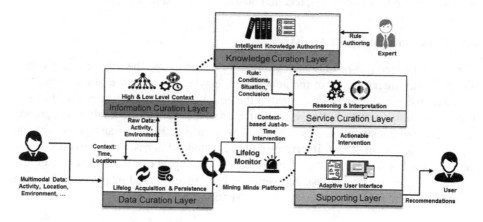

Fig. 2. Integration of lifelog monitor with wellness platform.

4 Experimental Setup

This work is focusing the unhealthy dietary habits and prolonged sedentary bouts. The context-based JIT intervention is provided to avoid the unhealthy habits of physical activities and dietary pattern. For this particular evaluation we have considered 12 volunteers with different gender and age. In order to assess the effectiveness of the JIT intervention, we have drawn the 12 scenarios on the basis of the profile information of our volunteers as shown in Table 1.

Table 1. Situations for monitoring the activities

Situation	Gender	Height (cm)	Weight (kg)	BMI	Activity level	Calories requirement	Recommended fat (gm)
S1	Male	178	92	30.9	Sedentary	2075	57
S2	Male	173	73	24.4	Active	2312	51
S3	Female	168	72	25.5	Sedentary	2020	45
S4	Female	164	56	20.8	Active	1982	40
S5	Male	179	69	21.5	Sedentary	2033	52
S6	Male	176	78	25.2	Active	2112	54
S7	Male	165	48	17.5	Sedentary	1676	43
S8	Female	164	68	25.3	Active	1931	43
S9	Male	165	78	28.7	Active	2042	52
S10	Male	180	98	30.2	Active	2298	59
S11	Female	164	58	21.6	Sedentary	1793	40
S12	Male	168	90	31.9	Sedentary	2100	53

The wellness platform has recorded the volunteers' activities for 21 days with at-least 4 consecutive days for a user. The intimation is generated just-in-time on the basis of detected prolonged activities, location, and the food that they logged.

4.1 Experimental Result Analysis

The context-based just-in-time lifelog monitor has monitored the activities of the user and generated interventions of the unhealthy lifestyle. The response of the volunteers increases when it considers the context of the volunteers while generating the interven-tion. After analysis of the lifelog, it is observed that the intimation for fats has improved the intake and consumption effectively as shown in Fig. 3(a). The analysis of the log represents that about 42% of interventions are unattended in case of context-less inter-vention. The result shown in Fig. 3(b) represents the impact of context-based interven-tion as compare to context-less intervention. The context-based intervention is about 17.5% more effective than context-less intervention.

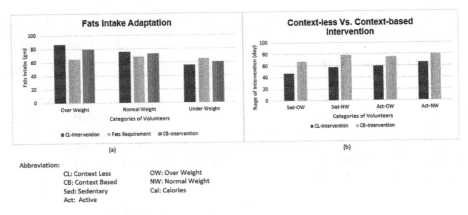

Abbreviation:

CL: Context Less	OW: Over Weight
CB: Context Based	NW: Normal Weight
Sed: Sedentary	Cal: Calories
Act: Active	

Fig. 3. Evaluation of intervention effectiveness on the basis of context

5   Conclusion and Future Work

The designed context-based just-in-time lifelog monitor, monitors the activities and generates the interventions about the alarming situation on the basis of the context. The push based indication to right person, at right time for alarming event helps the individual to change unhealthy behavior proactively. The novel approach of context-based moni-toring and just-in-time intervention generation has not only improved the dietary habits but also reduced the number of prolonged sedentary bouts. This precautionary approach can support to avoid chronic diseases by reducing weight and adopting active lifestyle. In future we want to use behavior theory to adopt healthy behavior by identifying the behavior status of the user and generate behavior based intervention.

Acknowledgments. This work was supported by Institute for Information & communications Technology Promotion (IITP) grant funded by the Korea government (MSIT) (No. 2017-0-00655) and and by the Korea Research Fellowship Program through the National Research Foundation of Korea (NRF) funded by the Ministry of Science and ICT (NRF-2016H1D3A1938039).

References

1. Ali, R., Afzal, M., Hussain, M., Ali, M., Siddiqi, M.H., Lee, S., Kang, B.H.: Multimodal hybrid reasoning methodology for personalized wellbeing services. Comput. Biol. Med. **69**, 10–28 (2016)
2. Banos, O., Amin, M.B., Khan, W.A., Afzal, M., Hussain, M., Kang, B.H., Lee, S.: The mining minds digital health and wellness framework. Biomed. Eng. Online **1**, 76 (2016)
3. Ardell, Donald B.: High Level Wellness, An Alternative to Doctors, Drugs, and Disease. Bantam Books, New York (1979)
4. Amin, M.B., Banos, O., Khan, W.A., Muhammad Bilal, H.S., Gong, J., Bui, D.M., Chung, T.C.: On curating multimodal sensory data for health and wellness platforms. Sensors **16**(7), 980 (2016)
5. Banos, O., Amin, M.B., Ali Khan, W., Ali, T., Afzal, M., Kang, B.H., Lee, S.: Mining minds: an innovative framework for personalized health and wellness support. In: 2015 9th International Conference on Pervasive Computing Technologies for Healthcare (Pervasive Health), pp. 1–8. IEEE, May 2015
6. Ahmad, M., Amin, M.B., Hussain, S., Kang, B.H., Cheong, T., Lee, S.: Health fog: a novel framework for health and wellness applications. J Supercomput. **72**, 1–19 (2016)
7. Kvaavik, E., et al.: Influence of individual and combined health behaviors on total and cause-specific mortality in men and women: the United Kingdom health and lifestyle survey. Archiv. Intern. Med. **170**(8), 711–718 (2010)
8. Petersen, K.E.N., et al.: The combined impact of adherence to five lifestyle factors on all-cause, cancer and cardiovascular mortality: a prospective cohort study among Danish men and women. Br. J. Nutr. **113**(05), 849–858 (2015)
9. Katz, D.L., Meller, S.: Can we say what diet is best for health? Ann. Rev. Pub. Health **35**, 83–103 (2014)
10. Azumio: Argus quantify your day-to-day (2015). http://www.azumio.com/s/argus/index.html
11. Thorp, A.A., Owen, N., Neuhaus, M., Dunstan, D.W.: Sedentary behaviors and subsequent health outcomes in adults: a systematic review of longitudinal studies, 1996–2011. Am. J. Prev. Med. **41**(2), 207–215 (2011)
12. Millennium Ecosystem Assessment: Ecosystems and Human Wellbeing: A Framework for Assessment. Island Press, Washington, DC (2003)
13. Khan, W.A., Amin, M.B., Banos, O., Ali, T., Hussain, M., Afzal, M., Hussain, S., Hussain, J., Ali, R., Ali, M., Kang, D.: Mining Minds: Journey of Evolutionary Platform for Ubiquitous Wellness
14. Sweeney, T.J., Witmer, J.M.: Beyond social interest: striving toward optimum health and wellness. Individ. Psychol. **47**, 527–540 (1991)
15. Witmer, J.M., Sweeney, T.J.: A holistic model for wellness and prevention over the lifespan. J. Couns. Develop. **71**, 140–148 (1992)
16. CSEP: Canadian Physical Activity guidelines (2017). http://csep.ca/CMFiles/Guidelines/CSEP_PAGuidelines_adults_en.pdf
17. USDA Food Composition Database. https://ndb.nal.usda.gov/ndb/
18. Portions per person. https://www.cookipedia.co.uk/recipes_wiki/Portions_per_person

Assessment of a Smart Kitchen to Help People with Alzheimer's Disease

Roberto Menghi[✉], Francesca Gullà, and Michele Germani

Department of Industrial Engineering and Mathematical Sciences,
Università Politecnica delle Marche, Via Brecce Bianche, 12, 60131 Ancona, Italy
{r.menghi,f.gulla,m.germani}@univpm.it

Abstract. The ageing population is leading to a significant impact on current society and it is introducing new challenges to find innovative solutions to help older adults to improve their quality of life, stay healthier, and live independently. In this context, the present paper provides a usability assessment of a Smart Kitchen developed to support people with the early-stage dementia in cooking activities. The smart system is managed through an adaptable user interface, which provides information on the meal preparation and allows to configure and manage all household appliances in a simple and intuitive way. Although this preliminary evaluation only included a small number of participants, the results showed that the system could be useful to help and guide people to remain independent in their own home environment for daily kitchen activities.

Keywords: Adaptive interface · Alzheimer's Disease · Smart home
Usability evaluation

1 Introduction

The aging of society has become a global trend due to the life longevity and declining birth rate. This phenomenon is even more acute and significant in the developed regions such as in Europe, where almost one-sixth of the population is aged over 65 and it is estimated that this proportion will increase up to one in four people in 2025 [1]. The aging of the population will be accompanied by rapid increase in the number of people with mental and physical impairments as well as various age-related chronic disease like cognitive decline. One of the most prevalent types of chronic disease within the older population is Alzheimer's Disease (AD) [2]. AD is a progressive, debilitating and chronic disease that affects one in twenty older people (over 65 years old) and it is characterized by a loss of brain function which degrades the ability to think cognitively, communicate, make reasonable decisions, behave in a lucid manner, and recall memory [3]. Early-stage impairment is related to difficulties in performing complex tasks and over the years, it can worsen until the inability to perform even the most basic functional activities.

Different studies have been carried out in recent years on how technology can improve the life quality for individuals suffering from cognitively debilitating disease [4, 5]. Modern technologies could so have an important role to satisfy main needs of

© Springer International Publishing AG, part of Springer Nature 2018
M. Mokhtari et al. (Eds.): ICOST 2018, LNCS 10898, pp. 304–309, 2018.
https://doi.org/10.1007/978-3-319-94523-1_30

users with dementia. However, one of the main problems of the developers is relating to the user interface usability. This topic is further complicated since dementia affects every individual differently and each person has his own specific set of conditions, disabilities and needs. To consider all users, and limit computational effort, the Adaptable User Interfaces have been developed. There are several contexts in which the adaptive systems have been used (e.g. in the smart home, in workplaces application and healthcare area), however the applications of adaptive systems to support people with disabilities and the elderly are not so common [6, 7].

In this context, this research work aims to evaluate the usability of a smart kitchen managed through an adaptive user interface, which provides information on the meal preparation (i.e. the list of ingredients, the quantities required and the steps of the preparation) and allows to configure and manage all household appliances in a simple and intuitive way. Adapting itself to the end-user capabilities and needs, the adaptive user interface assists the user by providing information and alerts in the event of unusual situations requiring warnings.

2   The Smart Kitchen

An overview of the smart kitchen and the user interface (UI) developed to help users in their daily kitchen tasks is given. The smart kitchen is composed by: several environmental sensors (e.g. brightness, temperature), the home automation platform that manages all information and controls all devices, and some household appliances (i.e. oven, dishwasher and the fridge) with smart functions (i.e. provide information regarding status, programming and controlling operations) [8].

The system is controlled and managed by an Application Core that defines the most comfortable adaptation according to user preferences through continuous communication with the Database Management System. The Application Core represents the brain of the entire application and it is composed of two adaptive mechanisms: (a) the adaptable engine that is focused on graphical interface features (e.g. text, size and type of font) and it is based on user features; (b) the adaptive engine that is based on the user-system interaction and the adaptation actions focus on the dynamic features such as preferences based on the history of user's interaction, information contents, icons, and layout [9].

Lastly, the UI has been designed to help the user in the kitchen's activities. To support the different user needs in the various stages of the cognitive disease, two interface versions have been developed: Normal UI and Wizard UI. The first one was designed to resemble the most common setting menu [10], where information is displayed on a single web page. The second one was designed to accomplish the task and minimizing the amount of information that the user should understand and manage. To prevent the user from being confused if too many options are presented at once, the information was provided through a setup-driven process [10]. Figure 1 shows an example of the meal preparation user interface in which the user is supported not only at the beginning of the activity (i.e. take the correct quantity of ingredients according to the number of diners) but also to carry on with it, with stepwise assistance during all preparation.

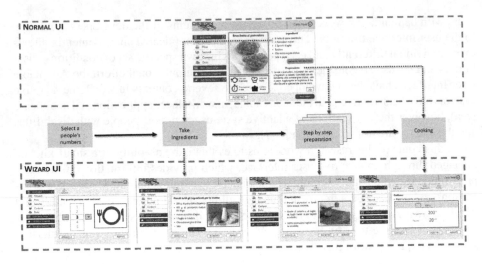

Fig. 1. Meal preparation UI (top: Normal UI, below: Wizard UI)

3   Methods

A usability evaluation has been carried out to investigate the reliability and the user-friendliness from the perspective of people with cognitive impairment. Volunteer subjects were recruited in facilities of the local municipality. The participants were primarily seniors, with early-stages of AD. In total the sample was composed of 15 participants, 5 males and 10 females, with a mean age of 72.2 years old (SD = 3.5). To be involved, the following inclusion criteria were fixed:

- Age 65 and older;
- Mini-Mental State Examination (MMSE) score between 22 and 28 (early and mild impaired patients who retained the physical and functional ability to participate in a cognitive or motor stimulation program);
- Familiarity with touchscreen devices (e.g. smartphone, tablet);
- Intermediate level of expertise in cooking.

The experiment took place in the usability Lab, which was set up to serve research purposes. The Lab was equipped with the smart kitchen, a table and a chair. On a large table, participants had at their disposal the tablet with the developed Application, the utensils and the ingredients needed. The Application was presented on a tablet (10.1″) and the setting was maintained the same for all participants.

On the day of the test, participants were first welcomed in one of the laboratory facilities and were debriefed regarding the overall activity and the goals of the experiment. Before the experiment began, participants were invited to redo the MMSE and to carefully read the informed consent and to sign it in only when the contents were clear. Then, the participants have been conducted in the Lab where they were told how the experiment will be performed. Given the typical poor confidence older adults have in their abilities to interact with new technologies, a training phase has been carried out to explain how the application was structured and how to operate it. Participants were asked to prepare a plumcake for two people.

The experiment consists of four tasks: (1) find the appropriate recipe through the specific menu on the interface; (2) take the necessary ingredients and the correct quantities; (3) process the ingredients; and (4) cook the meal by programming the oven. The experiment was conducted by using both Wizard UI and Normal UI. During the entire interaction, users were encouraged to express their thoughts, feelings and opinions aloud while the experimenter was taken annotation of the performance, errors and user attitudes. The experimental session was completed when the user has completed the two tasks.

4   Results

Tests show interesting results which partially confirm the existent literature [11] and partially reveal new findings that can be useful to improve the assistive technologies for people with early-stage of dementia. The following objective parameters have been collected for each task: task completion (C), errors made by user during the interaction (E), number of support requests made by user to the experimenter (Sr) and time in second of completed tasks.

By analyzing the results, it was found that Task 2 and Task 3 are the most complex tasks to be completed independently for users with Alzheimer disease (Figs. 2 and 3). In particular, for the Task 2, in the Normal mode, only five users involved are able to complete the task independently, with a success rate of 38%. In fact, most users often recur to the aid of the experimenter (Sr = 4.0; SD = 0.65), with an average error E = 2.5 (SD = 0.78). Instead, in the Wizard Mode, twelve users complete the task independently (C = 79.0%), with a sharp decrease in the help' requests and errors (Sr = 2.0, SD = 0.34; E = 1.3, SD = 0.36).

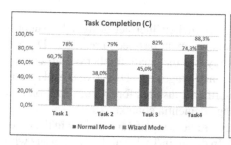 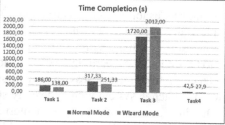

Fig. 2. Comparison between Wizard and Normal Mode: (a) Task completion (b) Time completion.

Regarding the Task 3, in the Normal Mode, the results show that the task was completed successfully by six users with an average number of errors E = 3.1 (SD = 0.49) and an average support requests Sr = 5.0 (SD = 0.48). Instead, in the Wizard mode, thirteen users complete the task independently, with an average error E = 1.5 (SD = 0.31). The wizard mode increases the success rate of the task (82.0%) and consequently the completion time. Moreover, the results show for Task 1, in the Normal mode,

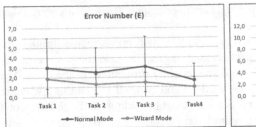 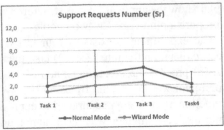

Fig. 3. Comparison between Wizard and Normal Mode: (a) Error and (b) Support request number.

a success rate of 60% with an error average E = 3.0 (SD = 0.25) and a support request Sr = 2.0 (SD = 0.33); on the other hand, in the Wizard Mode, the success rate reaches about 80% with a mean error E = 1.9 (SD = 0.25). Finally, for the Task 4 the results show that the task was completed successfully by eleven users with an average number of errors E = 1.7 (SD = 0.2) and an average support requests Sr = 2.1 (SD = 1.8), in Normal mode. Instead, in the Wizard mode, thirteen users have completed the task independently, with an average error E = 1.0 (SD = 0.16). The completion times for each task in the Wizard mode are generally lower compared to the Normal mode, except for the Task 3, in which the time increment is mainly due to the step by step procedure.

At the end of the session, users were also asked to answer to the SUS questionnaire [12]. The SUS analysis results show that the interfaces are considered very useful for all involved users. The Wizard Interface has obtained a higher score (SUS = 90.5) given by the greater amount of information available in this mode.

5   Discussion and Conclusion

A preliminary usability study of an adaptive smart kitchen interface designed to support people with early-stage dementia in kitchen management has been presented. Despite the interesting results, the limitation of this study was the small number of participants due to the difficulty of recruiting patients with early-stages of AD. The obtained results and feedback from the test session provide significant insights for the introduction of a new smart kitchen system within the early-stage dementia context.

Our findings show that the Wizard interface provides significant support in the independent kitchen activities to the user with AD. In detail, in Task 2 and Task 3, users who performed the assignments with the Wizard UI have obtained a higher success rate than using the Normal UI. In Task 2 (*"take the ingredients"*), the users have been supported by the Wizard mode into the selection of the correct quantities and ingredients to be taken. Furthermore, in Task 3 (*"process the ingredients"*), users have found benefits in the step by step process due to a decrease in cognitive load, in information to remember, and in the help availability. However, in this last task, due to the more detailed level of information the Time completion has been increased. In Tasks 1 and Task 4, the difference between using the Normal UI and the Wizard UI is less significant in terms of performance and time. However, it should be noted that the use of a wizard interface makes the user-system interaction easier. In Task 4 (*"oven setting"*), users reported a more user-friendly household appliance configuration by providing detailed information and control alerts. In Task 1 (*"find the appropriate recipe"*), user interaction is improved with step-by-step search help and with reminder messages. The support provided by the Wizard mode allows users to perform semi-autonomously the assigned tasks, reducing the help requests and the number of errors. Furthermore, the greater clearness of the information given in this modality impacts in terms of percentage of task completion and time.

This research work suggests that the system could be useful to help and guide people to remain independent in their own home environment for daily kitchen activities. The introduction of an adaptive smart kitchen system may then take into account the cognitive disabilities through its ability to adapt according to user needs. Future works will be focus on the integration and implementation of this system in real-life contexts with persons with early-stage and mild dementia.

References

1. Giannakouris, K.: Regional population projections EUROPOP2008: most EU regions face older population profile in 2030. Statistics in focus, Eurostat (2010)
2. Alzheimer's Association: 2009 alzheimer's disease facts and figures. Alzheimers Dement. **5**(3), 234–270 (2009)
3. Albert, M.S.: Cognitive and neurobiologic markers of early Alzheimer disease. Proc. Natl. Acad. Sci. **93**(24), 13547–13551 (1996)
4. Sauer, A.L., Parks, A., Heyn, P.C.: Assistive technology effects on the employment outcomes for people with cognitive disabilities: a systematic review. Disabil. Rehabil. Assist. Technol. **5**(6), 377–391 (2010)
5. Arab, F., Bauchet, J., Pigot, H., Giroux, A., Giroux, S.: Design and assessment of enabling environments for cooking activities. In: Proceedings of the 2014 ACM International Joint Conference on Pervasive and Ubiquitous Computing, pp. 517–526 (2014)
6. Letsu-Dake, E., Ntuen, C.A.: A case study of experimental evaluation of adaptive interfaces. Int. J. Ind. Ergon. **40**(1), 34–40 (2010)
7. Shakshuki, E.M., Reid, M., Sheltami, T.R.: An adaptive user interface in healthcare. Procedia Comput. Sci. **56**, 49–58 (2015)
8. Gullà, F., Ceccacci, S., Menghi R., Germani, M.: An adaptive smart system to foster disabled and elderly people in kitchen-related task. In: Proceedings of the 9th ACM International Conference on PErvasive Technologies Related to Assistive Environments, p. 27. ACM (2016)
9. Gullà, F., Ceccacci, S., Menghi, R., Cavalieri, L., Germani, M.: Adaptive interface for smart home: a new design approach. In: Cavallo, F., Marletta, V., Monteriù, A., Siciliano, P. (eds.) ForItAAL 2016. LNEE, vol. 426, pp. 107–115. Springer, Cham (2017). https://doi.org/10.1007/978-3-319-54283-6_8
10. Orso, V., Gullà, F., Menghi, R., Ceccacci, S., Cavalieri, L., Germani, M., Gamberini, L.: A digital cookbook for elderly people: investigating interface concept. In: Proceedings of the International Conference on Interfaces and Human Computer Interaction, pp. 159–166 (2017)
11. Wherton, J.P., Monk, A.F.: Problems people with dementia have with kitchen tasks: the challenge for pervasive computing. Interact. Comput. **22**(4), 253–266 (2010)
12. Brooke, J.: SUS-A quick and dirty usability scale. Usability Eval. Ind. **189**(194), 4–7 (1996)

Detection of Untrustworthy IoT Measurements Using Expert Knowledge of Their Joint Distribution

Ilia Nouretdinov[✉], Salaheddin Darwish, and Stephen Wolthusen

Information Security Group, RHUL, Egham TW20 OEX, UK
{i.r.nouretdinov,salaheddin.darwish,stephen.wolthusen}@rhul.ac.uk
http://isg.rhul.ac.uk/

Abstract. The aim of this work is to discuss abnormality detection and explanation challenges motivated by Medical Internet of Things. First, any feature is a measurement taken by a sensor at a time moment, so abnormality detection also becomes a sequential process. Second, an anomaly detection process could not rely on having a large collection of data records, but instead there is a knowledge provided by the experts.

Keywords: Anomaly explanation · Untrustworthy data
Internet of Things

This work was initially motivated by some security challenges in Medical Internet of Things (MIoT). An individual instance (data record) in this context is presented as a sequence of measurements generated by multiple sensors. Abnormality of a record usually becomes a reason to produce an alert to doctors, reporting a suspected critical health state of the patients. However, the task is to separate a real health alarm from threats and vulnerabilities of the MIoT system. The principal question is which of the measurements (features) are less trustworthy than the others. The key assumption is that some knowledge of the joint feature distribution is available before having the measurements. The information about feature dependencies may be extracted from data analysis or obtain from experts. Involving experts in data analysis is very desirable. This is discussed e.g. in [5] where a Bayesian causal network for diagnostic is provided with elements of human feedback. Expert knowledge may also include some prior knowledge collected from earlier research on different data sets (e.g. connection between pulse pressure and coronary heart disease in [6]). Therefore, we assume that prior knowledge comes in the form of elements of probabilistic model. It is important to mention that we rely neither on collected historical data nor on regular quick feedback. The work [1] develops a feature-related anomaly explanation approach *providing user with information about the combination of dimensions (an attribute subset) in which an outlier shows the greatest deviation*. This might suit our needs, but the solutions in [1] require a sufficient quantity of instances to learn about normal and abnormal ones. In MIoT modelling, the features appear

© Springer International Publishing AG, part of Springer Nature 2018
M. Mokhtari et al. (Eds.): ICOST 2018, LNCS 10898, pp. 310–316, 2018.
https://doi.org/10.1007/978-3-319-94523-1_31

to follow a sequential form, the output has to be updated on each step. This has something in common with on-line machine learning [3], but we have to interpret new measurements as features, not as instances. Sequential feature explanation is also addressed in [2] but unlike our setting, the order of features is not fixed.

1 Data and Prior Knowledge

Let the data *record* for a patient has the form $D = (d_1, \ldots, d_m)$ where d_j is j-th *feature (measurement)*, m is the overall number of measurements. In general, j-th feature is a measurement taken at time moment t_j from a sensor $s_j \in \{1, \ldots, q\}$.

The prior information known from the experts can be of the following types:

1. Information about joint distribution of the features.
2. Information about exceptions: explainable deviations from typical behaviour of the system. It may also include the recommended reaction:
   - **Ignoring**: to continue without any change.
   - **Deleting**: the feature(s) from the record.
   - **Closing**: as a compromise, it may be used for training, but not considered as an abnormality.
   - **Correcting**: to eliminate the contribution of an external factor.
   - **Switching** to the new pattern, with deleting/closing of the prehistory.

Example. We propose that each sensor has its own stochastic schedule. The distribution of the time between the measurements of a Sensor is exponential with variance $\lambda = 1$ for Sensor 1, $\lambda = 0.5$ for Sensor 2. We assume that the data record is the sum of two stochastic components. The first 'proper' one is related to the measured values themselves generated by a natural multi-dimensional Gaussian distribution. The second 'noisy' component reflects an influence of Sensor 1 on Sensor 2. Let the joint distribution of measurements from Sensor 1 be Gaussian with mean 0, variance 1 and covariance e^{-t} where t time between the measurements. Similar parameters for Sensor 2 are 0, 1.5 and $1.5e^{-2t}$. The covariance between a measurement of Sensor 1 and a measurement of Sensor 2 is $-e^{-4t}$. If the last measurement of Sensor 1 was done in less than $t_1 = 0.5$ time then the measurement of Sensor 2 is 'affected' i.e. enlarged by a random noisy component distributed uniformly on $[0, \lambda]$. We assume that $l_0 = 0.1 \leq \lambda \leq 0.5 = l_1$.

Two types of exceptions are included into the model:

1. An individual exception: The noisy influence of Sensor 1 on Sensor 2 may sometimes disappear (as if $\lambda = 0$).
2. A temporary shift: Assume that the time is measured in days, and the non-integer part of the time stamp is below 0.5 at night. Within the time intervals $(0, 0.5)$, $(1, 1.5)$ etc., λ may raise temporarily to its maximal value 0.5.

We use the following basic settings for simulation experiments:

1. Low noise: $\lambda = 0.1$ ended with a sensor fault at $t = 15$.
2. Medium noise: $\lambda = 0.3$ ended with a system fault at $t = 15$.

3. High noise: $\lambda = 0.5$ ended with a critical health state at $t = 15$.
4. Attack simulation (within-range negative shift) at a time point: $\lambda = 0.3$, changed to $\lambda = 0.1$ at $t = 15$.
5. Attack simulation (out-of-range negative shift) at the origin, $\lambda = 0.05$.
6. Attack simulation (out-of-range positive shift) at the origin, $\lambda = 0.6$.
7. Attack simulation (wave shift) at the origin, variable noise: $\lambda(t) = 0.3e^{sin(t)\sqrt{t}}$.

2   Testing for Abnormalities

We consider a data record as anomalous if it is anomalous even for the best fitting distribution of the distributions that agree with the prior knowledge. Therefore, we split the task of anomaly detection into two stages: (1) estimating of the best fitting distribution $\hat{P}$ (in Bayesian or Maximum Likelihood sense); (2) testing the data on agreement with this distribution.

The first testing question is whether any abnormality is caused by the last measurement added to the system. The statistical test related to this particular feature can be based on the residual i.e. the difference between the true value of the last measurement and one expected from $\hat{P}$.

What we also need is some form of accumulation of abnormality reflected in the sequential features. Therefore, we apply the second type of testing based on the elements of machine learning and ranking: try to predict each measurement from $\mathcal{P}$ and the remaining measurements, and to calculate the *probabilistic residuals* i.e. *p*-values measuring how likely the *true* value of this feature looks according to the predictive model, and to apply *i.i.d.* testing (in assumed way of measurements we can expect them to be nearly *i.i.d.* in a normal situation).

There still may happen that none of $P \in \mathcal{P}$ fits the data at a satisfactory level, but this is not explainable by abnormality of the last feature or a group of them. Let us imagine that the knowledge is two-level: there exists a hard model $\mathcal{P}$ and an extended model $\overline{\mathcal{P}}$. In that case, it is possible to compare best fitting $\hat{P} \in \mathcal{P}$ with the best fitting $\hat{\overline{P}} \in \overline{\mathcal{P}}$. The alert is produced if the difference in fitting degree is essential.

Example (continued). Let $\hat{\lambda}$ be the maximum likelihood solution. The following cases may appear:

1. $\hat{\lambda} < 0$: we reduce this case to $\hat{\lambda} = 0$, and go the point 2.
2. $0 \leq \hat{\lambda} < l_0$: the most likely parameter value is out of range; this may be a possible reason for a special alert, if the ratio of likelihoods at $\hat{\lambda}$ and l_0 is above the pre-selected threshold ϕ; otherwise we just reduce $\hat{\lambda}$ to l_0.
3. $l_0 \leq \hat{\lambda} \leq l_1$: we make further steps of analysis in assumption of this value;
4. $l_1 < \hat{\lambda}$: the most likely parameter value is out of range; this may be a possible reason for a special alert, if the ratio of likelihoods at $\hat{\lambda}$ and l_1 is above the pre-selected threshold ϕ; otherwise we just reduce $\hat{\lambda}$ to l_1.

Let $D = (d_1, \ldots, d_m)$ be the observed vector of measurements at a step m (with 'deleted' ones). It is needed to calculate *p*-values:

$$p_i = \hat{P}\{\tilde{d} : \delta_i(\tilde{d}) \leq \delta_i(d_i) | d_1, \ldots, d_{i-1}, d_{i+1}, \ldots, d_m\}.$$

If $p_m < \varepsilon_1'$ (strict alarm level) we detect an individual measurement error. This is also done if $p_m < \varepsilon_1$ (soft alarm level) unless another kind of error is reported.

Then, for each sensor i, we consider the sequence $(p_1^i, \ldots, p_{m_i}^i)$ of measurements from the sensor i. Let $\tilde{p}_{(h)}^i$ ($h = 1, \ldots, m_i - 1$) be the p-value produced by Mann-Whitney-Wilcoxon 'ranksum' test on $(p_1^i, \ldots, p_h^i)$ and $(p_{h+1}^i, \ldots, p_{m_i}^i)$. The group error is reported if $\min_h \tilde{p}_{(h)}^i < \varepsilon_2$.

3   Explanation

The aim of explanation is to analyse the visible contradiction between the data and the model. In our example, we assume that abnormal health state or system fault is reflected as group error of more than one sensors, unlike a fault of one of the sensors.

Example (continued). To check type 1 exception, exclude the latest measurement from the 'affected' list (temporary set $z_k = 0$), re-run the process of anomaly detection and check whether the alert is reproduced. Type 2 can be checked similarly: if error disappears if λ is changed to 0.5 for the same night.

The items in the following list are defined based on order of priority: each of them is used only if none of the preceding ones is applicable.

- *Normal work or detected exception.*
  Action for type 1 exception: 'closing' the latest feature.
  For type 2 exception: 'closing' all 'affected' features from the same night.
- *Measurement mistake.* An individual error (strict alert).
  Action: 'deleting' the measurement.
- *Alarm A/B: health state or system fault.* A group error for both sensors.
  Action: 'deleting' the measurements after the earlier splitting point.
- *Alarm C: sensor fault.* A group error for only one of the sensors.
  Action: 'deleting' the measurements of this sensor after the splitting point.
- *Measurement mistake.* An individual error (moderate alert).
  Action: 'closing' the measurement.
- *Special alert: information bias.* A general shift.
  Action: no immediate actions, just marking for investigation.

4   Experiments and Evaluation

Scenarios 1–7 follow Sect. 1. The measurement mistakes and exceptions of types 1–2 are imputed at arbitrary moments (8, 18–19, 32, 39–41, 49, 54, 52). We are modelling mistakes leading to out-of-range or rare measurements with big absolute values: 1 for Sensor 1 and 2 for Sensor 2 as examples.

Table 1. Effectiveness of the algorithms

Sc.	$\phi = 10, \varepsilon_2 = 0.05$		1. Meas. error $\pm$	2. Group error delay	3. False alerts	4. Explanation accuracy
	ε_1	ε_1'				
1	0.001	0.001	-10	-6	-8	N/A; gr+(S1)
	0.05	0.01	$+4/-6$	-4	-7	$+3/-1$; gr±(S2)
2 (*)	0.001	0.001	$+4/-6$	0	-11	$+4$; gr$-$(MM)
	0.05	0.01	$+2/-8$	-4	-13	$+1/-1$; gr$-$(S2)
3	0.001	0.001	$+6/-4$	0	-11	$+4/-2$; gr$-$(MM)
	0.05	0.01	$+2/-8$	0	-13	$-1/-1$; gr$-$(S1)
4 (*)	0.001	0.001	$+4/-6$	0	-11	$+4$; gr$-$(MM)
	0.05	0.01	$+4/-6$	-4	-13	$+2/-2$; gr$-$(S2)
5	0.001	0.001	-10	$-11(2)$	-8	N/A
	0.05	0.01	$+4/-6$	$-11(1)$	-10	$+3/-1$
6	0.001	0.001	$+4/-6$	$-11(9)$	-6	$+1/-3$
	0.05	0.01	$+4/-6$	$-11(17)$	-12	$+1/-3$
7 (*)	0.001	0.001	$+2/-8$	$-11(3)$	-9	$+2$
	0.05	0.01	$+4/-6$	$-11(6)$	-9	$+2/-2$

In Table 1, we apply the methodology of untrustworthy measurement detection to the data records created in 7 scenarios. The star mark (*) in the table means the setting is selected for graphical representation in Figs. 1, 2 and 3. For **measurements mistakes**, the evaluation criterion is the number of recognised vs. missed measurement mistakes. For **group errors**, we observe quickness of reaction: how many steps passed before an alert was produced. The change point is $t = 15$ (step 44) for scenarios 1–4, and the origin (step 1) in scenarios 5–7. In scenarios 1–4 we consider any alert as an evidence of reaction, while in 5–7 we are waiting for an alert of the proper type ('special alert'). Also, we have taken a note (in brackets) of the number of produced special alerts, and the amount of **false alerts** reported without any real causes. For true alerts, we check **accuracy of explanation**. For a measurement mistake and we calculate the number of examples with this (correct) explanation ($+$) vs. the others ($-$). An explanation of a group mistake may be correctly ($+$) or wrongly ($-$) assigned to one of the types: sensor fault; health state; global mistake. We consider it as partially right ($\pm$) if a sensor fault is recognised with a wrong sensor.

In our experiments, only a part of measurement mistakes is recognisable but this may be due to insufficient amount of data for analysis. Typically, some amount of collected features is needed for sensitivity of measurement mistake. On the other hand, elimination of suspicious measurement mistakes is useful for better detection of group errors. Group errors are recognised in some of scenarios/settings as individual measurement mistakes. This may hopefully be resolved by using extra 'strict' significance level for individual mistake. Group errors are likely to be recognised in this setting. However, detection of the exact cause appears to be harder; the easiest one for recognition is 'positive shift'.

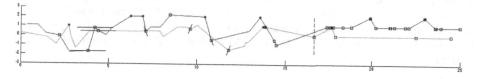

Fig. 1. Scenario 2: S1-2 fault

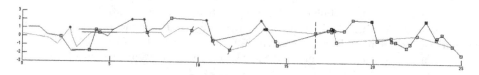

Fig. 2. Scenario 4: Late shift (decrease)

Fig. 3. Scenario 7: Early shift (wave) (The markers on these figures mean: a star is for an imputed measurement mistake; a square is for a produced alert (measurement mistake if no lines are attached); one oblique vertical line crossing the square is for sensor fault alert; two oblique vertical lines are for system fault or healthy state alert; a horizontal line is for a special alert.)

5   Conclusion

In this work, we shed light on the problem of untrustworthy measurement detection motivated by MIoT. The proposed solution is based on its interpretation as a form of anomaly detection and explanation. We take into account specific challenges: lack of reliable historical data and feedback, working only with the general experts' knowledge and one actual record, sequential addition of features. We have validated the approach using a synthetic data sample that includes imputed scenarios of measurement mistakes, exceptions, faults and attacks. It appears that individual mistakes are hardly recognisable at first steps of the work, but improves with growth of the amount of collected measurements. The group errors are quickly recognisable by statistical analysis, but detection of the exact cause may be not so easy. The reaction of the system attacks (global errors) to intentional attacks is promising. The prior task for the future work may be developing some kind watermarking as in [4], with elements of active learning in investigation.

Acknowledgements. This work was supported by Technology Integrated Health Management (TIHM) project awarded to the School of Mathematics and Information Security at Royal Holloway as part of an initiative by NHS England supported by InnovateUK, by European Union grant 671555 ("ExCAPE"), and AstraZeneca grant R10911.

References

1. Micenkova, B., Ng, R.T., Dang, X.-H., Assent, I.: Explaining outliers by subspace separability. In: Data Mining (ICDM), pp. 518–527. IEEE (2013)
2. Siddiqui, M.A., Fern, A., Dietterich, Th.G., Wong, W.-K.: Sequential Feature Explanations for Anomaly Detection. arXiv:1503.00038 [cs.AI] (2015)
3. Bottou, L.: Online Algorithms and Stochastic Approximations. Cambridge University Press, Cambridge (1998). ISBN 978-0-521-65263-6
4. Mo, Y., Weerakkody, S., Sinopoli, B.: Physical authentication of control systems. IEEE Control Syst. Mag. **35**(1), 93–109 (2015)
5. Zagorecki, A., Orzechowski, P., Holownia, K.: A system for automated general medical diagnosis using Bayesian networks. In: Lehmann, C.U., et al. (eds.) MEDINFO (2013). https://doi.org/10.3233/978-1-61499-289-9-461
6. Franklin, S.S., Khan, S.A., Wong, N.D., Larson, M.G., Levy, D.: Is pulse pressure useful in predicting risk for coronary heart disease? The Framingham heart study. Circulation **100**(4), 354–360 (1999)

System for User Context Determination in a Network of IoT Devices

Kushal Singla[✉] and Joy Bose

Samsung R&D Institute, Bangalore, India
{kushal.s,joy.bose}@samsung.com

Abstract. In order to build a user profile using data from various connected IoT smart sensors and devices, determination of the current context of the user is vital. We assume a hierarchy of contexts (such as party, trip, exercise) based on common daily activities of users. Knowing the context can inform about the actual activity being performed by the user and predict what the user might be interested in at a given moment. This can then be used to suggest appropriate services to the user. In this paper, we propose a system to infer the user context from input data from various devices. Our system includes an app classifier, a Points of Interest (POI) classifier and a motion classifier to make sense of the input sensor data. We describe the implementation details of a system and some results on real world data to measure our model performance.

Keywords: User modelling · Context · POI classifier · App classifier

1 Introduction

Smartphones, smart watches, pedometers and other smart IoT devices are widely used nowadays. Such devices continuously generate data related to the user's activities. We are interested in the problem of inferring the user's current activity based on the sensor data. Here we assume a scenario with a number of connected smart devices belonging to a user, along with a master device such as a smartphone that always stays with the user and receives data from other devices. All such data is rapidly changing, and the sensors and devices might be moving or stationary.

In this paper, we describe a system that takes sensor data from various IoT devices belonging to one user and generate a context, updated in real time. Our main contribution lies in defining a hierarchy of contexts, using a combination of rule and model-based approaches to identify the context, and using algorithms to better classify the current context based on sensor inputs. Our system runs on the user's primary device and generates the context in real time, which can be used to offer relevant services.

We define the user's context as made up of one of a hierarchy of contexts. We propose the following rudimentary context hierarchy, which can be extended as required: Meeting (office meeting, doctor appointment, dentist appointment), Shopping (mall, supermarket, movie), Socializing (nightclub, bar, house party), Exercise (Gym, football game, tennis game), Meal (Date, family meal), Moving (Work trip, leisure travel, commuting).

© Springer International Publishing AG, part of Springer Nature 2018
M. Mokhtari et al. (Eds.): ICOST 2018, LNCS 10898, pp. 317–323, 2018.
https://doi.org/10.1007/978-3-319-94523-1_32

2   Related Work

2.1   Context Generation in Real Time on Mobile Devices

Generation and identification of context in mobile devices has been an area of interest. Chon [1] developed a model running on a smartphone to identify the context to use for location based services, using the output of various types of device sensors. Lee [2] used a HMM based model on smartphone sensor data to recognize the user's current activity such as running, walking, moving on a bus etc. (Fig. 1).

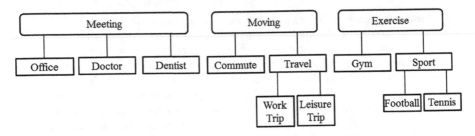

Fig. 1.   Illustration of a hierarchy of contexts, where each level gives a more detailed view of the type of context of the user.

2.2   Context Identification by Learning Patterns from the Data Generated by Multiple IoT Devices

There are a number of available works related to learning patterns from the data generated by IoT devices. Raento et al. [3] developed a system to infer contextual data. Otebolaku [4] developed a model to identify the context on the basis of data generated by IoT devices, using some preprocessing steps and a neural network to classify the input into one of seven possible contexts. Sharma [5] and Kannan [6] propose models in which data from sensors is used to identify activities such as walking, running etc.

The existing models generally do not personalize the context for individual users, but rather have a single model that works for all users. Also, they do not learn from the user's actions and dynamically changing contexts in real time. Most of their processing is performed offline. This is where our contribution lies.

3   System Overview

A system to identify the user's context can be based on any of the following methods:

- Rule based system: This can have static or dynamic rules to identify context.
- Model based system: This infers the context based on learning from the past labelled or unlabeled data from user devices, similar to Otebolaku [4].
- Hybrid system: This uses rules to define some sub-contexts or candidate contexts, along with a learning model to learn from the user's recent activity to fine tune the final context.

We use a point of interest (POI) classifier, an app classifier and a motion classifier to identify various aspects of the user's current activity from various sensors. Below is a brief description of the three classifiers (Fig. 2).

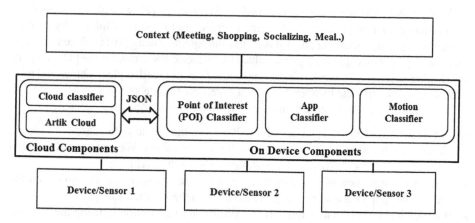

Fig. 2. High level architecture of our system to identify the current user context from device sensor outputs.

3.1 POI Classifier

The Point of Interest (POI) can be a useful indictor of the context of the user. If the user is in a home location, that could be an indicator that they are involved in a task at home, such as cooking a meal or watching TV. The POI classifier module takes the latitude-longitude values from the GPS sensor on the smartphone and outputs the type of location, e.g. park, mall, hospital, residence area such as apartment complex.

For our system, we first explored the feasibility of using third party POI related APIs. We first identified a few test locations such as a face (Café Coffee Day), a mall (Soul Space arena), a hospital (Rainbow hospital), office premises (Samsung office), and some residential premises using the latitude-longitude coordinates near the area of Doddane-kundi in Bangalore, India. We explored the following two maps APIs to get the POI information using the latitude-longitude coordinates: Foursquare API using a provided Sandbox account [8] and Google places reverse Geocoding API [9]. Our aim was to train a model to identify the type of POI from the POI information (within a certain radius of the exact coordinates supplied) obtained from the APIs.

We got some useful results, with the Foursquare API giving the place name (e.g. Café Coffee Day, Soul Space Arena mall) and place type information (Coffee Shop, Shopping Mall), and giving more relevant information than the Google API.

However, we also experienced a few issues with using the API calls:

- APIs may give incorrect location type, such as when it has recently changed.
- They gave information of more than one place for a given set of coordinates, e.g. for two POIs on different floors of a shopping mall.
- The GPS sensor also sometimes did not give the correct values.

- The categories identified were inconsistent. For example, in case of the POI identification upon giving GPS coordinates for one office, the API call gave the category as "Business Center", while for another office it gave "Office".

Similar problems were also highlighted by Shaw et al. [7], who also tried to solve the problem of mapping the current location coordinates to a point of interest by training a model using datasets of user check-ins from Foursquare. Zhang [10] explored a related but reverse problem, using the context values from check-ins to predict the POI category with higher accuracy. So we decided to make a dataset of labelled place names and train a classifier to classify the location type for a given coordinate set.

The steps in our classifier training are as follows:

- Get the latitude-longitude values of the POI from the phone GPS sensor.
- Identify the location using the latitude – longitude values. We use the public APIs from Foursquare and Google places Reverse Geocoding API [9].
- Extract features such as venue distance, name, Foursquare category name, and the address to train a classifier to map the location to the location id.
- We built a classifier to map the latitude-longitude to a location id using the location mapped address from Google Places Reverse Geocoding API [9].
- These two individual classifiers are used to build a robust ensemble classifier with a better accuracy as against the individual classifiers.

Figure 3 shows the high level architecture of our point of interest (POI) classifier.

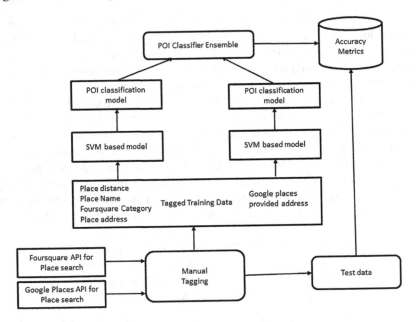

Fig. 3. Architecture of the POI classifier.

3.2 App Classifier

The apps being browsed by a person can be useful to identify several types of context cases. For example, when a person is travelling in a new city, they might be using a maps or navigation app such as Google maps. So the usage of such an app can be taken to indicate that the person is travelling. The app classifier module in our system takes the app name as input and outputs the type of app. This module takes as input a training set of app name to app type mappings. This training set is used to train an SVM classifier, which then gives the final app type.

3.3 Motion Classifier and Other Sensors

The motion classifier module takes as input the values from the accelerometer and Gyroscope sensors on the smart phone and/or fitness wearables. It processes the input data and classifies the motion as MOTION_WALK, MOTION_RUN and so on. Such models have been well studied and used, for example by Sun [11] and Alzantot [12]. Additionally, other sensors can infer the context of the user from their smartphone and other device usage. For example, if the TV or AC is on, it can be an indicator that they are watching a TV channel at home. The time spent by the user while in a certain context can be an additional factor. Also, the output of two or more modules or devices can be combined to get a better understanding of the context.

3.4 Voting Method to Decide Context

In our system, using the POI, app and other classifiers, we get an understanding of the user's context from a given device. We use the inputs from multiple IoT devices to get a better view of the context, as long as they have same location as the user. For example, the TV is not a valid input if the user is away from home. We use a modified Borda count voting method to decide the final context, where each device 'votes' for a particular context in each type (POI, app, motion). The context with the maximum number of votes is identified as the final context.

4 Implementation and Experimental Results

In our implementation, we made a proof of concept prototype which we ran on a Samsung Galaxy S8 phone. We implemented the POI classifier using a simple manually edited dataset of labelled places in Doddanekundi area in Bangalore. Our dataset of POIs includes 50 POI locations with 5 types of locations and 10 of each type, with the latitude-longitude values of each POI along with the type. Then we used the Foursquare API and Google reverse geocoding API to provide input features (name, address, distance and category) for a given latitude-longitude value, which we use in the input of the classifier as described. The classifier is trained to recognize the POI types in the area given the GPS coordinates. We wrote an app on the smartphone to detect active apps running in the foreground. Using this, we track the currently running app and use this as input to our app classifier to identify the app type.

We made a dataset of 100 apps, taking 20 apps in each of these 5 categories. We kept the training: test data ratio of 70:30. We used an SVM classifier to train the model, which is then used to predict the type of apps. We got 88% prediction accuracy for the app classifier across our app classes, and 92% for the POI classifier. As mentioned, we use the modified Borda count method for different IoT devices to vote for the final context. Stationary devices such as the smart TV and fridge get a lower weight than the smartphone and smartwatch, which are typically moving with the user. We implemented our context classifier on the smartphone, found the computed context values using Borda count voting from devices and used the rules to identify a few typical user contexts including the following: meal (POI type is restaurant, active apps include pay), gym (POI type is gym, active apps are music, health), work related meeting or trip (POI type is office) etc. We tested with five users and collected data and identified the contexts. We found we could identify the given contexts with reasonable accuracy for a variety of POIs in our Doddanekundi location.

5   Conclusion and Future Work

In this paper, we have presented a system for inferring the context in real time from user values. We defined a hierarchy of contexts and used a hybrid of a rule based and model based method, using the Borda voting method to find the final context using candidate contexts. In future, we plan to improve our model and test more thoroughly, and also increase the number of context categories.

References

1. Chon, J., Cha, H.: LifeMap: a smartphone-based context provider for location-based services. IEEE Pervasive Comput. **10**(2), 58–67 (2011)
2. Lee, Y.-S., Cho, S.-B.: Activity recognition using hierarchical Hidden Markov Models on a smartphone with 3D accelerometer. In: Corchado, E., Kurzyński, M., Woźniak, M. (eds.) HAIS 2011. LNCS (LNAI), vol. 6678, pp. 460–467. Springer, Heidelberg (2011). https://doi.org/10.1007/978-3-642-21219-2_58
3. Raento, M., Oulasvirta, A., Petit, R., Toivonen, H.: ContextPhone: a prototyping platform for context-aware mobile applications. IEEE Pervasive Comput. **4**(2), 51–59 (2005)
4. Otebolaku, A.M., Lee, G.M.: Towards context classification and reasoning in IoT. In: Proceedings of ConTEL. IEEE Press (2017)
5. Sharma, M., Srivastava, R., Anand, A., Prakash, D., Kaligounder, L.: Wearable motion sensor based phasic analysis of tennis serve for performance feedback. In: Proceedings of ICASSP (2017)
6. Kannan, R., Garg, A.: Adaptive sensor fusion technology for mobile and wearable applications. IEEE Sens. J. (2015)
7. Shaw, B., Shea, J., Sinha, S., Hogue, A.: Learning to rank for spatiotemporal search. In: Proceedings of WSDM 2013. ACM (2013)
8. Foursquare Developers: API Explorer. https://foursquare.com/developers/explore#req=users%2Fself

9. Reverse Geocoding: Google Maps Javascript API. Google Developers. https://developers. google.com/maps/documentation/javascript/examples/geocoding-reverse
10. (Yue) Zhang, D., et al.: Large-scale point-of-interest category prediction using natural language processing models. In: Proceedings of IEEE BIGDATA. IEEE Press (2017)
11. Sun, L., Zhang, D., Li, B., Guo, B., Li, S.: Activity recognition on an accelerometer embedded mobile phone with varying positions and orientations. In: Yu, Z., Liscano, R., Chen, G., Zhang, D., Zhou, X. (eds.) UIC 2010. LNCS, vol. 6406, pp. 548–562. Springer, Heidelberg (2010). https://doi.org/10.1007/978-3-642-16355-5_42
12. Alzantot, M., Youssef, M.: UPTIME: ubiquitous pedestrian tracking using mobile phones. In: Proceedings of WCNC 2012. IEEE (2012)

Author Index

Printed in the United States
By Bookmasters